INSIDERS' GUIDE® TO

SOUTH DAKOTA'S BLACK HILLS & BADLANDS

SIXTH EDITION

T.D. GRIFFITH & NYLA D. GRIFFITH

INSIDERS' GUIDE

GUILFORD, CONNECTICUT
AN IMPRINT OF GLOBE PEQUOT PRESS

All the information in this guidebook is subject to change. We recommend that you call ahead to obtain current information before traveling.

INSIDERS' GUIDE ®

Editor: Kevin Sirois
Project Editor: Heather Santiago
Layout Artist: Kevin Mak
Text Design: Sheryl Kober
Maps: XNR Productions, Inc. © Morris Book Publishing, LLC

ISSN 1539-3542
ISBN 978-0-7627-6476-1

Printed in the United States of America
10 9 8 7 6 5 4 3 2 1

CONTENTS

CONTENTS

Directory of Maps

ABOUT THE AUTHORS

Tom Griffith attended the University of London before he graduated from the University of Wisconsin–Eau Claire. He worked as a reporter, photographer, and managing editor of award-winning newspapers in Arizona, Montana, and South Dakota before serving as director of communications for the Mount Rushmore Preservation Fund, a nationwide campaign that raised $25 million to preserve and improve the mountain memorial. In addition to writing articles for dozens of newspapers and magazines, Tom is the author of six books, including *America's Shrine of Democracy* with a foreword by President Ronald Reagan; *South Dakota*, a comprehensive guide to the state; *Greeno, A Winning Tradition of Teaching and Coaching* with a foreword by NBC's Tom Brokaw. Also, *Outlaw Tales of South Dakota, Outlaw Tales of Nebraska*, and *Deadwood: The Best Writings on the Most Notorious Town in the West*, all published by Globe Pequot Press. He has co-authored more than 30 travel guides to date. Tom and his wife, Nyla, make their home in the Black Hills of South Dakota. In their spare time, they enjoy trout fishing, motorcycling, and travel.

A fourth-generation South Dakotan, **Nyla Griffith** is a successful photographer and author whose work has appeared throughout the US. She is the author of *Lucky Strike* and *Visible Breath*, two novels set in western South Dakota. Her travels have taken her to more than 50 countries.

ACKNOWLEDGMENTS

As a sixth-edition book, credit for much of the initial research and writing goes to the authors of the first edition, Barbara Tomovick and Kimberly Metz. Assisting these writers were a host of individuals well-versed in the life and character of the Black Hills, including photographers and *Rapid City Journal* staffers, real estate agents, and many individuals who have worked in public service and the Black Hills visitor industry for many years.

Thanks also are extended to the second-edition revisers, Bert and Jane Gildart, who provided some updated information and stunning photographs, and Dustin D. Floyd, who assisted in revamping this book's third and fourth editions.

Many of the first edition's sources were consulted for this sixth edition of the book, although a number of new faces deserve recognition. Among those are the staff of the Adams Museum and House; the employees of the Rapid City Parks and Recreation Department; the many helpful people at the chambers of commerce scattered throughout the Hills; the Deadwood Historic Preservation Commission; the Black Hills, Badlands and Lakes Association; the South Dakota Department of Tourism; Amanda Kille and Chad Blair at TDG Communications; Black Hills children's advocate Angie King; the Interpretation Centers of the many national and state parks in the Black Hills, particularly Judy Olson, director of resource education at Badlands National Park; the hundreds of small business owners across the region who answered their telephones and e-mail; and, of course, all the helpful—and sometimes anonymous—voices not mentioned here who provided us with the facts, figures, snapshots, and information you now hold in your hand. Last, but never least, editor Kevin Sirois also deserves recognition for his efforts to make this edition come together so smoothly.

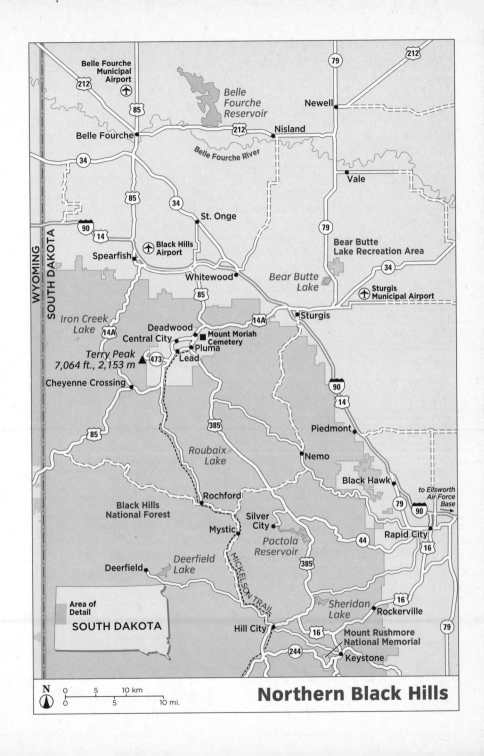

Northern Black Hills

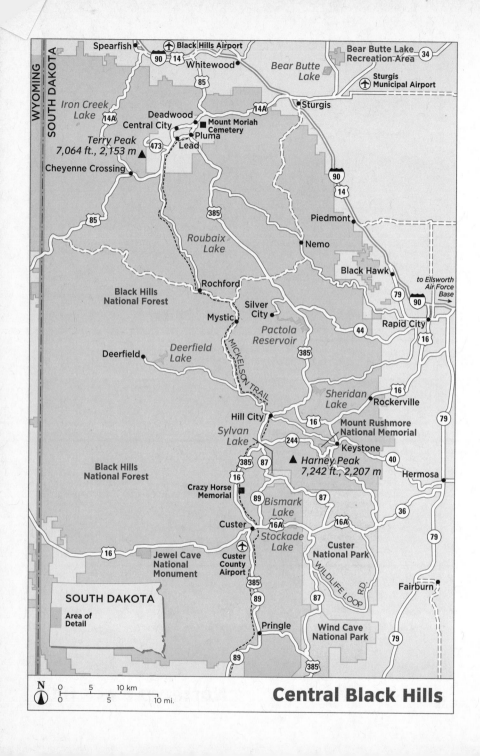

Central Black Hills

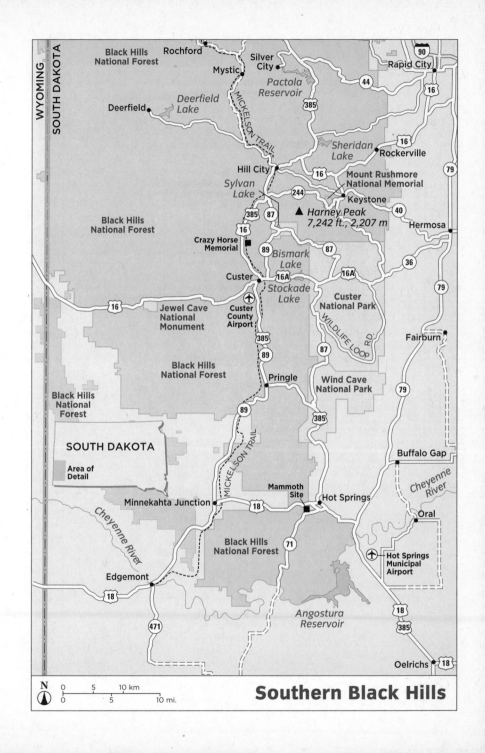

Southern Black Hills

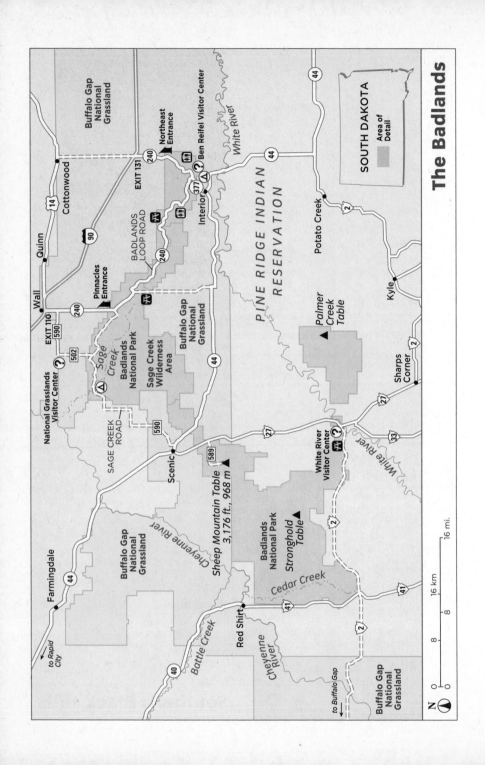

The Badlands

INTRODUCTION

The Black Hills and Badlands form a region of contrasts. The Hills are an uplifted island of mountains in the middle of prairie flatland, and the Badlands resemble a sometimes spooky, prehistoric moonscape. Considered together, as they are in this book, they form a place that is welcoming, accessible, and quietly magnificent.

The Black Hills and Badlands are bounteous and beautiful, but sometimes tough and challenging, too. You'll find natural beauty of great power here: craggy mountains, mysterious geological formations, sudden weather changes, towering evergreens, grassy prairie, alpine meadows and vistas that will make your heart ache. This is still a homey kind of place where the good-hearted residents look you in the eye and say hello, and where visitors are welcomed with smiles, questions, and helpful hints.

In addition to the natural wonders and welcoming atmosphere, the contrasts, we believe, are what make life here so extremely interesting. You'll find ghost towns and modern towns, high-tech commerce and country life, and a taste of the combined Old West, Midwest, and New West. We have trendy restaurants and rustic bars, sophisticated art galleries and quaint attractions, and cowboys and businesspeople and artists. Recreation ranges from rough-and-tumble rodeos to skiing, skating, mountain hiking, and biking. In some areas you can still view century-old wagon-trail ruts from modern highways. Life has changed quickly here in the relatively short history of settlement; yet, in other ways, it has hardly changed at all.

We've filled this book with places to visit, eat, and shop, fun activities for children, sights to see, trails to hike, history to discover, and much more. The table of contents will direct you to specific chapters, and the **How to Use This Book** chapter will help you use and enjoy some of the unique tidbits we've sprinkled throughout this book.

Whether you're an armchair traveler or tourist or new resident, we're glad for the opportunity to contribute to your enjoyment of our beloved Black Hills and Badlands. We think you'll love this place, too, and that you'll take pleasure in its delightful contrasts. We hope you'll feel at home here, just as we do.

Welcome. The Black Hills and Badlands await your exploration.

HOW TO USE THIS BOOK

Let's say you've just opened this book for the first time. The cover is bright and smooth, the page corners sharp, the spine a bit stiff. So you've opened it somewhat gingerly, wondering where to begin.

The fact is you'll get hooked on the Black Hills and Badlands no matter where you start your journey. Naturally, the table of contents will give you an idea of the sort of information you'll find here. The comprehensive index at the back will help you zero in on specific things you'd like to learn more about. But maybe you just want to chapter surf and get a feel for what this guide is all about. Go right ahead. The ride's on us.

To make it more fun, we've sprinkled interesting tips and trivia throughout the text, flagged with the **i** symbol. And because we wanted to make our book unique among the Insiders' Guides, we borrowed from the South Dakota state slogan, "Great Faces, Great Places" (a reference to the faces of Mount Rushmore National Memorial), to bring you vignettes about some outstanding people and places you might not otherwise hear about. You'll find those stories under the dozens of **Close-up** headings for an in-depth look at some of what makes this a special place.

Throughout the book you'll also find listings accompanied by the ✳ symbol—these are our top picks for attractions, restaurants, accommodations, and everything in between that you shouldn't miss while you're in the area. You want the best this region has to offer? Go with our **Insiders' Choice.**

Most of our chapters are arranged geographically, from north to south. Since locals customarily refer to various sections of the Black Hills as the Northern Hills, the Central Hills, and the Southern Hills, we've done that, too. The boundaries aren't necessarily hard and fast, so for our purposes we've divided the area up as follows:

- The **Northern Hills** include Belle Fourche in Butte County, all of Lawrence County (primarily Deadwood, Lead, and Spearfish), and Sturgis and Bear Butte State Park in Meade County.
- Piedmont and Black Hawk, in southwestern Meade County, come under **Central Hills** listings because those communities tend to be closely tied to Rapid City (in Pennington County) and are even listed under Rapid City in the phone book. Hill City, Keystone, Mount Rushmore National Memorial, and Harney Peak, all of which are in Pennington County, also come under the Central Hills umbrella.
- The **Southern Hills** in this book encompass Custer and Fall River Counties, which include the towns of Custer and Hot Springs, respectively, plus Custer State Park, Wind Cave National Park, Crazy Horse Memorial, and Jewel Cave National Monument.

Some might argue with our geography, and we would agree there's a certain amount of latitude in defining these locations. Nevertheless, we think our divisions will help you plan and navigate through the Black Hills and perhaps come to a better understanding of the area. You'll get better acquainted in the Area Overview chapter, which describes each region in detail.

In our chapters on **Attractions, Kidstuff, Gaming & Casinos,** and **Annual Events & Festivals,** you'll learn about fun and fascinating things to see and do. In the Campgrounds and Accommodations chapters you'll find out where to rough it and where to relax in comfort. The Restaurants chapter will point you toward the best places to eat, whether you want a plain bagel, a homemade pizza with the works, or an elegant multicourse dinner. And in our chapters on **History, Recreation, Parks & Mountains, The Badlands & Nearby,** and **Day Trips & Weekend Getaways,** you'll find out why we and so many others choose to make this area our home.

Moving to South Dakota or already live here? Be sure to check out the blue-tabbed pages at the back of the book, where you will find the **Living Here** appendix that offers sections on relocation, real estate, education, health care, retirement, and media.

We've done our best to be thorough in every chapter, but chances are you're still going to have to make some phone calls while you're here. Luckily, South Dakota is "small" enough to have just one area code, 605. Although there are no rules for which calls are long distance and which aren't, many calls between the Central Hills and Northern Hills are now considered local, but all calls to and from the less populated Southern Hills are long distance.

Some attractions include sales tax in their admission prices, and some add tax at the time of purchase. You'll need to inquire. Tax rates vary depending on where you are and what you're buying. Take note that state law requires groceries to be taxed, so don't be surprised if a checker adds on a few cents to your bushel of corn or fresh bison steaks.

We've included general credit card information in chapters that have to do with accommodations and dining, but when shopping or visiting attractions you should ask whether plastic is accepted.

You'll notice that we do a lot of cross-referencing among chapters, and that's because we want to make sure you don't miss anything.

You'll find, too, that the terms Native American, American Indian, and Indian are used throughout the book. The three are interchangeable, though most locals will use the latter two when referring to North America's aboriginal peoples. We also use both Sioux and Lakota in writing about the tribes of western South Dakota, because although all Lakota people are Sioux, not all Sioux are Lakota. We explain the distinction in a Close-up section in the **History** chapter.

Soon, we hope, the volume you hold in your hands will look a bit dog-eared, its pages filled with underlines and notes, and its spine creased from constant use, like well-earned laugh lines.

AREA OVERVIEW

The Black Hills are ancient, some of the oldest mountains in North America. Although they don't claim the same attention as younger, taller mountain ranges, such as the Rockies to the west , they're recognized for their quiet splendor.

But mountains they are; they could as easily have been christened the Black Mountains as the Black Hills. The Lakota Sioux named them Paha Sapa—*paha* meaning any "height," whether mountains or hills, and *sapa* meaning "black." It seems likely that early translators settled on Black Hills for this, the only mountain range in Dakota Territory, to avoid confusion with North Carolina's Black Mountains, a range of the rolling Blue Ridge.

But why black when the Hills are covered with thick stands of evergreens? Quite simply because from a distance these pine-covered slopes loom like a backlit silhouette against the vastness of the Great Plains. The Black Hills have been called an oasis in a sea of grass, a description you're likely to appreciate after a long drive across the boundless prairie to reach us.

We are no longer surprised to meet people who don't know where the Black Hills are or who think all of South Dakota is flat. Yet the Hills claim a substantial number of distinctions. For starters, this area is home to one of the largest concentrations of national parks, memorials, and monuments in the world. It's also a region rich with history, a land once trod by the likes of Crazy Horse, Sitting Bull, Lt. Col. George Armstrong Custer, Buffalo Bill Cody, Wild Bill Hickok, and Calamity Jane (see the History chapter), among others. In fact, the latter two are still here; they are permanent residents of Deadwood's Mount Moriah Cemetery.

OVERVIEW

The Hills are home to the nation's first national forest (discussed in the History chapter) and to one of our country's most prominent and defining symbols, Mount Rushmore National Memorial (see Attractions). Yet even among those who easily recognize Mount Rushmore, many don't know that the famous mountain carving is in the Black Hills, in South Dakota.

Nevertheless, some four million people from around the world find their way here each year, making tourism one of our top industries, along with agriculture. Visits to Mount Rushmore, Custer State Park (see the Parks & Mountains chapter), and Deadwood (see Gaming & Casinos and Attractions) are likely to capture your imagination. A climb to the top of Harney Peak or a trek in the Black Hills National Forest (see Recreation) could very well make you want to stay forever. But to understand the nuances of life here takes more time.

For in some ways Black Hills residents have a bit of an identity crisis. We cherish and brag about our area's natural beauty and fascinating sights while tolerating a profusion of billboards that mar the view and a small number of embarrassingly tacky roadside attractions. The vast majority of us are solidly politically conservative, yet we cry out for new industry and complain when our young people leave.

i You'll find copies of two free visitor publications, *South Dakota Vacation Guide* and *Exploring the Black Hills and Badlands,* at many area attractions, motels, and chambers of commerce. You can request copies from the Black Hills, Badlands, and Lakes Association, 1851 Discovery Circle, Rapid City, 57701; (605) 355-3600. The office is located off I-90, exit 61.

We proudly call ourselves South Dakotan, but we cite deep philosophical differences with our neighbors east of the Missouri River, which divides the state in half. In fact, "East River" is practically a curse in the Black Hills (as much as "West River" is a dirty word in Sioux Falls or Vermillion). East River, with its thicker population, rolling farmland, quaint villages, and conservative mind-set, is decidedly Midwestern. West River, on the other hand, with its rough-and-tumble gold-rush past, ranches, arid plains, granite peaks, and even deeper conservative thinking, is clearly western. We Black Hills residents feel more akin to our neighbors in Wyoming, Montana, and Colorado, who share our mountain time zone, than we do to our East River brethren, who all happen to be on central time. Indeed, we commute to Cheyenne, Billings, Fort Collins, and Denver more often than we travel to Sioux Falls, Minneapolis, or Omaha, which are about as far. The two sides of South Dakota are two different worlds. Of course, that's not taking into account the Badlands (see The Badlands & Nearby chapter), which seem to belong on another planet altogether.

Some locals like to call the Black Hills "God's country," but like any earthly paradise, this one has its imperfections. For instance, most of us work hard for dishearteningly low wages, and although some argue that our cost of living is lower than in many other places, few families here can survive on a single paycheck (more about that in the Child Care chapter). For too many would-be homeowners, "affordable housing" is an oxymoron, and for all of us property taxes are high. Limited career options and low pay drive many of our best and brightest young people to other states. So when locals say they live here for the quality of life the area offers, they're talking less about material objectives and more about intangibles such as neighborliness, clean air, elbow room, and a sense of safety.

Add the fact that only a portion of the Black Hills is privately owned. The rest is public land and, for the most part, unspoiled. The Black Hills National Forest takes up 1.2 million acres, or about 2,000 square miles— that's about one-third of our total area. National and state parks, monuments, and recreation areas make still more of the land surface off-limits to expansive development. All of this makes the Hills an extraordinarily unfettered playground.

The Hills are remarkable in other ways as well. There is a strong Native American presence, particularly in Rapid City, that manifests itself in our public art, museums, interior design, local products, and even architecture (see the Arts chapter). The same holds true for our Scandinavian pioneer heritage. Jokes about Norwegian bachelor farmers abound, as do surnames that end in *son* or *sen*, *ahl* or *al*.

Place names are revealing, too, often summoning images of land formations and wildlife. Many towns were named for their natural features, straightforward descriptions consisting of the plainest word combinations: Belle Fourche (French for "beautiful fork"), Spearfish, Deadwood, Rapid City, Hill City, Hot Springs.

Roads meander as if they had minds of their own, seeking out the irregular more than the smooth spots. It's not uncommon to see riders sweeping across the foothills on horseback. And only in the harshest winter weather do we fail to pass roadside bicyclists or joggers on even our most mundane jaunt into town.

Nestled within the Hills are a couple of dozen small towns, each with a personality all its own. Rapid City, with a population of more than 60,000, is the largest city by far. Yet even in Rapid City it's practically impossible to go anywhere without pausing to talk to someone you know. To our way of thinking, that's one of the best reasons to live here.

The information below is meant to serve as an introduction, a verbal handshake from people all over the Black Hills. Not every community is included, though, so we urge you to check a map, explore on your own, and get acquainted with us face to face. And be sure to check other chapters in this book such as Relocation, Education, Health Care, and the Arts for additional information about our Black Hills hometowns.

NORTHERN HILLS

Northern Hills residents enjoy small-town life enhanced by the presence of a four-year liberal-arts college (see the Education chapter) centrally located in Spearfish. To the north is Belle Fourche, to the east is Sturgis, and to the south are the twin cities of Deadwood and Lead. Each of these communities is unique in character and contributes something in the way of goods, services, and employment to the area as a whole.

Belle Fourche

As the northern gateway to the Black Hills, Belle Fourche, the Butte County seat, is a prairie town with close ties to the Northern Hills community. Near the fork of the Belle Fourche and Redwater Rivers, it's home to about 4,500 people, small enough that one longtime resident described it this way: "Even if you dial the wrong number, you still know who you're talking to." With its railroad tracks and rodeo grounds, it's not hard to imagine Belle Fourche when it was a dusty cow town. Although tamer now than in its heyday as a cattle and sheep shipping center (see History), the downtown business district retains a strong ranching flavor with stores that cater to folks who work on the land.

The town was built on cattle, but sugar beets and sheep also were big industries in the early days. Though not as lucrative as they once were, they remain economic pillars of Belle Fourche; the wool warehouse, livestock exchange, and grain elevator are community landmarks. Today, bentonite mining is the big industry, although the school system and hospital are major employers, too.

The city's real crown jewel is its community center, built in 1992. There are racquetball courts, basketball courts, a theater, walking track, exercise room, and indoor pool with a waterslide. Residents from all over Butte County—numbering upward of 9,000 and growing—come here to relax and work out.

Deadwood & Lead

The Lawrence County towns of Deadwood and Lead (with about 1,300 and 3,000 people, respectively) are so closely associated with each other that it seems appropriate to couple them here. Through the years their list of cooperative efforts has included anything from a school district to a street sweeper. The mountainous twin cities were at the heart of the Black Hills gold rush and quickly prospered after San Francisco–based Homestake Mining Company acquired the area's richest gold deposit in Lead in 1877 (see History).

Until it closed in 2002, Homestake Gold Mine remained the economic pillar of the Northern Hills for more than 120 years, which made it the nation's longest-running underground gold mine. Both communities knew the yellow metal would run out eventually, so the closure was no surprise. And today, the 8,000-foot-deep mine is being readied as the nation's new deep underground science laboratory.

In the 1980s, Deadwood was dying. Most miners and supporting businesses had established themselves in Lead, and Deadwood's elegant brick storefronts and Victorian mansions, holdovers from its Wild West heyday, were left to crumble. Citizens saw an unlikely savior in the form of gaming, and in 1989 Deadwood became the third venue in the nation after Nevada and Atlantic City, New Jersey, to legalize gambling (see the Gaming & Casinos chapter). Today, Deadwood's streets are once again paved with brick, its mansions restored, and its Main Street bustling with up to 2 million annual travelers seeking their fortunes. The gaming industry has helped to market the Black Hills as a world-class destination and is Deadwood's current economic cornerstone. In fact, there are more jobs in Deadwood than there are residents.

i It sometimes seems that Deadwood is home to as many special events as slot machines. On virtually any weekend of the spring and fall shoulder seasons, you can stumble on events ranging from classic car shows and Octoberfests to Wild Bill Days and the Deadwood Jam, a two-day musical celebration featuring top acts. Go online at www.deadwood.com to check out the special event calendar.

Lead, on the other hand, was harder hit by the mine's closure. While new casinos, hotels and resorts have revived Deadwood, no single industry has come in to save Lead—at least not yet. Plans are in the works to build a science and engineering laboratory deep underground in the old mine, funded by the National Science Foundation. At the bottom, shielded by 8,000 feet of limestone and granite, scientists could conduct subatomic experiments with minimum interference from cosmic radiation. In 2007, the NSF selected the Homestake Mine as the site of the nation's new Deep Underground Science and Engineering Laboratory (DUSEL), and with a $35 million commitment by the State of South Dakota and a $70 million donation from South Dakota philanthropist T. Denny Sanford, the lab's future seems secure. The hope is that the lab would provide jobs for several dozen people and attract similar high-tech industries to the area that might employ hundreds or perhaps thousands more.

In the meantime, Lead is capitalizing on its proximity to downhill skiing and some of the best cross-country skiing and snowmobiling in the world. Lead's smalltown atmosphere, historic Homestake Opera House, and location near the mouth of stunningly beautiful Spearfish Canyon attract more and more visitors each year (see the Recreation chapter).

Spearfish

Black Hills State University and an accessible location off I-90 have provided Spearfish with some priceless advantages. The town has grown quickly in recent years, boosted to a population of nearly 10,000 (with another 3,500 in the surrounding 3-mile area) in part by retirees who succumb to its charms: a progressive outlook, tidy appearance (notice the pretty porches on houses along Main Street), convenient shopping, assorted medical facilities, and handy recreational opportunities. The Donald E. Young Sports and Fitness Center on the BHSU campus is open to community members, and an 18-hole golf course and outdoor swimming pool (see the Recreation chapter) are situated at the mouth of Spearfish Canyon. The unspoiled canyon, which beckons with stunning views of cliffs and streams, offers excellent trout fishing in Spearfish Creek (see the Recreation chapter for information about licenses and regulations).

The creek runs through town, not far from an attractive city hall–library and a paved 2-mile-long bike path. With a couple of large department stores, a Super Wal-Mart, strip malls (see the Shopping chapter), and a vital downtown, Spearfish is the subregional shopping center for the Northern Hills.

i *Outside* magazine named Spearfish Canyon one of the 50 best bicycle rides in America. The publication recommends biking from the town of Spearfish to Spearfish Canyon Lodge at Savoy and back. That makes the 25-mile round-trip doable with one vehicle but ignores the scenic riches of the stretch from Savoy to Cheyenne Crossing.

Ranching, the timber industry, retail stores, health care, light manufacturing, and the school district are top employers, along with the university. Pope & Talbot Sawmill, which in May 2008 sold to International Forest Products Ltd., has operated here for close to two decades; a Premier BankCard call center is in one of three industrial parks on the east edge of town. For those familiar with the town, Spearfish has long been a favorite place to conduct meetings, and that has meant plenty of business for the town's convention center.

Sturgis

Although best known as the home of the annual Sturgis Motorcycle Rally (see Annual Events & Festivals), Sturgis is much more. The Meade County seat of about 6,500 residents is a retail and service center for those who live on outlying farms and ranches. Located roughly a half hour's drive from both Spearfish and Rapid City, it's also home to professional couples who go their separate ways to work each day. Sturgis citizens are proud historians as well, and they love reenacting the 1870s at Fort Meade during the annual Calvary Days celebration.

We don't know of any town that gets more use out of its community center, either. Everything, it seems, takes place at

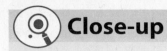

Close-up

Saga of Sue

In some ways the saga of **Sue** is a classic, the tale of a simple country girl transformed into a superstar worth millions of dollars. Thrust unwillingly into the spotlight, she quickly became world famous. Men fought over her, and one even went to prison. Today Sue is in Chicago, a skeleton of her former self—just as she has been for millions of years. Sue, you see, is a nearly complete set of *Tyrannosaurus rex* bones and for now, anyway, the largest, most complete T. rex ever found.

Sue the dinosaur fossil was named for Sue Hendrickson, a field-worker for the Black Hills Institute of Geological Research in Hill City. After Hendrickson found the giant skeleton on land belonging to rancher Maurice Williams in 1990, the institute paid Williams $5,000, and workers removed Sue's remains for restoration. But before long there were allegations that institute president Pete Larson, his brother, Neal, and their partner, Bob Farrar, had been stealing fossils from public land. An investigation started.

In 1992 the FBI confiscated Sue along with other fossils and records from the institute, and a federal indictment charged the Larsons and Farrar, among others, with 153 crimes. None of the charges had to do with Sue, but the institute couldn't get her back. The courts said Williams couldn't sell the fossil without government permission because his land, which is on the Cheyenne River Indian Reservation northeast of the Black Hills, was held in trust. So the government kept custody of Sue, and Williams kept the

---

the center, from recreation and meetings to concerts and school plays. Fort Meade Veterans Administration Medical Center (in the Health Care chapter) is the town's top employer, with the school district, the local hospital, and Black Hills Special Services Cooperative also providing jobs. Majestic Bear Butte (turn to Parks & Mountains for details) rises from the prairie northeast of town, a landmark for recreation and Native American spiritual rites.

> **i** Many Black Hills towns post signs at their city limits proclaiming "GOLD Community." In this context, GOLD stands for Guide to Opportunities for Local Development, a resource every bit as precious as the yellow metal. The program is administered by the governor's Office of Economic Development.

CENTRAL HILLS

Hill City

After the national magazine *Men's Journal* declared Hill City one of the country's 25 "truly cool" places, the little village that accurately calls itself the Heart of the Hills seemed poised for a population boom—and soaring property values. But a scarcity of available houses and building sites made the town's "cool" phase short-lived, no doubt to the relief of many of the 800 or so people already living here (and worried about their property taxes).

Part of the town's charm is its ready access to hiking and mountain biking trails and some of the Hills' most popular bodies of water: Sheridan and Deerfield Lakes and Pactola Reservoir. Sylvan Rocks Climbing School & Guide Service, an accredited climbing school, is located here, convenient to

institute's money, saying it was payment for disturbing his land. A federal jury ultimately rejected most of the charges in the federal case against the fossil hunters, but Pete Larson spent 18 months in federal prison for transporting undeclared traveler's checks through customs.

Meanwhile, Williams asked the government to sell Sue for him, and in October 1997 the 65-million-year-old fossil went on the auction block at Sotheby's in New York. In less than nine minutes she was sold to the highest bidder for $8.3 million. Williams became a multimillionaire, and the Field Museum of Natural History in Chicago became Sue's new owner. However, Walt Disney World Resort and McDonald's had put up most of the money to buy Sue. So, although the fossil will be properly curated and exhibited at the museum, a full-size cast of Sue eventually will be on display at DinoLand USA. McDonald's-sponsored DinoLand is part of Disney's Animal Kingdom, a feature of Walt Disney World in Florida.

After the auction, the Black Hills Institute kept the rights to the registered trademark name "Sue," and "Dakota" was chosen as the winning entry in a contest to rename the fossil. The institute later relented so Sue could keep her name, but paleontologist Bob Bakker (who is not affiliated with the institute) already had figuratively pinned a new tag on the world's most famous T. rex. Because of her star power, Bakker called Sue "the Marlene Dietrich of dinosaurs."

some of the area's foremost climbing spots (see Recreation chapter).

As seasonal shops along Main Street attest, a certain number of residents rely on tourism for their livelihood, and Black Hills Central Railroad/The 1880 Train (see the Attractions chapter) has long been the main tourist draw. Some residents find year-round work at the Rushmore Forest Products sawmill, the Black Hills Institute of Geological Research, the school district, and the forest service; others commute to jobs in Rapid City. The Railroad Avenue truck bypass and the inviting Old World Plaza boutique mall on Main Street show that Hill City is on the move; further proof comes from the infusion of excellent art galleries showcasing regional talent.

In 2009, the community's chamber of commerce and economic development corporation moved into spacious new quarters on Hill City's eastern edge. The former US Forest Service building also now houses the Hill City Area Arts Council, *Art of the Hills* magazine, the Black Hills Playhouse office, a CCC Museum, and a sheriff's substation. Visitor consultants provide information on what to do, see, and eat while in the area, and displays, video presentations, and brochures are available.

Keystone

Mount Rushmore is the *raison d'être* for Keystone, a town that at first glance looks like a T-shirt mecca but bears closer scrutiny. True, you could probably fill several pickup trucks with logo-emblazoned shirts, fudge, and jewelry made of Black Hills Gold (see the Close-up in the Shopping chapter) from the 40-plus summer tourist shops that line Winter Street—known as the Strip.

But there are major attractions here, too (as you'll see in the Attractions chapter), such as the Borglum Historical Center (Rushmore-Borglum Story), Big Thunder Gold Mine, and Beautiful Rushmore Cave. And although fewer than 250 people live in Keystone year-round, a keen interest in local history—gold and tin oxide were among the minerals mined here decades ago—has spawned the impressive West River History Conference, held each Sept at the Keystone Community Center.

i Phone book listings for Rapid City and Keystone alone include some 70 businesses that start with Rushmore, and another 10 that include Mount Rushmore in their names.

Rapid City

Rapid City, with nearly 70,000 residents, is the largest community in the Black Hills—and all of western South Dakota for that matter. Not surprisingly, then, this gateway to the Hills off I-90 is also the medical, educational, cultural, air transportation, and shopping hub for the entire region. But even in the face of ongoing expansion, Rapid City remains a low-key place with friendly shopkeepers and minimal traffic hassles. Its 22 parks (one of which surrounds Canyon Lake) and the paved 13.5-mile bike path that runs beside Rapid Creek are some of its most attractive features. The bike path is symbolic of the city's ability to survive tragedy: After a 1972 flash flood killed 238 people and injured more than 3,000 others, the city established a parklike floodway along the creek so no one could build there and live in harm's way again. Even today, Rapid City and its longtime residents continue to define themselves in terms of "before the flood" and "after the flood."

While Rapid Creek divides the city into north and south, the forested ridge known as Skyline Drive splits it the other way. To the east lie the oldest development, the downtown core, and Central High School; the west side, with its newer housing, golf courses, expansive Sioux Park, and Stevens High School, is almost a community unto itself. In fact, to get across town, you either have to loop several miles north and take I-90, or you have to pass through the Gap, a narrow canyon carved by Rapid Creek that barely has room for two six-lane roads. These streets are among the busiest in South Dakota, and congestion there inspired a bypass over the ridge several miles southwest of the city.

i The nonprofit InterTribal Bison Cooperative in Rapid City, www .itbcbison.com, provides financial and technical assistance and other services to Indian tribes that want to restore bison to tribal lands, primarily for cultural and spiritual purposes.

The Rapid City economy depends heavily on Ellsworth Air Force Base to the northeast of the city (read about the base in the History chapter). Ellsworth employs some 3,000 military personnel and another 500 or so civilians, injecting about $140 million a year into the local economy in wages alone. Other major employers include several Black Hills Gold manufacturers, Rapid City Regional Hospital, the school district, Green Tree Financial Servicing, the federal government, and the state of South Dakota, to name just a few.

When not working, Rapid citizens enjoy recreational opportunities at a massive indoor aquatic center and ice rink (see the Recreation chapter), cultural events, entertainment and hockey games at Rushmore Plaza Civic Center (listed in Annual Events & Festivals), and artistic expression at the expanded Dahl Fine Arts Center (see the Arts chapter). Other advantages include the Journey Museum (see Attractions), South Dakota School of Mines and Technology (see Education), Rapid City Regional Airport (see Getting Here, Getting Around), and easy access to I-90.

SOUTHERN HILLS

Like the Northern Hills, the Southern Hills are characterized by small towns, but the pace might even be a step slower.

Custer

Custer is home to fewer than 2,000 people despite the extraordinary landmarks that lie right outside its borders. Incomparable Custer State Park (see the Parks & Mountains chapter)—at approximately 71,000 acres one the nation's largest state parks—is just minutes east of town; inspirational Crazy Horse Memorial (see Attractions) is to the north. Although summer brings a flood of visitors to both, as well as to Flintstones Bedrock City and other attractions (see Kidstuff), Custer lacks the spit and shine and amenities of, say, Cody, Wyoming, a sophisticated tourist town that has made the most of its location near Yellowstone National Park.

Indeed, when the visitors vanish in the fall, Custer emerges as what it really is: a tightly knit community whose citizens are united by their love of high school basketball and who faithfully attend games whether they have a relative on the team or not (read about the team's accolades in the Education chapter). Social life revolves largely around school and youth activities, banquets, and church events. The Custer Youth Corrections Center, a state-run boot camp for juvenile offenders, is south of town; headquarters for the Black Hills National Forest is on the north end. Both are major employers, as are the school district, Custer Regional Hospital, Crazy Horse Memorial, and the park. Ranching, lumbering, and mining (primarily feldspar, mica, and quartz) also add to the town's economy.

Hot Springs

When desirable attributes were being handed out, Hot Springs must have been near the front of the line. For starters, the southernmost town brags that it has the best climate in the Hills, and we wouldn't argue to the contrary. Pick a day, any day, and it's likely to be warmer and drier here than anywhere else nearby. Other marvels of this city include the thermal waters that made it a health resort for buttoned-up Victorians with or without physical complaints. They probably walked right over the top of what is now the Mammoth Site of Hot Springs, the serendipitously discovered spot where ancient elephant-like mammals succumbed to the forces of nature and were preserved for all time (see Attractions). Visitors and residents alike must have delighted in the area's lovely pink sandstone that positively begged to be turned into eye-catching buildings in the town and, in fact, was (see the Close-up in the Attractions chapter).

Southern Hills Municipal Golf Course, historic Evans Plunge warm-water swimming pool, and nearby Angostura State Recreation Area are other bright gems in the crown of this prom queen called Hot Springs. So it makes sense that the Miss South Dakota pageant takes place here the third weekend of June each year. Likewise, it seems fitting that the health care industry is a key employer for Hot Springs' 4,000-plus citizens, along with the school district. Hot Springs Veterans Administration Medical Center and the State Veterans Home are here.

A sense of well-being is furthered by well-placed city parks and the Freedom Trail hiking and biking path beside the Fall River, which runs through town. If you can tear yourself away, you'll find unspoiled, uncrowded recreational spots in just about any direction, including Wind Cave National Park to the north (see the Parks & Mountains chapter) and Cascade Falls to the southwest, on the way to the Black Hills Wild Horse Sanctuary (see Attractions).

GETTING HERE, GETTING AROUND

Set in the middle of the country, the Black Hills are landlocked, a bit remote, and far from any huge metropolitan area. Still, getting here is easy enough and not too inconvenient, and their relative remoteness allows the not-yet-spoiled Hills to remain their charming selves. Most of us who live here wouldn't want it any other way.

Once you get here, however, you have quite a variety of options for getting around. There are bus, van, airplane, helicopter, and balloon tours, as well as some great bike paths and rentals. Of course, there are taxis and rental cars, too. Still, your best bet is to drive and see the Hills at your own pace. Although the Black Hills encompass 6,000 square miles, it's easy to get around quickly via I-90 and some well-maintained US and state highways. But because the fastest way isn't usually the most interesting way, we've included lesser-known scenic roads, too. These more lightly traveled routes meander through some of the most pleasant scenery in the Hills. Although it may take you twice as long to get where you're going via these routes, you'll have twice as much fun getting there. And fun is why you're here, isn't it?

If you're from a metropolitan area, you'll be pleased to note that South Dakota drivers are laid-back and patient with slow-traveling visitors. Angry honks are rare, but passing is not. Black Hills residents, who have grown up navigating the narrow canyons, like to speed. Law enforcement officials are usually tolerant of moderate speeding, but don't expect much leniency at night, when animals are more likely to bound across highways, or for drunk driving.

OVERVIEW

Though the Black Hills don't have the parking difficulties you'll find in big cities, parking is trickier here than in other, similar-size places. The increased traffic brought by visitors is one factor, but so is the simple issue of space. When you build towns in narrow mountain gulches, you barely have room for businesses and homes, let alone parking lots. Hill City and Keystone are challenging only during the day in summer, though Deadwood can be troublesome on evenings and weekends year-round, especially during popular special events.

In Rapid City the only parking problems you'll find are downtown though things improve after the summer tourist rush subsides. Traffic, however, can be quite slow all year during "rush hour"—which is nothing like its big-city counterpart. All the same, cars frequently back up in the Gap, the narrow corridor between east and west Rapid City. Things can be further complicated by trains, which tend to lumber through the Gap shortly after 5 p.m.

Overall, transportation problems are few here, making the Black Hills a beautiful and exciting place to travel any time of the year.

GETTING HERE

By Air

If you fly in on a commercial flight, you'll land at **Rapid City Regional Airport,** one of the fastest-growing airports in the US. If you're flying your own plane, you have more choices.

Northern Hills

**BLACK HILLS AIRPORT–
CLYDE ICE FIELD**
300 Aviation Place, Spearfish
(605) 642-4112, (800) 843-8010
Planes both small and large land here. The airport can even handle large corporate craft; in fact, Kevin Costner's big private jet occasionally sets down here. There are two grass strips, one is 4,000 feet and one is 2,000 feet long; one 6,400-foot asphalt strip; two large overnight hangars; and four county hangars with 11 slots each. The airport also has an instrument approach. Fuel, maintenance, and repair services are available (though no food service), and you can even camp on the grounds. Rental cars are available. The airport is 3 miles east of Spearfish. It is managed by Eagle Aviation, which also offers Eagle's View Air Tours (see listing under Eagle Aviation) and provides aircraft rental, flight instruction, and Cessna service and parts.

STURGIS MUNICIPAL AIRPORT
13345 Alkali Rd., Sturgis
(605) 347-3356
www.sturgiscityofriders.com/airport.php

This small, city-owned airport is 5 miles east of Sturgis on SR 34, then another mile down Alkali Road (turn right off the highway onto Alkali). The airport has 4,600 feet of asphaltic concrete runway; fuel, hangars, and maintenance service are available. You can't buy food or rent a car here.

C&B Aviation manages the airport, which can accommodate small planes and jets, turboprops, and twin-engine craft.

Central Hills

RAPID CITY REGIONAL AIRPORT
4550 Terminal Rd., Rapid City
(605) 394-4195
www.rapairport.org
This city-managed regional airport is a user-friendly, family-oriented facility that is among the fastest growing airports in the US. And, it offers convenient daily connections to Chicago, Minneapolis, Denver, Dallas and Salt Lake City, as well as weekly flights to Las Vegas and Phoenix.

Inside the 90,000-square-foot terminal, which is cozy and pleasant, you'll find thoughtful services, including free wireless Internet. The airport is one of only two in the country originally built with nurseries. The unattended nursery room—furnished with sink, chairs, and diapers—gives moms and dads a chance to let a child nap, change a baby's diaper, or find a moment of peace and quiet for themselves. Each elevator, escalator, and restroom has information in Braille, and there is one TDD phone in the terminal. The public-address system broadcasts outside the terminal entrance, so you won't miss important information if you leave the terminal. Increasingly busy, expansion of the facility is slated to begin in 2011.

The airport, 10 miles from downtown Rapid City off SR 44, has several runways for commercial and general aviation use. Jets the size of 747s and 757s can land here, but larger jets and international flights are not accommodated.

Car rental agencies with desks at the terminal include: **Avis,** (605) 393-0740, (800) 331-1212; **Budget,** (605) 393-0488, (800) 676-0488; **Hertz,** (605) 393-0160, (800) 654-3131; **National,** (605) 393-2664, (800) 227-7368; and listings of additional car rental agencies are in the Getting Around by Rental Car section of this chapter.

Airport Express Shuttle, (605) 399-9999 or (800) 357-9998, serves the airport. Other shuttle and taxi services are available, but you must call them to schedule service. All are listed later in this chapter in the Getting Around by Taxi, Shuttle, and Limo section.

If you fly your own plane into Rapid City Regional Airport, two fixed-base operators can service your plane while you tour the Hills: **Westjet Air Center,** 4160 Fire Station Rd., Rapid City, (605) 393-2500, (800) 888-4270, provides full maintenance services, pilot lounge, tie-downs, hangers, catering and aircraft sales. **Rapid Fuel,** 3900 Airport Rd., Rapid City, (605) 393-4317 provides self service fueling, pilot lounge and tie-downs.

Southern Hills
CUSTER STATE PARK AIRPORT
Custer State Park, Custer
(605) 255-4515
You can fly your small plane into Custer State Park, land on the paved runway, park, and tie down your plane (no hangars are available). No car rentals or pickup services are available, however, and whoever picks you up must purchase a state park entrance license. The airstrip is in the east-central portion of the park, off Wildlife Loop Road. You need to obtain permission before landing.

HOT SPRINGS MUNICIPAL AIRPORT
SR 79 South, Hot Springs
(605) 745-3555
The city of Hot Springs manages this airport, which has one asphalt runway (4,500 feet) and one turf runway (4,000 feet). It can handle aircraft such as business planes or small jets. The airport has no maintenance service. Tie-downs are available but you may want to bring your own. They also offer self-service fuel, car rentals, and a customer lounge area. The airport is 7 miles from Hot Springs.

By Bus

The Black Hills are apparently considered so remote that Greyhound buses don't directly serve the area. Fortunately, if you favor traveling by bus, you can make connections from Greyhound routes to two regional bus services, which operate out of **Milo Barber Transportation Center** in Rapid City and share a local telephone number and ticketing staff. The small transportation center terminal has a pleasant waiting area and vending machines but no food service.

JEFFERSON LINES
Milo Barber Transportation Center
333 6th St., Rapid City
(605) 348-3300,
(612) 332-8745 (charters and tours),
(800) 451-5333 (schedules)
www.jeffersonlines.com
Jefferson offers bus service to points east of Rapid City. The staff can schedule your entire trip, even the portions you'll travel by Greyhound. Rapid City is the only Black Hills town at which Jefferson buses make stops. The company also offers charters and sightseeing tours for groups.

POWDER RIVER COACH USA

Milo Barber Transportation Center
333 6th St., Rapid City
(605) 348-3300, (800) 442-3682
1700 East US 14, Rapid City
(307) 682-0960

Powder River has service to points west of Rapid City. You can schedule your complete route, even the Greyhound connections, through the transportation center. In addition to stops in Rapid City, buses make scheduled stops in Sturgis and Spearfish. Powder River also provides charters and sightseeing tours to groups. A second location is at 1700 East US 14 (307-682-0960), also in Rapid City.

By Car

Denver is about 400 miles from the Black Hills; Kansas City, Missouri, is nearly 700 miles away; the Twin Cities of Minneapolis and St. Paul are about 600 miles distant; and Omaha, Nebraska, is some 500 miles away.

The major (and easiest) route to the Hills is I-90, which skirts the northern and northeastern boundaries of the Black Hills. I-90 has convenient exits to Rapid City, Sturgis, and Spearfish. Alternatively, if you're crossing the northern Midwest on I-94, you can exit at Belfield, North Dakota (near Dickinson), onto US 85, which goes south to Belle Fourche. I-80 runs through the midsection of the Midwest, where you can catch US 26 at Ogallala, Nebraska, then US 385 at Northport, Nebraska, and head north to Hot Springs, South Dakota, at the southern edge of the Black Hills.

Check out the rules of the road in the Getting Around by Car section that follows, so you'll be aware of South Dakota's traffic regulations as soon as you cross the state line.

i Temperature differences in the Northern, Central, and Southern Hills can be as much as 10 to 15 degrees. You may leave Rapid City, for example, on a warm afternoon only to find it much cooler in Deadwood or windier in Hot Springs. Pack the proper clothing for your drive.

GETTING AROUND

By Air

If you're a fan of flying, try an air tour or a balloon or helicopter ride. For those who fly a private plane into the Hills, there are several places mentioned in the "By Air" section to park your aircraft, have it serviced, and leave it safely while you go off to sightsee. Two balloon companies in the Hills can take you for a very special ride. **Black Hills Balloons** in Custer, (605) 673-2520, is listed in the Recreation chapter under Ballooning. A helicopter ride is another thrilling way to see the Black Hills. **Black Hills Aerial Adventures** north of Custer, (605) 673-2163, is listed in the Attractions chapter under Tours and Byways.

Northern Hills

EAGLE AVIATION

300 Aviation Place, Spearfish
(605) 642-4112, (800) 843-8010
www.eagleaviationinc.com

Eagle Aviation, which is based at and also manages Black Hills Airport—Clyde Ice Field, offers Eagle's View Air Tours for two to five people in a Cessna high-wing aircraft (the wings are above the windows for unobstructed views). Fly over gold country (Lead, Deadwood, Spearfish Canyon, and the Homestake mines) or Devils Tower, Mount Rushmore, and Crazy Horse Memorial on 20- to 120-minute tours. Upon request, pilots can fly you over some nearby Wyoming and Montana attractions. Eagle Aviation also has a charter service.

By Bicycle

Bicycling is a great way to see the Hills up close, at a more leisurely pace. If you didn't bring your own equipment, you'll find bike rental information in the Bike Tours and Rentals section of the Recreation chapter.

Rapid City has a wonderful bike path that meanders 13.5 miles through the city, following sparkling Rapid Creek and bisecting the city's extensive park system. And, two new bike trail systems are under construction. This foresighted city's policy is that all new streets will incorporate bike paths in their construction. The town of Sturgis has a Centennial Bike Path that runs from Brown High School, east of town, to SR 34 on the south side of town.

Spearfish has a bike path that runs in sections (some are concrete paved, others are sections of streets) from the northwest side of town to the south side. Even the streets of most small towns that lack official bike paths are usually lightly traveled, which makes biking them a treat.

The best-known bike paths in the Black Hills, however, are recreational gems: the **George S. Mickelson Trail** and the **Centennial Trail** (both multiuse and open to bicyclists, hikers, horseback riders, and cross-country skiers). You'll find more about both in the Recreation chapter.

By Bus & Van Tour

Many companies will customize your tour; just tell them what you'd like to see and they'll take you there. We recommend you write or call for a brochure to determine if the tour fits your plans, then call to schedule before you arrive. Some companies adjust their operating hours for winter weather.

Northern Hills
ALKALI IKE TOURS
Deadwood
(605) 578-3147
www.alkaliiketours.com
These are history-packed, narrated, one-hour tours of Deadwood and Mount Moriah Cemetery. Look for the ticket booth in front of Old Style Saloon No. 10 at 657 Main St. Tours begin at that location five times per day. Alkali Ike Tours' 46-passenger buses operate from May through Oct 1, weather permitting.

BOOT HILL TOURS
Deadwood
(605) 578-3758
www.boothilltours.com
This tour company provides one-hour narrated tours of Deadwood and Mount Moriah Cemetery in a 40-passenger bus. Tours start at the Bodega, 662 Main St., five times each day.

DAKOTA BUS SERVICE
631 South 32nd St., Spearfish
(605) 642-2353
This service offers shuttles to Deadwood as well as charters and customized sightseeing tours to destinations in the Black Hills and throughout the country. It accommodates only groups.

ORIGINAL DEADWOOD TOUR
Deadwood
(605) 578-2091
www.originaldeadwoodtour.com

Since 1974, the Original Deadwood Tour has provided factual, entertaining, and humorous one-hour narrated tours of Deadwood and Mount Moriah Cemetery conducted in 40-passenger buses. The ticket booth is located in front of the Midnight Star at 677 Main St., where the tours begin.

i In 2003 the South Dakota Department of Transportation and the South Dakota Highway Patrol joined several other states in launching a 511 information system. Anyone in the state can dial 511 toll-free to receive complete weather and road construction reports that are updated regularly.

WESTERN TRANSPORTATION, INC.
Sturgis
(605) 347-5066
Take a sightseeing tour around the Hills or a chartered trip across the country. Customized and escorted tours are offered in 47-passenger coaches. Step-on guide service is available, too, which means a Western Transportation guide will accompany and narrate any tour. If you wish to write for tour information, send a request to P.O. Box 700, Sturgis, SD 57785.

Central Hills
AFFORDABLE ADVENTURES
Rapid City
(605) 342-7691
A very flexible tour company, Affordable Adventures offers jaunts all over western South Dakota and serves domestic and international clients. The owner is a "receptive operator," which means she can customize your tour to your needs and specifications. Vehicles are 7- and 11-passenger vans, but larger vehicles are available, too. The tours

are informative, are conducted by knowledgeable guides, and accommodate parties from two up to 100 people. To write for information use P.O. Box 903, Box Elder, SD 57719.

GRAY LINE OF THE BLACK HILLS
Rapid City
(605) 342-4461, (800) 456-4461
www.blackhillsgrayline.com
Gray Line is a worldwide company, and this locally owned franchise has 50 years of experience. It offers four- to ten-hour narrated sightseeing tours around the Hills and customized package tours that include accommodations and attractions. Gray Line also has a nationwide charter service. Many campgrounds, motels, and hotels can arrange a Gray Line tour for you, so inquire where you're lodging.

STAGECOACH WEST
Rapid City
(605) 343-3113, (888) 343-3113
www.mountrushmoretours.com
Groups of 1 to 100 or more can take both standard and customized narrated tours with Stagecoach West. Tours depart daily from Fort Hays located on US 16 between Rapid City and Mt. Rushmore. Cost for the tour only is $54 for adults, $27 for children ages 5 to 12. Children 4 and under, who sit on an adult's lap, are free. A nine-hour tour which includes a cowboy music show and meal is also available. The company also offers nationwide charters. If you'd like to write, send queries to P.O. Box 264, Rapid City, SD 57709.

Southern Hills
GOLDEN CIRCLE TOURS
Custer
(605) 673-4349
www.goldencircletours.com

Golden Circle's owners say 14-passenger vans travel roads that large buses can't. The buses pick up passengers at their Custer area lodging. The seven-hour tours include park entrance fees. They add that their drivers are experienced and knowledgeable and that their tours (including available narrated tours) are flexible. For more information write to P.O. Box 4033, Custer, SD 57730.

By Car

The Black Hills provide a majestic backdrop to any car ride, from multiday tours to grocery-store runs. Roads are wide and traffic laws are few, but there are some things you should know before making major forays into the Hills.

First, motorcyclists love it here. Thousands of visitors and locals alike ride their steel horses through South Dakota every summer. If you're used to watching for automobiles, you might find motorcycles easy to overlook—so keep an eye out. Only bikers under the age of 18 are required to wear a helmet. The only other equipment motorcyclists are required to have is eye protection (or a windshield) and rearview mirrors.

Second, remember that there is an abundance of wildlife here. It's common to see deer, antelope, porcupine, and even the occasional coyote or elk standing on the shoulder, especially at dawn or dusk. It's just as common for them to dart out in front of passing vehicles, so be vigilant and keep a finger on the horn.

The narrow, winding quality of Black Hills roads makes traveling fun, but only if you keep your eyes on the pavement. Let the passengers do the *oohing* and *aahing*, or you might end up approaching a tight corner too quickly. Most major bends have suggested speeds posted before the turn—many signs

South Dakota's Low Profile

In 1987, Frank and Deborah Popper of Rutgers University in New Jersey proposed turning parts of the Great Plains (which include South Dakota) into a Buffalo Commons—a game preserve of sorts.

They predicted that climatic and economic hardship, and even the landscape, would drive away what remained of the already sparse human population. Two years later an article in *Newsweek* magazine included our fair state in what it called "America's Outback," a region on the brink of decay.

At the same time, publisher Rand McNally omitted South Dakota, North Dakota, and parts of other apparently insignificant states from portions of its *Photographic World Atlas* for lack of space. Insulting? Not really. The truth is, we kind of like it when others think we live in a throwaway state. As Custer State Park once noted in a promotional piece, "Out Here" a traffic jam is when the bison herd crosses the highway in the park.

recommend speeds appropriate for RVs, but some suggested speeds may seem tight even for compacts. If in doubt, slow down.

South Dakotans hate it when anyone tries to dictate their behavior. All the same, the state's seat-belt laws are getting more aggressive. Any adult in the front seats must wear a belt, but you cannot be ticketed for not wearing a seat belt unless you have been pulled over for another offense. On the other hand, anyone under the age of 18 may be cited for not wearing a safety belt even if you weren't pulled over for something else.

Drinking and driving is not taken lightly in South Dakota. A person is legally intoxicated with a blood-alcohol content of .08 or more. Highway patrol officers carry digital breath-analyzer devices. If you're suspected of driving under the influence, you'll be asked to take the test. If you are arrested for DUI and refuse, your driver's license will be confiscated at the time of arrest. And if the officer smells alcohol on your breath, you can be taken directly to jail.

i South Dakota has a "move over law" which requires motorists on a four-lane highway to use the left lane if a law enforcement vehicle is pulled off on the right shoulder and is flashing amber lights.

The speed limit on South Dakota interstate highways is 75 mph, except through cities, where it is reduced to 65 mph. Most state and US highways have a speed limit of 55 through the Black Hills.

Right turns on red are permitted in South Dakota unless otherwise posted.

If you're traveling on school days, you may meet school buses on the roads. When the yellow lights of a bus flash, prepare to stop. When the red lights flash, all drivers (in all directions) must stop at least 15 feet from the bus and remain stopped until the lights no longer flash. When the bus's yellow hazard lights flash (for example, at a railroad crossing), motorists must stop and then proceed with caution. Bus drivers are authorized to turn in the license numbers of offenders.

The Faster Routes

NORTHERN HILLS

If you need to get where you're going in a hurry, I-90 is the route to travel. It follows the boundaries of the north and northeastern Black Hills and, thus, is the ideal route to Sturgis (exits 30 or 32) and Spearfish (exits 10, 12, or 14). From those towns you can pick up routes to take you farther north to Belle Fourche or south to the towns of Lead, Deadwood, Nemo, Rapid City, and others.

CENTRAL HILLS

From I-90, use exits 55 through 61 to reach Rapid City. If you're heading to the Central Hills, US 16 South has four lanes from Rapid City to Keystone. US 16A to Mount Rushmore, which branches off US 16 near Keystone, is also a four-lane highway. From that area, US 16 South becomes a two-lane road.

i In Rapid City, Main Street runs one-way west and St. Joseph Street (locally known as "St. Joe") runs one-way east. West Boulevard and East Boulevard mark the west and east borders of downtown, and numbered streets from First to Ninth run north and south between them. Mount Rushmore Road (US 16) is sometimes called 8th Street or Rushmore Road by longtime residents.

SOUTHERN HILLS

The fastest route to the Southern Hills is SR 79, which runs from Rapid City, past Hermosa, to the Hot Springs area. SR 79 rolls through prairie hills and Buffalo Gap (where legend says the buffalo entered the Black Hills). It intersects US 385, which will take you 3 miles west into Hot Springs. There you can

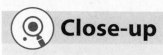 **Close-up**

Nellie Zabel Willhite, Pioneer Aviatrix

In the early days of aviation it took a courageous person to fly those "orange crates"—rickety biplanes that would never pass the aircraft safety standards of today. That's why the pilots were called daredevils, for only truly daring people risked life and limb to soar through the air, betting skill and wild courage against the high odds they'd never make it safely back to the ground.

In the 1920s, in the midst of excitement over aviation's arrival in the area—which brought wing walkers, barnstormers, stunt fliers, and ride-for-a-dollar pilots—came **Nellie Zabel Willhite**. She was skilled and adventurous, brave and strikingly pretty, with determined eyes and a bright smile . . . and she was deaf.

Nellie was born in a log cabin in Box Elder in 1892. Her father, Charley "Pard" Zabel, was also a pioneer. He left Wisconsin for the Black Hills when he was 17 and took up freighting: driving oxen teams loaded with merchandise over the Fort Pierre-Deadwood route. Nellie's uncle was the famous Russ Madison, known as Mr. Rodeo for his role in founding many rodeo events as well as the organization that would later become today's Professional Rodeo Cowboys Association.

When Nellie was two, a bout with measles robbed her of her hearing. When she was eight, her mother died. She was unable to communicate, so her grieving father took her to the State School for the Deaf, where she was taken in by a kindly doctor and his wife, who taught her lipreading and other skills. She later studied drawing at Yankton College and music at the Boston Conservatory.

But it was another talent that changed Nellie's life in a most dramatic way. In late 1927 she learned to fly, just five days before her 35th birthday. She was the 13th student at the Dakota Airlines Flying School in Sioux Falls. She soloed on Friday, January 13, 1928, after 13 hours of instruction, then landed smack-dab in a mud puddle. Thereafter, 13 was her lucky number.

The first licensed woman pilot in South Dakota, and probably the first woman in the state to pilot an airplane, Nellie told her father of her dreams to fly. He promptly bought an old Eaglerock biplane, which she christened with the number 13 and the nickname "Pard" in Charley's honor. He returned the compliment by joyfully telling her she had "the instincts of a wild goose" when she found her way, using road maps and with Charley aboard, to Wisconsin.

Nellie and winged Pard barnstormed the country, racing, stunt flying, and giving rides to awed onlookers. Once they were swept up into a tornado and went from 2,000 to 8,000 feet in a matter of seconds. Keeping her head, Nellie pushed Pard into a downward 3,000-foot spiral and restarted the stalled engine, escaping with only badly shaken nerves. Her most memorable experience, however, was the time "at the top of a loop-the-loop maneuver two or three mice fell out from somewhere in the floor of my plane—and I hoped there wouldn't be any more of them."

Nellie belonged to the "99s," the prestigious club of women pilots of which Amelia Earhart was the first president. She was a friend and student of Clyde Ice, another early South Dakota aviation pioneer, for whom the field at Black Hills Airport in Spearfish is named.

Nellie Willhite passed away at the age of 99 in 1991. Before she died, however, she was inducted into the South Dakota Hall of Fame and the state's Aviation Hall of Fame in recognition of her achievements as both a pioneer aviatrix and a woman whose handicap never got in her way.

journey farther south on SR 71 to Angostura State Recreation Area or use US 18 to go farther west or east.

The Scenic Routes

Ah, the scenery! That's what you came here to see, and there's no better way to view it than on scenic routes. We can truthfully say there are no unscenic highways in the Black Hills, but we've listed our favorites below. Take a leisurely drive through some of the most picturesque landscape west of the Mississippi, with plenty of opportunities to pull over, park, and look around.

If you favor quiet, little-traveled routes known only to locals, we have plenty to offer. The Black Hills National Forest is positively laced with county and forest service roads—most graveled and rather narrow—where you'll see sights only locals usually see. If you have a good sense of direction and an adventurous spirit, you'll love exploring these roads. Get a detailed road map and plenty of gasoline first, and be prepared for emergencies or car trouble, because you may not meet another car, and you'll be far from help should you need it.

i It's a good idea to fill your gas tank before touring the Black Hills, especially if you're using back roads and scenic routes. Gas stations are sometimes few and far between, and you'll be driving for miles, possibly quite far from the nearest town. You don't want worries about running out of gas to spoil your enjoyment of the scenery.

NORTHERN HILLS

The 19-mile **Spearfish Canyon State Scenic Byway, US 14A,** is one of the best drives

around. It runs between Spearfish and Cheyenne Crossing, and you'll meander along the paved road, following pretty Spearfish Creek past towering limestone cliffs, waterfalls and evergreen and aspen forests.

There are some great places to hike just off the highway, including Roughlock Falls and Spearfish Peak, and there's information about biking, climbing, and crosscountry skiing in Spearfish Canyon in the Recreation chapter. You'll find more information on the Spearfish Canyon State Scenic Byway in the Attractions chapter.

US 14A also runs east and west between Deadwood and Sturgis, through beautiful Boulder Canyon. Traveling west, you'll reach a wide valley that is being developed with houses and businesses, then the road enters the canyon again and twists, turns, and climbs. The last mile or so is a steep grade that drops down into the town of Deadwood.

CENTRAL HILLS

A great Central Hills drive is along **SR 44** (Jackson Boulevard west from Rapid City), then US 385 North. SR 44 is known as the **Rimrock Highway.** It passes Cleghorn Springs State Fish Hatchery, Thunderhead Underground Falls, and other attractions (there's information about these in the Attractions chapter). It runs along Rapid Creek through spectacular canyons, where rimrock cliffs tower above you, and the little town of Johnson Siding. Rimrock Highway dead-ends into US 385, the Black Hills Parkway, from which you can head north to Deadwood and Lead, taking side trips on county roads to the little towns of Rochford, Silver City, or Mystic. You can also follow the road south, past Pactola Reservoir and Sheridan Lake to Hill City, Custer, and Hot

Springs. The Black Hills Parkway bisects the Hills, north to south, from Deadwood/Lead to Hot Springs.

Nemo Road (Pennington/Lawrence CR 234) begins at West Chicago Street in Rapid City and winds through lovely woods to the quaint town of Nemo. The road ends at US 385 south of Deadwood and Lead.

Pennington County Road 323, the Old Hill City Road, will take you from Keystone to Hill City through some pleasing scenery. The narrow road follows Battle Creek and crosses and recrosses (several times) the tracks used by The 1880 Train (see Attractions). Watch out for the train in the summer. You'll see some gorgeous rock formations along this winding route, too.

One of our favorite drives is **Forest Service Road 17** from Hill City to Deerfield Lake. The road occasionally runs parallel to the George S. Mickelson Trail, which is detailed in the Recreation chapter. This area has interesting and surprising examples of rolling prairie in the middle of the pine-covered Black Hills. From Deerfield, FR 17 (this section is unpaved) turns north and intersects with FR 231, which leads to the whimsical mountain town of Rochford, founded in 1878.

SR 40 travels from the subtle prairie plains of the Hermosa area to the wooded foothills around the little town of Hayward, then into the higher hills of Keystone. As you drive toward Hayward, look to your left (the south side of the road) to see Mount Rushmore in the distance.

SOUTHERN HILLS

You simply must not miss the exquisite **Peter Norbeck National Scenic Byway**, 70 miles of road that loops through the Black Hills National Forest, Norbeck Wildlife Preserve, and Custer State Park. The byway includes the Needles Highway (SR 87/89), Horse Thief Lake Road (SR 244), and Iron Mountain Road (US 16A).

You'll see historic sites, wild animals, nifty switchbacks, pigtail bridges, lakes, and towering granite spires as you pass through tiny tunnels. Because we consider the byway a major attraction, you'll find complete information in the Attractions chapter, but note that sections of Iron Mountain Road and the Needles Highway close during the winter.

Custer State Park's Wildlife Loop is another drive you mustn't miss. Its 18 miles of paved road literally loop through the beautiful park. You will probably see bison, deer, hawks, pronghorn antelope, prairie dogs, and the park's begging burros. If you're really lucky, you'll also spot Rocky Mountain goats, bighorn sheep, elk, and coyotes. There's more about Custer State Park and its wonderful roads in the Parks & Mountains chapter. We also recommend SR 36 from Hermosa to Custer State Park, a delightful road that winds through pretty farm and ranch country. The landscape becomes increasingly beautiful as you approach the park. Near the park entrance, SR 36 becomes US 16A.

i Most interstate information centers (plus one at Mount Rushmore and one at Custer State Park) have interactive kiosks. Touch the screen to find information on attractions, accommodations, and routes. Some centers stock travel tapes. For $20, you can listen and learn about the sights as you drive across the state. When you return the tape you receive $15 back.

By Public Transportation

Unfortunately, the Hills lack public transportation systems, except for the two below.

Northern Hills
DEADWOOD TROLLEY
City of Deadwood
102 Sherman St., Deadwood
(605) 578-2622

Not many communities with fewer than 2,000 residents can afford a public transportation system, let alone one this complete. Trolleys run from one end of town to the other seven days a week, stopping at all the major hotels, casinos, and attractions. From Memorial Day to mid-Sept, trolleys operate 7 a.m. to 1:30 a.m. Sun through Thurs and 7 a.m. to 3 a.m. Fri through Sat and hit each stop as often as every 10 minutes, although the coming of winter sees a trolley at each stop every hour, and only until midnight or 2 a.m. Fares are simple—one ride costs $1—and though the system was designed primarily for tourists, locals love its convenience. Alas, the trolleys themselves are rubber wheeled, but steel-wheeled trolleys have been suggested by historic preservation consultants on multiple occasions. Still, the vehicles are very distinctive, marked with bright green and gold paint, with wooden benches and open-air seating in summer.

Central Hills
RAPIDRIDE/DIAL-A-RIDE
333 6th St., Rapid City
(605) 394-6631

These small buses operate Mon through Fri, 6:25 a.m. to 6 p.m. Fares are $1.50 for adults and 75 cents for seniors 60 and older and disabled individuals. Those with transfers from another route and children younger than age five (with adults) ride for free. The RapidRide office is in the Milo Barber Transportation Center. Its five designated routes cover schools, the hospital, the mall, the library, and popular shopping areas rather than visitor attractions, so it's more a service for residents than for tourists. If you want to try it, however, get a schedule at the transportation center so you'll know where the buses stop. A new City View Trolley hits the Journey Museum, Stavkirk Chapel, Storybook Island, Dinosaur Park, and other local attractions and provides a narrated tour. Adults are $2, children under 12 and seniors over 60 are only $1. Call (605) 394-6631 for schedules and more information.

By Rental Car

We list the nationally recognized companies plus some local businesses. Some automobile dealerships also rent vehicles (look under Auto Renting in the Yellow Pages). Many rental car companies have SUVs, trucks, and vans, too; inquire if you need something bigger and more rugged than a passenger car.

In the Black Hills are **Avis,** (605) 393-0740, (800) 331-1212; **Budget,** (605) 393-0488, (800) 676-0488; **Dollar,** (605) 342-7071, (800) 800-4000; **Enterprise,** (605) 399-9939, (800) 325-8007; **Hertz,** (605) 393-0160, (800) 654-3131; **National Car Rental,** (605) 393-2664, (800) 227-7368; and **Thrifty Car Rental,** (605) 393-0663, (800) 847-4389. Budget also has a second location at 1947 Deadwood Ave. in Rapid City, (605) 341-9040.

Local rental car companies include Rent-A-Wreck and Casey's car rentals in Rapid City. **Rent-A-Wreck,** located at 1600 E SR 44, (605) 348-3050, (800) 733-WREK, provides pickup and return service as does **Casey's,** 1318 5th St., (605) 343-2277.

By Taxi, Shuttle, and Limo

Many of these services also offer customized sightseeing tours; call ahead if you're interested.

Northern Hills
DAKOTA TAXI
(605) 920-2020
www.dakotataxi@rushmore.com
Serving primarily the northern Black Hills communities of Deadwood, Lead, Sturgis, and Spearfish, Dakota Taxi also provides shuttles to Rapid City Regional Airport.

Central Hills
AIRPORT EXPRESS SHUTTLE
Rapid City
(605) 399-9999, (800) 357-9998
You'll find drivers waiting at Rapid City Regional Airport during scheduled flight arrivals, or you can call them for a pickup. They'll take you where you want to go, whether that's from the airport to downtown Rapid City, to your hotel, to Deadwood, or on a tour.

DIAMOND PREMIER LIMOUSINE & SIGHTSEEING TOURS
Rapid City
(605) 787-6796, (800) 718-8544
www.blackhillslimo.com
Rent a fifteen-person luxury stretch Hummer limo for any occasion, including tours through the Black Hills and to Deadwood, or ride to the airport in style. They offer several luxury vehicles from which to choose.

PRESIDENTIAL LIMOUSINE
Rapid City
(605) 390-3691, (800) 357-9998
Available 24/7 for airport transfers, events or tours with vehicles accommodating 6 to 14

passengers. Rent a special nostalgic vehicle built by Jesse James on the Discovery Channel named the "Red Rockin Limo."

RAPID TAXI
Rapid City
(605) 348-8080
This taxi service will take you around town or out of town.

By Train

✳BLACK HILLS CENTRAL RAILROAD/ THE 1880 TRAIN
222 Railroad Ave., Hill City
(605) 574-2222
www.1880train.com
You can take an old-fashioned train ride from Keystone to Hill City and back again on this delightful train. There's information in the Attractions chapter on these 20-mile round-trip train rides, which are a terrific way to see the Black Hills the way the old-timers used to.

Specialty Transportation

WHEELCHAIR SERVICE OF THE BLACK HILLS
(605) 341-2577
This company specializes in nonemergency transportation for people in wheelchairs. Although its drivers usually transport people on errands and to appointments, the service also offers sightseeing tours around the Hills. Its vans with lifts have a capacity of three wheelchairs. Operating hours are 8 a.m. to 5 p.m. Mon, Wed and Fri. Call ahead to arrange a customized tour.

HISTORY

In geologic terms, Black Hills history dates back millions of years. Because that part of our past is covered in the Natural World chapter, this chapter focuses on what is known about humans' presence here. (For a history of the Badlands, please see the Badlands & Nearby chapter.) It's an abbreviated account, however, because so much took place in a very short time. Scores of books have been written on the subject, and you'll find many of them in libraries, bookstores, and gift shops.

South Dakota attained statehood on November 2, 1889, more than a decade after pioneer settlement of the Hills had begun in earnest in 1875–76. From that time forward the story has been one of boom and bust, fire and flood, hunger and plenty—but always one of diligent efforts toward the building of strong, enduring communities.

Black Hills history, however, isn't just about the spread of European civilization on the western frontier. For the Native inhabitants, white encroachment on the Black Hills region was an invasion of a bountiful and cherished domain, and the struggle for its control was long and bloody. Although American Indians and non-Indians later learned to coexist, bridging the ideological and cultural chasm between the two groups is still a work in progress.

Tensions flared anew in 1973 when members of the American Indian Movement (AIM) rioted and set the Custer County Courthouse on fire to protest the killing of an Indian by a white man. The conflict grabbed national headlines when AIM members occupied Wounded Knee village on the Pine Ridge Indian Reservation, staging a symbolic 71-day standoff to protest the treatment of American Indians in general. Wounded Knee II, as it came to be called, is considered a turning point in modern American Indian life, but it took almost another two decades before Indians and non-Indians in South Dakota reached out their hands in friendship. Accepting a challenge by then *Indian Country Today* newspaper publisher Tim Giago, the late Gov. George S. Mickelson declared a Year of Reconciliation in 1990, the 100th anniversary of the infamous Wounded Knee Massacre. It was the first step of a long journey.

WHO WAS HERE FIRST?

Archaeological evidence indicates the presence of prehistoric hunters called Paleo-Indians in the area as early as 11,000 years ago. Believed to have originated in Asia and crossed the Bering Land Bridge to the New World, these nomads and their successors left a record over the course of several millennia. Their ancient petroglyphs have been found carved, painted, and pecked into the rock at various places in the southern Black Hills; you'll get to examine some of them if you tour the Black Hills Wild Horse

Sanctuary near Hot Springs (see Attractions). More recently, roughly between 200 and 500 years ago, aboriginal peoples left evidence of hunting activity at the Vore Buffalo Jump west of nearby Beulah, Wyoming (see Day Trips & Weekend Getaways).

That American Indians were here when the first Euro-Americans arrived is undisputed, but there is disagreement about much else. According to a Sioux creation story, the Lakota (Western, or Teton, Sioux) tribes have always lived here. They entered the world through Wind Cave, lured from their subterranean home by a trickster who falsely promised them wealth. However, anthropologists say the Lakota didn't arrive in the Dakotas until the 18th century. In fact, their homeland was farther east in Minnesota and Wisconsin—perhaps even as far east as Virginia. But other tribes, outfitted with guns and pressured by white settlers, drove them to the plains. Before the Lakota were free to settle the region, however, they had to drive out the preexisting Crow and Arikara tribes.

Whatever the date of their arrival, events since the last quarter of the 19th century are clearly documented. The United States' last great gold rush forever changed the Black Hills and ended a way of life for a proud, powerful people who found themselves confined on desolate reservations and reduced to poverty and government dependence.

We might never know the name of the first person who set foot in the Black Hills, but we do know that a white man traveled through during the late summer of 1823—it was none other than fearless, pious Jedediah Smith, on his way west. But while Smith's presence is little more than a footnote in history, the unfinished chapter on the ultimate battle for control of the Black Hills begins with the name of bold, brash Lt. Col. George Armstrong Custer. For it was Custer who led an 1874 expedition authorized by the war department to gather information and also, perhaps above all, confirm rumors of gold in the streams and soil of Paha Sapa.

i Some early-day denizens of the Black Hills had colorful nicknames. Cold Deck Johnny, Swill Barrel Jimmy, Three Sixes Joe, Slippery Sam, Bummer Dan, Mineral Jack, Bedrock Tom, and Madame Mustachio are monikers that arouse conjecture about their owners.

TREATIES & LAND CLAIMS

As the westward push brought competition for land, the US government devised treaties that set aside territory for exclusive use by Indian tribes in exchange for promises that westering pioneers and settlers would not be harmed. The Fort Laramie Treaty of 1868 was one such agreement; it ceded western Dakota Territory (which included the Black Hills) and parts of neighboring states to the Sioux—oblivious to claims that might legitimately have been made by other tribes.

Enter Custer and a series of events that changed minds in the nation's capital. First, the Custer expedition—which was itself illegal by the terms of the Fort Laramie Treaty—confirmed and greatly exaggerated the presence of gold in the Black Hills. That left the government powerless, and soon unwilling, to turn aside the wave of prospectors that quickly followed. In addition, the gold rush of 1876 coincided not only with the nation's centennial but with Custer's death at the hands of Indian tribes in the Battle of the Little Bighorn. We can assume that federal officials and the nation as a whole did not look kindly on Indians after that. Congress, determined to annex the Black Hills, demanded in 1877 that they be sold, and opened the area for settlement in spite of Sioux resistance. Refusing to accept the terms, the tribes filed suit in 1923, claiming that the Black Hills had been seized unlawfully.

i The Homestake Gold Mine caused the city of Lead to be rearranged several times. Before mined-out tunnels were properly backfilled, streets and buildings had to be moved as the ground above the mine gradually sank. In the 1990s the mine rerouted US 85, the city's Main Street, and moved buildings to allow expansion of the surface mine.

More than half a century later, in 1979, the US Court of Claims agreed, awarding the tribes compensation and damages in excess of $100 million, a decision upheld by the US Supreme Court the next year. However, the Sioux have refused to take the money, which has approximately tripled in interest-bearing accounts in the Sioux Nation's name. Now there are demands for the return of the land itself in accordance with the Fort Laramie Treaty.

US Sen. Bill Bradley of New Jersey tried to settle the controversy in 1985 with a bill that would have given the Sioux all federal land in western South Dakota except Mount Rushmore National Memorial, along with natural-resource and jurisdictional rights as well as the settlement money. The Bradley bill never made it to the Senate floor, however, and a second attempt failed as well.

There is a great deal of opposition to the concept of conveying the Black Hills to Native American ownership, for several reasons. To many in the wider society, this concept appears as a threat to the social and economic order that has taken hold over the last century. In addition, there are those who argue that the Fort Laramie Treaty was broken by both sides and is no longer valid or even relevant; that whites acted no differently from Lakotas in displacing prior occupants of the land.

There is also disagreement over the role of the Black Hills in American Indian life. Plains-dwelling Indian tribes are not known to have lived within the boundaries of the Hills but did enter the area at times for various purposes and do consider them sacred.

If consensus about who can rightfully claim the Black Hills is ever reached, it's not likely to happen anytime soon.

BLACK HILLS OR BUST

Once word of the Custer expedition's discovery of gold in French Creek was out, adventurers began organizing illegal forays to the Black Hills. The first group to evade the military units assigned to keep fortune hunters out was the Gordon Party, which departed from Sioux City, Iowa, in late 1874. Among the party were Annie Tallent, the first white woman known to enter the Black Hills, and her nine-year-old son, Robert. Arriving at French Creek on Christmas Eve, the invaders set about building a sturdy log stockade. Their presence was soon detected, however, and the next April they were escorted out of the Hills by blue-coated soldiers. Today you can visit a re-creation of the Gordon Stockade in Custer State Park (see the Parks & Mountains chapter).

The escapade made headlines, and soon prospectors were entering the Hills in a brazen fashion. By 1876 a full-blown gold rush was under way. Although early efforts to find treasure focused on the French Creek and Custer areas in the Southern Hills, news of a gold strike in Deadwood Gulch quickly shifted the action north—so quickly, in fact, that the population of Custer City dropped from an estimated 6,000 or more to just 14 in a mere two weeks.

The first workings were placer (rhymes with Vassar) deposits that could be washed out of the gravel where gold had been dropped by slow-moving streams. As the easy diggings played out, miners began looking for rich hard-rock lodes on which to patent claims. The most famous of these was the Homestake, discovered in 1876 by brothers Fred and Moses Manuel and sold to George Hearst in 1877. By that time, the Hills were teeming with tens of thousands of prospectors, many of whom eventually returned home with empty pockets. Others successfully developed mining properties, harvesting gold, silver, or other minerals; in time, many of the deposits were mined out, and once-thriving communities decayed into ghost towns.

The Homestake Gold Mine in Lead had a different fate, continuing to produce gold decade after decade and making mining the cornerstone of the Northern Hills economy for generations. Mining and related business opportunities provided secure jobs and cash flow for the area, attracting immigrants of many nationalities who often formed their own ethnic neighborhoods in the new country. Some of these can still be seen in Lead today.

The roster of early-day citizenry also included many characters whose names and exploits are legendary. James Butler "Wild Bill" Hickok, dubbed the Prince of Pistoleers, was an early arrival in Deadwood. So was Martha Jane Cannary-Burke—Calamity Jane. Wild Bill, already famous as a lawman and a dead shot, made a grand exit when he was murdered during a card game by drifter Jack McCall. Salty-tongued Calamity, who often wore buckskins and carried sixguns, was reputed to be a down-and-out, not altogether honest, but kindly drunk who nursed the sick during a smallpox epidemic before succumbing to alcoholism in 1903. The origin of her nickname is uncertain, but many accounts attribute it to a venereal calamity that befell the gentlemen with whom she consorted. She and Wild Bill ("the only man I ever loved," she claimed after his death in 1876, although the then-recently wed Hickok doesn't seem to have returned the compliment) are buried along with other Deadwood notables in Mount Moriah Cemetery in Deadwood (see the Attractions chapter). Elfin 4-foot 3-inch prospector Potato Creek Johnny, martyrized Preacher Smith, and quick-witted Sheriff Seth Bullock also found their final resting place there, and a considerable tourist industry quickly took hold around all their legends. You can learn more about them at the Adams Museum in Deadwood, which you'll find listed in the Attractions chapter.

Tourism has become a top industry in the Black Hills, but it was mining that sustained the area during the Great Depression, when the federal government promised to pay top dollar for all the gold that was produced. Many who had lost their livelihoods found work as miners, and the value of Homestake stock soared. The company continued to prosper and pay good wages, and a new gold rush began after the price of gold reached $800 an ounce in the early 1980s. New heap-leach technology and

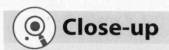 **Close-up**

The Custer Expedition of 1874

When **George Armstrong Custer** led an expedition into the Black Hills in the summer of 1874, he handed himself his own death certificate. The illegally conceived Custer expedition led to the gold rush of 1876, which triggered the US government to forcibly take the sacred Black Hills from Sioux control. This land seizure contributed greatly to the Indian Wars of the late 1870s and 1880s. One of the ensuing battles, fought near the Little Bighorn River, would take Custer's life.

Word of the gold found during Custer's trip might have been the catalyst that released wave after wave of white fortune-seekers, but the flood had been building for years. In fact, Secretary of the Interior Columbus Delano wrote a letter as early as 1872 bluntly spelling out the government's plan:

> I am inclined to think that the occupation of this region of the country is not necessary to the happiness and prosperity of the Indians, and as it is supposed to be rich in minerals and lumber it is deemed important to have it freed as early as possible from Indian occupancy.
> I shall, therefore, not oppose any policy which looks first to a careful examination of the subject. . . . If such an examination leads to the conclusion that country is not necessary or useful to Indians, I should then deem it advisable . . . to extinguish the claim of the Indians and open the territory to the occupation of the whites.

Although Delano was supposed to protect Plains Indian territorial rights, his words clearly contradicted the Fort Laramie Treaty of 1868, which prevented whites from ever setting foot in the "country" he mentioned. Nevertheless, two years after Delano's letter, Custer was off to conduct a "scientific survey" of the protected Great Sioux Indian Reservation.

Custer, his troops, and a small contingent of scientists arrived at the Belle Fourche River before entering the Black Hills on its western side. For two months the Seventh Cavalry scaled the mountainsides of the Lakota's Paha Sapa, collecting samples and writing reports about the valleys, the forests, and, eventually, the gold. These reports were regularly sent west to Fort Laramie, where they were telegraphed to army posts farther east.

Even if the official military reports hadn't leaked out, the journalists Custer took with him would have informed the country immediately on their return. In a matter of months prospectors were preparing to invade the forbidden Black Hills. The military was officially dispatched to escort any intruding pioneers off the protected Sioux lands, but it gave up in 1875, permitting thousands of gold seekers to descend upon the Black Hills. The Sioux, outraged over the broken Laramie Treaty, did their best to launch an organized rebellion. They scored their greatest victory in 1876 at the Battle of the Little Bighorn, where Custer and most of the men who were with him on the Black Hills expedition were killed.

But the resistance was doomed before it began. The Sioux, along with their Cheyenne and Arapaho allies, were ultimately defeated and forced onto the much smaller reservations we see on maps today. Their once-protected territory, land that covered parts of present-day Wyoming, Nebraska, and both Dakotas, was divided and sold to ranchers and prospectors.

the development of giant earthmoving machines led to the resurrection of mines that had closed decades before, and in the mid-1980s modern-day surface mining was introduced to the Black Hills. State permits were granted for operations that would dig deep pits totaling hundreds of acres and use cyanide solution to treat huge piles of crushed ore—as well as provide good jobs and substantial tax revenues.

Those developments produced a passionate, bitter conflict between environmentalists and mining supporters that ruptured the community and ruined friendships. In early 2004, local politicians reached an agreement with Barrick Gold Corporation, owner of the now-defunct Homestake Mine. The state government agreed to indemnify Barrick of various environmental liabilities in exchange for a free-and-clear donation of the mine for use as a National Underground Laboratory. As a result, the legislature has been allocating funds to construct a temporary lab at the mine's 4,850-foot level, which opened in 2009. The National Science Foundation selected Homestake as its preferred site for the permanent lab and South Dakota leaders continue efforts to attract high-technology firms to the region in anticipation of scientific research at Homestake.

LAW & ORDER

A death a day was the rule when a tent city sprang up in Deadwood Gulch in 1876. In no time at all there were 75 saloons in the town, and the local newspaper deplored the presence of claim jumpers and dance-hall girls. "The summer air is filled with profanity and curses," an editorial protested. Was Deadwood much different from any other western mining camp? Likely not. Things began to settle down, though, when court

was called to order on May 10, 1877. (One account says it was the first court session held in the Hills; another has the first session taking place about the same time in now-defunct Sheridan.)

Meanwhile, a Canadian hardware dealer who had come to Deadwood by way of Montana had become the first officially appointed sheriff in the Black Hills. An imposing figure, mustachioed Seth Bullock gained a reputation as the lawman who never killed anyone. He went on to success in many ventures, including a stint as the first Black Hills forest supervisor. He also became a close friend of Theodore Roosevelt, who was his frequent guest. A Belle Fourche rancher, he's even credited with introducing alfalfa to South Dakota.

Law officers in Belle Fourche probably could have used Bullock's help when handsome Harry Longabaugh—the Sundance Kid—and a group of outlaws tried to hold up the Butte County Bank there on June 28, 1897. The bungled job netted a trifling $97, but most of the bandits were quick enough to get as far as Red Lodge, Montana, before they were captured. They later escaped from the Deadwood jail and were never prosecuted for their crime.

i The original name of the town of Deadwood was "Dead Wood Gulch." The hills around the mining camp had suffered a forest fire years before the first prospectors arrived, and dead trees were everywhere. It wasn't long before enterprising entrepreneurs were selling firewood and the town had become known simply as "Deadwood."

History books recount many hair-raising stories of drunken judges and astonishing jury verdicts in the region's early days. But on some occasions irate citizens took the law into their own hands, as when masked vigilantes broke into a temporary jail in Rapid City and hanged three alleged horse thieves the night of June 21, 1877. Many people believed one of the executed men, 19-year-old Jas. (presumably James) "Kid" Hall, was innocent. The incident caused a rift among the citizenry and earned Rapid City the unflattering nickname Strangle Town. A dead tree on Hangman's Hill on Skyline Drive in Rapid City may or may not be the actual tree used in the lynching, but, rooted in cement, it serves today as a grizzly reminder of do-it-yourself frontier justice.

Nowadays, judgment is handed down in hushed courtrooms according to uniform, codified laws that take up many volumes on law library shelves. But even after the law became more organized and orderly, a wild streak persisted in the Black Hills for many years. Brothels like Pam's Purple Door continued to operate in Deadwood until an FBI raid closed them down in 1980. The bust made national news, and Deadwood once more made headlines as a sinful city.

i In 2009 South Dakota ranked sixth in the nation in total ethanol production. This could be an important asset as vehicle manufacturers increase production of vehicles that can run primarily on ethanol.

RANCHING

While others were busy with the pursuit of shiny yellow metal, would-be cattle barons had their sights set on green gold. To them, the waving grass on the fringes of the Black Hills looked like a giant pasture for fattening livestock. Soon cattle herds that plodded up the dusty trails from Texas were grazing on vast spreads where, not long before, huge bison herds had roamed. White hunters, eager for buffalo robes, had decimated the native animals and by so doing, driven a stake into the heart of Plains Indian life.

The first herd of cattle turned loose on the range was driven away by the Sioux, but in 1875 a Coloradan named Joe Reynolds brought Hereford stock to the Central Hills and established the area's oldest ranch. Historic Reynolds Stage Stop is still a working ranch.

Once settlers arrived for good in the Black Hills and it became clear that there weren't enough gold mines to go around, some turned their attention north to the wide-open grasslands of what is now Butte County. Ranching flourished there, and so did the city of Belle Fourche in its southwest corner. By the end of the 19th century, Belle Fourche had become the cattle-shipping capital of the world, with herds lined up for miles waiting to be loaded into railroad cars bound for eastern markets.

Early on, however, in the 1880s, an enterprising Minnesota judge noticed that the short-grass prairie would also be ideal for raising sheep. H. J. Grant brought the first sheep to western Dakota Territory from Texas in the 1880s, much to the indignation of the cattle ranchers. They listed all kinds of ways sheep would ruin their grazing land and contaminate their water. They were wrong, it turned out, and when they discovered that wool could be at least as profitable as beef, some either switched altogether or added sheep to their operations. Today, a wool warehouse in Belle Fourche still buys wool from ranchers in a wide area and sells it to mills all over the country.

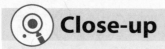

Close-up

The Sioux

Tepees. Buffalo hunts. Beadwork. Feather headdresses. The movie *Dances with Wolves*. This is how the **Sioux** are most often portrayed. Is it an accurate picture? Yes and no.

The term "Sioux" refers to a group of American Indian tribes originally united by a common language, Siouan. The name is a French-English corruption of the Ojibwa (Chippewa) *nadow-is-iw,* a derisive term meaning "adders," or "snakelike." But many don't realize that the people known today as the Sioux are made up of three divisions that have distinct dialects and cultural attributes. The primary divisions are Dakota (Santee, or Eastern), Nakota (Yankton, or Middle), and Lakota (Teton, or Western), and each of these has further subdivisions.

Dakota and Nakota tribes, who settled in woodland and river areas respectively, often lived in bark dwellings or earth lodges and grew crops. The largest and most powerful division, the Lakota, was made up of nomadic, tepee-dwelling, horse-mounted bands that dominated the Great Plains when white settlers arrived. The Lakota came to represent the quintessential Plains Indians.

Lakota subdivisions, known as the "Seven Tents," are Oglala (Red Cloud was a famous chief), Hunkpapa (Sitting Bull's people), Minneconjou (Big Foot's followers), Sicangu (also called Brule), Sans Arcs, Sihasapa (Blackfeet, distinct from the Algonquian Blackfeet), and Oohenanpa (Two Kettle). The Pine Ridge Indian Reservation east of the Black Hills is home to many members of the Oglala Lakota tribe.

Skilled buffalo hunters, the Lakota also became well known for their bold geometric quiltwork and beadwork. Today, many examples of traditional Lakota artwork, both old and new, can be seen in Black Hills museums and stores (see the Attractions, Arts, and Shopping chapters).

By the way, the book *Dances with Wolves* is about a Comanche tribe. The multiple-award-winning movie is about a Lakota tribe because, according to author Michael Blake, it was hard to find anyone who spoke fluent Comanche. (Native Americans in the film speak Lakota with English subtitles.) And anyway, the movie was filmed in South Dakota, including several locations in the Black Hills.

Ranching is important to the modern Belle Fourche economy, and its heritage is celebrated each year during the Black Hills Roundup. You can read about this three-day festival in the Annual Events chapter.

Between 1898 and 1910 the grand-daddy of local ranching celebrations took place in Rapid City. Cowboys from all over the region as well as dignitaries from Chicago and other faraway places looked forward to April each year so they could attend the three-day meeting of the South Dakota Stock Growers Association. Stockmen's Days was their time to buy supplies and have fun as they raced their horses down Main Street, played games, danced, and generally made a racket.

The celebration died out, some say because the ladies of Rapid City found it too boisterous, but the Stock Growers Association is still headquartered in the foothills town staked out by energetic Denver hotelier John Brennan. Brennan, who quickly gave up a hard miner's life in favor of civic development, envisioned a new Denver when he chose a town site near the banks of Rapid Creek. Rapid City began life as a hay camp where freight crews could revive themselves and their animals before pushing on to the mining camps deep within the Hills. The town quickly became the area's commercial center, a role it continues to play today while retaining a good deal of its cowboy flavor.

i The community of Hisega west of Rapid City is said to have been named for six young ladies who had a picnic there: Helen, Ida, Sadie, Ethel, Grace, and Ada.

TIMBER & THE FOREST

Once prospectors arrived in the Hills, primitive lumbering operations couldn't produce board feet fast enough to meet the demand for mine shorings, buildings, and fuel. It didn't take long for steampowered sawmills to get up and running just about everywhere, but by the mid-1880s, railroad construction increased the need for timber still further. Much of the area was clear-cut as a result. The situation was exacerbated by a rash of major forest fires in 1893, moving President Grover Cleveland to establish the 1.2-million-acre Black Hills Forest Reserve in 1897. The next year the nation's first commercial timber sale on federal forested land was authorized here, with Homestake Mining Company as buyer. In 1907 the reserve was renamed the Black Hills National Forest, having come under the jurisdiction of the USDA Forest Service two years earlier.

During the Depression, the forest provided jobs for Civilian Conservation Corps laborers who worked at improving timber stands, preventing and fighting forest fires, and numerous other tasks. Historical markers along many roads remind us of the CCC's contributions during those tough times. Its legacy remains intact at the Black Hills Playhouse, a once-abandoned CCC camp in Custer State Park where theatrical performances are staged each summer (see the Arts chapter).

The Black Hills National Forest has been a leader in the concept of multiple use, a practice that became law with the 1960 Multiple Use–Sustained Yield Act. This law ensures that national forests are managed for a variety of public uses, from logging to wildlife habitat and recreation, while maintaining productivity of land and harvestable resources. Logging and the manufacture of wood products remain important industries in the Black Hills today, employing more than 1,800 people in logging and milling alone. In addition, timber sales provide 97 percent of income from the forest (25 percent of those receipts go to counties with national forest acreage). But in recent years timber sales have come under a barrage of challenges by environmentalists who think too many trees are being cut and too many roads are being built for logging.

i In 1898 the first commercial timber sale on federal forested land in the United States was authorized in the area of Jim and Estes Creeks near the town of Nemo.

THE RAILROAD

Because the Black Hills were part of the Great Sioux Reservation and off-limits to the railroads, iron horses bypassed the area during the height of the 19th-century rail boom. In the first decades of white settlement, people

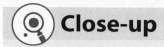

Close-up

Babe the Blue Ox & the Beginning of the Black Hills

Geologists will argue, but we think this whimsical tale of mythological giant lumberjack Paul Bunyan and his beloved blue ox, Babe, offers a perfectly good explanation for the creation of the Black Hills.

One morning, so the story goes, Babe spied a batch of pancakes baking for the logging crew's breakfast. The sight made her so hungry that she gobbled up all 400 flapjacks, but even that wasn't enough to quiet her rumbling stomach. So with one bite, Babe devoured the scorching hot griddle and then gulped down the cookstove, flames and all. Suffering from the worst case of indigestion ever known, Babe galloped off with a mighty bellow, tearing up the prairie in her distress.

When Paul finally found her, poor Babe was flat on her back, feet sticking straight up in the air, dead as a post. Grieving, Paul started to dig a grave but changed his mind and instead covered his pet with a layer of dirt and rocks. Babe's burial mound became the Black Hills, and if you don't believe it, we have proof: The Belle Fourche River and South Fork of the Cheyenne River still flow all the way to the Missouri with the tears Paul shed while performing this sad task.

came on horseback, in ox-drawn wagons and, later, in stagecoaches.

Nevertheless, narrow-gauge rail lines were used within the Hills to carry fuel and materials to the mines. Homestake Mining Company built the first such railroad in 1881. The first outside train arrived in Rapid City during the 1886 Fourth of July celebration after the Fremont, Elkhorn & Missouri Valley Railroad built a branch from Chadron, Nebraska, to the Black Hills. The Elkhorn soon laid track to the Northern Hills, reaching Whitewood in 1887, Belle Fourche in 1889, and Deadwood in 1890. Other lines such as the Chicago, Milwaukee & St. Paul Railway Co., the Grand Island Railroad, and the Chicago, Burlington & Quincy Railroad brought supplies and tourists to the area. You can still ride part of the old CB&Q route on the Black Hills Central Railroad (The 1880 Train) in Hill City (see Attractions).

i Pactola Reservoir and Sheridan Lake bear the names of gold-rush towns that were flooded when the lakes were built.

Because it was a destination resort, Hot Springs had two rail lines that delivered visitors eager to soak in its mineral baths, starting in 1892. Ironically, though, western South Dakota didn't connect via rail to the eastern part of the state until the next century, and one historian has speculated that the continued isolation may help to account for ongoing differences between "East River" and "West River" South Dakota (see the Area Overview chapter).

Competition for invaluable rail service was stiff and often underhanded. In the push for the first train, Rapid City got the upper hand when citizens executed a legal maneuver that skirted a ban on financial aid to railroads while raising money for a depot and other improvements. To the north, Seth Bullock cut a deal granting the Elkhorn a right-of-way across his acreage in exchange for a station that would give rise to the town of Belle Fourche, even as residents of nearby Minnesela were negotiating for a depot in their town. (Belle Fourche later "stole" the county seat away from the now-abandoned town of Minnesela, too.) It just goes to show how vital rail service was for economic and social progress.

Railroads declined in importance as interstate highways and airlines provided efficient alternatives. Many miles of track were abandoned, and now, through a rails-to-trails project, a 114-mile section that belonged to the Burlington Northern Railroad has new life as a recreational trail. You can read about the George S. Mickelson Trail in the Recreation chapter.

ℹ️ Creosote, a substance used as a wood preservative, is commonly found in the railroad timbers that crisscross South Dakota and can cause neurological disturbance if inhaled in strong concentration.

The Burlington Northern Santa Fe Railway still has a crew change point in Edgemont, and the Dakota, Minnesota & Eastern Railroad chugs along the eastern slope of the Hills. In fact, the now–Canadian Pacific–owned DM&E is in the midst of a $2 billion project, the country's largest railroad expansion since the Civil War. The proposal, which includes building and upgrading 1,000 miles of track to Wyoming's coalfields, has been under legal attack since 1998. But federal agencies continue to rule in the company's favor, making the project's future more certain.

EDUCATION & REFINEMENT

The first business to get a foothold in any rough-and-tumble mining camp was generally a saloon, and a newspaper often followed on its heels. Once respectable women and children arrived, settlers lost little time in starting schools, churches, and other cultural institutions.

At first many of these activities took place in crude shared or rented quarters, but within a few years pupils were attending classes in schools built just for them. The area's first teacher arrived long before that, though: Annie Tallent, the first white woman in the Hills, was a teacher. After she and the rest of the Gordon Party were expelled from their stockade in 1875, she returned to the Black Hills and, after being deserted by her husband, taught school and later became a school superintendent. She also wrote a book, *The Black Hills, or Last Hunting Grounds of the Dakotahs*. Her typically 19th-century views on Native Americans later branded Annie Tallent a bigot in some people's minds, and a Rapid City elementary school named for her was rechristened South Park Elementary School.

A prevailing philosophy in Tallent's day was that Native Americans' best interests would be served through acculturation. With that in mind, the federal government chose Rapid City as the site for an Indian school much like the one at Carlisle, Pennsylvania, where students were forced to cast off their Native dress, language, and religion and try to become Christian farmers and ranchers. Rapid City Indian School opened in 1887 and operated for several decades.

Perhaps some of the teachers at the Indian school were trained at Spearfish Normal School, which opened in 1883. And perhaps some of their students went on to study at Dakota School of Mines, where classes were offered for the first time in 1885. Both schools have grown and undergone name changes over the last century-plus, and you can read about Black Hills State University and South Dakota School of Mines and Technology in the Education chapter.

Many early settlers must have gone to school and learned to read before arriving here, because newspapers were in demand from the beginning. Not surprisingly, the first paper was published in Deadwood, where the action was. Deadwood was first, that is, if you don't count the single issue published in Custer by W. A. Laughlin and A. W. Merrick before they packed up their press and headed north. Before long their *Black Hills Pioneer*, founded in 1876, had lots of competition, and at one point Deadwood had three dailies and three weeklies.

In 1878 pioneer newspaperman Joseph Gossage arrived from Nebraska to start the *Black Hills Weekly Journal* in Rapid City. But Gossage's industrious, intelligent wife, Alice, gets much of the credit for the newspaper's success and longevity as well as for breaking ground for early women reporters. Together, and with help from the talented reporter Richard B. Hughes, the Gossages built the paper into an outstanding daily publication. Today the *Rapid City Journal*, as it's now called, is the largest newspaper in all of western South Dakota.

News on the spiritual front showed notorious Deadwood to be a leader, a reassuring achievement given the town's early reputation as a wicked place. Congregationalists founded the area's first religious institution there in 1876, although they didn't get a church building until almost a year later—and then they shared it with two other Protestant sects. Catholic worship came first

to Deadwood in 1877 as did Baptist church services in 1881.

The Black Hills got its first martyr when Henry Weston Smith was found shot outside Deadwood in 1876. Though Indians were blamed for the murder of the staunchly Methodist Preacher Smith, the crime was never solved. Some historians believe he was killed by prospectors and gamblers who didn't take kindly to his fiery sermons. Today, however, most Black Hills residents consider themselves devoutly religious; you can read more about that in the Worship and Spirituality chapter.

For entertainment, settlers joined fraternal organizations such as the Masons and Oddfellows, and many immigrant groups had their own ethnic societies. Theater troupes were often among the first to arrive in a new settlement, and as cities gained a foothold, elaborate theaters were built. The Matthews Opera House in Spearfish was the most ornate theater in South Dakota when it opened in 1906; it was quickly upstaged by the Homestake Opera House in Lead, constructed eight years later. Though both eventually decayed (the Matthews from neglect, the Homestake from fire damage), the Spearfish theater has been restored and hosts regular performances, while Lead's opera house continues to undergo massive restoration with occasional productions.

By 1881 Rapid City had its first public building, Library Hall, and the townspeople used it for all kinds of civic and social activities. As the city became the area's population center, it also became the cultural center, and today western South Dakota's largest city, with a population of nearly 70,000, hosts most of our major cultural events. (Turn to the Arts chapter for an in-depth look at the local cultural scene.)

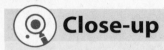
Close-up

The Lawrence County Courthouse

The fight to save the **Lawrence County Courthouse** in Deadwood didn't provoke gunplay, but it had all the intrigue of a full-blown range war.

The Beaux Arts–style courthouse, with a cupola on top and handpainted murals on the walls inside, opened for business in 1908. Three years later President William Howard Taft came for a visit, and the courthouse was decorated in his honor.

As time went by, county offices grew cramped, and in the 1970s a new public safety center was added on. But a decade later the original part of the courthouse was declared structurally unsafe, and everybody had to move out. That's when the fighting started.

At first, the Lawrence County Board of Commissioners couldn't decide whether to fix the building or demolish it. So a citizens group, Save the Courthouse, held a rally on the front steps and got up a petition to have county voters decide. Then the commissioners voted to tear the building down, but the public vote went the other way. That meant the commissioners had to figure out how to renovate the building and accommodate ongoing expansion in county government at the same time, and also how to pay for the mandated work. The discussion lasted more than three years. In the meantime there were efforts to stop the county from issuing bonds to pay for the project, a proposal to move the county seat to Spearfish, a dispute over land for a new courthouse annex, and an attempt to block the annex project altogether. In addition, a leader of Save the Courthouse was convicted of arson for setting fire to her own restored Victorian home in an attempt to collect insurance money.

Fortunately, though, the courthouse was repaired, and while the job was in progress, workers uncovered all kinds of beautiful artwork that for decades had been hidden under false ceilings and behind wall panels. Restoration experts cleaned and touched up murals and refurbished original stenciling with paint and gold leaf. When the building reopened in 1991, the citizens of Lawrence County reaffirmed what they'd known all along—they had saved a national treasure.

Not surprisingly, the Black Hills today are home to many talented artisans who appreciate living in such an aesthetically pleasing environment. Two of the most conspicuously inspired pieces wrought by local artists, however, can't be seen in any gallery. Mount Rushmore National Memorial near Keystone and Crazy Horse Memorial near Custer are monumental works whose very existence makes their creators themselves seem larger than life. You can read about both of them in the Attractions chapter.

THE MILITARY

From the arrival of the first warrior society to the present, the Black Hills have had a military presence. It wasn't until 1878, however, that Fort Meade, east of Sturgis, became the first official military post in the area. By then, there was little fighting left to do on the frontier, and the soldiers' role was largely one of peacekeeping and community service. What remained of the Seventh Cavalry after Custer's defeat built Fort Meade, and many of the regiment's major players were in service there. Among them was Maj. Marcus Reno, the senior surviving officer of the Little Bighorn. Reno's troubled career ended in an 1880 court-martial at Fort Meade after he was accused, unjustly it is now believed, of window peeping at the home of his commander, Col. Samuel Sturgis. Another renowned Little Bighorn survivor, the horse Comanche, lived out his life as a pampered mascot at Fort Meade (see the Retirement chapter for a write-up on Comanche).

Relations between the fort and the nearby town of Sturgis were not always amicable. Racial tensions arose when a black soldier from the 25th Infantry, Cpl. Ross Hallon, was hanged by vigilantes for allegedly killing a Sturgis doctor in 1885. And in 1924 citizens were shaken when two soldiers fired machine guns on a burning cross erected by the Ku Klux Klan. The Klan was so well organized in the Black Hills at that time that newspapers reported on the activities of its hooded members, which included giving money to churches and marching in parades.

Overall, though, Fort Meade was a community asset where civilian girls attended dances and military operations continued for 66 years, far longer than the average army fort. During World War I, South Dakota National Guard troops trained there, and during the Depression the facility was headquarters for all South Dakota CCC camps. In 1942 the Fourth Cavalry's horses were retired and exchanged for motorcycles and light tanks. The next year, Fort Meade became a training ground for glider troops, and then, in 1944, it ceased to be a military post and in 1945 became a prisoner-of-war camp for German soldiers. Today Fort Meade is the site of a Veterans Administration primary care facility (see the Health Care chapter) and houses a fine museum.

The same year Fort Meade soldiers turned their horses out to pasture, the army gained a new foothold in the isolated southwestern corner of South Dakota. Work began in 1942 on the Black Hills Ordnance Depot (later called the Black Hills Army Depot), a long-term storage facility for weapons and supplies, and soon a whole new community had sprung up near the tiny hamlet of Provo. The new town called itself Igloo, after the igloo-shaped concrete bunkers used for storing ordnance at the site. The depot brought a degree of prosperity to the area, where the agriculture-based economy had suffered tremendous losses during the Dust Bowl years. The depot closed in 1967, and much of the land reverted to livestock grazing. Igloo is now deserted, a veritable ghost town.

i The USS *South Dakota* was the most decorated battleship of World War II.

About the same time that work first started on the depot, the army also established an air base near Rapid City as a place to train B-17 bomber crews. Unlike the depot, Rapid City Army Air Base shut down for about six months after World War II, but it soon reopened under the auspices of the US Air Force. It became a permanent installation in 1948 and after a series of name changes was dedicated to the memory of Brig. Gen. Richard E. Ellsworth in 1953. Ellsworth, commander of the 28th Strategic Reconnaissance Wing, and a crew of 23 died in a plane crash while returning from a routine mission in Europe.

A study of Ellsworth Air Force Base prompts contemplation about some of the critical developments in modern-day world events. For example, during the Cold War increasingly sophisticated weapons, from surface-to-air missiles to intercontinental ballistic missiles (ICBMs) were assigned to the base. Nuclear warheads were stored in 150 heavily guarded underground silos under base command. A new age dawned, however, with the toppling of the Berlin Wall and the Strategic Arms Reduction Treaties between the United States and Russia. Ellsworth began deactivating its missile silos in 1991 and finished destroying them in 1996. A silo and launch capsule east of Wall has been preserved as a Minuteman Missile National Historic Site, the only such landmark in the US. Tours are by reservation only and give the general public a very real glimpse into the heart of the nation's military during the Cold War.

As recently as 1992 Ellsworth was dubbed the Showplace of Strategic Air Command, home to four wings plus two squadrons with separate missions of their own. It's a smaller operation now, due to general military cuts, but the base remains a key heavy-bomber facility. The 28th Bomb Wing, which started at Ellsworth and fought in World War II, is still based there, in charge of a fleet of B-1B bombers and still adapting to the nation's military needs. Today it stands ready for conventional rather than nuclear warfare.

i In 2006 Ellsworth Air Force Base outside Rapid City was selected as the new location for a consolidated financial services center, as well as a 24-hour call center for use by all air force personnel. This, just months after the Base Realignment and Closure Commission voted to remove Ellsworth from its list of bases slated for shutdown.

Ellsworth is the largest, but not the only, military presence in the Black Hills today. The South Dakota Army National Guard established itself in Rapid City and other Black Hills towns almost two decades before Ellsworth was built, in fact. Camp Rapid, the army guard's state headquarters, was established in the mid-1920s.

The South Dakota National Guard itself formed in 1862 to protect settlers while regular troops were busy with the Civil War. Under the command of the state governor, today's guard fulfills a threefold mission that includes providing reserve forces for federal service, helping local agencies during emergencies, and being active in community service. Local units, which are based in Belle Fourche, Spearfish, Sturgis, and Custer, as well as Rapid City, have helped quell forest fires, served in overseas conflicts, completed construction projects, and performed numerous other vital tasks. Along with Ellsworth, the guard provides government jobs and purchasing power that have a significant impact on the local economy.

TOURISM

Modern Black Hills tourism began at the end of the 19th century in the Southern Hills, where thermal springs along Fall River, long revered by indigenous Indian tribes for their healing powers, were a trendy sell to Victorian visitors from metropolitan areas. Clever marketing, along with a railroad connection and a few modern resorts, captured the interest of travelers from all over the country who came to soak their aching joints in the warm waters.

It wasn't long before the rest of the Black Hills caught on. The Sylvan Lake Hotel, built right on the shore of Custer State Park's crown jewel in 1895, was an upscale regional hot spot until it burned to the ground 40 years later. Deadwood, ever on the cutting edge of technology, saw its first automobile in 1891; highways and roadside motels were quick to follow.

However, President Calvin Coolidge—"Silent Cal"—gets much of the credit for bringing widespread tourism to the Black Hills in the 20th century. Coolidge and First Lady Grace came for a three-week vacation, and ended up staying three months. The reticent Vermonter decided to make Custer State Park his summer home in 1927, and while he was here he took time out from trout fishing and running the country to dedicate Mount Rushmore (see the Attractions chapter). Newsreels of the day gave untold numbers of Americans—many of whom apparently didn't know where or even what the Black Hills were—their first glimpse of the area's pine-covered mountains and dramatic rock outcroppings.

And so it was that tourism in the Black Hills expanded northward. Today, most visitors to the area come to see Rushmore, America's Shrine of Democracy, or the revived streets of Deadwood. Of course, while they're here they take time to view wildlife, explore caves, hike hillsides, snowmobile down narrow canyons, ride motorcycles around forested bluffs, and visit the dozens of other attractions in the region, among other things.

Tourism is critical to the economy of the Black Hills, bringing in more than four million people—and many times that in dollars—to the region every year. Residents proudly point out that over half of the state's visitor dollars are spent in the Black Hills, proving that the area is secure in its position as the regional capital of commerce, culture, and art.

THE NATURAL WORLD

For many visitors, the natural world of the Black Hills is the awe-inspiring main attraction, their primary reason for coming. And this delightful aspect of the Black Hills makes so many other activities and attractions possible. For example, camping and recreational opportunities abound here. We also have some great art, as well as geology- and paleontology-based museums and sites. Many accommodations boast gorgeous locations; some restaurants serve Black Hills trout. All of these are inspired and sustained by our natural world.

We talk a lot about nature and its many facets throughout this book—it's integral to our way of life—and we'll make a point here of directing you to the Recreation chapter, which provides thorough information on outdoor activities. In this chapter, however, we'll tell you a bit about our natural history: the Hills' elements and how they came to be; the animals, birds, fish, and flora you can expect to see; the insects you'll likely swat; and the weather you will alternately bask in and curse (sometimes all in the same day).

GEOLOGY

The Black Hills are a unique geologic formation. They rise out of the Great Plains like an oasis and are unlike the landscape of the rest of South Dakota. Do know, however, that Hills is a misnomer; they're definitely mountains, smaller than the Rocky Mountains but higher than the Appalachians. From a distance, they look black—the effect of dense pine and spruce cover.

The Hills' Precambrian formations have been estimated at 1.7 billion to 2.5 billion years old. During the Cambrian period the area was covered by ancient seas, and changes during the Mississippian period left the lower deposits of limestone, sandstone, and shale some 300 million years ago. Younger rocks cover and surround these deposits, including a purple limestone at least 230 million years old. Higher layers are composed of more sandstone, limestone, and shale, including Pierre shale and Niobrara chalk, remnants from the bottom of a Cretaceous sea.

The Black Hills were uplifted during the Paleocene epoch, some 63 million years ago, by the same geologic forces that created the Rocky Mountains. Although the mind envisions this as a noisy, cataclysmic, cinematic event, it actually happened very slowly, and over the span of eons the Hills changed many times.

Over the slow millions of years, the area was arid, then subtropical, and then nearly buried in volcanic ash. New rivers and streams carved their own paths, and rain and wind carried away surface particles. Toward the end of the Eocene era, the climate became arid once again, turning South

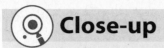

Close-up

Bear Butte: A Lakota Legend

In Lakota mythology, Maka is the Earth spirit, second only to Inyan, who created her. Inyan's spirit is Wakan Tanka (The Great Mystery), and Maka's is Makaakan (Earth Goddess). Their home is the Black Hills, The Heart of Everything That Is.

Long, long ago, Maka became deeply disappointed by the behavior of her children, whose many nations had grown away from her and so had begun to fight among themselves. She called to them, but most ignored her, so she shook herself, causing earthquakes, floods, and volcanoes, breaking the surface of the Hills, and changing life for all the inhabitants.

The four-legged creatures held a meeting to discuss this disaster, and Buffalo declared that the two-legs should be destroyed, since they had caused all the trouble. Magpie heard this discussion and flew back to the winged creatures, who held a meeting of their own. Owl made the point that Bear was a two-legged creature and the symbol of wisdom, which must be spared at all costs. The winged creatures declared that the two-legs must, therefore, be saved. A great race was proposed; the winners would decide the fate of the two-legs.

Four times, over many days, the creatures ran and flew clockwise around the sacred Black Hills. Magpie didn't stop except to sleep for a bit at night; many times he passed exhausted animals who were forced to rest. The pounding feet, hooves, and paws left a red trail of blood on the racetrack, and the earth shook with the running. With Buffalo nearing the finish line at Bear Butte, clever Magpie hitched a ride on his back, then flew ahead at the last moment to win the race and save the two-legs.

During the contest, a strange swelling had risen from beside Bear Butte, which you can still see there today. They opened it and found Inyan's sacred staff there. In commemoration of Bear, whose wisdom was spared that day, Maka named Bear Butte his home. She left the trail of blood, the Red Racetrack, in place to mark the sacrifice of her children and to remind all the creatures—the four-legs, the two-legs, the winged, and the growing things—to always live in peace as equals and to remember that we are all relatives.

Dakota into a windy desert. Hundreds of feet of clay and sand nearly covered the Hills and buried the Badlands. Nature sculpted the eerie Badlands formations through erosion by wind and water, then supplemented them with sediments washing and blowing eastward from the Black Hills.

During those days the Black Hills formation became elliptical, and today the area is approximately 50 miles wide and 120 miles long. Much of it is now the Black Hills National Forest. But the land hasn't changed much since Lt. Col. Richard Irving Dodge viewed it. Dodge accompanied the Jenney-Newton expedition here in 1875; it was the second government-sanctioned visit to the mysterious and then-unknown territory. He wrote: "There can scarcely be a country where the scenery is more varied. From the top of some lofty peak the explorer gazes in wonder at the infinite variety at his feet. Grand mountains, frowning crags, gloomy abysses, dense forests, and intricate jungles alternate with lovely parks, smooth lawns [grasslands], and gentle slopes. Each portion of the Hills has its own especial peculiarities of scenery. One struggles through dense, apparently interminable thickets, over masses of broken rocks, up and down steep ravines, to emerge at the most unexpected moment upon a smooth, well-kept flower-covered lawn, as varied and beautiful in form . . . as was ever conceived by the most enthusiastic landscape gardener. One finds himself continually saying, 'What perfect taste.'" More than a century later, visitors and residents still agree with his assessment.

The geologic island that is the Hills is made up of four distinct subregions. The Great Hogbacks form the outer ring. These sandstone ridges were turned upward when the dome of the Hills broke through the surface of the earth and pushed skyward. They got their name because their sharp ridges look like the backs of razorback hogs. The best-known break in the Hogbacks is at Buffalo Gap, where SR 79 cuts through it.

i Rose quartz is the South Dakota state mineral. You can find large and small specimens and gifts made from the pink mineral in local rock and gift shops.

Just inside the Hogbacks is the Red Valley, or Red Racetrack, a lower, narrow feature composed of the red sandstone of the Spearfish Red Beds. It drops down sharply from the Hogbacks and is from a quarter mile to 2 miles in width. The Lakota knew this valley, and their mythology includes a wonderful legend about its formation, which you'll find in this chapter's Legends and Lore. A limestone plateau lies inside the Red

Valley, circling the core of the Hills. The western portion of this plateau is wider and higher than the eastern, in places reaching some 7,000 feet above sea level and rivaling only Harney Peak—the Hills' tallest mountain—in height. Within this plateau lies our famous network of caves and caverns, although no one knows for sure if they are actually connected to each other. The soft limestone was deeply carved by water and time, resulting in modern-day Wind Cave National Park, Jewel Cave National Monument, and many privately owned and operated caverns (the latter are listed in the Attractions chapter).

The fourth region, the inner core of the Black Hills, is crystalline. This is where the oldest rocks and the tallest mountains can be found. Eighteen peaks higher than 7,000 feet are here, including Harney Peak at 7,242 feet above sea level and Terry Peak at 7,064 feet. Harney, by the way, is North America's highest point east of the Rockies.

The crystalline core was formed from volcanic magma about 1.7 billion years ago, and it's estimated that the crystallization occurred some 8 miles deep in the earth. This core was later transformed during the geologic uplift into quartzite, granite, schist, and mica. The soft schist and mica eroded away, leaving the tougher granite to form craggy mountain peaks (some geologists believe that if Harney Peak had never eroded, it would be 15,000 feet above sea level). This area also contains deposits of gold, silver, and other minerals as well as the less financially valuable but more accessible granite needles, which are the result of erosion.

The bones and fossils of prehistoric creatures have been discovered in the Black Hills and Badlands regions. The most famous is Sue, the *Tyrannosaurus rex* who has her own

Great Faces feature in the Area Overview chapter. Another is a genus of dinosaur discovered by paleontologist O. C. Marsh of Yale University on Piedmont Butte. In 1889 Marsh spotted a bone fragment displayed at the Piedmont Post Office, visited the site where it was found, and named his new find *Barosaurus*. Mammoth Site of Hot Springs is an ancient sinkhole; you can visit its mammoth graveyard (see the Attractions chapter). The remains of a "big pig," an Archaeotherium or wild boar, were found in the Badlands, which has its own abundance of fossils and finds. If you're fascinated by paleontology, you'll thoroughly enjoy a visit to the Museum of Geology at South Dakota School of Mines and Technology in Rapid City (see Attractions) and to the Black Hills Institute of Geological Research in Hill City.

Rock hunters will enjoy searching for clear and white quartz and, less often found, rose and smoky quartz, as well as feldspar, apatite, mica, columbite, agate, jasper, tourmaline, petrified wood, and beryl. Near the town of Keystone, you may find pieces of schist containing tiny but lovely rough garnets. Just make sure you're on land where collecting is allowed before you dig or take anything away with you.

If you'd like to further explore the geology of this area and see the natural roadside (and off-road) attractions most visitors whiz right past, we recommend John Paul Gries's fine book, *Roadside Geology of South Dakota*. You'll find other books in local bookstores on dinosaurs, fossils, rockhounding, and natural history. Our Badlands & Nearby chapter talks about the geologically wondrous Badlands and the natural treasures you will discover there.

WILDLIFE

Here in the Hills, perhaps more often than in many other states, you're likely to come across animals you've never seen in the wild and those you've always wanted to see. Perhaps it's because they are abundant here, or perhaps it's because the wilderness areas that are their homes are so close to our towns and cities.

If you want to meet some of these animals up close and personal, where they can't run too far away, try Bear Country U.S.A., Black Hills Wild Horse Sanctuary, or Reptile Gardens, all detailed in the Attractions chapter. It's more difficult, but also more rewarding, to get out into the Hills and find these animals on your own, on their turf, and under more natural conditions.

Remember to keep your distance (the animal's reaction will tell you if you're too close), and never feed a wild animal. Use extra caution during rut (mating season) and when viewing mother animals with their young. Keep your camera and plenty of film handy. We recommend a telephoto lens so you don't have to get close. If you come upon a wild animal while hiking, it's usually best to stop immediately and back away slowly, making some noise and avoiding direct eye contact. Like you, most animals prefer to avoid a confrontation and will do so unless they feel threatened. Please also watch out for wildlife while you're driving; many species cross roads at all times of the day and night.

The early morning and evening feeding hours are the best times to see wildlife. Most species virtually disappear during broad daylight, preferring to rest and conserve energy before resuming their quest for food.

Nothing quite defines South Dakota like the buffalo, pounding across the plains and

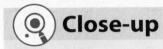

Close-up

Prairie Dog

If you stop in certain grass-clipped prairie areas of Wind Cave, Custer State Park, or the Badlands and hear a barking sound, chances are you've stopped at the home of the **prairie dog**, one of the most social of all mammals. Once entire "cities" stretched hundreds of miles across the prairies of the West. Because prairie dogs cut all plants growing within 100 feet of their burrows, and because their "towns" required such expansive areas, these communities eventually had to give way to agriculture.

As social animals, prairie dogs communicate with one another using body language and often calls. You might see them grooming one another, for they are fastidious. Wait long enough and you might also see them standing erect and whistling or "throwing" themselves backward. Gestures such as these have evolved as survival techniques, serving as warnings that their homes are about to be invaded by a hawk, coyote, snake, or ferret, and that it may be time to seek refuge in their burrow.

Life for the prairie dog centers around the burrows. Invariably, each member in the community has a guardroom located about 3 to 6 feet below the entrance. Though the room itself may be little more than a shelf, nevertheless it is adequate as a sanctuary from predators. From the guardroom a tunnel turns horizontally and leads to a bathroom and a separate bedroom. To prevent flooding during times of heavy rainfall, generally these two chambers are elevated above the level of the guardroom.

For increased surveillance, prairie dogs reduce grass heights around the burrows to about 6 inches, which in turn serves to attract other species of animals. Bison are attracted to the barren grounds to wallow in the dust on hot summer days. The short grass and burrows attract one of the most interesting species of owls, the diminutive burrowing owl, which you might well see should you stake yourself out for an early morning watch. All in all, biologists say prairie dog communities attract more than 26 different species of animals, including the endangered black-footed ferret, which preys on the prairie dog.

Because the "dogs" serve as such wildlife magnets, we are fortunate the Black Hills provides a safe haven for these remarkable creatures.

hills the way their ancestors did so long ago. Actually, the animals you see today are bison (North American bison, to be exact), but most everyone calls them buffalo. We discuss these immense creatures in the Parks & Mountains chapter, where we extol the beauty of Custer State Park, home of a fine and easily viewable herd. Small groups also live at Bear Butte State Park and Wind Cave National Park (also detailed in that chapter) and in the Badlands.

When driving through these areas, you may come upon shaggy bison standing in the road. It's best to just enjoy the awesome view and wait until they move—you wouldn't want your car gored by a perturbed buffalo. You're on their turf, after all. We'll say this several times in this book: Bison are wild and unpredictable. If harassed, the 2,000-pound beasts can pursue you at speeds in excess of 30 mph.

i In 2005 the South Dakota Game, Fish & Parks Department opened mountain lion hunting season in the Black Hills, as well as other portions of South Dakota, for the first time.

Custer State Park and Wind Cave National Park are probably the best places to see elk, although they are shier than bison. Elk were reintroduced here from Yellowstone National Park in the early 1900s, after being exterminated by overhunting. You may need to hike off the road a ways, at sunset or sunrise, to see a herd moving down into a valley to feed. If they see you first, which they likely will, they will move away. Carry binoculars to get a better view. You haven't lived until you've heard an elk bugle. During the fall rut, males call females with a strange hooting, echoing sound that really can't be described, but it will give you goose bumps.

You may see shaggy white mountain goats standing precariously on the rocks above you at Mount Rushmore National Memorial and in the Needles area. Their ancestors came to Custer State Park from Canada as a wildlife display, but the wily creatures escaped and made their way to the Northern and Central Hills, where their progeny live happily today. They consider these high, rocky areas safe and cozy.

The Audubon bighorn sheep native to the Black Hills unfortunately became extinct in the 1920s. Rocky Mountain bighorn sheep were introduced years later to the Badlands, the area around the Stratosphere Bowl near Rockerville, and Custer State Park. They have done well, despite an early die-off caused by disease.

Unfortunately (although ranchers and farmers wouldn't agree), grizzly bears and wolves were eliminated from this area by the early 1900s, although rare sightings of black bears, wolves, and wolf–dog crossbreeds are still reported. There were even sightings of two moose in the Black Hills in 2003. Where do these transients come from? Either Wyoming's Bighorn Mountains, 150 miles to the west, or Minnesota's woodlands, 500 miles east.

Though you'd never know it by observation, mountain lions and bobcats are more abundant. Both of the reclusive species have made a comeback in recent years, thanks to legal protection and plenty of prey. Even lynxes, which are rare and very shy, are growing in number. All the same, you'll be lucky if you find any tracks or scat to mark the presence of these nocturnal hunters.

If you're out in the Hills in the evening, far away from the lights and noise of civilization, count on hearing eerie howls and screeches echoing through the forested valleys. Though coyotes, the state animal, are as abundant in the pines as they are on the prairie, don't expect to spot these skittish, stealthy creatures. It takes a sharp eye to catch a glimpse of one slinking between some trees.

Delicately beautiful creatures you'll see plenty of are mule deer, white-tailed deer, and pronghorn antelope. The deer, with their ghostly gray-brown coloring, are easy to miss, especially in low light. Antelope, with their bold splashes of white, are easier to spot. You'll often see both grazing on distant hillsides, even in the middle of the day, and you can see them close up at state and national parks, especially Custer State Park.

Custer State Park is also populated by the notorious "begging burros." Introduced into the park in the 1920s, they are great fun to watch (from your car, because they can be

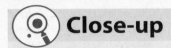

Close-up

Black-Footed Ferret Reintroduction Project

The rarest mammal in North America is making a comeback in South Dakota. Endangered **black-footed ferrets**, once common in the Black Hills and Badlands, are being reintroduced here through a project of the National Park Service and the USDA Forest Service.

Ferrets live in prairie dog towns, because their required diet, prairie dogs, lives there, too. Decades ago, poisoning and shooting were common means of exterminating prairie dogs to prevent their burrowing on ranch land. With their decimation came a decline in their predators, the ferrets, until the only known group of black-footed ferrets in the world survived in Mellette County, South Dakota.

Captive breeding of black-footed ferrets was attempted unsuccessfully, and eventually they disappeared. The species was considered extinct in the late 1970s. Then one day in 1981 near Meeteetse, Wyoming, a rancher's dog brought him a black-footed ferret, and the human race had a second chance to save the species. The total population of the Meeteetse group was estimated at 129. The group was monitored for four years, until an outbreak of deadly canine distemper struck in 1985 and 1986; officials then captured 24 animals, of which 18 survived to become the core of the reintroduction program.

Black-footed ferrets have been successfully bred and released into Badlands National Park and Buffalo Gap National Grassland since 1994. More litters of wild kits are born each year, including 73 litters in 2007. However, a flea-borne sylvatic plague confirmed within the park in 2008, impacting both prairie dog and black-footed populations, reduced new litters of Badlands ferrets to just three in 2010. The forest service estimates that more than 35 wild black-footed ferrets lived in the Badlands National Park in 2010, and at least 200 more lived in the Conata Basin outside the park in Buffalo Gap National Grassland.

Park officials don't plan on releasing any more captive-born animals in the area, although officials are considering taking some of the wild-born ferrets from the Conata Basin and moving them to the prairie dog towns inside the park boundaries of the Badlands.

aggressive). Park officials don't want you to feed them, which will annoy the burros very much, but your consolation is an almost-assured sighting of the shy little foals that hang back from the group and watch you with their big, dark eyes.

Kids and grown-ups alike will love the prairie dog towns at Custer State Park, Wind Cave National Park, and Badlands National Park. These little critters chirp, whistle, and bark (but not like a dog does); dive underground and poke their heads up again; and

sit up to nibble at food held in their paws. You'll swear they're performing and long to feed the cute little fellows, but don't do it. They're wild, and their cute little teeth are uncommonly sharp.

You may also see jackrabbits and cottontails, foxes, squirrels and chipmunks (great photo subjects), skunks, badgers, marmots, porcupines, raccoons, mink, and beavers (along with their beautifully engineered dams and the pointed stumps of the trees used to build them).

Ferret breeding season begins in March, and kits are born in May and early June. In July and August, mother ferrets take their offspring above ground to learn, explore, and play. Nighttime spotlight surveys by volunteers estimate the range and size of the population. Volunteers stay awake from 8 p.m. to 6 a.m. sidestepping prairie rattlers and watching for bison, and wield high-powered spotlights that reveal animals by their eye shine. A ferret's eyes glow emerald green due to a corneal film that reflects that color. (A rabbit's eyes shine red, an antelope's glow green-yellow, and a coyote's reflect green, but not that distinct ferret emerald.) Since ferrets are solitary, several dancing emerald-green eyes mean a mother and her kits—and success for the program.

Bill Perry, district ranger for Buffalo Gap National Grassland and the regional black-footed ferret coordinator for the forest service before he moved to a USFS position in Washington, D.C., says the reintroduction program is the most exciting he has participated in during his career. He has helped reintroduce big-game animals such as Rocky Mountain bighorn sheep and mountain goats, but he has a special fondness for the ferrets, which he calls "enchanting." "We're dealing with an animal threatened with extinction," he says. "If we can't make this program work, there's very little hope for the ferret."

On a visit to the Black Hills and Badlands, you'll see plenty of prairie dogs. You probably won't see a ferret, though, because they've adapted to nocturnal hunting to capture their diurnal prey. Sleeping prairie dogs are perfect targets for wily ferrets, and—despite their enchanting faces—a fight between the two is anything but cute. "Pound for pound," Perry says, "the only fighter more vicious than a ferret is a wolverine." This is especially impressive when you consider that prairie dogs are more than twice the size of ferrets.

Read the Badlands & Nearby chapter and read about Buffalo Gap National Grassland in the Parks & Mountains chapter. If you'd like to participate in a spotlight survey (volunteers are especially needed during July and Aug), call the National Park Service at (605) 433-5361 or the forest service at (605) 279-2125.

Birders will love the Black Hills. Because of their proximity to the Rocky Mountains, the Platte River, and the Missouri River, there is a good mix of western and eastern birds here. Expect wild turkey, pheasant, ruffed and sharp-tailed grouse, magpies, golden and bald eagles, turkey vultures, and many species of owls and hawks. There are plenty of smaller birds, including eastern and western meadowlarks, mountain bluebirds, mountain chickadees, dippers, and a type of dark-eyed junco that only inhabits the land in and around the Black Hills.

i There are 18 peaks in the Black Hills that rise to an elevation of greater than 7,000 feet. It is possible to climb to the summit of each one.

Amphibians and reptiles to watch for include prairie rattlesnakes, bull snakes, western painted turtles, snapping turtles, and various lizards and toads. If you're hiking or climbing, watch out for the prairie rattler, the only poisonous reptile in the Black Hills and very common. To avoid rattlers, a good rule is to never put your fingers or feet where you can't see what you're touching, especially behind logs and rocks. If you are bitten, get help immediately.

The streams in the Hills afford blueribbon fishing, and that includes Rapid Creek, which winds its way through Rapid City. We can't name many cities where people can fly-fish downtown.

Trout are the big draw, including brown and brook trout, rainbows and splake, but you'll also find some walleye, perch, crappie, bluegill, and bass. The trout aren't native, but they have been raised and stocked here since the late 1800s. Anglers can visit the D.C. Booth Historic Fish Hatchery and the National Fish Culture Hall of Fame and Museum in Spearfish, or the Cleghorn Springs State Fish Hatchery west of Rapid City (all discussed in the Attractions chapter) to learn about the process of stocking sparkling streams with healthy, hearty, feisty trout.

FLORA

The Black Hills are home to a great variety of wildflowers, plants, trees, and native grasses. The Hills are, in fact, unique due to the combined effects of climate, geology, topography, relative isolation, and location where several botanical zones meet and overlap, creating interesting diversity not seen elsewhere.

Some of the trees and shrubs you'll see here include ponderosa pine, white spruce (recognizable by its drapery of lichen on the lower branches), ground juniper, quaking aspen (which turns a beautiful yellow in the fall against a backdrop of dark spruce), western red cedar, mountain mahogany, currant,

buffalo berry, and sumac. Ponderosas grow above the 4,000-foot elevation mark, preferring rocky soil and drier growing conditions. Spruce prefers moist, northern exposures. At lower elevations you'll see burr oak, box elder, American elm, cottonwood, willow, and much more.

A small population of lodgepole pines grows on 150 acres in Lawrence County, some 150 miles from the nearest stands in Wyoming's Bighorn Mountains, where it commonly occurs. A tiny population of limber pines grows near Harney Peak; again, the nearest stands of this species are in the Bighorns. Botanists believe both have been growing in the Black Hills for more than 200 years, but no one knows for sure how they arrived and came to thrive here in relative isolation from their kin.

i Obnoxious weeds can be spread when people pick wildflowers and take them home or to their campsite. Weed seeds can stick in the tread of automobile tires or boots, or lodge on a sleeping bag or tent. What can you do to contain the spread of weeds that choke out necessary plants and sometimes poison livestock? Drive and walk only on established roads and trails, don't pick unknown flowers, and feed your horse certified weed-free hay and feed.

Just outside the Great Hogbacks that surround the Hills are grasslands, with mixed grasses and shrubs such as prairie June grass, buffalo grass, blue grama, little bluestem, and western wheatgrass, plus prickly pear cactus and yucca. Inside the Hills, however, you can see examples of high-elevation prairie. Gillette Prairie and Reynolds Prairie are west of Deerfield, in the Central Hills, and

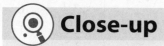

Close-up

Celebrating a Species of Pine

Essentially, because of a species of tree rare in the Black Hills, in 1977 Congress proclaimed the **Cathedral Spires Trail** a Registered National Natural Landmark. **Limber pine**—a five-needled pine tree—grows a ways in from the trail. To find this same species elsewhere, one must travel hundreds of miles north or go west to the Bighorn Mountains.

Core samplings indicate that the limber pines here are hundreds of years old. The question is: How did they ever establish themselves along this remote trail deep within the Black Hills of South Dakota? Glaciologists say that some 10,000 years ago, massive ice fields isolated these stands of *Pinus flexilus*. Botanists theorize that the trees' seeds could have been transported into the area in bird droppings. Whatever happened, limber pine now grows along this trail as an isolated group that remains peculiar to the Black Hills. By hiking the Cathedral Spires Trail, you'll have an opportunity to see stands of this beautiful species as well as a multitude of other aspects such as the area's geological features. Still, it's the trees for which Congress designated the trail, and it's the trees that will make you want to take the short hike of less than one hour.

beautifully illustrate a striking transition from coniferous forest to grassland. Another high-elevation prairie is in Danby Park, west of Custer in the Southern Hills. Although their existence is a bit of a mystery, these small prairies are beautiful examples of nature's unaccountable whims and fancies.

There's an incredible variety of landscapes to view here—at all seasons of the year—but we hope you won't overlook the understated but lovely changes on prairies and plains. Native grasses and plants put on subtle shows all the time: in fertile spring, high summer, winter, and chilly fall, when grasses as well as trees change color. Mountain sunsets are wonderful, but prairie sunsets are, too; we think you'll love watching pastel evening light flood over the prairie, sinking every hollow and draw into deep shadow.

Romantically named wildflowers and herbs found locally are prairie coneflower, Indian paintbrush, black-eyed Susan, wood

lily, yarrow, wild bergamot, fleabane, yellow lady slipper, blue larkspur, Rocky Mountain iris, and aster. There are many more, but our favorite is that harbinger of spring, the pasqueflower, South Dakota's state flower (also called wild crocus or mayflower). This dainty, tuliplike, white-to-purple beauty pops up through the melting snow in late winter and early spring, determined to share news of the coming warm season.

Because the climate of the Hills varies so drastically from region to region, and because elevations range from high mountains to low valleys, with the varied moisture and light levels that accompany such differences, we can't tell you where to find all these examples of flora. Instead, we recommend a good field guide, which you can find at local bookstores. Put on some sturdy shoes, long pants, a light heart, and a sense of adventure, and take an exploratory trip into the Black Hills.

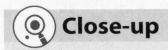 **Close-up**

Disasters in the Black Hills

Frontier life is traditionally connected with natural disasters, and nowhere is that more evident than in the historical records of early Black Hills mining towns. Paging through books and newspapers, you can't help but notice that tragedies, especially those weather related, seem to come one right after the other in the 1870s and 1880s, perhaps giving the impression that seasons were harsher back in the "old days."

And while our grandfathers' assertions that they walked uphill both ways to school in 10 feet of snow would support that impression, in fact the climate probably hasn't changed much in the past century. On the other hand, building methods have. The first waves of settlers and prospectors quickly erected humble shacks and hastily constructed mines, paying little attention to where or how they put structures up. Hundreds of wooden shacks constructed just inches apart, on cliffs and the bottoms of narrow gulches, all without building codes, were a temptation too great for fate to resist.

Since Deadwood was long the most populous gold town in the Black Hills, records on disasters here abound. With its founding the city faced trouble when a series of blizzards struck in 1876 and 1877. These were just a premonition of the blizzard that would come in March 1878, when a light rain turned to three days of snow that reached a height of 7 feet and produced drifts over 20 feet deep. The flimsy wooden roofs of Deadwood's early buildings snapped under the weight. Fortunately, the snow quickly melted. Unfortunately, it created a flood that was followed in April by more heavy rains that washed out bridges, roads, houses, stores, and mines. A second destructive flood came through in 1883, causing $250,000 worth of damage. Black Hills Historian Watson Parker notes that while the waters wiped out the city school and Methodist Church, the Gem Theater and most of the saloons were left virtually untouched.

Water was a terrible enemy, but so was fire. The great fire of 1879 was relatively small when it broke out in a downtown bakery, but the situation quickly turned tragic when flames spread to a nearby hardware store and ignited eight kegs of gunpowder. The resulting explosion spread burning timber across town, resulting in the eventual destruction of 300 buildings and $3 million worth of property. Deadwood had been wiped out twice by flood and once by fire in a five-year period. Afterward, property owners rebuilt their structures with brick and stone, giving them the ornate Victorian facades visitors to the town can still see today.

Although Black Hills residents have gotten more careful over the years, disasters still happen. In fact, one of the most destructive floods in the history of the United States occurred in 1972 in the Black Hills. One million metric tons of water doused the region, causing $165 million worth of damage, destroying or damaging more than 4,000 homes and killing 238 people, most of them in Rapid City. Forest fires continue to be a threat; the Westbury Trails blaze in 1988 drove hundreds from their homes in West Rapid City, while the Grizzly Gulch fire in 2002 forced the evacuation of Deadwood and half of Lead.

INSECTS

Since there are more than two million acres of pine forests, grass prairies, and clear-flowing streams in the Black Hills, you're bound to run into a number of bugs. Fortunately, the Black Hills are dominated by a mostly dry, mountainous climate, which means that less desirable creepy crawlers (mosquitoes for instance) aren't nearly as numerous as they are farther east and north.

Abundant wildflowers draw colorful butterflies (including the famous orange and black monarch) each spring. Other pleasant insect species native to the Hills include lightning bugs and dragonflies. Of course, there are biting or stinging insects in the area, such as yellow jackets, spiders (including wolf spiders and black widows, which are poisonous but rarely lethal), ticks, and carpenter ants. Since spring typically doesn't arrive in the Black Hills until late April and the first frost usually comes in mid-September, insects are only around for a few short months.

WEATHER

This is a region of weather extremes. Our weather has something for everyone's taste, often at the same time. The Southern Hills are usually warmer and drier than the Central or Northern Hills, which receive more snow in the winter and thunderstorms, hail, and rain in the summer.

However, anywhere in the Hills, summer temperatures in the 90s are not unusual, and winter sometimes brings temperatures well below zero and windchill factors considerably lower than that. On the other hand, the Rapid City area is sometimes called the Banana Belt because of its relatively mild climate compared with other parts of the Hills. It's known for an average of 300 days of sunshine each year and snowfalls that often melt before the next ones arrive. January thaws usually occur throughout the Hills, bringing warmer temperatures and a few days of blessed relief from winter's cold—as well as lots of mud.

Many first-time visitors have heard all about nearly mythical South Dakota weather: raging blizzards, howling prairie winds, dust storms, intense heat. Generally speaking, however, the Black Hills don't experience those events regularly, although our weather is indeed variable due to our elevation and location near the center of North America.

Gardening isn't always easy here, with an average frost-free date of May 20, a short growing season, and the possibility of snow or a freeze every month in the Northern Hills. However—and this points to the differences in regions—Hot Springs has a growing season a full 35 days longer than Deadwood's.

Usually winters are relatively mild (compared to the rest of South Dakota), although blizzards come through occasionally. Spring is often wet and wild, with fluctuating temperatures and snow well into summer (again, depending on the region). Summer is typically warm and sunny, with chilly nights, thunderstorms, and frequent hail. Fall arrives in September with pleasant, warm days and cool nights, sometimes with temperatures dipping below freezing. Tornadoes don't occur often, but high winds are frequent. Statistically, Rapid City is windier than Chicago, the Windy City.

If you're visiting in the summer, watch out for thunderstorms, lightning, and some pretty large hailstones. Our storms are spectacular, but hail hurts (it can even cause concussions), so take shelter under a covered area, preferably in a hardtopped vehicle or building.

ACCOMMODATIONS

Whether you're visiting the Black Hills for pleasure or business, your accommodations are an important component of a pleasant visit. In this chapter you'll find a selection of accommodations that includes hotels, cottages, vacation homes, cabins, ranches, and bed-and-breakfasts. Although the Hills have literally hundreds of lodging possibilities—including inexpensive chain or mom-and-pop motels and single rooms in private homes—we've selected only the most interesting, comfortable, and enjoyable.

You may assume the accommodations in this chapter do not allow indoor smoking or accept pets and are not wheelchair accessible. If these features are important to you, read the write-ups closely, because we'll indicate all exceptions. You may also assume that each accepts credit cards, requires an advance deposit, and expects advance notice of cancellation.

The Black Hills tourist season runs from Memorial Day weekend through Labor Day weekend. Some accommodations are open before and after those holidays, and some close as soon as the season ends. Many remain open all year, catering to fall travelers and winter recreation enthusiasts. We'll give you the approximate dates of operation, but these dates are not set in stone, as they sometimes change with the weather.

Many lodging operators raise their rates during tourist season and lower them in the off-season, and almost all of them raise their rates during the Sturgis Rally & Races (more about that in the Annual Events & Festivals chapter).

During rally time, the first two weeks of August or so, the Hills are filled to the brim with visitors, and available accommodations are scarce, even if the rates are higher than usual.

Price Code

The following price ratings are based on the cost of one night's lodging for two people (double occupancy) at in-season rates. Some businesses lower their rates during the off-season; inquire when you call. There is often an extra charge (not included in this code) for each extra person or child.

$.................	Less than $90
$$	$90 to $120
$$$	$120 to $150
$$$$	More than $150

ACCOMMODATIONS

Robins Roost Cabins, Hill
   City, 65
Strawberry Bed & Breakfast,
   Deadwood, 56

Whispering Pines
Campground & Lodging,
   Rapid City, 65

$
Deerfield Lake Resort, Hill
City, 62

BED-AND-BREAKFAST INNS & RANCHES

In most bed-and-breakfasts, you get the chance to talk with the owners, meet other guests, and be pampered. Some of the Hills' B&Bs are ranches, too, offering you a taste of the western experience.

Northern Hills

BLACK HILLS HIDEAWAY
BED-AND-BREAKFAST $$–$$$
11744 Hideaway Rd., Deadwood
(605) 578-3054, (877) 500-4433
www.enetis.net/~hideaway
It's a tribute to the tranquillity of this property that it was selected by the owners, two corporate dropouts from the East who, after vacationing in the Hills 10 years, "downsized" themselves and created their hideaway in the forest. Now it's your turn. You can downsize your hectic life here, at least for a while, and bask in the peaceful mountain air. Once the site of a 1904 mining claim, these 67 acres are bordered by the Black Hills National Forest.

The owners invite you to "come and be pampered" in one of their eight guest rooms. They offer a full, hot country breakfast that features their trademark dishes: homemade blueberry coffee cake and egg skillets. Cookies and snacks are available during the day and a commercial kitchen can accommodate small parties (both at extra charge).

You can hike and mountain bike on the premises; snowmobile, ski, and golf nearby; and drive to Deadwood and Lead for gaming and sightseeing. But you may want to stay right here, soak in the hot tub or whirlpool, and just listen to the silence. Inquire about bringing children.

Black Hills Hideaway is 7 miles south of Deadwood off US 385. Watch for the Tomahawk Country Club, then turn onto Hideaway Road and drive one mile.

FIRST DEADWOOD COTTAGES $$$
388 Main St., Deadwood
(605) 920-1512
www.firstdeadwood.com
Conveniently located on Main Street in Deadwood, it is a short walk to the action of downtown and the Days of '76 Rodeo Grounds. There is plenty of free parking, a bonus for this central Deadwood location. The three cottages have at least two bedrooms and two have a full kitchen and laundry. The Bullock Cottage has three bedrooms and three baths. All are nicely furnished. There is a hot tub in the common area.

STRAWBERRY BED &
BREAKFAST $–$$$
21291 Strawberry Hill Lane, Deadwood
(605) 578-2149, (866) 578-2149
www.strawberrybnb.com
Strawberry Hill is infamous among locals for its steep slopes and deep snow in winter, which can make for difficult driving. Fortunately, two summers' worth of construction straightened and widened US 385, which

goes right up and over this local landmark. This makes it much easier to get to the Strawberry Bed & Breakfast, perched near the summit of the mountain. Located about one-tenth of a mile from the highway in a stand of ponderosas, the inn provides private and secluded accommodations within 3 miles of Deadwood's city limits.

Privacy is further enhanced by the type of accommodations here. Guests don't have rooms; they have small cottages connected to the main house by a series of decks. As with most bed-and-breakfasts, each guest room is decorated differently. One has yellow and white country-style furnishings, one is made up to look like a hunting lodge, another has lacy Victorian accents, and one is contemporary, decorated in the forest-and-mauve color scheme you find in many hotels. Each cottage has its own modern bathroom and parlor/game area, but for breakfast guests must use the decks to climb to the main house. Breakfast is typical western fare, including eggs, sausage, and coffee, although waffles with spiced pears add some nice culinary color.

Two sleeping cabins are located farther down the hill. Set off from the other buildings in the forest, they're more rustic. Neither has its own bathroom, but there is a separate, heated shower house. These lodge-style accommodations are especially popular with hunters in autumn. In winter, snowmobilers practically take over the place, and with good reason: A groomed snowmobile trail runs right across the property. If that weren't enough, two ski slopes are located only a few miles away.

YESTERDAY'S INN $$–$$$$
735 North 8th St., Spearfish
(605) 644-0210, (866) 5898-1616
www.yesterdaysinn.net

Located within walking distance of downtown's shops and restaurants, the inn is open year round. The house is on the National Register of Historic Places and the house and grounds are well tended. The inn has four rooms and a newer, two bedroom cottage, all decorated in tasteful Victorian reproductions. The backyard gardens and pond are a quaint setting for weddings and other events. During the summer breakfast is served on the wrap-around porch. Snacks are served daily in the evenings. Open year round, children and pets are not welcomed.

Central Hills

THE ANCHORAGE
BED & BREAKFAST $$$$
24110 Leaky Valley Rd., Keystone
(605) 574-4740, (800) 318-7018
www.anchoragebb.com

Jim Gogolin promised his wife, Lin, that in return for her sacrifices during his years as a naval officer and their travels around the world, she could choose their retirement home. Although she could have selected Majorca, the Philippines, or other lovely places, Lin chose the Black Hills and announced that she wanted to open a bed-and-breakfast inn. Thus the name the Anchorage and the navy-eclectic decor.

Some accommodations are in a separate, private building called the Chart House. It sleeps up to eight people and is rented to just one party at a time. The kitchen is fully equipped, even supplied with some staple items, and there's a hot tub on the deck where you can watch the stars and the deer that come out of the woods. It's a real home with a handmade quilt, books, and a game table, but it doesn't have a television or telephone. Then there are four rooms in the main quarters, each with private bath, fireplace, and access to a hot tub. The houses sit on the rim of a lovely valley with a view of Harney Peak. You may see bobcats and coyotes and hear the whistle of the Black Hills Central Railroad/The 1880 Train as it chugs past. The Centennial Trail is just over the hill. There are 20 acres to play on here; if you need more room, you can go next door to national forestland.

The most-used word in the guest book is "wonderful," but that is hardly adequate for Anchorage breakfasts. "Spectacular" may be more apt. The specialty breakfast is pumpkin waffles with hot apple butter, smoked turkey sausage, rhubarb cake, and a compote of mango and fresh blueberries. Other delights include pepper and sausage quiche, wild raspberry crepes, and huge pecan caramel rolls. You might get to try Jim's Baked Pancakes, filled with apples, nutmeg, pecans, and sour cream, served with ham and muffins. Breakfast is served in the main house.

✳AUDRIE'S BED AND BREAKFAST AND DAS ABEND HAUS COTTAGES $$$$
23029 Thunderhead Falls Rd., Rapid City
(605) 342-7788
www.audriesbb.com
This glorious old-world estate was the Black Hills' first bed-and-breakfast; it was founded in 1985 and is still owned and operated by the same family. Its handsome antique furniture, purchased when the family was in Europe, adorns each room. The beautiful buildings on the property are the Old Powerhouse (built in 1910 for watergenerated electricity), and the chalet-style das Abend Haus (German for "the Evening House") Cottages. Each has two suites. You can also stay in one of seven big, high-ceiling log cottages, each of which is delightfully decorated. All are available for weekly or monthly vacation rentals. The rooms, suites, and cottages are elegant and luxurious. They're beautifully furnished in rich colors, fabrics, and woods. Each has a private bath and entrance, latticed deck or porch, hot tub, cable television, refrigerator, and microwave. Breakfast is placed in each refrigerator so guests can heat and enjoy it in privacy. It includes bacon-and-egg quiche for two, homemade baked goods, fruit, cereal, and juice.

Audrie's is in a pretty, quiet, and secluded canyon 7 miles west of Rapid City. You can easily drive to any Central Hills attraction, or you can take a walk, explore the Black Hills National Forest around the property, fish for trout in Rapid Creek, which flows right through the estate (you'll need a license—see the Recreation chapter), or bicycle up the road. Fishing poles and bicycles are provided for guests. Dedicated to comfort and privacy, Audrie's does not allow children or pets, and guests are asked not to bring visitors. The hot tubs can't be used after 11 p.m. or before 7 a.m. so that everyone can enjoy the nighttime peace and silence.

BLACK FOREST INN
BED & BREAKFAST LODGE $$$
23191 US 385, Rapid City
(605) 574-2000, (800) 888-1607
www.blackforestinn.net
You'll love the spaciousness here (10,000 square feet and 10 rooms), especially the huge great room with its rock fireplace. A wonderful deck overlooks the lawn and surrounding forest and holds a hot tub that's waiting just for you. Or settle into the game room, where you can read, play pool or games, or watch television. A homemade breakfast is served in courses on silver and crystal. Meeting rooms are available for retreats and workshops. This is an especially

lovely place for reunions, weddings, and anniversary celebrations. Black Forest Inn is centrally located: It's near Pactola Reservoir, Sheridan Lake, Mount Rushmore, and Rapid City, as well as within a 30-minute drive of every attraction in the Central Hills.

ℹ️ Many of the businesses listed under this heading are members of the Bed & Breakfast Innkeepers of South Dakota (BBISD). Members must meet standards for hospitality, cleanliness, and safety and must pass an association inspection conducted by state-trained inspectors. For additional information, or to request a member directory, call (888) 500-INNS.

COYOTE BLUES VILLAGE
BED & BREAKFAST $-$$$$
P.O. Box 966, Hill City 57745
(605) 574-4477, (888) 253-4477
www.coyotebluesvillage.com

The Swiss owners have given their bed-and-breakfast inn a contemporary European flavor. "Experience a piece of Europe in the Black Hills," they like to say. You'll love the original art scattered throughout the house, the huge deck, and the views across open land and forest. Breakfast includes home-baked breads and other culinary delights including fruit, French toast, eggs, and another specialty, Swiss muesli, as well as deli meats and specialty cheeses. When they purchased the property, the owners were intrigued by the nocturnal howling of coyotes, which they decided was coyote singing; thus the Coyote Blues name. You'll still hear the coyotes nearly every night, but that's about all; the peace and quiet will astound you. The owners offer seven theme rooms (one a suite), three basic rooms, and a conference room. There's a

sitting area, a table tennis table and a piano (for those who want to exercise only their fingers); the guest reading room has a large-screen TV and DVD. Coyote Blues Village is 12 miles from Hill City and 22 miles from Rapid City, just south of Pactola Lake off US 385.

DEERVIEW BED &
BREAKFAST $$-$$$
12110 Deerfield Rd., Hill City
(605) 574-4204, (888) 622-5274
www.deerviewbb.com

Deerview is a beautifully appointed and carefully designed bed-and-breakfast that reflects the owners' attention to detail. The pine-studded property is bordered by national forest, where you can hike, snowmobile, look for old gold mines, or fish at Deerfield Reservoir, just 9 miles away. It's only 5 miles to Hill City along scenic Deerfield Road. The cottage is set in the pines, apart from the main house, and has two rooms. A separate space between the rooms houses the shared hot tub. A third room is in the main house but has its own entrance and a private hot tub outside. Deerview also boasts two vacation homes: a five-bedroom, three-bath and a two-bedroom, one-bath. Each room has a microwave (with complimentary popcorn), small refrigerator, satellite television, and a coffeemaker. The owners are proud of their full, delicious breakfast, which is served in your room.

HIGH COUNTRY
GUEST RANCH $$$-$$$$
12172 Deerfield Rd., Hill City
(605) 574-9003, (888) CABIN28
www.highcountryranch.com

This one's not a dude ranch or a working ranch, but a real guest ranch where you can spend a few nights, relax, eat a cowboy breakfast, and still do your sightseeing. Read about trail rides in the Recreation chapter. Other offerings include a pool, outdoor movies, a cowboy supper, and bicycle rentals. If you're looking for a place to both ride and bask in some luxury, there are 21 cabins here, and they're not rustic. Some have vaulted ceilings, bay windows, hot tubs, and fireplaces. Even your horse can be comfortable; board your equine for an extra charge (feed and hay are not furnished). Alcohol use is limited and rooms are nonsmoking. A traditional western breakfast is served, with simple but hearty food. Guests say the pancakes are "the best in the world," and breakfast is served in the spacious dining hall. Other meals can be reserved for groups (ask about picnic lunches or steaks cooked on pitchforks) for an extra charge. This ranch is "off the beaten path but close to everything," say the owners. The George S. Mickelson Trail goes right through the property. The ranch is open all year but trail rides and activities are available Memorial Day through Labor Day.

NORMARKE FARMS $$-$$$$
12203 Nemo Rd., Nemo
(605) 578-2125
http://normarkefarm.homestead.com/
cover.html
A massive log home, Normarke sits on 87 acres of wooded hills and meadows about 17 miles south of Deadwood. The owners welcome visitors with traditional Scandinavian heritage and hospitality. Each of the five bedrooms is named for a Scandinavian country and sleeps two and each has a private bath. Relax by the large stone fireplace in the living room and take the chill off. A nearby small fishing lake is stocked with pan trout three times a year. A full, gourmet-style breakfast is served in the dining room each morning.

SHARI'S SWEETGRASS INN
BED AND BREAKFAST $$-$$$
9356 Neck Yoke Rd., Rapid City
(605) 343-5351
www.sweetgrassinn.com
This eight-room inn off US 16 boasts a great location between Rapid City and Mount Rushmore, with convenient access to many major attractions in the Central Hills. A spacious common room, a large parking area, and private entrances to each room are additional attractions for road-weary travelers who may be getting tired of cramped cookiecutter chain hotels. The eclectic decor suggests charming Victorian country, with floral-print furniture. Half of the rooms, which are all named for flowers, have their own whirlpool tubs, but a hot tub on the back deck is open to all guests during the summer months. Rooms have their own TVs, and coffee pots, and the common room has a fridge and microwave. Wildlife roams the inn grounds, from the family of rabbits that lives under the porch to wild turkeys that shuffle past in the early morning hours. There is a two-night minimum from June through Sept but they will accept a one-night stay if a room is available.

VIXIE'S VICTORIAN VILLA
BED & BREAKFAST $$$
10430 Big Piney Rd., Rapid City
(605) 343-9234, (877) 343-9234
www.bbonline.com/sd/vixiesvilla
This is a bed-and-breakfast inn locals like to use as a getaway. The owners describe the three-story redwood home nestled in the peaceful pines of Black Hills National Forest as "an oasis of rest where you can experience old-fashioned hospitality and the simple pleasures of a full country-style breakfast." Each of the four suites has a hot

tub, television, and small refrigerator. All the rooms look out on peaceful views. Breakfast is served in the rooms, and the menu varies daily. Coffee is available in the rooms. When you wake in the morning, you may see deer, rabbits, squirrels, and chipmunks outside. Vixie's is centrally located near Rapid City, 30 miles from Deadwood, across the road from a fine restaurant and lounge, the Fireside Inn.

WILLOW SPRINGS CABINS
BED & BREAKFAST $$$$
11515 Sheridan Lake Rd., Rapid City
(605) 342-3665
www.willowspringscabins.com

Two beautiful cabins and some wonderful breakfasts define the secluded Willow Springs accommodations. Tucked away in a quiet valley, surrounded by national forest, the cabins are decorated with family heirlooms and are cozy, comfortable, and private. The Willows Cabin sleeps four and is open all year. The Frontier Cabin sits on a little hill, sleeps two, and is open from May through Sept. Each has a private bath, hot tub, television and DVD, air-conditioning, stereo, microwave, coffeemaker, and small refrigerator. It's an easy drive to Rapid City, Sheridan Lake, and Pactola Reservoir, but you might want to stay right here and bask in the peace and quiet of 140 acres, where the wind still combs the branches of age-old ponderosa pine. Walk down to Spring Creek, fish (license required) and swim on the property, ice-skate in the winter, and get to know the friendly resident cats and dog. Breakfast is served in the dining room of the house or brought to your cabin. The owner calls it "a wholesome and hearty gourmet breakfast." The cabins are stocked with coffee, tea, and popcorn. A two-night stay is required.

i On the third Saturday in September, the Bed & Breakfast Innkeepers of South Dakota sponsor a Pumpkin Festival and Open House. You can tour a member inn or ranch and meet the owners. Pumpkin treats are served and entertainment or activities are offered at each inn. Not every BBISD member inn participates, so call (888) 500-INNS to request a list by mail.

Southern Hills

CUSTER MANSION
BED & BREAKFAST $$–$$$
35 Centennial Dr., Custer
(605) 673-3333, (877) 519-4948
www.custermansionbb.com

This gorgeous and fascinating historic home is a charmer. Of Gothic design from the Victorian era (it was built in 1891), it is a tribute to both the success of the rancher/civic leader who built it and the current owners, who lovingly restored it. Listed in the National Register of Historic Places, it has seven gables, two staircases, transoms, stained-glass windows, a butler's pantry, and two rooms and three suites, all quaintly decorated. The mansion is filled with antiques, heirlooms, and lovely old framed prints from the owners' collection. Breakfast often includes a buttermilk sauce for your pancakes or waffles. You'll rest well in the gorgeous four-poster king bed in the Evergreen Room. Or you might choose to relax in the gabled-wall Shenandoah Room, which has a Jacuzzi. The Evening Star family suite has two rooms connected by a tiny charming hallway, and the bathroom features an antique claw-foot tub. You may also choose the Rose of Sharon Room or the Morning Dew Room. Whichever room you choose, you'll enjoy discovering the delightful idiosyncrasies of this historic house. Alcohol use is limited.

CABINS & COTTAGES

Camping cabins, cottages, and housekeeping cabins offer privacy and scenic settings, with facilities ranging from rustic to luxurious.

Northern Hills

CHEYENNE CROSSING $$
21415 US 14A
Spearfish Canyon, Lead
(605) 584-3510, (800) 529-0105
Built near the site of one of the old Deadwood–Cheyenne stage stops and locally known for home cooking, Cheyenne Crossing offers a three-bedroom lodge, with one bath, a living room, and dining area. Fish for trout right out the back door.

WICKIUP VILLAGE $$–$$$
US 85, Cheyenne Crossing Lead
(605) 584-3382, (800) 505-8268
www.spearfishcreekcabins.com
The setting is the best amenity here. These 20 log housekeeping cabins are surrounded by Black Hills spruce and near lovely Spearfish Creek at the head of Spearfish Canyon. They are heated by gas-log fireplaces and furnished with everything you'll need, except groceries. Each cabin has its own bathroom and shower. Leashed pets are allowed. Here you'll be within just a few miles of Lead, Deadwood, and Spearfish.

Central Hills

DEERFIELD LAKE RESORT $
11321 Gillette Prairie Rd., Hill City
(605) 574-2636
www.deerfieldlakeresort.com

Deerfield Lake Resort has four heated cabins, each with one large room, two double beds and futon couch, a kitchenette, private bath, satellite TV, and Wi-Fi. It's a year-round resort, and there's always something to do here. Deerfield Reservoir is next door, with great fishing in both summer and winter, and Hill City is just 14 miles away. Winter, however, is the resort's busiest season, as the property is adjacent to popular snowmobile trails; you can even rent a snowmobile here. From mid-Dec through Mar breakfast is available. They also offer canoe and 4-wheeler rentals, horse corrals and a country store for essentials and fuel.

**ELK CREEK CAMPING
  RESORT AND LODGE** $–$$$$
Elk Creek Road, Piedmont
(605) 787-4884, (800) 846-2267
www.elkcreekresort.net
This 11-acre resort has 4 cabins and 5 ranch-style houses that enclose 17 "cottage rooms." The vacation home has four bedrooms, two kitchens and a garage. Each motel-style cottage room shares only a wall with adjoining rooms and has a private bath, coffeepot, and refrigerator. Some rooms have kitchens, too. Cabins have one main room and a small bunk room that sleeps up to eight people. The cabins have no plumbing (shower facilities are nearby), but they do have air-conditioning and refrigerators. They also offer on-site RV rentals. An outdoor, shared hot tub is on the premises, as is a heated pool. Breakfast is available for purchase on summer weekends. Your pet is welcome, but an additional deposit is required. One cottage is wheelchair accessible. Elk Creek Resort is open year-round, and a campground is also on the property. To get there, take I-90 to exit 46.

HARNEY CAMP CABINS $-$$$
24345 SR 87, Hill City
(605) 574-2594
www.harneycamp.net

Sixteen housekeeping cabins share this quiet, secluded property in the tall pines. Each has a private bath and sleeps from two to eight people. Sunday Creek runs through the property, and you can select a cabin that is accessible by a little bridge across the creek. Fire pits, grills, and a playground are available, and pets are allowed (please inquire). There's a hot tub and sundeck by the creek, and you can hike on the forest service land that surrounds Harney Camp. The cabins are open from Apr through Oct. Call to make reservations.

HOLY SMOKE RESORT $$-$$$
US 16A, Keystone
(605) 666-4616, (866) 530-5696
www.holysmokeresort.com

This great place is tucked off the highway in Buckeye Gulch, the site of old gold, silver, and copper mines. Legend has it that well-known western writer Stewart Edward White prospected for gold here for six months in 1901, then holed up in a log cabin on this site while he penned *The Westerners, The Claim Jumpers,* and *The Blazed Trail.* You may stay in one of 19 cabins, including an 1893 mining-camp cabin, Stable your own horse for $10 per day May 15 through Memorial Day and after Labor Day, or rent one for a trail ride, or hike on the fire roads that lace the 75-acre property. The cabins have one or two bedrooms. A duplex unit is perfect for two couples traveling together. The Holy Smoke is open from mid-May to Sept 30. Register at the nearby Holy Smoke Restaurant and Lounge (see the Restaurants chapter), just down the road.

LITTLE ELK CANYON CABIN AND COTTAGE $$$-$$$$
12645 Dalton Lake Rd., Nemo
(605) 578-2012
www.littleelkcabin.com

This beautiful 1930s cabin was built by the Civilian Conservation Corps and moved to its present site in Vanocker Canyon. It's just 3.5 miles from the little town of Nemo, close to Dalton Lake and great hiking in Little Elk Canyon, yet right off Lawrence County Road 26 for convenience. Set in a pleasant meadow and surrounded by tall pines, it feels quite secluded. You may see deer, elk, or eagles during your stay. The cabin was lovingly restored by its talented owners and is charming, modern, comfortable, and air-conditioned. It sleeps several people in the one bedroom, a loft with two twin beds, and a sofa bed in the living room. The owners have added to the property a lovely new cottage with two full bedrooms. Lounge under the open beam ceiling and skylights, or relax next to the fireplace. Privacy is guaranteed, as each guesthouse sits on its own five acres. Both the cabin and the cottage have a warmly glowing wood interior, furnished kitchen, full bathroom, microwave, telephone, satellite TV, DVD, baseboard heat, and a picnic table and grill outside. Bedding and towels are furnished. The friendly owners live just "over the hill and through the woods."

THE LODGE AT PALMER GULCH RESORT $$-$$$$
SR 244, Hill City
(605) 574-2525, (800) 562-8503
www.palmergulchresort.com

Palmer Gulch Resort has a lovely 62-room lodge and 30 cabins. Some of the one- to three-bedroom cabins have kitchens of various sizes and some are sleeping cabins. Six new executive lodges, some with three and four bedrooms, feature hot tubs, gas grills, and commanding views of the Harney Range. All have private baths. Outdoor and indoor hot tubs and two outdoor pools are available for use. The cabins are open only from May 1 through Oct. The lodge has both rooms and mini-suites, which have fireplaces (some mini-suites also have kitchenettes and balconies). It's a popular place for family reunions, as it has meeting facilities, a conference room, indoor sauna and hot tub, a reunion hall with kitchen, a picnic shelter outside, and a restaurant and lounge across the parking lot. Pets are allowed, and the lodge is wheelchair accessible (one room has a roll-in shower). The lodge is open from Apr 15 through Oct 15. Smoking is permitted in the cabins, but not in the lodge. The resort is 5 miles west of Mount Rushmore. See the Campgrounds chapter for information about the Mount Rushmore KOA, which is located at Palmer Gulch.

**MYSTERY MOUNTAIN
RESORT** $$-$$$$
13752 South US 16 West
Rapid City
(605) 342-5368, (800) 658-2267
www.mysterymountain.us
You have your choice of 23 lodging facilities that offer seven different kinds of accommodations. There are camping cabins (one room, no bathroom, and lower rates than those designated by the above price code), guesthouses, and the big reunion cottage with five bedrooms, two baths, and kitchen with microwave and dishwasher. Some units remain open throughout the year, except for the camping cabins and one small cabin. Pets are allowed. You can enjoy the rest

of Mystery Mountain while you're there, too: pool, hot tub, playground, mini golf, camp store, and laundry. There's also a campground, which you can read about in the Campgrounds chapter.

NEMO GUEST RANCH $$$
Main Street, Nemo
(605) 578-2708
www.nemoguestranch.com
There are 14 cabins and houses at the Nemo Guest Ranch, with private baths and one to five bedrooms that sleep 4 to 13 people. Some have kitchens or kitchenettes. Pets on leashes are allowed, but no smoking in the guesthouses. Some units are open year-round. The ranch is rustic and designed for outdoor fun; there are no televisions or phones (except pay phones), but Wi-Fi is available. Campground and horse accommodations are available (see the Campgrounds chapter). You can shop for supplies at the late-1800s general store, dine at the Branding Iron Cafe, or have beer or wine at the Ponderosa Bar, all nearby. The ranch is on Lawrence County Road 234, which is also called Nemo Road, and is 16 miles northwest of Rapid City and 30 minutes from Deadwood.

PINE REST CABINS $$$-$$$$
P.O. Box 377, Hill City 57745
(605) 574-2416, (800) 333-5306
www.pinerestcabins.com
You can get your rest in rustic little cabins with their backdrop of pine forest, yet they're only 1 mile south of Hill City. There are seven one-bedroom cabins, one guest room, and four two-bedroom cabins with fireplaces to choose from. Some have kitchenettes with basic utensils, coffeepot, toaster, and outside grill and picnic table. Linens and towels are provided. Your pet is welcome in some

rooms at an additional charge. There is cable television, Wi-Fi, a playground for the kids, and a hot tub. The George S. Mickelson Trail is across the highway. Call for reservations.

ROBINS ROOST CABINS $-$$$
12630 Robins Roost Rd., Hill City
(605) 574-2252
www.robins-roost-cabins.com
Seven housekeeping cabins and three-bedroom, and two bedroom homes are on the property. The fully furnished cabins have private baths and showers, fireplaces, two double beds, and furnished bedding and towels. Wi-Fi, charcoal grills and picnic tables are available at each cabin. The larger homes sleep up to 10 people. Some of the cabins have been set aside for pet owners; please inquire. Robins Roost is in a pretty pine setting close to Hill City, just 12 miles from Mount Rushmore, and near tiny Mitchell Lake, which is reported to have great fishing.

SPOKANE CREEK RESORT $-$$$$
US 16A, Keystone
(605) 666-4609
www.spokanecreekresort.com
This family-oriented resort is just a mile from Custer State Park and has some fine amenities, too, such as laundry facilities, trout fishing, a deli/general store, heated outdoor pool, miniature golf, fresh cinnamon rolls each morning, and a playground for kids. There are 21 cabins on 29 acres, two of which have no bathrooms or kitchens but do have electricity and use of the nearby shower and require that you bring your own bedding. The 15 housekeeping cabins have private baths and from one to four rooms that sleep two to eight people. All cabins come with a picnic table and fire ring. The resort is open from mid-May to mid-Sept.

There's information about the resort's campground in the Campgrounds chapter.

SPRING CREEK INN $$-$$$$
23900 US 385, Hill City
(605) 574-2591, (800) 456-2755
www.springcreekinn.com
This pretty property is just off the highway and a short distance from Hill City. You can rent the cottage house, two log cabins or one of three chalets. The cottage house has two bedrooms, two bathrooms, kitchen, air-conditioning, and outside picnic tables. The chalets have three bedrooms, one or two bathrooms, living rooms, decks, kitchenettes, and air-conditioning. They also offer two small log cabins and a two-bedroom A-frame home with a hot tub. The facility is open Apr 1 to Nov 30. Motel units are also available. Spring Creek runs through the property, which is surrounded on three sides by forest service land. Barbecue grills, an outdoor fireplace, volleyball and basketball courts, a playground, and a picnic shelter round out the experience. You should inquire before bringing your pet along.

WHISPERING PINES CAMPGROUND & LODGING $-$$$
22700 Silver City Rd., Rapid City
(605) 341-3667, (877) 341-3667
www.blackhillswhisperingpines.com
Four camping cabins are for rent here, surrounded by stands of aspen and ponderosa. These are simple one- and two-bedroom sleeping cabins without bathrooms (facilities are nearby), you bring your own bedding. A campground is on the property, too, with a general store and snack bar where breakfast specials are served, and the coffee is always on and free. Nightly cookouts and movies are offered to campers and cabin renters.

Whispering Pines also has two luxury vacation homes, which you can read about in the Vacation Homes and Condominiums section of this chapter. The property is on the Centennial Trail (see Recreation) and close to Pactola Reservoir and Central Hills attractions.

Southern Hills

AMERICAN PRESIDENTS CABINS & CAMP $$$–$$$$
US 16A, Custer
(605) 673-3373
www.presidentsresort.com

A serene country setting makes American Presidents a popular place for family reunions. There are 45 cabins on 50 acres, all with private bathrooms, although a few are sleeping cabins. The more luxurious cabins sleep from 10 to 12 people, have several bedrooms, two bathrooms, and their own decks. Other cabins vary in size; ask which will best suit you. Guests can use the 60-foot-by-40-foot heated pool and hot tub, surrounded by a 5,000-square-foot deck, then hit the convenience store for snacks. One cabin is wheelchair accessible, as is the shower house on the grounds. American Presidents has a campground (see the Campgrounds chapter), and the facility is open from approximately Apr through Oct 1.

ANGOSTURA STATE RESORT $$$
Angostura Recreation Area, Hot Springs
(605) 745-6665, (800) 364-8831

Angostura State Resort is located on one of the largest lakes in Western South Dakota and just minutes from Hot Springs. The 100-slip marina is within easy walking distance of the cabins. Of the six cabins, four have two bedrooms and two have three bedrooms; all have kitchens and bathrooms. The resort includes a large heated swimming pool and convenience store. Angostura Reservoir is noted for great fishing, beaches and boating.

BLUE BELL LODGE AND RESORT $$$–$$$$
Custer State Park SR 87, Custer
(605) 255-4531,
(888) 875-0001 (reservations)
www.custerresorts.com

The expanded Blue Bell Lodge houses the dining room, with family-style dinners, a lounge, and a small meeting room. Around the lodge are 29 log cabins, including sleeping cabins, a honeymoon cabin with one room and fireplace, and housekeeping cabins that accommodate four, six, or eight people. The Commissioner's Cabin has four rooms, a full kitchen, and sleeps eight. Some cabins are open in winter. Blue Bell is favored for its stables and trail rides. You'll also find a new general store with gifts and supplies.

CALAMITY PEAK LODGE $–$$$$
US 16A, Custer
(605) 673-2357, (800) 591-5949
www.blackhills.com/calamitypeak

If you stay here, you'll be just 2 miles east of the town of Custer and look out on French Creek and Calamity Peak, a craggy granite mountain across the highway, all surrounded by the beauty of Black Hills National Forest. You have your choice of accommodations. A house that sleeps 10 is available. One cabin sleeps four people, the other sleeps six; both have a kitchen and private bath. Motel units are also available, including two that sleep six people and have fully furnished kitchens. Grills and picnic tables are outside, and each unit has free satellite TV and Wi-Fi. An extension of the popular Mickelson Trail runs through the property. Calamity Peak Lodge is open only from May through Oct.

CUSTER MOUNTAIN CABINS & CAMPGROUND $-$$$$
US 16A, Custer
(605) 673-5440, (800) 239-5505
www.custermountain.com

The eight rough-hewn log housekeeping cabins at this well-run resort has two or three bedrooms, private baths, and decks. They also offer two small camper cabins, an alternative to camping but you still bring your own gear and bedding. A three bedroom house is available and sleeps up to 10 with two baths and a full kitchen. You can hike on the adjoining forest service land, and you'll be near both the city of Custer and Custer State Park. There's a campground on the property, too, and you'll find information about it in the Campgrounds chapter.

i Need help finding accommodations in the Black Hills and Badlands? Call the Black Hills, Badlands, and Lakes Association, (605) 355-3600, or visit Black Hills Visitor Information Center, 1851 Discovery Circle (exit 61, I-90), Rapid City. You can also call or visit the Rapid City Convention and Visitors Bureau, (605) 343-1744; 444 Mount Rushmore Rd.; www.visitrapidcity.com.

LEGION LAKE RESORT $$$-$$$$
Custer State Park, Custer
(605) 255-4521
(888) 875-0001 (reservations)
www.custerresorts.com

Another pretty little spot in Custer State Park, Legion Lake has a store, a gift shop, and dining room, plus 25 houskeeping and sleeping cottages, some with kitchens. The lake is small and great for families who want to swim, fish or rent a paddle boat. Get your coffee fix at Starbucks in the lodge.

STATE GAME LODGE & RESORT $$$$
Custer State Park, Custer
(605) 255-4541,
(888) 875-0001 (reservations)
www.custerresorts.com

The charming State Game Lodge and Resort offers cottages or motel units on its grounds. Built in 1920, the Game Lodge was used as the summer White House by President Calvin Coolidge in 1927 and is listed on the National Register of Historic Places. Cottages range in size from one room with two double beds to the Reunion Cabin which accommodates up to 16 people. The 4,200 square foot Reunion Cabin has four bedrooms, including two with a fireplace, and a loft with bunk beds. The housekeeping cabins have kitchens or kitchenettes and fireplaces and sleep up to eight people. Sleeping cabins are smaller but all have private bathrooms. The 30-unit Creekside Lodge opened in 2008, and has a large lobby, two meeting rooms, and over-sized guest rooms with microwaves and refrigerators. If you'd prefer to stay in the lodge, you can read about it in the Resorts and Lodges section of this chapter.

✴SYLVAN LAKE LODGE $$$-$$$$
Custer State Park, Custer
(605) 574-2561,
(888) 875-0001 (reservations)
www.custerresorts.com

Thirty-one one-room sleeping cabins on the lodge grounds have fireplaces and television. Housekeeping cabins have televisions, and the Senator's Cabin accommodates up to 10 people. It has four rooms, full kitchen, fireplace, three beds, and two sofa beds. The Honeymoon Cabin is a favorite of many guests. The view is spectacular. All of the cabins were completely renovated in 2008.

You can also stay in the lodge's guest rooms; see the Resorts and Lodges section.

HOTELS

Found in the heart of Black Hills towns, these hotels give you easy access to historic and cultural sites.

Northern Hills

BULLOCK HOTEL $$$
633 Main St., Deadwood
(800) 336-1876
www.historicbullock.com
Deadwood legend Seth Bullock, the town's first sheriff and a friend of Teddy Roosevelt, built this elegant and charming hotel in 1895. It soon became known as one of the finest hotels in the region. When Deadwood's renovation began in 1989, the Bullock was meticulously restored to its early grandeur. Today, you can bask in the fascinating history of the building while enjoying some very modern luxuries. The old ballroom is now a casino, and you can dine beside the ornate fireplace in Bully's Restaurant and Lounge (named in Teddy's honor). Seth's Cellar can accommodate your private party or banquet. Like many Deadwood hotels, the Bullock offers tour packages (food, lodging, and gaming) for groups. The hotel also operates the Branch House, 37 Sherman St. (about a block away), which offers mostly suites; rates are slightly higher than the Bullock's. Reservations are made through the Bullock Hotel at the above number.

FIRST GOLD HOTEL & GAMING $$-$$$
270 Main St., Deadwood
(605) 578-9777, (800) 274-1876
www.firstgold.com
Although not a historic hotel, the newly expanded First Gold has a lot to offer, including two restaurants (one with a bar), 11 casinos, two hotels with more than 200 rooms, 80 covered parking spaces, and meeting and banquet facilities. The main hotel has three suites with Jacuzzis; two of the suites have kitchens. First Gold's Terrace Casino is smoke-free. Pets are permitted in certain rooms (deposit required).

HISTORIC FRANKLIN HOTEL $$-$$$
709 Main St., Deadwood
(605) 578-3670, (800) 584-7005
www.silveradofranklin.com
The Franklin has a rich and lively Deadwood-style history. Built in 1903, it was the site of the first South Dakota radio broadcast, and it is the traditional place to stay for visiting celebrities, from Babe Ruth and John Wayne to Kevin Costner and country music stars Big & Rich. It also was a famous gambling house, even though the practice was outlawed until 1989. In fact, rumor says that an illegal poker game was being held in the hotel's basement in the moments leading up to legalization. The Silverado casino across the street purchased the Franklin in late 2005 and closed it for remodeling. The completely renovated main floor reopened in July 2006. Among other things, the new owners restored the front entrance to its original appearance, revealing portions of the original tin ceiling that were covered up over the years, investing more than $100,000 on chandeliers, and constructing a new wing on the Franklin's western side. A multimillion-dollar renovation of the guest rooms will be completed in phases.

MINERAL PALACE HOTEL $$-$$$
610 Main St., Deadwood
(605) 578-2036, (800) 847-2522
www.mineralpalace.com
The Mineral Palace is a new hotel, at least compared to others in town that are housed

in historic buildings. Each of its rooms and suites has a big bathroom, television, and clock radio. Some rooms are wheelchair accessible, and you can request a nonsmoking room. The Royal Suite has a Jacuzzi, wet bar, and fireplace. The multiroom casino and restaurant are on the first floor of the hotel. A three-story expansion with additional hotel and casino space opened in 2006.

Central Hills

ALEX JOHNSON HOTEL $$$
523 6th St., Rapid City
(605) 342-1210, (800) 888-ALEX
www.alexjohnson.com

The Alex was built in the 1920s by the businessman whose name it carries but the owners have recently completed a multimillion-dollar renovation of the property. The hotel is one of the treasures of Rapid City's historic downtown (six US presidents have stayed here, and you've seen Cary Grant here in the 1959 Alfred Hitchcock classic *North by Northwest*), and its lobby is beautifully furnished with Lakota art and artifacts. Here you'll be in the heart of town, yet within an hour or so of every attraction in the Black Hills. The 143 rooms are elegantly furnished. There are three suites: the Executive; the Bridal, with a hot tub; and the impressive Presidential with two separate bedrooms and a full kitchen. Some rooms are wheelchair accessible. The Landmark Restaurant is on the first floor, as is Paddy O'Neill's Pub and Casino, and meeting and banquet facilities are available.

*RADISSON HOTEL $$$
445 Mount Rushmore Rd., Rapid City
(605) 348-8300, (800) 333-3333
www.radisson.com/rapidcitysd

We've included this chain hotel here because it's in the heart of Rapid City and has special accommodations for business travelers. It is located on the corner of busy Mount Rushmore Road and Main Street. The rooms have coffeemakers, microwaves, and dataports. Other amenities include free shuttle to and from Rapid City Regional Airport; restaurant and lounge; banquet facilities; indoor pool and hot tub; exercise area; and business center with fax, copier, and computer. Four rooms are wheelchair accessible. The restaurant at the hotel—Enigma—offers one of the classiest continental dining experiences in the region. Read more about it in the Restaurants chapter.

RUSHMORE PLAZA HOLIDAY INN & CONFERENCE CENTER $$$–$$$$
Rushmore Plaza Civic Center
505 North 5th St., Rapid City
(605) 348-4000, (800) 315-2621
www.rushmoreplaza.com

This eight-story chain hotel values service and is adjacent to the Rushmore Plaza Civic Center—convenient for those attending conventions, meetings, or events there. The hotel's amenities include a lovely atrium, indoor pool, sauna, whirlpool/hot tub, exercise room, cable television and HBO, the Tiffany Grille restaurant, and the Fountain Court lounge. The Presidential Suite has its own Jacuzzi. Pets are allowed (please ask, deposit required). Rapid City also has two Holiday Inn Express hotels (750 Cathedral Dr. and 645 Disk Dr.), which have no restaurant or lounge but do offer free continental breakfast.

Southern Hills

SOJOURNER INN $$–$$$$
1729 Minnekahta Ave., Hot Springs
(605) 745-3361, (605) 890-0692
www.sojournerinn.net

This three-story, historic hotel was originally built as a hospital, in the day when the nearby hot mineral springs were considered a miracle cure-all. Open year round, the hotel is located in the downtown district and thus within walking distance to the major attractions including Evans Plunge. The one and two bedroom suites are beautifully decorated and some offer a full kitchen and private patio. What makes the Sojourner Inn special is the mineral water bath and meditation garden. The outdoor natural pool is constantly filled by flowing mineral water. The Sojourner Cabins are located on a ranch between Hot Springs and Wind Cave National Park. The five newer cabins are creatively decorated and have two to three bedrooms and well-equipped full kitchens.

RESORTS & LODGES

Black Hills resorts offer lodging, restaurants, and other conveniences in a single setting.

Northern Hills

DEADWOOD GULCH RESORT $$
US 85 South, Deadwood
(605) 578-1294, (800) 695-1876
www.deadwoodgulch.com
Deadwood Gulch is a complete resort, with something for everyone, including 98 motel rooms of various sizes and styles. The resort is on the Mickelson Trail—the part that can be accessed by snowmobiles. It has a convention center, two casinos, a fitness room, a large indoor hot tub, and a restaurant favored by the locals.

✳THE LODGE AT DEADWOOD $$–$$$$
US 85, Deadwood
(605) 334-2731
www.deadwoodlodge.com

This new upscale resort and convention center is destined to become its own attraction and a major destination for conventions, corporate events, board retreats, trade shows, weddings, and private catered functions. Opened in the fall of 2009, the $47 million property affords sweeping, panoramic views of the Black Hills and the plains of western South Dakota. The resort sports 140 luxury hotel guest rooms and suites, a convention center large enough to accommodate up to 1,700 people, a first-class restaurant, sports bar, year-around indoor water park, and a Las Vegas–style casino with poker, blackjack and slot machines.

i Tourist season in the Black Hills and Badlands begins Memorial Day weekend and ends Labor Day weekend. But spring, fall, and winter are great seasons in which to visit and enjoy the scenery and recreation (although many attractions are closed), as well as to take advantage of lighter traffic and smaller crowds.

✳SPEARFISH CANYON LODGE AT LATCHSTRING VILLAGE $$$–$$$$
US 14A, Spearfish
(605) 584-3435, (877) 975-6343
www.spfcanyon.com
This relaxing 54-room resort in glorious Spearfish Canyon offers lodging, conference facilities, gift shop, restaurant, a lounge, and a sports center. The accommodations vary in size from guest rooms to suites, with amenities like coffeemakers, fireplaces, balconies, and microwaves. At adjacent Latchstring Village you'll also find trails, fishing, a botanical garden, and snowmobile rentals. Although you'll be close to Deadwood, Spearfish, and Northern Hills attractions, the incredible

scenery may entice you to stay right here. Check out the short hikes to nearby Little Spearfish Falls and Roughlock Falls, the latter of which received major upgrades in 2008, leaving it handicapped-accessible and better than ever.

Southern Hills

STATE GAME LODGE AND RESORT $$$–$$$$
Custer State Park, Custer
(605) 255-4541, (888) 875-0001
www.custerresorts.com
This beautiful structure was President Coolidge's summer White House in 1927, when he intended to take a two-week vacation and ended up staying three months. You're likely to enjoy it as much as Silent Cal. The charming lodge is listed on the National Register of Historic Places and is one of the treasures of Custer State Park. You can stay in one of the lodge's seven guest rooms, which come in a variety of styles and sizes and accommodate up to four people each. The Creekside Lodge which opened in 2008 features a large lobby, two meeting rooms, and over-sized guest rooms with microwaves and refrigerators. While you're there, dine in the remodeled and expanded Game Lodge Dining Room or have a drink in the lounge. But, don't miss the Buffalo Jeep Safari. Meeting and banquet facilities are available, too. Cabins and motel rooms are also for rent; there's information in the Cabins and Cottages section of this chapter.

✳SYLVAN LAKE LODGE $$$–$$$$
Custer State Park, Custer
(605) 574-2561, (888) 875-0001
www.custerresorts.com

This is a cozy lodge next to picturesque Sylvan Lake, close to the trails to the summit of Harney Peak, and on the way to both Mount Rushmore National Memorial and Crazy Horse Memorial. Enjoy cocktails on the veranda, sit by the pleasant fireplace in the lobby, or have dinner in the dining room. The lodge has 35 rooms that vary in configuration and size and accommodate from one to six people. Read about the cabins on the grounds in the Cabins and Cottages section of this chapter.

VACATION HOMES & CONDOMINIUMS

For longer visits to the Hills, consider renting a vacation home or condominium.

Northern Hills

BAREFOOT RESORT $$$–$$$$
21111 Barefoot Loop, H.C. 37, Lead
(605) 584-1577, (800) 424-0225
www.barefootresort.com
Located on the site of the historic Barefoot mining claim, and (at 6,400 feet) higher than any other lodge east of the Rockies, these 45 condos are across the road from the Terry Peak Ski Lodge and 15 minutes from Deadwood. One- to four-bedroom units are available, and each has a private bath, kitchen, living and dining room, fireplace, and a great view from the balcony. A pool and hot tub are on the premises. Time-share programs are available, as is one four-bed cabin.

MOUNTAIN STREAM ESTATES $$$$
Rochford Rd., Lead
(605) 229-1619, (888) 213-2414
www.mountainstreamestates.com
These two luxurious vacation homes are near Cheyenne Crossing, deep in the Hills

ACCOMMODATIONS

and close to Deadwood, Spearfish, skiing, snowmobile trails, and hiking. A stream runs close by, and there's a trout pond near the houses. Each fully furnished house has five bedrooms, three baths, and kitchen with dishwasher and microwave. Both houses have a jet-spray tub and garage. One house has an outdoor Jacuzzi.

TERRY PEAK CONDOS $$$–$$$$
H.C. 37, Lead
(605) 584-2723, (888) 584-2723
www.terrypeaklodge.com
These 17 condos are attached to the main lodge, which faces the Terry Peak Ski Area. Each has its own private entrance. Seven of the condos have two bedrooms and two baths; the remainder have one bedroom and bath. This is nice but simple lodging for people more interested in being outdoors— the condos have no phones, cable television service, or air-conditioning, but they do have fully equipped kitchens. Guests have access to an indoor pool, hot tub, and game room.

Central Hills

EDELWEISS MOUNTAIN
LODGING $$$$
US 385, Rapid City
(605) 574-2430
www.edelweissmountain.com
A dozen vacation homes are available through Edelweiss Mountain Lodging in the summer, and several of those are available in the winter. The office is off the highway, between Sheridan Lake and Pactola Reservoir; the homes are all in the immediate area. Homes with one to four bedrooms and private baths are available. Some have hot tubs and pool tables, and all but one have fully furnished kitchens. Some of the homes are accessible to the disabled. All have great views of the surrounding pine-covered hills.

WHISPERING PINES CAMPGROUND &
LODGING $$$$
22700 Silver City Rd., Rapid City
(605) 341-3667
www.blackhillswhisperingpines.com
Whispering Pines has one vacation home— a spacious three-bedroom, two-bath, fully-furnished home that will sleep up to nine. Kitchen, toiletries, linens and cooking utensils are provided. Whispering Pines also rents an 8-by-30-foot fully furnished travel trailer, four camping cabins and provides camping via 46 pull-through RV spots with full hook-ups, and up to 40 tent sites. Fire pits and picnic tables are supplied. The property is on the Centennial Trail (see Recreation) and close to Pactola Reservoir and Central Hills attractions.

CAMPGROUNDS

Thousands of people come to the Black Hills each summer to camp among the pines, and both public and private campground operators are happy to oblige them. Whether you want to pack all your amenities on your back and hike to a primitive tent site, settle down with cable TV in your RV, or bring your horse with you, you'll find plenty of choices that meet your needs. We've listed a number of fine places we would recommend to our camping friends, but understand that these entries merely scratch the surface. There's an abundance of well-run camping spots from one end of the Hills to the other.

Many of the campgrounds in this chapter offer a wide range of creature comforts, but you'll find the owners have also done a commendable job of preserving the natural surroundings that beckon people to the Hills in the first place. And even those with the most campsites have a spacious feel—the great outdoors is all around you. Listen closely and you'll probably catch the strains of a coyote serenade at dusk. Of course, you're more apt to see wildlife if you hike deep into the forest, find a flat spot of ground, and pitch your tent. As long as you don't want a campfire and pack all of your supplies in and out, this is a pleasant (and free) option almost anywhere in the Black Hills National Forest.

OVERVIEW

Privately owned campgrounds often have swimming pools and other recreational opportunities on-site, and many are located near major attractions. But if you'd like to go touring and let someone else do the driving, be sure to ask whether any bus tours stop for passengers where you intend to stay. If you're looking for a public campground with fewer amenities, refer to the listings for state and national parks and recreation areas. You'll find 26 public campgrounds operated by the USDA Forest Service (see the Black Hills National Forest heading later in the chapter). Lastly, we have a separate section for horse camps.

For information about camping in or near the Badlands, consult the Badlands chapter. If you're looking for a cabin to rent, the Accommodations chapter is your best source.

Unless we state otherwise, the campgrounds listed here have showers, flush toilets, and RV dump stations. Full RV hookups mean water, sewer, and electricity; partial means electricity and water or electricity only. Each listing includes a breakdown of RV and tent sites to help you gauge which campgrounds suit your camping style. And unless a listing states otherwise, assume your major credit card will be accepted and your pet is welcome on a leash.

You'll notice that many campgrounds give opening and closing dates "depending on the weather." Well, that's just the way we operate here, where winters can be long and blustery—or comparatively brief and mild. Be aware that campgrounds and other accommodations are apt to be packed in early August during the Sturgis Rally & Races (see Annual Events & Festivals). Although it's a good idea to make advance reservations any time you're coming to the Hills, it's especially wise to do so for stays during Rally week.

Whenever you arrive, and wherever you stay, don't be surprised if you find a family reunion or two in progress. Black Hills campgrounds are a popular choice for such activities, and when you think about it, what better way to spend time with those you love?

CAMPGROUNDS

Northern Hills

**BEAR BUTTE STATE PARK
CAMPGROUND**
SR 79, Sturgis
(605) 347-5240
**http://gfp.sd.gov/state-parks/directory/
bear-butte/campsites.aspx**
If beautiful views and peaceful solitude are your top priorities, you'll appreciate the opportunity to stay here. On clear days you can see Bear Butte reflected in Bear Butte Lake, which is just a short walk from the campground. To the south, the Black Hills form an inviting silhouette on the horizon. You'll find 15 campsites for tents and RVs, but amenities are limited to a pit toilet and a hand pump for water; there are no showers, hookups, or dump stations. Also, because trees don't grow well here, shade is scarce.

State Park Camping Reservations

The state reservation center handles summer reservations for campsites, cabins, and picnic shelters in South Dakota state parks and recreation areas from early Jan until early Sept. (To make arrangements for the off-season, fall through mid-May, call the individual parks.) In general, your stay is limited to 14 days, and all fees, including a small processing fee for out-of-state residents, must be paid in advance. Call (800) 710-CAMP, or go to www.campsd.com to make reservations up to 90 days in advance. For general park information, call (605) 773-3391; for information about a particular park, call the park.

But there's a picnic shelter for you to use, and, of course, the lake for you to play in (see the Recreation chapter for boating information). East of the main camping area are four fairly well-shaded tent sites with a vault toilet and no water. Overflow camping is available during the Sturgis Rally & Races.

Since the campground is not heavily used except during the Sturgis Rally in Aug, you should have no trouble finding a site on a first-come, first-served basis. There's a self-registration fee of $10 per camping unit (such as a tent or RV) but no park entrance fee to use the campground. If you drive into the eastern portion of the park to see the visitor center or use the hiking trails, you'll need a park entrance license. If you walk over (a hike in itself), you can get in for free. The campground is open all year, although the water is shut off during the winter. To get there, go 3 miles east of Sturgis on SR 34, turn left onto SR 79, and go about 4 miles. Turn left again onto the dirt road where you see the campground sign and go another mile.

CHRIS' CAMPGROUND
701 Christensen Dr., Spearfish
(605) 642-2239, (800) 350-2239
www.blackhills.com/chriscampground
Two-legged kids will delight in the opportunity to bottle-feed the four-legged variety at the petting farm here. Baby animals such as goats, lambs, and calves from local ranches spend the summer at this shady, grassy campground, which has been owned and operated by the Christensen family for nearly 50 years. Feedings are at 8 a.m. and 5 p.m., and guests are welcome to join in. The rest of the time, a heated pool with slide, rec room, and playground are good places to pass the time, and you'll find free wireless Internet. There are 132 campsites: 45 basic ones for tents or trailers and the rest with full or partial RV hookups. Six camping cabins offer another option for summer nights. Laundry facilities, paved interior roads, a convenience store, cable TV, volleyball, horseshoes, a basketball court, and lovely mountain views all make your stay that much more enjoyable. Weather permitting, you can visit between mid-Apr and mid-Oct. Limited camping is available all winter. Rates for four people range from $19 to $32.

ELKHORN RIDGE RV PARK
20189 US 85, Spearfish
(605) 722-1800, (877) 722-1800
www.elkhornridgervpark.com
One of the classiest RV parks and campgrounds in the Black Hills, this new 75-acre resort also is among its most luxurious. And with a location in the Centennial Valley near I-90 and US 85 between Spearfish and Deadwood, there's no lack of things to do nearby. Nevertheless, the campground developers saw fit to construct a heated outdoor swimming pool, hiking trails, a playground, and courts for horseshoes, basketball, and tennis. There are Internet and satellite television hookups available for RVs, full laundry facilities, a fenced dog park, and a new pavilion and outdoor amphitheater. A new 18-hole golf course has recently opened nearby.

Because the campground is fairly new, there isn't a great deal of greenery. A stand of mature trees sits on the northern edge, and new plants have been included in the landscaping, but it will be several years before this becomes a well-shaded place to pitch a tent or park your rig. In the meantime, large berms (topped by tasteful statues of elk and other wildlife) have been sculpted to separate the campground from the adjoining highways, which ensures relative privacy for the 186 full hookup sites, 20 tent sites, and 36 cabins. RV sites run $48 and tent sites $35 and it is open year round.

The campground is located on the Frawley Ranch property, an estate once owned by a pioneer Deadwood lawyer. Indeed, the entire Centennial Valley was once a major source of food for the once bustling city of Deadwood, which lies only a few miles above in the hills. Many of the original homestead structures have been preserved and make up one of the few National Historic Landmarks inside South Dakota's borders. Although the ranch buildings are normally closed to the public, they are opened on special occasions. If you're interested in a peek at this piece of frontier history, inquire at the front desk about the next time the ranch's unusual stone buildings—including a one-room schoolhouse and a traditional dugout—might be open for public viewing.

GLENCOE CAMPRESORT
20555 Glencoe Dr., Sturgis
(605) 347-4712, (800) 272-4712
www.glencoecamp.com
A magnificent view of Bear Butte greets you as you turn off SR 34 into Glencoe CampResort. Glencoe is open mainly during the annual Sturgis Motorcycle Rally but will accept groups of 200 or more during the rest of the year. The 1,000 RV sites with full hookups are close to the entrance, and then the dirt road winds around to more than 100 cottonwood-shaded, creekside acres for tent camping. Chemical toilets and water faucets are located throughout the grounds. During the Sturgis Rally & Races each Aug, campers can buy meals that are prepared in an enclosed kitchen and served in a covered eating area with seating for 320. Campers are required to purchase a $200 wristband during Rally week, as the owners bring in top name entertainment nightly, and campsites are extra. The campground is 3 miles east of town.

MOUNTAIN VIEW CAMPGROUND
625 Christensen Dr., Spearfish
(605) 642-2170, (800) 365-2170
www.mountainview-campground.com
Trees and grassy areas make this a homey little place to stay in your tent or RV, and the heated pool, game room, free Wi-Fi, and small playground provide good family recreation. There are 80 sites altogether, most with partial or full hookups. Laundry facilities and a convenience store provide more comforts. Some of the picnic tables have shelters to keep you out of the rain. The

campground is open from early May until mid-Oct, weather permitting. Rates for up to four people range from $17 to $30.

SPEARFISH CITY CAMPGROUND
404 South Canyon St., Spearfish
(605) 642-1340
www.spearfishparksandrec.com/
campground
Don't be fooled by the name; this quiet, shady campground is on the outskirts of town, alongside Spearfish Creek and D.C. Booth Historic Fish Hatchery and little more than a stone's throw from the mouth of incomparable Spearfish Canyon. Thousands of people descended on the campground in 1989, when the National Horseshoe Pitchers Association held its annual tournament here, but the dust has long since settled. The campground offers 150+ non-hookup sites; 57 full-hookup sites with electricity, water, sewer and cable TV, Wi-Fi; and 5 premium sites. There are about 60 sites that may be reserved. Depending on the weather, you can camp here from early May through Sept. Prices start at $18 for one person at a basic site and $30 for up to four people using full hookups. Children ages 5 and younger stay for free.

WHISTLER'S GULCH RV PARK & CAMPGROUND
235 Cliff St., Deadwood
(605) 578-2092, (800) 704-7139
www.whistlergulch.com
Like just about everything in Deadwood, this campground a mile south of historic Main Street is situated on a hill. But the brief climb brings you to 126 immaculately groomed, level campsites, camping cabins, and a fabulous view across the gulch. Twenty-six of the sites are reserved for tents, and the rest have

full hookups for RVs. You won't find a dump station, but other comforts include a sports court, a heated outdoor pool, arcade games, laundry, and a small store. The Deadwood Trolley stops here and for a buck takes you downtown to casinos and restaurants. The campground operates May 1 to Oct 1, weather permitting. Rates for two adults start at $26.50 for a tent site, $41 for an RV site with full hookups, and $58 for a camping cabin, although special event pricing does apply, so call for exact rates. Stay six nights and get the seventh free except during special events.

Central Hills

*MOUNT RUSHMORE KOA AT PALMER GULCH RESORT
SR 244, Hill City
(605) 574-2525, (800) 562-8503
www.palmergulch.com
If you're looking for a home away from home, this is it. Just about everything your family needs or wants is here, from recreational opportunities to nondenominational Sunday-morning worship services. That's because the resort, which started as a guest ranch in the mid-1930s, pays close attention to customer surveys. The state tourism department recognized its efforts with the George S. Mickelson Hospitality Award.

The list of services is impressive. Besides a grocery store, Palmer Gulch Grapes and Grinds offers specialty coffees and South Dakota wines. Palmer Creek Outfitters offers active outdoor adventure gear, camping supplies, and squares cut from huge slabs of fudge. A resort fee covers an 18-hole minigolf course, the waterslide, splash park, jumping pillow, trail rides, Wi-Fi, and cable TV; or you can watch a free movie every evening. Two outdoor pools, two hot tubs, two

wading pools, two playgrounds, bicycle and paddleboat rentals, and a free trout pond (you do need a fishing license) will probably occupy a good deal of your time. At night, free family activities are on tap, including hayrides and Native American dancing, and there's free transportation to evening lighting programs at nearby Mount Rushmore and Crazy Horse memorials. Other popular activities are the horse-drawn hayride to a chuck wagon cookout in the pines and the customizable trail rides to the top of Haney Peak.

If all the activity leaves you with hunger pangs, a restaurant serving three meals a day, a lounge with a full bar, an ice-cream parlor, and a sandwich shop come to the rescue. You can even rent a car and fill the gas tank here! And—need we say so?—there are laundry facilities and cable TV. All this is set against the Black Hills National Forest.

In case you find time to sleep, there are 150 tent sites, 185 partial hookups and 130 full hookups for RVs, 35 full deluxe sites, a group camping area, and 55 camping cabins. There's also an attractive new lodge and a number of furnished cabins (see the Accommodations chapter). The resort, 5 miles west of Mount Rushmore, is open from May 1 until Oct 1. Prices for campers range from $26 to $72 a night. Camping cabins start at $52. Tent spaces are $26.

RAFTER J BAR RANCH CAMPGROUND
US 16/385, Hill City
(605) 574-2527, (888) RAFTERJ
www.rafterj.com
Meadows, mountain views, and spacious campsites are among the first features you notice at this pristine campground. If you like outdoor recreation, you could spend your whole vacation right here, riding horseback,

bicycling, and hiking, because the George S. Mickelson Trail borders the property. The Rafter J offers a new wagon ride and chuck wagon dinner, as well as an impressive new playground. A swimming pool, rec room, and hot tub are good places to spend the day, too. In the evening you can watch cable TV in your RV or join fellow campers for a free movie or other family entertainment. The Ranch Store sells supplies, groceries, and gas for your car (your own or one you've rented at the campground), and there's a laundry for your convenience. There are some 220 campsites, more than half of which have full or partial RV hookups. Some of the tent sites have electricity, too. There are 23 heated camping cabins, 12 with kitchens and bath; the other 11 are sleeping cabins. The campground, 3 miles south of Hill City, is open from May 1 to Oct 1. Nightly rates in-season for two people range from $31 to $48 for a campsite. Cabins are $55 to $159 a night for two. There's no charge for children seven and younger, but horse and bicycle rentals cost extra.

i **Two wheelchair-accessible campsites** are located at Pactola Lake and one at Sheridan Lake. The sites have raised tent pads and other features that make them user-friendly. See the Black Hills National Forest listing for reservation information.

SPOKANE CREEK RESORT
24631 Iron Mountain Rd., Keystone
(605) 666-4609, (800) 261-9331
www.spokanecreekresort.com
You're just a mile north of Custer State Park and a short drive south of Mount Rushmore when you camp here. Plus, this campground in the Norbeck Wildlife Preserve is along

what many consider to be the most interesting road in the Black Hills—also known as Iron Mountain Road—with rock tunnels and curly "pigtail" bridges. If that doesn't entice you, perhaps the thought of waking up to the scent of freshly baked cinnamon rolls will. You can buy them, along with breakfast sandwiches and coffee, in the general store each morning; later in the day you can munch on pizza made to order and sub sandwiches prepared on fresh bread. When not eating or exploring, you can swim in the outdoor heated pool or play a variety of sports, including nine-hole minigolf.

The campground has 31 sites for tents and 30 RV sites with full or partial hookups. Three of 18 cabins are for roughing it without plumbing, and the rest have bathrooms and kitchen facilities. (See the Accommodations chapter for more about the cabins.) A picnic pavilion with electricity and room for 100 can be reserved for family reunions and other events. The cost for two people in a tent starts at $22.50, and cabins start at $45. The campground is open from mid-May through Sept.

Southern Hills

AMERICAN PRESIDENTS CABINS & CAMP
US 16A, Custer
(605) 673-3373
www.presidentsresort.com
Its location a mile east of Custer places this campground within minutes of many of the Black Hills' biggest attractions, including Custer State Park, Crazy Horse Memorial, Jewel Cave, and Mount Rushmore. The place has bragging rights to a heated shower house, a spa, and a heated outdoor pool advertised as the Hills' largest. There's also space for basketball, volleyball, horseshoes,

minigolf, a playground, and an arcade. A convenience store and laundry simplify life on the road. You'll find 36 sites with full or partial hookups and 30-plus shaded tent sites. There is no dump station, but the management will let you empty your RV holding tank at a vacant full-hookup site if you need to. Water spigots are plentiful, and picnic shelters are available for family reunions or other gatherings. See the Accommodations chapter for information about the 45 cabins and 15 motel units here. The campground opens around mid-Mar if the weather permits, but water might not be available until Apr 1. The place shuts down around mid-Nov, but you probably won't get a shower here after Oct. Prices for two people range from $36 to $49. Inquire about off-season rates.

ANGOSTURA STATE RECREATION AREA
Off US 385, Hot Springs
(605) 745-6996, (800) 710-CAMP
http://gfp.sd.gov/state-parks/directory/angostura

Angostura Reservoir is the star attraction in this 1,125-acre park, and if you can't bear to leave after a day of water sports, you might as well plan to stay at one of 167 campsites spread among four campgrounds. Three of them—Cascade, Hat Creek, and Horsehead—are along the shore; the fourth, Cheyenne, is 150 yards distant. Cascade, close by the marina and with two camping cabins is the shadiest and most popular. The Breakers Beach Club serves a beachside burgers-and-beer menu during the summer, and there's a convenience store with camping and boating supplies. The concessionaire also has six fully furnished, two-bedroom cabins for rent; call (605) 745-6665 for more information.

The campgrounds 10 miles southeast of Hot Springs are open all year, but the comfort stations close when it gets cold in Oct. You'll have to settle for vault toilets from then until spring, but you can still have electricity for a small fee. Peak-season rates, from mid-May through Labor Day, range from $12 to $16; camping cabins with heat and air-conditioning rent for $35 a night. When you make your reservation, be sure to ask whether to reach your campground by the north or south entrance.

BEAVER LAKE CAMPGROUND
US 16, Custer
(605) 673-2464, (800) 346-4383
www.beaverlakecampground.net

Once the kids find out about the 360-foot waterslide at this campground, you might have no other choice than to stay here. But think of the benefits to yourself, too. While the youngsters are happily sliding (and burning off a great deal of energy), you're taking your leisure under a pine tree or beside the heated pool. And the owners make the following promise: If their restrooms aren't the cleanest you've ever found, your stay is free. There are approximately 99 campsites here, about 37 of which have full or partial hookups for RVs. A year-round full-service cabin is available also. Your family will have the use of a laundry, small convenience store, arcade, and playground. They also offer a range of cabins from which to choose or rent the Native tipi. The campground, 3.5 miles west of Custer, is open from May to Oct. Peak season (early June to late Aug) rates start at $23 for four people, with an additional charge for hookups and use of the waterslide. Inquire about off-season, monthly, and group rates. Children ages 5 and younger stay for free. Pets are welcome.

ℹ️ If road grime has you ready to trade your firstborn child for a shower, Beaver Lake Campground west of Custer has a far less drastic solution for you. For a small fee ($4.50), you can use the showers there and be on your way, your family still intact.

COLD BROOK AND COTTONWOOD SPRINGS RECREATION AREAS
Hot Springs
(605) 745-5476
http://corpslakes.usace.army.mil/visitors
If you're looking for solitude and outdoor activities rather than modern amenities, these small recreation areas run by the US Army Corps of Engineers are excellent choices. Somewhat remote, both are situated at reservoirs that are off-limits to noisy, high-speed watercraft. Cold Brook, reputed to have the clearest, warmest water in the Black Hills, has a small beach for swimming; Cottonwood doesn't have a beach but offers fine fishing. Both have hiking opportunities, a wildlife area, and playgrounds. Neither campground has hookups or showers, but Cottonwood Springs has flush toilets and running water. Reservations are not accepted: It's first-come, first-served only. Cold Brook has 13 campsites and is open year-round; Cottonwood Springs has 18 sites that are open from mid-May to mid-Sept or longer if the weather permits. Both cost $5 a night, payable through self-registration. Cold Brook is less than a mile northwest of Hot Springs; follow Evans Street and take the hard left that leads to the project. Cottonwood Springs is west of town off US 18; follow the signs from either direction, then go 2 miles on gravel roads. Credit cards are not accepted.

CUSTER MOUNTAIN CABINS & CAMPGROUND
US 16A, Custer
(605) 673-5440, (800) 239-5505
www.custermountain.com
If quiet, spacious, shady, and close to wildlife are the words you'd use to describe your ideal campsite, you'd do well to check out this place. You'll be nearly surrounded by USDA Forest Service land that invites you to follow wildlife trails on a hike. (There are no marked trails.) Smack-dab between the city of Custer to the west and Custer State Park to the east—either one is just 1.5 miles away—the campground can accommodate more than 30 tents in a grassy meadow. For RVs there are 21 full-hookup sites plus several more with electricity only and cable TV. Two camping cabins are also available. See the Accommodations chapter to find out about the modern, year-round log cabins. Tents and RVs are welcome between mid-Apr and late Oct. Prices are $24 for a tent site and $29 to $33 to park your RV. Camping cabins are $57 a night.

*CUSTER STATE PARK
Custer
(605) 255-4515, (800) 710-CAMP (2667)
www.campsd.com (reservations)
www.custerstatepark.info (information)
Campsites in Custer State Park are in great demand among out-of-staters, and, in fact, the state reservation center starts handling requests (Jan 2) for Custer several weeks ahead of those for other parks. You'll find a variety of camping opportunities in the park, all with showers and some with electrical hookups. Yet each of these campgrounds has its own personality.

Center Lake Campground (no flush toilets) is, naturally, near Center Lake and adjacent to the Black Hills Playhouse. Set amid dramatic granite outcroppings, Sylvan Lake's popular namesake campground has a higher elevation that ensures cooler summer temperatures. Blue Bell, the southernmost site, is handy to a stable offering trail rides and is a good place to watch for wildlife. All three of these campgrounds offer total shade.

Stockade Lake Campground is shaded on the west side and offers good access to Mount Rushmore and Crazy Horse Memorials. Centrally located Game Lodge Campground (the only one with a dump station) is ideal for large motor homes but also has well-shaded sites along Grace Coolidge Creek. Grace Coolidge Campground, also centrally located, is mostly shaded and close to the park's walk-in fishing area.

Legion Lake Campground is in a valley setting across the road from a playground and a lake and lodge of the same name. It's also close to the Badger Hole (see the Parks & Mountains chapter for a Close-up on South Dakota poet laureate Badger Clark) and the Centennial Trail.

Sites at Center Lake are first-come, first-served; Blue Bell, Game Lodge, Legion Lake, Stockade Lake North and South, Grace Coolidge, and Sylvan Lake campgrounds are reservation only—but if you show up before noon, you might be able to reserve an unclaimed site on the spot. Game Lodge is open all year with limited facilities and reduced rates during the winter; the others are open from early May until late Sept, with variations due to weather and maintenance schedules. Except at Center Lake, where the fee is $16, nightly rates are $18 per camping unit (such as a tent or camping trailer) per site; $22 with hookup. French Creek Horse Camp is $25 with hookup and one corral.

Group camping is available near two of the developed campgrounds as well. Game

Lodge group area has showers and flush toilets; Stockade Lake doesn't, but they're within walking distance. The rate is $4 per person per night, with a $80 per night minimum. Reservations are required.

Hikers might prefer picking their own primitive campsite anywhere within the French Creek Natural Area in the approximate center of the park. Hike in a mile from French Creek Horse Camp on the west end or 2 miles from the Wildlife Loop on the east end. The fee is $4 per person per night. Open fires are prohibited in this area. For more information call (605) 255-4464 or stop at the Peter Norbeck Visitor Center from May to Oct.

For information about French Creek Horse Camp, see the Horse Camps section of this chapter. Information on Custer State Park's cabins and lodges is in the Accommodations chapter. To find out what makes this park such a popular place, read the Parks & Mountains chapter.

ELK MOUNTAIN CAMPGROUND
Wind Cave National Park
US 385, Hot Springs
(605) 745-4600
www.nps.gov/wica

Like the rest of the park, this serene campground is unspoiled and beautiful, with rolling, grassy hills and a wide prairie sky. A self-guided nature trail loops around the campground for about a mile. On summer nights, free ranger-led programs start around sundown in the outdoor amphitheater that has bench seating and a projection booth for slide shows. Check the park's visitor center for the program schedule, because it varies as the days get shorter. The 75 campsites have no hookups, and there's no dump station or showers. The sole modern comforts—flush toilets and running water—are

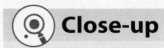

Close-up

Custer Campsites

By the time Lt. Col. George Armstrong Custer and his Seventh Cavalry arrived in the Black Hills in 1874, rumors of gold had been trickling out of the area for years. Up to that point the US government, determined to honor the Fort Laramie Treaty of 1868 (which ceded the Hills to the Sioux), had refused to provide military escorts for prospectors eager to invade the forbidden territory in search of riches. Inevitably, however, the war department at last authorized a Seventh Cavalry expedition to explore the Black Hills. It was to be a reconnaissance mission only, but Custer took miners along to look for gold. (At 23, the vain and daring Custer, who graduated last in his class at West Point, had become the Civil War's youngest general. But the "boy general" was dropped to captain after the war and later made a lieutenant colonel in the Seventh Cavalry, the rank he held on this mission. Nevertheless, you'll often see references to "General Custer" in the Hills.)

One of Custer's party, Horatio Ross, did indeed find specks of gold in French Creek on August 2, and by the end of the year a band of adventurers led by John Gordon had snuck in, intending to stay. Little more than a year later, the Black Hills gold rush of 1876 was in full swing. Today you can pull off the highway at Wheels West Campground, 3 miles east of Custer on US 16A, and read a historical marker at the site of Custer's base camp. The expedition stayed here for five days, and its leader named the area Golden Valley. A half mile farther east, the Gordon Stockade has been re-created.

Another more obscure Custer campsite is 5 miles south of Bear Butte in Meade County. At the intersection of SR 34 and County Road 12C, County Road 6L heads south. As it narrows you'll find a flagpole and a stone monument with a hand-lettered sign that reads: CAMPSITE, GENERAL CUSTER EXPEDITION, AUGUST 14–15, 1874. ENTIRE COMMAND OF SEVENTH US CAVALRY CONSISTING OF 1,200 MEN AND HORSES, 110 WAGONS AND EQUIPMENT. Custer, on the return trip and two weeks' ride from home, wrote a note to his wife, Elizabeth ("Libbie"), here, saying, "I have the proud satisfaction of knowing that our explorations have exceeded the most sanguine expectations."

operational from mid-May until mid-Sept. The campground in the west central part of the park is open year-round. The rate is $12 per night during peak season, half that when the plumbing is shut off. Reservations are not accepted, and payment is by self-registration, but there's always a volunteer host on hand to welcome you and answer questions. During extremely dry conditions, a campfire prohibition will be posted. Credit cards are not accepted.

i Volunteers contribute more than $150,000 worth of labor each year to help maintain the Black Hills National Forest.

FLINTSTONES BEDROCK CITY CAMPGROUND
US 16 West, Custer
(605) 673-4079, (605) 673-4664
www.flintstonesbedrockcity.com

You'll especially want to consider staying here if you have little ones who will appreciate the adjacent Flintstones amusement park (see the Kidstuff chapter for more about that). For one thing, your stay allows you unlimited entries to the park once you've paid admission. In addition to 127 tent and RV sites—52 with full hookups—the 30-acre campground on the edge of town has laundry facilities, a game room, outdoor heated pool, nine holes of miniature golf, plus volleyball, basketball, and horseshoe courts. The campground is open mid-May to Labor Day. Prices range from $20.50 to $27 for two people. Six cabins are also available at $43 for two people.

BLACK HILLS NATIONAL FOREST

NATIONAL FOREST SUPERVISOR
R.R. 2, Box 200, Custer
(877) 444-6777 (reservations only)
www.fs.usda.gov/blackhills
The South Dakota portion of the Black Hills National Forest has 30 designated campgrounds, from lakeside to rugged. None of these campgrounds have utilities, but that's probably one reason you wanted to camp in the forest. In most cases, though, you do get the luxury of drinking water. Most have spacious RV sites with lots of trees and bushes for privacy. More than half of the campgrounds are open or partially open all year, but what services do exist are shut down during the winter, and you have to carry out your trash yourself. Be aware that snow can close the roads, blocking your way in or out.

About half operate on a first-come, first-served basis, but others have reservable sites. Your stay is limited to 14 days. In general, fees are charged between Memorial Day and Labor Day weekends only. Rates range from $8 to $17 a night, except at four remote campgrounds that are maintained with the help of donations, and at the Bear Gulch and Sheridan Lake group areas, where fees start at $40. Inquire about specifics. If your horse will be traveling with you, see the Horse Camps listings below. Also see the Hiking & Backpacking section of the Recreation chapter to learn about backcountry camping in the forest.

i You can pitch your tent just about anywhere in the Black Hills National Forest (except at highly developed areas such as lakes), but state law and federal regulation allow open fires only in the fire grates in designated campgrounds and picnic areas. Build a fire anywhere else and you could be fined $1,000, jailed for a year, and ordered to pay civil damages.

HORSE CAMPS

Horse camps cater to visitors who wish to explore the Black Hills with their equine friends.

Northern Hills

NEMO GUEST RANCH
Main Street, Nemo
(605) 578-2708
www.nemoguestranch.com
The atmosphere at this well-kept ranch in Paradise Valley is nothing short of charming, with its western-style buildings and hitching-post trim. There are plenty of comforts, too, from the Ponderosa Bar and Brandin' Iron Cafe to the turn-of-the-20th-century Nemo Mercantile general store, which also houses a laundry. You can even gas up your truck right here. Take your pick of 14 modern cabins and houses with one to five

bedrooms, which rent from $75 to $350 a night; a nearby motel (see the Accommodations chapter for complete information about those units); and 25 RV sites with full hookups or unlimited tent sites—but leave your horse in one of the corrals. The ranch is open year-round. Nightly rates range from $20 to $30 for a campsite. Horses stay for $10 per night. The ranch is 21 miles from the junction of US 385 and Nemo Road, southeast of Deadwood, or 16 miles northwest of Rapid City from the other end of Nemo Road, also called CR 234.

Central Hills

DEERFIELD LAKE RESORT
11321 Gillette Prairie Rd., Hill City
(605) 574-2636
www.deerfieldlakeresort.com
This year-round facility actually caters to many types of sporting, so depending on the season, you can bring your horse, fishing pole, hunting rifle, or even your snowmobile. Snowmobile and ATV rentals are available for use at the resort, too, and a maintenance shop is right there. You'll find more than 66 miles of marked and mapped horse trails as well as more than 340 miles of groomed national forest snowmobile trails that depart from the resort. Deerfield Lake gleams quietly across the dirt road, offering top-notch trout fishing and no-wake boating for a small fee, payable at the lake. For lights-out you can either reserve one of four two-bed, heated housekeeping cabins (see the Accommodations chapter) or, mid-May through Sept, pick a spot for your tent or RV—all 25 sites have electricity, and six have full hookups. There's no dump station, but there is a gas pump as well as a convenience store where you can purchase hunting and fishing licenses, five-day snowmobile

permits, groceries, fishing tackle, and worms. From mid-Oct to Mar, a small cafe on the premises serves meals. Camping fees are $17 to $30 per night; cabins start at $75, double occupancy. Horses board for $12.50 a day in corrals, and a barn is available. You must be 18 or older to rent a snowmobile or a fourwheeler. Call for rates and reservations.

i All hay and other feed brought into Custer State Park and Black Hills National Forest campgrounds must be certified weed free.

Southern Hills

BLACK HILLS NATIONAL FOREST
(877) 444-6777
www.recreation.gov
The national forest has two public horse camps with sheltered hitching areas, Willow Creek and Iron Creek. Of the two, Willow Creek is the more deluxe: It has drinking water. Neither has showers or utility hookups. Reservations are recommended at both during the summer. Iron Creek, east of Custer, has nine campsites but cannot accommodate rigs over 50' in length; Willow Creek, on SR 244 between Hill City and Mount Rushmore, has eight group sites. Rates are $22 per night at Iron Creek; at Willow Creek, group rates apply.

FRENCH CREEK HORSE CAMP
CSP No. 4, Custer State Park
(605) 255-4515, (800) 710-2267
www.campsd.com
No more driving 3 miles to Blue Bell Campground to take a shower when you stay here. A new era began in 1998 with the opening of a comfort station housing showers, flush toilets, and sinks with hot and cold running water from a newly drilled well. The familiar

vault toilets were left in place, though, to save you a potentially lengthy hike in the middle of the night. There are no hookups or dump station at this horse camp on North Lame Johnny Road. The campground has three camper cabins and 22 reservable sites with electricity and two that are available on a first-come, first-served basis. As popular as this place is, it's a good idea to reserve a site well in advance, especially for the summer months. You can begin booking sites on Jan. 2 of each year. The campground, 3 miles east of Blue Bell Lodge, is open all year with limited facilities from Nov until May. With reservation, each site gets a corral. The fee is $25 per night per camping unit, and $45 for a cabin. Once here you can ride just about anywhere in Custer State Park except the Sylvan Lake watershed area and the walk-in fishing area that links Grace Coolidge and Center Lake Campgrounds. Both areas are posted. Four trails depart from the campground; see the Recreation chapter for more information.

RESTAURANTS

After hiking and biking the boundless backcountry of the Black Hills or working the backwaters into a froth while fly fishing, most outdoor adventurers head home with a healthy appetite. But even here in the middle of cattle country, hidden culinary treasures and outstanding wine cellars await the discerning diner. Frankly, you can eat anywhere, and even in the Black Hills, buffets are as ubiquitous as strip malls. But, if you're looking for a calming atmosphere coupled with the best refreshments and entrees to please your palate, you do have a handful of exceptional choices in western South Dakota.

Prime rib reigns supreme here, and you'll find any number of steak houses, restaurants, and cafes that cater to those who relish a hearty slab of beef. Indeed, some of the best steak and prime rib in the world is served right here. And while you won't find the diverse array of exotic cooking you might see in a more metropolitan area, the Black Hills has begun to branch out from the traditional steak house. New ethnic eateries are popping up all the time, and some restaurants now serve dishes for vegetarians (still a dirty word in some small ranching towns).

OVERVIEW

We've arranged the restaurants in this chapter by cuisine type with geographic subheadings under each. Some restaurants serve breakfast, lunch, and dinner, and some serve only one or two meals a day; the individual listings will tell you. The write-ups under Sweet Treats direct you to places you'll want to go for snacks and desserts. Most eateries are open seven days a week year-round, and we've noted those that aren't as well as those that extend their hours during the summer—that is, between Memorial Day weekend and Labor Day. If you plan to dine out on a holiday, it's a good idea to call ahead, because some restaurants close to give their owners and employees those special days off.

We've provided general price information with each listing, and unless you see the notation "no credit cards," assume you can pay for your meal with a major card. South Dakota prohibits smoking in any public building unless it possesses a liquor license. Most of the restaurant listings here include information on smoking policies, but if in doubt, follow this rule of thumb: If you can order a beer, you can smoke. Otherwise, you'll have to take it outside. If you don't see any mention of alcohol in a write-up, none is served in that particular establishment. We've noted which places provide parking; at others you'll need to park curbside or in a public parking lot.

If you didn't believe that the Black Hills were in the West, here's your proof: There isn't a single restaurant here that requires a tie. Even at Jake's, a Kevin Costner–owned establishment on Deadwood's Main Street and arguably the classiest restaurant in the state, blue jeans and a cowboy hat are the standard. Of course, you may feel more comfortable at places like this in a sport coat or dress, but you'll be just as welcome in less-formal attire.

The listings below, while comprehensive, are not exhaustive. Your wanderings will take you near many fine eateries, including

well-known chains not listed here because we assume you know them by reputation.

Price Code

Prices are the average cost of dinner (or lunch, for coffee and sandwich shops) for two adults. Drinks, appetizers, dessert, and tip are not included.

$................. Less than $12
$$ .... $12 to $25
$$$ .... $25 to $40
$$$$ .... More than $40

Rushmore Supper Club & Lounge, Keystone, Eclectic, $$–$$$, 102

Sage Creek Grille, Custer, Eclectic, $$–$$$, 103

Saigon Restaurant, Rapid City, Asian, $$, 99

Sanford's Grub & Pub, Spearfish, American, $$, 90

Seven Grill, Spearfish, Eclectic, $$$, 101

Shooters Restaurant & Sports Bar, Rapid City, American, $$, 95

The Stadium Sports Grill, Belle Fourche, American, $$, 91

Stampmill Restaurant & Saloon, Lead, American, $$–$$$, 92

State Game Lodge Dining Room, Custer, American, $$$, 96

Sylvan Lake Lodge Dining Room, Custer, Eclectic, $$$–$$$$, 103

Tiffany Grille, Rapid City, Eclectic, $$$, 102

The Windmill Restaurant, Rapid City, American, $$, 95

AMERICAN

Listed here you'll find restaurants and cafes that specialize in familiar foods such as steak, hamburgers, chicken, fish, and seafood. Some of these places are plain, some are fancy, but each has a definitive place in its community.

Northern Hills

BUFFALO STEAKHOUSE   **$$**
658 Main St., Deadwood
(605) 578-1300
www.buffalo-bodega.com

This buckaroo-theme restaurant practically shouts "beef" and moos. The eating establishment at the back of the gaming hall serves prime rib as its special daily from 3 to 11 p.m. It's open summers from 8 a.m. to 2 a.m. How 'bout the steak, steak tips, burgers, ribs, or chicken for lunch? Lunch begins at 11 a.m. And you want a beer or a glass of wine to go with that? Sure thing, partner. Live entertainment daily Memorial Day to Labor Day

DEADWOOD GRILLE   **$$–$$$**
The Lodge at Deadwood
100 Pine Crest, Deadwood
(605) 584-4800, (866) 290-2403
www.deadwoodlodge.com

As the newest restaurant in the Northern Black Hills when it opened in late 2009, the Deadwood Grille had a lot to do to earn the respect of locals. But, they did it in short order. The beautiful restaurant and adjoining sports bar quickly became a favored hangout and the Grille has set a new benchmark for eating establishments in the region. Surrounded by Mission-style woodwork, native stone, oak floors and friendly waitstaff, it's hard not to be impressed. Then the food arrives. Opening with a baked brie en croute, diners might select from any number of exceptional entrees ranging from a coffee-rubbed filet mignon and premium ribeyes to a potato-crusted salmon or a fresh-water trout. And, the desserts are to die for. Diners can extend the night by stepping into the adjacent casinos or Oggie's Sports Bar & Emporium.

✳**DEADWOOD SOCIAL CLUB**   **$$–$$$**
657 Main St., Deadwood
(605) 578-1533
www.saloon10.com

Downstairs you'll find the infamous Saloon No. 10, the establishment listed on the National Register of Historic Places as the world's only museum with a bar. But, one of the best-kept secrets in Black Hills dining is found upstairs. The Deadwood Social Club opened its doors in 1994 with a welcome variety of Northern Italian cuisine, coupled with outrageous steaks, a seemingly bottomless wine cellar, and an ambiance replete with historical photographs and wood booths that beckon the Wild West. Guests discover a collection of Deadwood history, and the walls have been painted to make these photos stand out. It is warm, inviting and comfortable with a trace of the old wood accents of yesteryear combined with faux painting resembling marble and, in other cases, dramatic Victorian draperies.

The Social Club's menu, devised by manager Louie Lalonde and executive chef Doug Hanson, includes steaks, pasta dishes, a wide array of seafood, house-made breads, soups and dressings, and irresistible. If you love your grapes, the Social Club features 182 wines in its collection ranging from $16 to $300, including representatives of Northern California, Italy, France, Australia, Chile, and Argentina. The restaurant has 160 seats, and features wine flights, an outdoor fire pit, rooftop dining, and a wine and martini bar. Hours: 11 a.m. to 10 p.m. daily. When dinner is done, head downstairs and enjoy your favorite cocktail at the newest addition to the Saloon No. 10. Brought back from the edge of the Custer Battlefield, the 30-foot, historic Brunswick back bar complements the vintage western feel for which the No. 10 is famous. Bring the kids for a sarsaparilla— they're welcome until 8:30 p.m.

LATCHSTRING INN RESTAURANT AT SPEARFISH CANYON RESORT $$$
US 14A, Spearfish Canyon
(605) 584-3333
www.spfcanyon.com

Pan-fried trout is the signature menu item at this beautiful log restaurant overlooking Spearfish Creek, and the management was generous enough to share the recipe with us. You'll find it, along with some fascinating background about this historic eatery, in the Close-up in this chapter. We make it a point to stop at the Latchstring for a cold drink on the deck after summer bike rides through Spearfish Canyon, but you don't have to work that hard to enjoy a pleasant, leisurely meal in the restaurant's fabulous surroundings. Here it's equally lovely indoors and out because the dining room is decorated with antiques from the original Latchstring Inn (see the Close-up). Look around and you'll see a Stalwart bobsled, a shaggy buffalo hide, Calamity Jane's gun, and much more. Plaques that accompany many of the displays provide a mini-tour through local history. In the evening, the electric lights are dimmed to enhance the romantic glow of candles. Every window offers a dazzling view of the canyon, and a bird book will help you identify the little creatures that frequent the feeder out back.

For breakfast you can order trout, deep fried or pan fried (and with the head removed if you so request), along with eggs and hash browns or eggs and pancakes. Omelets and other items also are available. For lunch, burgers, sandwiches, buffalo stew, and salads provide a hearty midday energy boost. Trout makes an encore appearance on the dinner menu, prepared amandine. Walleye, rib eye, beef steaks, and chicken prepared in a variety of ways are other choices. Beer and wine can accompany your meal, which you'll want to polish off properly with crème brûlée, bread pudding, or Chocolate Decadence. Don't worry about the calories, because after you eat you can hike

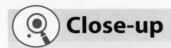

Close-up

Black Hills Trout at the Latchstring Inn

Imagine a weary 1876 prospector laying down his tools at the end of another fruitless day, eyeing the sparkling stream that refused to make him wealthy, and reckoning that if he couldn't have a gold pan full of riches he'd just as soon have a frying pan full of fat, fresh trout. Unlike today's vacationer though, that unhappy fortune seeker would have considered himself doubly unfortunate, because as recently as the Black Hills gold rush (see the History chapter), there were no trout in Black Hills streams. It wasn't until the 1880s that enterprising pioneers brought sloshing wagonloads of trout to this area, and, luckily for anglers ever since, the slippery swimmers took to the habitat like . . . well, like fish to water.

Anglers have come to the Black Hills in search of rainbows, browns, and brookies for more than a century now, and one of their favorite fishing spots has always been Spearfish Canyon. From the late 1800s until the 1930s, when a flood washed out the tracks, they would ride the Chicago, Burlington & Quincy Railroad to the canyon, fish all day, and take the train back to wherever they were staying. Or they might stay several days at Savoy, a bend in the canyon road between Spearfish and Cheyenne Crossing, where an inn has operated since the early 20th century. At first it was called Glendoris Lodge, but in 1919 it became the Latchstring Inn, a cluster of rustic cabins and a restaurant that started as a lumber company office in 1892 and was added onto. For decades, cooks at the inn happily fried up trout caught in nearby streams by proud, hungry anglers.

But by 1989 the beloved Latchstring had aged beyond repair, and the owner, Judy Woodworth, sold it to Homestake Mining Company. Homestake razed the old buildings and put up a beautiful log structure that houses the new Latchstring Inn Restaurant at Spearfish Canyon Resort. In the restaurant are many antiques from the old Latchstring

to Spearfish Falls or Roughlock Falls. Both are nearby, so ask for directions. Reservations are recommended for dinner at the Latchstring all year. Parking is provided.

SANFORD'S GRUB & PUB　　$$
545 West Jackson Blvd., Spearfish
(605) 642-3204, (800) 504-6840
www.thegrubandpub.com

You don't need to be a car buff to appreciate the automotive-repair-shop humor that went into naming the dishes served here. For instance, the Bent-Bumper sports a chicken breast, mozzarella, bacon and barbecue sauce, while the Crash Test Dummy features a half-pound burger with fried egg, cheese, and bacon. Then there's the Dip Stick, a sliced roast beef sandwich au jus on a sourdough roll. The number of choices on the menu is mind-boggling! In addition to burgers and sandwiches, you'll find appetizers (Tune Ups), Cajun food, pasta dishes, salads, steaks, shrimp, chicken, fajitas, meatless items, and rich desserts. And that's just the food—Sanford's has one of the largest selections of draft beers in the state. You can also top off your tank with wine, alcohol, and ice-cream drinks (they have a full bar). Sanford's is non-smoking. Getting to the Spearfish location is a little confusing, though—turn where you see the Sanford's sign on Jackson Boulevard and look for the corrugated metal

Inn, but another precious relic has been preserved as well: a simple recipe for pan-fried trout that dates back so far that no one, not even Woodworth, knows when it was first used in the Latchstring kitchen. Pan-fried trout is reported to be the most popular item on the menu even today, and the management graciously shared the recipe with us. The measurements are imprecise, but that only adds to its charm.

Latchstring Inn Pan-Fried Trout
Bread crumbs
Italian seasoning to taste
A dash of paprika
A pinch each of parsley and rosemary
A touch of thyme
A sprinkle of sage
Seasoning salt and black pepper to taste
Flour
Egg
Vegetable oil
Combine bread crumbs and seasonings. Filet the trout open. Dip in flour, then in beaten egg, then in seasoned crumbs. Pan fry in vegetable oil until the eyes turn white and pop out of the sockets. Serve at once and enjoy—but watch for bones!

(In case you're wondering whether the Latchstring Inn Restaurant serves trout caught from Spearfish Creek, which runs behind the restaurant, the answer is no. The entree on your plate came from a nearby trout farm.)

building tucked away in the alley. You'll pass it on your left on your way to the parking lot, which is clearly marked. Rapid City's location at 306 7th St. (605-721-1463) is easy to find—just look for the big warehouse and sign on Omaha Street. Sanford's is open from 11 a.m. to 10 p.m. May through Sept, and 11 a.m. to 9 p.m. during the off-season. See the Nightlife chapter for more.

THE STADIUM SPORTS GRILL $$
818 5th Ave., Belle Fourche
(605) 723-9521
www.stadiumsportsgrill.net
With menu items such as Slam Dunk Sandwiches, what sports fan wouldn't want to eat

here? The Stadium in Belle Fourche has lots of advantages for game buffs, too, as you'll see in the Nightlife chapter. But it's also won renown for its Stadium beef tips, a specialty acquired from the once-famous (but now defunct) Rancher Bar and Lounge formerly in the nearby hamlet of St. Onge. The restaurant, once known as Prime Time, was dubbed one of the nation's top 10 places to eat and its tenderloin tips called one of the unique meals in the United States. However, you can also order 8-ounce steaks; seafood; homemade soup; lemon-pepper chicken; salads and other tasty lunch and dinner items; plus Oreo fried ice cream to top it off. Handcut meats, generous portions, and a

RESTAURANTS

full bar are hallmarks of the Stadium Sports Grill, and you'll enjoy the pub's atmosphere (take note of the hand-built oak bar) Smoking is prohibited. A Sunday brunch is offered. There's plenty of seating, so you won't need reservations unless you're in a party of 15 or more. In any case, it should be easy to find a space in the Belle Fourche parking lot.

The Stadium In Spearfish at 744 North Main St. (605-642-9521) serves up just the kind of food you want to accompany your favorite game. Choose shrimp, onion rings, nachos, hot wings, burgers, sandwiches, salads, Indian tacos, steaks, chili, and more from the tabloid-size, newsprint menu, then read the sports pages while you wait for your lunch or dinner. The Stadium in Spearfish has a full-service bar as well as nonalcoholic beverages to go with your food.

STAMPMILL RESTAURANT & SALOON $$-$$$
305 West Main St., Lead
(605) 584-1984

Back in gold-rush days, the local stamp mills kept up a steady pounding, pulverizing ore so the gold could be extracted. This friendly restaurant in the heart of Black Hills gold-mining country pays tribute to the industry that created and sustained the city of Lead for more than a century. Fittingly, then, the Stampmill occupies an 1897 sandstone structure that is one of the oldest buildings in town. Beautifully renovated by a previous owner, it features a brick-and-wood interior with high ceilings and a gas fireplace to warm those snowy winter nights in the Northern Hills. Lunch items, named for some of the old stamp mills, are mainly burgers and sandwiches on homemade buns. For dinner, try a New York steak, or three rib selections, including garlic

rosemary, Thai and smokey barbecue. A full bar is available, as are dessert selections that include cheesecake, chocolate cake and an ice cream truffle. Be sure to take a look at the old mining photos on the wall while you're waiting to be served.

Central Hills

ELK CREEK STEAKHOUSE & LOUNGE $$-$$$
I-90 and Elk Creek Road, Piedmont
(605) 787-6349

Western garb fits right in at this popular restaurant, and you'll see many customers enter the ranch-style building in their best hats and boots. Steaks and seafood are the main menu items, but the kitchen also cooks up such varied dishes as chicken cordon blue, pasta and its signature prime rib. Steak sandwiches are available, but don't overlook the barbecued buffalo ribs and New York steaks, for a genuine taste of the Old West. The lounge has a full bar where you can order your beverage of choice. Elk Creek opens nightly for dinner, and reservations are recommended on weekends. The lounge opens at 4 p.m. on Sun and will serve food. Live music on Fri, Sat, and Sun. Take I-90 exit 46 and you'll be there.

✳FIREHOUSE BREWING COMPANY $$
610 Main St., Rapid City
(605) 348-1915
http://firehousebrewing.com

South Dakota's first brewpub isn't just about beer, although the 15 varieties made here (only a few available at a time) provide many reasons to visit the Firehouse. (See Nightlife.) This is also an excellent place to stop if you're looking for a hearty, appetizing meal in memorable surroundings. As the name and phone number suggest, the restaurant occupies Rapid City's historic 1915 fire station, which is listed in the National Register of Historic Places. Firefighting equipment of yore is suspended near the high ceiling, and garage doors are still in place in the front of the building. There's seating for diners downstairs near the rectangular bar, but nonsmokers will want to climb the stairs to the mezzanine, where the brewing vats are on display behind giant windows.

The menu changes with the season, but the food is always filling and plentiful. Popular dishes include the Reuben sandwich and Brewer's Burger. When you're in the mood for just a beer or cocktail and a snack, you'll find Fire Fightin' Nachos (jalapeños optional) among the tasty appetizers. Or you might find that Gorgonzola ale soup, made with the pub's Wilderness Wheat brew, hits the spot. Be sure to sample the freshly baked beer bread, too, and maybe order a loaf (with 24-hour notice) to take home. And yes, you can buy beer by the half gallon. The Firehouse is open for lunch and dinner Mon through Sat. On Sun, when it is open for dinner only, kids 12 and younger (one per family) eat for free.

THE GAS LIGHT $$$
13490 Main St., Rockerville
(605) 343-9276
www.thegaslightrestaurant.com
Rockerville was once a bustling gold camp. Thousands of miners settled in this section of ponderosa forest south of Rapid City, enough to warrant the construction of a flume to carry water from Spring Creek more than 20 miles away. Over time the gold ran out, the flume rotted, and nearly everyone left. The town tried to reorganize in the 1950s as a tourist attraction, hoping to catch

visitors on their way to Mount Rushmore, but it seemed that Rockerville was destined to become a ghost town. It almost is, save for the Gas Light. Decorated in Old West memorabilia and antiques, this spacious restaurant is popular with groups and parties who like the meeting rooms in the back and with hungry travelers on their way to the Central Hills.

You could start with a cocktail, beer, or glass of wine at the bar. For an appetizer, you might try their incredible buffalo wings, followed by a salad. The lunch menu includes sandwiches and buffalo burgers, and dinner offers many choices in chicken, pasta, seafood, and steaks. A special list of "old-world delights" such as prime rib and chicken Oscar includes recommendations for the appropriate bottle of fine wine. The Gas Light is open daily 11 a.m. to 9 p.m. for lunch and dinner between Memorial Day and Labor Day weekends. During the winter, dinner is served from 4 to 9 p.m. weekdays, and 11 a.m. to 9 p.m. Sat and Sun. The Gas Light is 12 miles south of Rapid City via US 16. Reservations are recommended, and parking is plentiful.

HOLY SMOKE RESTAURANT &
LOUNGE $-$$
US 16A, Keystone
(605) 666-4616
www.blackhills.com/holysmoke/
restau.html
The proprietors vow you won't find a can opener here, but we'll get to the food in just a minute. First we want to rave about the restaurant itself, which is an authentic log cabin with a southwestern flair. The dining room features an adobe fireplace, a knotty-pine floor, and a center post that was cut and peeled right on the property. Mexican

furniture and a beehive-shape stucco-and-lath fireplace invite you to enjoy a cocktail in the comfortable lounge. And who could resist the opportunity to dine alfresco on the deck on a warm summer evening? Back in the kitchen, hand-cut steaks, barbecued ribs, and homemade desserts are the Holy Smoke's culinary hallmarks. New in 2010, three different sizes of rib dinners starting at $8.95 were so popular the Holy Smoke served more than two tons of ribs. Chicken dishes and home-grown buffalo are available, too. Smoking is not allowed inside, but is allowed on the outdoor patio. Reservations are accepted for parties of six or more. The restaurant serves dinner from 4 to 9 p.m. daily from mid-May through Sept 30. It is 1.25 miles north of Keystone.

HORSE CREEK INN $$$–$$$$
23570 US 385, Rapid City
(605) 574-2908

If the topic were real estate, Horse Creek Inn would meet all three criteria: location, location, location. Not only is this quaint mid-20th-century cabin just a short drive from all the fun at Sheridan Lake, but it has a horse pasture out back where you're likely to see deer and coyotes. Formerly known as Old Wheel Inn, the pine-interior restaurant and lounge has retained its rustic ambience and simple furnishings, making it a delightful place to enjoy some fine food: Beef—top sirloin and filets—is the most popular item here, but chicken, seafood, pork chops, and a couple of vegetarian dishes (fettuccine primavera and Oriental stir-fry) are available as well. You'll see them all listed on the hand-drawn and lettered menus that are framed and propped up on easels in the dining room. Steaks are hand cut and can be ordered with Cajun spices, and you can

request a hamburger or appetizer to eat in the lounge, where there's a full-service bar.

During the summer you can take your drink or sandwich out to the deck, although you won't actually be served there. Nightly specials are offered, and the soups, salads, and desserts (such as mud pie and German chocolate cake) are made on the premises. The inn is open daily for lunch and dinner from May through Sept, for lunch Sat and Sun all year, and for dinner Mon through Sun the rest of the year. Reservations are recommended on weekends. The restaurant and lounge are nonsmoking, but you can smoke in the lounge. The inn, with its own parking lot, is one-quarter-mile north of Sheridan Lake Road on US 385, 18 miles west of Rapid City and 7 miles north of Hill City.

POWDER HOUSE $$
US 16A, Keystone
(605) 666-4646
www.powderhouselodge.com

You'll do more than dine at this well-known eatery—you'll be transported back to the time when a real powder house stored explosives for local mines. Built at the site of the original (the area was called Crossville then), the Powder House dishes up old-time Black Hills atmosphere in a log cabin furnished with pine-board tables and a working fireplace. The menu offers traditional western fare such as steaks and buffalo stew but appeals to other palates as well. You can get an assortment of chicken and fish entrees, fettuccine primavera topped with feta cheese, or even a veggie burger. Full bar service provides you with the cocktail, beer, or wine of your choice. For dessert, there's Bourbon Street bread pudding accompanied by a cup of freshly ground coffee. The Powder House, which is a mile north of town, is open for breakfast (trout and eggs, anyone?), lunch, and dinner, seven days a week from mid-May until Sept 30. Reservations are recommended for dinner during the summer. Smoking is not permitted in the dining room. Parking is provided.

SHOOTERS RESTAURANT & SPORTS BAR $$
2424 West Main St., Rapid City
(605) 348-3348

Warning: Parental permission is required for the hottest of Shooters' famous hot wings. The menu even says so. You're allowed to order spicy chicken wings mild, hot, or thermonuclear on your own, but you need a note from your mother to go all the way to extreme. Not to worry, though, because Shooters has plenty of other menu offerings, from appetizers, soups, and salads to wrap sandwiches, burgers, steaks, ribs, chicken, southwestern fare, pasta, and stir-fries. You can also choose from a large selection of beers, cocktails, premium wines, and single-malt scotches from the full bar. Desserts include homemade cheesecake and peanut butter pie. What's more, four satellites bring the wide world of sports to Shooters' TV sets. The clientele includes people of all ages, from 8 to 80, and you can find a table for up to 12 or 15. Shooters is nonsmoking. Ample parking is available.

i Although red wine is meant to be served at room temperature, some Black Hills bartenders keep it chilled and even serve it (or any wine) on the rocks. If you're particular, it's a good idea to ask before you order.

THE WINDMILL RESTAURANT $$
2803 Deadwood Ave., Rapid City
(605) 342-9456

If you're a fan of truck-stop food, this is your kind of place. And it's open 24 hours a day, ready to get your order from the kitchen to the table in five minutes no matter what time hunger strikes. Breakfast is available around the clock, and the truckers' specials (various meat and egg combinations) come with a choice of toast, biscuits, or cake. You'll also find satisfying hot and cold sandwiches, burgers, fried foods, Indian tacos, John's homemade meat loaf, barbecued ribs, a soup and salad bar, and ice-cream treats on the menu. If you like, try the Monday two-for-one hamburgers, the Friday all-you-can-eat fresh fish, or the Saturday and Sunday breakfast buffet. Beer and wine are available, and both smokers and nonsmokers will find a comfortable place to sit. As you can imagine, there's plenty of parking. Take I-90 exit 55 and you can't miss this place—just look for the big windmill.

Southern Hills

BLUE BELL LODGE AND RESORT $$
Custer State Park SR 87, Custer
(605) 255-4531
www.custerresorts.com

You won't find much to criticize at Blue Bell, either in the expanded saloon-style lounge (with a full bar and saddle barstools) or the family-style dining room. You'll find plenty of menu items based on wild game, from steak to meat loaf. You'll also find trout, walleye, and other entrees, but no matter what you order, everything comes to the table in big bowls so you can serve yourself, just like at home. You'll have to refrain from smoking. The Blue Bell complex (see the Accommodations chapter for lodging information) on the west side of Custer State Park takes its name from the Bell Telephone symbol, honoring the phone company executive who built Blue Bell in the 1920s. This is also the departure point for Blue

Bell's chuck wagon cookouts, which you can read about in the Attractions chapter. You can park for the restaurant right outside.

STATE GAME LODGE
DINING ROOM   **$$$**
State Game Lodge
Custer State Park
US 16A, Custer
(605) 255-4541
www.custerresorts.com
Welcome to the dining room of American presidents. Both Calvin Coolidge and Dwight Eisenhower took meals in the State Game Lodge's dining room during their presidencies. Just as you'd expect, game is the specialty here, so buffalo, venison, and the South Dakota state bird, pheasant, figure prominently on the menu. You might begin your meal with buffalo short ribs, then progress to a cowboy rib eye sautéed with garlic and topped with mushrooms on wild rice. Or perhaps you'd be interested in smoked pheasant pasta. If fish is your game, you might prefer a flavorful rainbow trout, roasted Altantic salmon, or Alaskan halibut. Lunch features a deli-style sandwich buffet, buffalo stew, elk burgers, and other items. In spring 2009, crews completed a $3 million restoration of the lodge. Reservations are recommended for dinner in the smoke-free game lodge, which is open from May through mid-Nov. Parking is available at the lodge in the northeastern quadrant of the park.

ASIAN
Northern Hills

CHINATOWN CAFE   **$$**
649 Main St., Deadwood
(605) 578-7778
www.heartofdeadwood.com

Chinese immigrants played an important role in early-day Deadwood, and this restaurant honors their contribution to local history. Your order is prepared individually from fresh ingredients and seasoned to your taste while you sip tea or a beer or wine-based cocktail from the bar. Lunch and dinner feature many standard Chinese favorites, from egg rolls and wonton soup to chop suey, chow mein, fried rice, and sweet-and-sour chicken, shrimp, or pork. However, you'll find plenty of more complex dishes such as Szechuan beef, walnut shrimp, orange-flavored chicken, and two kinds of war ba served on sizzling platters. Daily luncheon specials offer a choice of sweet-and-sour pork or another dish. Although you'll probably be focused on your meal, take a moment to notice the graceful Chinese lanterns and unusual circular seating arrangement. Chinatown accommodates nonsmokers as much as possible, so be sure to state your preference. The restaurant is on the second floor of Miss Kitty's gaming hall.

Central Hills

GREAT WALL RESTAURANT   **$$**
315 East North St., Rapid City
(605) 348-1183
You'll find several varieties of Asian food here, such as Cantonese Triple Delicacy pan-fried noodles, Mandarin-style sesame beef, Szechuan beef Taiwanese Happy Family, and Shanghai-style minced lobster with pine nuts. Those are a few of the house specialties, and you'll find tried-and-true lunch and dinner favorites on the menu as well, such as egg drop soup, chow mein, broccoli beef, almond chicken, and sweet-and-sour shrimp. You can also get vegetarian meals here, and there's never any MSG added to your food during cooking. Subdued lighting

and a saltwater fish tank create a somewhat mysterious mood in the dining area. Beer and wine are available. Reservations are recommended for five or more people. Parking is provided right outside the door.

HUNAN $$
1720 Mount Rushmore Rd., Rapid City
(605) 341-3888

A huge menu is just the beginning at this popular Chinese restaurant. The health conscious will be pleased to know that the food here is MSG free, and that special low-fat, sugar-free, and salt-free dishes are available. The regular menu includes everything from egg rolls and wonton soup to a Peking duck so elaborate it must be ordered 24 hours in advance. Although beef, pork, seafood, and vegetarian selections are offered in abundance, chicken—hot and spicy or sweet and sour—seems to be a favorite with guests. Beer and wine can accompany your meal, and cheesecake or lychee nuts (a Chinese fruit) can be your dessert. Take note of the magnificent photos in the entryway and behind the cash register, which are the work of owner Robert Wong, a native of China. We're sure you'll be impressed, not only by his skill as a photographer but also by the many ribbons, medals, and trophies he has won for his breathtaking images. His work has been featured in *National Geographic*. The prizes are on display in a cabinet in the restaurant. Smoking is prohibited at Hunan. Ample parking is provided. Hunan is open for lunch and dinner.

SAIGON RESTAURANT $$
221 East North St., Rapid City
(605) 348-8523

Vietnamese food must build brain cells, because the people who run this popular restaurant have phenomenal memories. It doesn't matter how long ago you ate here, they remember what you ordered and if you prefer your glass of water without ice. They recall what Harrison Ford had on his plate when he ate here in 1995 and which vegetarian dish Lindsay Wagner had in 1997. Wagner, TV's bionic woman, could have been speaking for all of the Saigon's loyal clientele when she sent proprietress Mai Goodsell an autographed photo that says, "Mai, both you and your business are a joy!"

Mai, a native of Vietnam, and her daughter, Rebecca, are the most visible members of the staff, but we suspect the kitchen harbors a team of wizards who whip up magical dishes for lunch and dinner. The menu contains many items you'd expect to find at an Asian restaurant, but you'll also find unusual dishes such as tofu lemongrass, a combination of noodles, bean sprouts, herbs, and tofu sprinkled with chopped peanuts and served with fish sauce; or chicken pad thai with shredded cabbage, carrots, cilantro, bamboo, rice noodles, and peanuts. The staff is amazingly flexible, so spicy items come in varying degrees of "heat," and you can request that the cook not use MSG in preparing your order.

When the restaurant moved into a spacious new building, the great food and welcoming atmosphere moved in, too. Longtime patrons will recognize the exquisite enamel and mother-of-pearl pieces from the former location amid the new decor, which features oval windows and interesting interior angles. Beer and wine are on the menu. There's handy parking in front. The Saigon closes on Sun and in late Jan.

i Although South Dakota isn't premier grape-growing habitat, two vineyards grow fruit and produce wine here. You can find products from Hill City–based Prairie Berry Winery (877-226-9453; www.prairieberry.com) at Black Hills restaurants and liquor stores. Wines from Valiant Vineyards (605-624-4500, www.buffalorunwinery .com), located in the east part of the state, also are common.

COFFEE & SANDWICH SHOPS

Although these places specialize in breakfast and lunch, some serve dinner or stay open long enough for a late-afternoon or early-evening meal. Be sure to check the other categories for places that serve early in the day; you'll find a couple of 24-hour establishments listed under American cuisine.

Northern Hills

COMMON GROUNDS $
135 East Hudson St., Spearfish
(605) 642-9066,
This gourmet coffee shop offers a full line of espresso drinks (including icy java slushes) and Italian sodas plus muffins, bagels, soups, salads, and wrap sandwiches for the vegetarian and carnivore alike. An eclectic mix of furniture and displays of student and local artwork make this a homey place to relax with a newspaper or good book while you munch and sip, and the rich aroma of bulk coffee you can buy to brew in your own kitchen just adds to the comfortable atmosphere. The cafe serves breakfast and has an all-day deli bar. Hours are 7 a.m. to 7 p.m. Mon through Fri, 7 a.m. to 6 p.m. Sat, and Sun 6 a.m. to 5 p.m. Smoking is not permitted.

Central Hills

B&L BAGELS $
512 Main St., Rapid City
(605) 399-1777
There's nothing quite like a fresh bagel to start the day or provide a pick-me-up at lunch. Bagels are mixed from scratch, then boiled and baked on a stone hearth the old-fashioned way. You'll have around 15 kinds to choose from, and you can order your bagel plain or spread with any of 15 flavors of light (less fat) cream cheese or another topping such as hummus or honey peanut butter. Or order it stuffed with a sandwich filling such as turkey, pastrami, roast beef, veggies, or cream cheese and lox. Soups and fat-free pasta salad round out your meal, but if a snack is all you need, try something from the bakery case, including scones, rolls and cookies. A full espresso bar offers java or tea or a refreshing Italian soda. Smoothies are available. The shop is open daily, except Sun, for breakfast and lunch. Smoking is prohibited.

THE BEANERY "DELI & BAKERY" $
201 Main St., Rapid City
(605) 348-6775
An expanded menu makes this an exceptional eating experience. Check out owners Chris and Lisa Holbrook's daily specials and the four or five soups handcrafted each day. The decor is marked by bright colors; fuchsias, blues, and teals, with accents of black, complement the movie star portraits from the 1950s and '60s that hang on the walls, and a beautiful jukebox in the dining rooms. You'll find cold and grilled sandwiches, as well as the signature sloppy joes. Lemonade, iced tea, coffee, soft drinks, beer, and wine are available, as are homemade pies, and cookies. Meeting rooms and catering are

available. The Beanery is smoke-free and located in the lower level of the historic Fairmont Creamery Building on the corner of Main and Second Streets. Check out the dinner show each Friday and Saturday night, starting at 6 p.m. Open 10:30 a.m. to 2 p.m. Mon through Fri.

BLACK HILLS BAGELS $
913 Mount Rushmore Rd., Rapid City
(605) 399-1277
www.blackhillsbagels.com
In addition to 28 kinds of bagels, 18 cream cheeses, and a variety of bagel sandwiches, you'll find tasty homemade salads and fresh fruit. Or, if you're in the mood for a snack, a homemade cookie, muffin, or cinnamon bagel knot—the low-fat alternative to doughnuts—could be just the thing. Try the Bourbon Street bagel pudding. A full espresso bar serves a wide variety of coffees plus Italian sodas and frappe freezes. The shop is open from 6 a.m. to 3 p.m. Mon through Fri and 7 a.m. to 3 p.m. Sat and Sun. There is no smoking in the restaurant. Limited parking is available front and back. Their newest venture is the Black Hills Bagels Express-O, located on Haines Avenue, which is a drive-through only establishment but offers a selection of many favorites from its big sister store.

ECLECTIC

The restaurants listed here serve dishes that cross many culinary borders. They often have a good selection of vegetarian offerings, and in fact, you'll see that we've even included a vegan eatery. But extraordinary meat dishes are on many of these menus, too.

Northern Hills

THE BAY LEAF CAFÉ $$
126 West Hudson St., Spearfish
(605) 642-5462
The menu describes the cafe's rosemary linguine this way: "Oh sigh. Oh heavy sigh." We suspect a few sighs of delight will have escaped your lips even before you see the menu, though, because the Bay Leaf itself is a collection of lovely architectural features. Right off you'll notice the beveled, stained-glass window in the front door and the ceramic tile floor. Regional artists' works hang on the walls.

Entrees run the gamut from trout amandine, elk, and buffalo rib eye to tempeh with sautéed vegetables and Cajun-style Bourbon Street pasta, plus ever-changing daily specials. Beer and wine are available, and after your meal rich cup of coffee, Italian soda, or herbal tea goes well with the rich, chocolaty homemade desserts. The food here is completely MSG free and largely preservative free as well. And in keeping with the emphasis on health, smoking is not permitted. The Bay Leaf serves lunch and dinner daily during the summer, and because that's an especially busy time of year, it's a good idea to call ahead and ask whether reservations are needed. The cafe is closed on Sun from early Oct until Memorial Day weekend. Hours vary in the off-season, so call ahead for evening reservations.

DEADWOOD THYMES
CAFÉ & BISTRO $$$–$$$$
87 Sherman St., Deadwood
(605) 578-7566
www.deadwoodthymes.com
Set among a row of brick office buildings about 2 blocks from the busy tourist traffic on Deadwood's Main Street, the Deadwood

Thymes is modest and unassuming. Unless you talk to the locals (who dine here regularly), you probably won't find it advertised anywhere, and a small wooden sign above the lonely brick facade is the only indicator of what lies inside. Even the interior—a remodeled funeral parlor—is relatively plain, accented only with some Old World–themed paintings and wrought-iron chairs and tables.

Despite the plain appearances, this is easily one of the best restaurants in Deadwood. The talented culinary staff creates a constantly changing array of European-inspired dishes for breakfast, lunch, and dinner. Brioche French toast, smoked salmon quiche, Thai burrito with peanut sauce, roast beef on rye with cream cheese horseradish and alfalfa sprouts, pecan encrusted shrimp and lobster cakes, breast of duck with orange sauce and forbidden rice, and pork prime rib with raspberry jalapeño salsa have all appeared on past menus. It is especially noteworthy that everything—from granola and doughnuts to salad dressings and the parsley gin sauce that accompanies the lamb chops—is homemade in the bistro's kitchen.

The Deadwood Thymes is open Tues through Sat for breakfast and lunch, but dinner is available only on Thurs, Fri, and Sat evenings. Brunch on Sun gives you the option of sampling a full range of the bistro's signature dishes.

JAKES $$$$
677 Main St., Deadwood
(605) 578-3656, (800) 999-6482
www.themidnightstar.com

You just can't help feeling glamorous when you dine at Jakes, located on the top floor of the Midnight Star casino. Although you're not likely to rub elbows with the glitterati here (but it's not impossible, either), just knowing this splendid restaurant was created by Hollywood celebrity Kevin Costner and his brother, Dan, lends panache to the evening. Jakes opens each night for dinner on the top floor of the 1879 Phoenix Building, Deadwood's first brick structure—and the only building in town that had a three-story privy out back (demolished in the 1940s). The Deadwood City Council held its first meeting in this space in 1881, but it's doubtful the early-day city leaders had as much fun as you will in this lofty chamber of cherry, mahogany, and double-lead crystal. (The original third floor was torn off several decades ago because of damage from a leaky roof, but the Costners' replacement is architecturally faithful.) With its tall windows and domed skylight, this is an exciting place to be during a summer thunderstorm, but you don't need a taste for thrills to appreciate the amenities. A propensity for stellar cuisine will do you just fine, because there's plenty of that at Jakes.

Begin with a tasty appetizer such as escargot, roasted portobello mushrooms, buffalo carpaccio, shredded pheasant quesadillas, or duck satay. After your salad, let the sorbet intermezzo, served on a lemon leaf, cleanse your palate for full enjoyment of an entree, such as sautéed walleye, honey-glazed shrimp, grilled pork tenderloins with cinnamon plum sauce, steak fillets, or Cajun seafood tortellini. These are just a few of the selections from the menu, which varies a bit every few months. What remains constant is the elegance of the food, including handmade desserts, such as macadamia white-chocolate cheesecake. The luxury of two fireplaces, a full bar, and live piano music Tues through Sat are the final exquisite touches. Because this is a popular place, reservations are recommended. Jakes is open daily for dinner.

The Midnight Star has a sports bar, Diamond Lil's, which serves lighter fare, and you'll find it listed in the Nightlife chapter.

SEVEN GRILL $$$
447 North Main St., Spearfish
(605) 717-5701

The Seven Grill is actually two different eateries in one—a soup shack and a steak house. The soup is homemade, as is just about everything on the menu, including the salad dressing. Try starting your meal with creamy potato or tomato bisque soup, and top your salad with creamy dill or Italian vinaigrette dressing. The soup is served with warm, fresh-baked bread, usually made with wholesome grains or herbs and sun-dried tomatoes and the cuisine is as distinctive as South Dakota—in other words, big, fresh, tasty meals. Chefs use steak and fish from the Black Hills and add their own creativity to the dishes. The signature rum-cured salmon is absolutely delicious. Of course, Seven Grill also serves prime steaks such as rib eye and tenderloin. It offers nightly specials, including the popular prime rib on Friday and Saturday nights.

The Seven Grill has fast become a local favorite, especially among the younger college crowd in Spearfish. The interior is warm and inviting, with a wooden bar and tables and a large stone fireplace. The outside patio has a fire pit, and it is covered in cold weather for those who still wish to dine outside. Local artwork decorates the walls, and regional musicians are frequently invited to play and entertain the crowd. It's open year-round for lunch and dinner until 11 p.m., but the bar stays open until the crowd tapers.

Central Hills

*ALPINE INN $$
225 Main St., Hill City
(605) 574-2749

For dinner you have your choice of filet mignon or filet mignon—that is, you may order the six-ounce filet or the nine-ounce, depending on the size of your appetite. For such a small menu, this restaurant in the 1886 quarters of the former Harney Peak Hotel has a big reputation and a loyal clientele. Those who want more variety wait for dessert, when there are some 30 selections, including homemade apple cheese strudel and bread pudding. Or they come here for lunch, which features a good choice of sandwiches served with sides such as Swabian German potato salad. Hearty bratwurst and schnitzel are on the menu, but so is more delicate fare such as a turkey croissant Parisienne and a cheese board. Beer, wine, and lattes are among the beverages served. Reservations are not accepted, but if your party has eight or more people, call ahead and the staff will do its best to make space available for you. The inn is closed on Sun. When it's nice out you can eat on the veranda for lunch (assuming there's a free table!), but if you eat indoors be sure to note the hotel's original wooden banister on the staircase and the sturdy old safe beneath the cash register. Credit cards are not accepted.

*ENIGMA $$$$
445 Mount Rushmore Rd., Rapid City
(605) 348-8300
www.enigmarestaurant.com

Sitting in a quiet corner of Enigma, it would not be difficult to imagine yourself dining on the banks of the Seine or sipping cocktails off Broadway after a show. This small, unobtrusive restaurant is incredibly intimate, with a quiet atmosphere and contemporary cuisine found only in metropolises 10 or 20 times the size of Rapid City. Located off the lobby of the downtown Radisson Hotel, Enigma has fewer than 20 tables; most of them are booths with a distinctive cozy, private feel. All the same, the dining room maintains a warm and open ambience, due in part to the large pieces of continental artwork hanging on the walls and soft lighting from candle sconces. More striking light comes from the blue neon sign on the far end of the restaurant, proudly reminding patrons that Enigma has one of the only martini bars in the five-state region.

This is the domain of restaurant maitre'd Ibrahim, an ethnic Moroccan who was trained in France, Cassablanca and Florida. He keeps a well-stocked bar complete with European and North African liqueurs; if you're feeling adventurous, ask for bombas. The kitchen is run by Chef Sergio, and Chef Gunter, the latter trained by the Master Chefs of Austria. Items on the menu vary with some regularity but can range from a simple Greek salad and filet mignon to more elegant tortellini a la Provençale with beef, peppers, and garlic sauce and saltimbocca a la Romana, with prosciutto ham, pasta, vegetables, and a sage cream sauce. Traditional European desserts include crème brûlée, fruit tarts, and other gastronomic delights. The wine list is impressive, but don't be afraid to opt for the fine quality house red or white. Also on the menu is the Mystery Dinner, a four-course, two-hour affair that lets you hand over the creative fate of your meal to the chefs.

RUSHMORE SUPPER CLUB & LOUNGE $$–$$$
253 Swanzey St., Keystone
(605) 666-4501

This popular restaurant, formerly called the Historical Rushmore Grill & Bar, is a block and a half east of the Strip (Winter Street, the town's main drag) in Keystone, but its reputation for authentic, made-from-scratch Mexican food draws hungry crowds in search of the cook's famous fajitas and other specialties served in heaping portions for lunch and dinner. Cajun blackened prime rib is on the menu, and so are half-pound buffalo and beef burgers, steaks, Cajun chicken sandwiches, and shrimp and taco salads, to name a few of the choices. A So-Sweet Burrito filled with apple and pineapple pie filling, deep fried and garnished with ice cream, three toppings, whipped cream, and a cherry is a special-request-only dessert that could pose as a meal in itself. The bar—note the ornate, century-old back bar from a longago Custer watering hole—serves highly regarded margaritas frozen, blended, or on the rocks, as well as beer, wine, and other cocktails. After many years of operation, the restaurant moved into larger quarters and added a sports bar in the basement. There's also a covered deck for outdoor dining. During the summer when it's busy, reservations are recommended for parties of seven or more.

i If you see Rocky Mountain oysters on a restaurant menu and wonder what they are—well, ask your waitstaff. All we'll tell you is that they're not seafood.

TIFFANY GRILLE $$$
505 North 5th St., Rapid City
(605) 348-4000

This elegant restaurant, lushly decorated with live greenery, is in the spacious atrium lobby of the Rushmore Plaza Holiday Inn. The serving day begins with traditional breakfasts accompanied by a cappuccino cart on weekdays; on Sunday the brunch buffet features a pastry bar and made-to order omelets. At midday you can order a lunch of a turkey club on a spinach wrapper; a Reuben, chef, or Caesar chicken salad; vegetarian wrap; or something equally delicious. Dinnertime is when the kitchen pulls out all the stops, however. Tempting dishes include rib eye, fillets of beef, Key West chicken breast with a blend of Caribbean spices and pineapple salsa, almond walleye, pork medallions, herb-crusted orange roughy filet, or roasted-vegetable lasagna. While you're waiting for your order, you might ready your palate with crab-stuffed mushrooms with Mornay sauce. All of the breads are tasty, as are the pies you'll see grouped with Chocolate Obsession Cake and other rich offerings on the dessert tray. Tiffany Grille has a full bar, and plenty of parking. Smoking is prohibited. Groups of 10 or more should make a reservation.

Southern Hills

*SAGE CREEK GRILLE $$-$$$
611 Mt. Rushmore Rd., Custer
(605) 673-2424
With its unique blend of local dishes, including buffalo and elk, the Sage Creek Grille has evolved into one of the most popular restaurants in the southern Black Hills. Opened in 1999 by owner/chef Nancy Gellerman, the 50-seat Sage Creek touts exceptional nightly specials and all cuts of South Dakota–certified steaks, as well as a pan-seared buffalo tenderloin that you'll remember long after the Black Hills fade away in your review mirror. Gellerman's desire to "keep it fresh and fun and filling" manifests itself in a menu that changes every three weeks. Sage Creek Grille has a small menu bolstered by buffalo burgers, elk and walleye dishes, salmon and

seafood entrees, combined with an excellent wine list of 50 varieties, including value wines with wonderful flavors. Diners relax in atmosphere surrounded by light oak and earthtones. Because the restaurant does not take reservations, some guests wait as long as 90 minutes to be seated. But, it's worth the wait. Local shops and galleries will keep you occupied in the meantime. Hours: Lunch, 11 a.m. to 2 p.m. and 5 p.m. to closing Mon through Sat in season, closed Sun and Mon as well as shorter hours in the off-season.

SYLVAN LAKE LODGE
DINING ROOM $$$-$$$$
Sylvan Lake Custer State Park Resort
SR 87, Custer
(605) 574-2561
www.custerresorts.com
The first hotel on Sylvan Lake was built in 1895, just six years after the lake itself. Unfortunately, a fire destroyed the popular Victorian-style inn in 1935, but its replacement opened just two years later. Today stone-columned Sylvan Lake Resort hosts Custer State Park's most elegant restaurant. Dinner specials the night we stopped in included bacon-wrapped elk tenderloin, sautéed calamari with red chili pasta, and grilled orange roughy with creamed crab. Beef fajitas with guacamole, buffalo steak, grilled Black Hills trout, and South Dakota ring-necked pheasant also were on the menu. On this same late-summer evening diners were relaxing on the stone veranda that overlooks the quiet lake, chatting and sipping cocktails from the bar. The resort, which is in the northwestern corner of the park, serves breakfast, lunch, and dinner daily from mid-May until late Sept. Smoking is prohibited as it is in all state-owned buildings. Parking is provided.

GERMAN

Southern Hills

THE BAVARIAN INN RESTAURANT AND LOUNGE $$$
US 16/385 North, Custer
(605) 673-4412
www.bavarianinnsd.com
This restaurant's name is your cue to its specialties, which are of the German persuasion. Rouladen, a stuffed, rolled topround steak, is the most popular item on the menu, according to the staff. Many diners come here for the prime rib au jus, but the restaurant also has a solid reputation for its schnitzel, bratwurst dinner, sweet-and-sour cabbage, spaetzle and gravy, rib eye, and sirloin steak. Fish and seafood, vegetarian lasagna, bratwurst sandwiches, mesquite-flavored steaks, and a burger deluxe satisfy all kinds of appetites, and the bar serves cocktails, beer, and wine to complement the food. A large selection of desserts includes German chocolate cake and, during the summer, homemade apple dumplings. The inn is open only for dinner through the winter, but from late May until Labor Day breakfasts are also served. Closed Sun.

The inn offers a nice outdoor deck for candlelight dining (in warmer weather) and has a 200-seat banquet hall for receptions, weddings, and reunions. Another added attraction is the menu for children under age six. Smoking is prohibited, parking is provided, and reservations are recommended.

INDIAN

Central Hills

CURRY MASALA $
2050 West Main St., Suite #7
Rapid City
(605) 716-7788
www.currymasalainc.com

One doesn't dine at Curry Masala for the ambience. Set in a nearly empty office suite on the west side of Rapid City, the restaurant's dining room is little more than a few wooden tables, a handful of folding chairs, and some secondhand booths that remain unattached to the wall—a section of which is formed from white canvas stretched across a wide doorway. Traditional and pop Indian music drifts pleasantly from a boom box in the open kitchen, from where the staff will serve you your food buffet-style on foam plates with plastic flatware. In fact, the entire restaurant can be summed up in one word: cheap. That said, the food here is spectacular. Owner Al Rodriguez keeps six curries on the menu at any one time, along with rice, naan bread, chai tea, and rotating selections of dessert items. Despite its somewhat hidden location and lack of publicity, the restaurant has gained a steady local following, thanks to the quality of the cuisine. The price point doesn't hurt, either—a lousy $5.95 will buy you more food than you could hope to eat in one sitting. To keep up with the growing crowd who come here to dine, Rodriguez has begun to schedule small community events in his establishment, including Bengali language classes and an Indian cooking school. The restaurant is open every day for lunch and dinner, except Sun when only lunch is offered.

ITALIAN

Northern Hills

✳ROMA'S RISTORANTE $$–$$$
2281 East Colorado Blvd., Spearfish
(605) 722-0715
Search the West and you'd be hard-pressed to discover a restaurant more inviting than Roma's in Spearfish. With a beautiful new building in 2010, you'll find this restaurant

open and airy, but the bonus is in the food. The owner and executive chef, Leigh Kamstra, calls it, "Italian with a twist." Even though it's upscale, it's not stuffy. Attire is casual. Roma's signature dishes include smoked pheasant ravioli, traditional lasagna, and the carbonara, as well as the house-baked bread and the house salad with balsamic vinaigrette topped with goat cheese. But diners also discover an exceptional blend of chicken dishes, pastas, steaks, seafood, and vegetarian selections, as well as a wine bar. Private room available as well as outdoor seating. Hours: Lunch 11 a.m. to 2 p.m. Mon through Sat, dinner 4 p.m. to close every day. Live music on Fri and Sat.

Central Hills

BOTTICELLI RISTORANTE $-$$$
523 Main St., Rapid City
(605) 348-0089

A local favorite, Botticelli Ristorante has been packing customers in for more than a decade with its convenient downtown Rapid City location, northern Italian cuisine, and quaint atmosphere. Owner Michelle Peregrine did such a marvelous job with the bricked walls and Venetian plasters, sipping a robust Chianti, you'll swear you're sitting in Tuscany. The menu boasts a decidedly European flare and has remained the same since the restaurant opened. But, frequent specials, fresh seafood daily, and chef's features add a new dimension each day. Diners find elegant selections of pastas, crème sauces, seafood and more than 100 wines in the cellar in this 122-seat establishment. Wines from all the usual suspects range from $19 to $140, and Botticelli's also features a dozen varieties of US and imported beers. (Insider's tip: The fettuccini a la Teresa is out of this world, but don't dismiss the daily specials.

Fish lovers should sample the salmon, opah, cioppino, or red sculton.) Regular hours: Lunch 11 a.m. to 2:30 p.m. Mon through Fri; 11:30 a.m. to 10 p.m. Sat. Dinner 5 to 10 p.m. Fri, 5 to 9 p.m. Mon through Thurs and Sun.

*PIESANO'S PACCHIA $-$$
3618 Canyon Lake Dr., Rapid City
(605) 341-6941
www.piesanospacchia.com

Don't be fooled by the amusing play on *paesano*, the Italian word for "countryman." Piesano's takes pacchia—Italian for feast—very seriously. Everything is homemade. Piesano's attracts a loyal clientele with scrumptious gourmet pizzas—sweet-and-sour cashew chicken is popular, but you can also order chicken Bar-B-Q, healthful vegetable, Happy Hawaiian, and more conventional varieties including primo, with the works. New combinations appear from time to time. Pizzas are created on hand-tossed dough made fresh daily, and we're told that the owners are so fussy they follow the wheat crop to make sure they get top-quality flour. Pizzas come in four sizes, including an 8-inch noon special; other choices include sub sandwiches, salads (with hand-torn lettuce), and special meals such as calzones on Tuesday and Friday, lasagna on Wednesday, prime rib subs on Thursday and Saturday, and Italian chicken breast subs for Wednesday lunch. And for dessert there's cheesecake. It was no surprise to learn that the Black Hills Restaurant Guide named Piesano's the best local pizza establishment several years in a row. You can have a bottled beer with your meal, but not a smoke. New offerings include a wine list and outdoor patior seating, and an updated decor featuring gold, green, and maroon colors with an Italian flare. There's plenty of parking right out front.

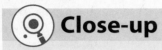

Close-up

Aunt Sally

Aunt Sally Sarah Campbell called herself "the first white woman that ever saw the Black Hills." But anyone who knew jolly "Aunt Sally" must have chuckled upon hearing that. For Aunt Sally was African American, and we can assume she meant she was the first non–Native American woman in the Hills.

Aunt Sally arrived here with the goldseeking expedition led by Lt. Col. George Custer in 1874, which you can read about in the History chapter. The only woman to go along on the trip, she had hired on as a cook for John Smith, a civilian trader who sold food, spirits, and other goods to the soldiers. After engineer Horatio Ross found sparkling flecks of gold in French Creek, a young newspaper reporter who had accompanied the excursion, William Curtis, interviewed the corpulent, well-liked cook for the Chicago Inter-Ocean. Curtis affectionately called her "a huge mountain of dusky flesh" and reported that she was more excited than anyone else about finding gold.

After all, Aunt Sally had left her comfortable home in Bismarck, North Dakota, and undertaken the journey for the sole purpose of seeing the Black Hills. Perhaps surprised to find that the Hills were in fact green rather than black, Aunt Sally apparently decided bright yellow was her favorite color and lost no time in filing a mining claim—illegally, we might add. The expedition was soon on its way again, but not before Aunt Sally had decided to return to the Black Hills at the first opportunity.

And return she did, although just when is not known. In time she filed a new claim at Elk Creek in Lawrence County and lived nearby, befriending her pioneer neighbors. They appreciated her cooking and midwifery skills, enjoyed her amusing anecdotes and tall tales, and took her pipe smoking in stride. At some point Aunt Sally reportedly adopted a 10-year-old white orphan boy, whom she had found crying in the street in Deadwood.

Aunt Sally lived to a ripe old age for her day. When she died on April 13, 1888, she was in her 70s. With fondness and respect, her friends laid her to rest on Vinegar Hill west of Galena, an old silvermining district in Lawrence County. Flattering obituaries appeared in two local newspapers, acknowledging her stature in the community. Though gone, Aunt Sally was never to be forgotten, and today the simple wooden marker that first graced her grave is on view in the Adams Museum in Deadwood.

MEXICAN

Northern Hills

GUADALAJARA MEXICAN
  RESTAURANT $$
US 14, Spearfish
(605) 642-4765

The Rodriguez family, owners of all Guadalajara restaurants in South Dakota, has brought a little piece of Old Mexico with them to the small college town of Spearfish. Dagoberto (Dago for short) played soccer for several teams in Mexico before he and his wife, Claudia, made the move from (you guessed it) Guadalajara, Mexico, to the states. They run the restaurant in Spearfish with the help of several other family members, including their two children, who pitch in occasionally. But everyone is family at Guadalajara, and the staff goes out of its way to make you feel welcome. You'll catch Dago making the rounds, shaking hands, and he'll speak Spanish with you if you'd like him to.

Great service is not the only noteworthy feature here—the food is as authentically Mexican as the family who makes it. Everything is made from scratch, from the chips and salsa all the way to the fried ice cream and sopapillas. You'll find all the traditional Mexican favorites, but the chimichangas are a local favorite. The sauces add flair to any dish; the Rodriguezes make their own red, green, and mole (pronounced "mow-lay") sauces, but there is also the delicious red ranchero sauce and other concoctions they refer to as "special" sauces. Portions are large, food is served piping hot, and a full bar can provide you with all the best Mexican drinks (be sure to try the margarita). Lunch is always a good deal at Guadalajara, but there are dinner specials every night and a kid's meal for 99 cents on Sun.

The experience doesn't end there—Guadalajara's decor reflects the old country. Everything is brightly colored, artwork and crafts all come from a small market town back home, and chairs and booths are brightly painted hand-carved wood made by one of Dago's friends in Old Mexico. The Rodriguezes have also brought traditions along with them, and if they find out it's your birthday, they'll plop a gigantic sombrero on your head, sing "Happy Birthday" in Spanish, and take a picture so you can remember the embarrassment! Guadalajara is open every day of the week. There is a smoking section by the bar.

i Deadwood casinos sponsor clubs that entitle members to free meals once they accumulate enough points. Inquire at those that house your favorite restaurants.

Central Hills

LA COSTA $$
603 Omaha St., Rapid City
(605) 388-8780

This south-of-the-border-style restaurant has built its reputation on fajitas and fast service while preparing food the old-fashioned way, from scratch. That means tomatoes and peppers for your complimentary salsa are roasted each morning, and the tamales are encased in real cornhusks. You'll find all your Mexican favorites here, along with seafood, combination plates, and weekday lunch specials. Popular entrees from the menu include fajitas, costenas with char-broiled beef or chicken accompanied by sautéed shrimp and crab, and char-broiled carne asada steak. The sopapillas topped with honey, cinnamon sugar, and whipped cream get rave reviews for dessert. You can order beer, including several Mexican varieties, and wine with your meal. La Costa is open for lunch and dinner seven days a week. And there's always a premeal bonus, because in addition to the obligatory homemade chips and salsa, your waitperson will bring refried beans to your table. Reservations are recommended for groups of more than 10. Ample parking is provided.

SWEET TREATS

Like people everywhere, Black Hills locals develop regular cravings for ice cream and other desserts. Luckily, we have industrious purveyors who are more than happy to cater to our collective sweet tooth.

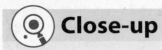 **Close-up**

Insider's Craving—No Trip without Turtles, No Travel without Truffles

Traveling through the scenic byways of the Black Hills, passing panoramas of ponderosa pine, peaks that reach the sky, and grazing buffalo herds, just wouldn't be complete without stumbling on one of those out-of-the-way, no-franchise operations that will keep you smiling, even after the chocolate is gone. Such is **Chubby Chipmunk Hand-Dipped Chocolates** in Deadwood, where Mary "Chip" Tautkus's decadent handcrafted truffles, toffee, and caramels could keep Weight Watchers in business.

"I started cooking when I was four years old, and they couldn't keep me out of the kitchen," Chip says. "The chocolate that I create is made so people have the most pleasurable experience that they can legally have. To watch someone bite into a truffle, close their eyes, sway back and forth and sigh, 'Oh my God, that is good!' just makes me feel great."

Since starting her business in a former Sinclair gas station on Deadwood's southside in 2005, Chip's concoctions, made purely with "butter and love," have created quite a stir. An editor with *Every Day With Rachael Ray* magazine discovered Chubby Chipmunk, then featured it in the publication. More than a year later, the magazine's readers still saunter in the door and have Chip sign the article. Then came local media coverage, a feature on a Seattle cable television show, and an appearance in United Airline's *SkyWest Magazine*.

Chip says she's still making her confections the same way she started. "Everything is still rolled and dipped entirely by hand," she says. "They are not your normal-sized truffles and some people have suggested I make them smaller. My philosophy is they are big enough to share, although you really don't have to."

To sample Chip's divine truffles, turtles, and chocolates, stop by Chubby Chipmunk at 420 Cliff St. in Deadwood, (605) 722-2447, or online at www.chubbychipmunk.net.

Northern Hills

CHUBBY CHIPMUNK HAND-DIPPED CHOCOLATES $
420 Cliff St., Deadwood
(605) 722-2447
www.chubbychipmunk.net
Don't even think about driving past this place, featuring over-the-top truffles, toffee and chocolates that will bring fond memories even after the Black Hills have faded in your rearview mirror. See related Close-up.

i One way to satisfy your sweet tooth in the Black Hills is to cover it in homemade saltwater taffy. Rushmore Mountain Taffy Shop (605-666-4430, www.rushmoremountaintaffy.com) in Keystone offers dozens of flavors, including huckleberry, buffalo berry, piña colada, cotton candy and key lime.

Central Hills

ARMADILLO'S ICE CREAM SHOPPE $
202 Main St., Rapid City
(605) 355-0507

The two families that run Armadillo's are masters of deliciously smooth ice cream. All of their ice cream is soft serve, and the decor adds to a 1950s feeling. The shop is located in an old gas station in downtown Rapid City, but the new look includes a black-and-white checked floor and redtop stools. But flash-backs are not what droves of people come here for; Armadillo's is known in the area for its inventive sundaes and fabulous sherbet. Family members and employees concoct both familiar and unfamiliar sundaes and tag them with their own name. Mike's Peach Cobbler has fresh peaches, caramel, and pecans; Rosie's Apple Pie has flame-roasted apples, caramel, and pecans; Tyler's Turtle simply has fudge with caramel and pecans. The creamy, smooth, low-fat sherbet is a local sensation, with flavors such as straw-berry cheesecake, wild blackberry, raspberry, strawberry, and root beer. Armadillo's serves only one flavor of sherbet each day and alternates the flavors every couple of days, but you can ask for a schedule of flavors in the summer.

There is more to this little shop than ice cream. Armadillo's also serves malts, fresh market-deli sandwiches, steamburgers (they're like sloppy joes), and homemade soups. As at any quality ice-cream parlor, prices aren't the lowest, but the portions are unusually large. The shop is open Mar through Oct from about 11 a.m. to 10 p.m. Lines are long in the summer, but it is worth the wait. No smoking inside, of course, but there are tables and benches outside.

NIGHTLIFE

The Black Hills are known for many things: unspoiled alpine vistas, herds of wild-roaming bison, epic mountain carvings, and woolly western legends. Nightlife, however, does not immediately spring to one's mind when the words "South Dakota" are uttered in conversation. In fact, the idea never occurs to many who visit here; there's even a good number of residents who never go for a night out on the town.

All the same, the Black Hills have a significant number of places that don't open until the sun sinks below the horizon. Rapid City's population base and Spearfish's college crowd make both communities regional nightlife capitals, though Deadwood's saloons, casinos, and frequent free concerts on Main Street make it the busiest night-life headquarters in a 500-mile radius.

In fact the following listings feature a few bars and pubs that have been here since gold-rush days. You'll find coffeehouses where you can hear live music and sometimes poetry, sports bars with TVs galore, a couple of nightclubs, and comedy clubs for a truly lighthearted night out.

OVERVIEW

A state law requires businesses that serve wine or hard liquor to also serve food if they're open on Sunday, even if the fare is just hot dogs, snacks, microwave pizza, or sandwiches. The South Dakota Department of Revenue calls this Sunday privilege. We call it your guarantee that you can at least find a snack or a meal at a bar or pub on Sunday. Remember that the drinking age in South Dakota, as in the rest of the country, is 21. Expect to be carded anywhere, but especially in Deadwood. We can't guarantee that you'll be able to buy wine or liquor in a package store on Sunday or certain holidays, because those regulations vary from town to town. And our source at the revenue department tells us hard liquor can neither be sold nor served anywhere in South Dakota on Memorial Day or Christmas. Keep in mind that the South Dakota Highway Patrol doesn't take kindly to drunk drivers, and penalties can be aggressive. Checkpoints in Rapid City and outside Deadwood are common.

As of November 2010, smoking has been outlawed in virtually all public places in South Dakota, including bars, restaurants, liquor stores, and video lottery establishments. The few exceptions are found at tobacco shops and cigar bars in Sioux Falls and Deadwood. Although video lottery machines (see the Gaming & Casinos chapter) remain controversial, you'll find machines in just about any establishment where you can buy a drink. Because they're so prevalent, we've noted those places that don't have them.

We've handled closing time the same way—unless otherwise noted, it's 2 a.m. You also can assume a business is open seven days a week unless we've mentioned that it's closed on certain days. Most bars and pubs offer discounted drinks during a late-afternoon or early evening weekday happy hour, so we've noted only the exceptions or those that serve food as an accompaniment. And because so few of our bars and pubs require a cover charge, we tell you those that do.

BARS, LOUNGES, & PUBS

At the following establishments you'll experience our unique Black Hills culture and meet interesting residents. A few of these places may be a bit rough around the edges—they're not exactly Planet Hollywood. But all the bars listed here are great places to mingle with locals. If you're a fan of bars as cultural icons, you'll find the following a fascinating addition to your Black Hills adventure.

Northern Hills

B&B LOUNGE AND BACK PORCH
703 North Main St., Spearfish
(605) 642-8292, (605) 642-2134
www.backporchbar.com
A popular nightspot for dancing and listening to rock 'n' roll music by local bands and DJs, the B&B boasts a clientele whose ages generally range from 21 to 50-something. It has a full bar and serves snacks and fried foods. When you get tired of dancing, you can play pool.

FLANAGAN'S IRISH PUB
729 7th St., Spearfish
(605) 722-3526
www.flanagansirishpub.us

Big dark beams and the atmosphere of an Irish pub give this place a wonderful feel. Stop in for a pasty and a pint, with 16 different lagers, ales, and stouts on tap. Outdoor seating in summer and live music every weekend. Open at 4 p.m. seven days a week.

MOONSHINE GULCH SALOON
FR 231, Rochford
No telephone
The Moonshine Gulch is a local secret—a remote mountain bar with no telephone, a handful of electric lights, and genuine western character. This is a real saloon—a bit wacky, pretty funky, and gloriously idiosyncratic. The rustic old building has a wooden front porch where you can lounge on a bench and view the tiny town of Rochford, pretending you've gone back in time to its decades-ago mining days. Inside there's simply too much to look at: wildlife trophies, hundreds of hats, antiques, junk everywhere, and stuff covering the walls in a visual extravaganza. Even the restrooms have quotable quotations on their walls. The food is great—homemade fries, burgers, and sandwiches—and you can have a brew with your meal. You won't find video lottery here, but you will find real locals enjoying real life, deep in the Black Hills. Moonshine Gulch is on the main road through Rochford, a town so small that—if you find it—you can't miss this saloon: It's the main attraction.

i Back in the good ol' days, state law prohibited the buying or serving of spirits on election day. Sometime before 1971, lawmakers changed their minds. Perhaps they were hoping for a different outcome at the ballot box!

✳OLD STYLE SALOON NO. 10
657 Main St., Deadwood
(605) 578-3346, (800) 952-9398
www.saloon10.com

Local color is an understatement at the Saloon No. 10, a place tagged as the only museum in the world with a bar. A quick look around at the cluttered interior and you'll agree. The decor is much the same as it was in the early 1900s, with sawdust on the floor, western artifacts all around, and pictures of Deadwood's good, bad, and ugly surrounding you anywhere you sit. One face you're sure to see is that of Wild Bill Hickok, who in 1876 sat in the wrong chair at the Saloon No. 10 and played his last game of poker before getting shot from behind. You can watch this scene if you'd like—from Memorial Day through mid-Sept, the shooting of Wild Bill is reenacted daily at the bar.

Of course, there's plenty of gambling at the Old Style, and you're sure to have better luck than Wild Bill on that fateful day. The blackjack and poker tables have a room all to themselves, and there are also slot machines. With all that history under their belt, people at the Saloon No. 10 know how to entertain. Enjoy service by saloon girls in lacy period costumes or dance each weekend to a live band. If you get hungry, just step upstairs to the classy but casual Deadwood Social Club for some fine northern Italian dining and exceptional wine (read more about the Social Club in the Restaurants chapter). There's also the Charlie Utter Theatre, which hosts live shows (many related to Deadwood's history) throughout the year. Call the Saloon No. 10 and ask for theater show information.

SANFORD'S GRUB & PUB
545 West Jackson Blvd., Spearfish
(605) 642-3204, (605) 721-1463
www.thegrubandpub.com

Sanford's decorative theme is "junkyard chic." This charming place is full of antiques, old Coke machines, aging bicycles suspended from the ceiling, and memorabilia from nearby Black Hills State University. It opens at 11 a.m. for lunch and closes at 10 p.m., seven days a week in the summer. Call for winter hours. You'll want to read more about Sanford's menu in the Restaurants chapter, but you'll find foods in jumbo portions, half-pound burgers, crawfish, barbecue, pasta, steaks, and seafood—and nightly dinner specials. Choose from among more than 99 beers and 20 taps. This pub offers hard liquor, beer, and wine. For recreation, after putting away all that food and drink, you can play pinball or pool, or watch one of the 25 televisions. A second location is in Rapid City at 306 7th St. (605-721-1463).

Central Hills

BRASS RAIL LOUNGE
624 St. Joseph St., Rapid City
(605) 341-1768

This tiny bar might be in the middle of Rapid City's bustling downtown, but it's fairly quiet, very down to earth, and the sort of place where—if you showed up often enough—everyone would indeed know your name. It's so casual, in fact, that it may close before 2 a.m. if business is slow. The jukebox has a good selection of tunes, and electronic dartboards stand along one wall. You won't find a pool table, live music, or meals (just sandwiches, pizzas, and snacks). Instead, you will find interesting Rapid City residents and friendly bartenders. The sign over the bar that reads SALOON No. 8 refers to the fact that the Brass Rail holds the eighth liquor license issued in South Dakota after Prohibition, making it one of the oldest bars in Rapid City.

i South Dakota's legal blood-alcohol limit is 0.08—the approximate result of one drink per hour. If a law enforcement officer suspects you're driving under the influence of alcohol, you'll be asked to submit to a breath analysis. If you refuse and are arrested for DWI, your driver's license will be confiscated, and if the officer should smell alcohol on your breath, you may be jailed.

CHEERS LOUNGE AND CASINO
Grand Gateway Hotel
1721 North Lacrosse St., Rapid City
(605) 342-2273, (800) 2RAMADA
www.grandgatewayhotel.com/
dining.php

This hotel bar is popular with locals, businesspeople, hotel guests, and travelers. It's a relaxed place to hang out, whether you're staying at the hotel or elsewhere. Snack foods are always served at happy hour. Karaoke Mon through Sat starting at 9 p.m. The bar serves wines a good selection of wines as well as liquor and a dozen beers on tap. In the winter Cheers may close earlier than 2 a.m.

445 LOUNGE AT THE RADISSON HOTEL
445 Mount Rushmore Rd., Rapid City
(605) 348-8300
www.hotelrapidcity.com/dining.htm

Nearly 70 martinis are on the menu at this fashionable downtown venue that caters to the generation that values what they do after work as much as during work. A great hang-out lounge. You'll relax on ultra-modern sofas while you watch the HD TVs, and

from 5 to 7 p.m. weekdays, the happy hour attracts a good show of downtown businesspeople. Live bands provide entertainment on weekends, one of the lone bars in town to do so. The loud and boisterous patrons of the bar often mix with the quiet and dressy diners headed for the hotel's restaurant, Enigma, in the lobby, which separates the two very different venues. Read more about Enigma in the Restaurants chapter.

FIREHOUSE BREWING COMPANY
610 Main St., Rapid City
(605) 348-1915
http://firehousebrewing.com

The Firehouse—which occupies the historic 1915 Rapid City firehouse building—has something for everyone. The restaurant welcomes families with its cuisine (see the Restaurants chapter). Both the rectangular bar and the second-floor mezzanine are comfortable places to relax and watch the crowd. In the summer the big, partially covered patio is a perfect place to eat and listen to the bands that play on its stage. It even has overhead radiant heaters for chilly nights.

The Firehouse brews its own terrific beer on the premises. Several recipes are rotated, and you'll find five to six on tap at any time, ranging from Wilderness Wheat (a light beer served with lemon) to Smokejumper Stout (a dark, coffeelike, and heavy-bodied brew).

PADDY O'NEILL'S PUB & CASINO
523 6th St., Rapid City
(605) 342-1210, (800) 888-2539

This classy pub is part of the Alex Johnson Hotel and is named for the hotel's first guest, who registered on July 1, 1928. Paddy's clientele includes businesspeople and hotel guests, but the live music by local

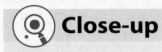 **Close-up**

Carry A. Nation

The most famous and feared leader of the temperance movement, hatchet-wielding Carry Nation, twice visited the Black Hills. Born Carrie Amelia Moore, she married Rev. David Nation and legally changed her name to **Carry A. Nation,** to better express her iron-willed commitment to ending the use of alcohol as well as its kindred sins, smoking and gambling. Many saloons and gambling halls came under her attack, and she was not averse to using rocks, canes, iron rods, and anything else she could get her hands on to break bottles, destroy furniture, and physically punish the sinners.

Rapid City storyteller Carl Leedy, in his book *Golden Days in the Black Hills,* says that Carry visited Rapid City in 1905 but refrained from breaking any saloon windows. However, he tells that she jerked a pipe away from a smoker and angrily stomped on it, and during her speech to the crowd she addressed more smokers at the back of the auditorium. "You fellows down there by the door," she shouted, "if the Good Lord had intended you to smoke he would have turned your noses up the other way, for a smoke stack."

In 1910 Carry visited Sturgis. Apparently, passionate activism agreed with her. "Carrie [sic] is a pretty spry old lady for her age [she was 64] and moved around like a young girl at the age of 16," the *Sturgis Weekly Record* reported. Four brave male community leaders accompanied her to nearby Fort Meade for a visit, without telling her that two of them—between whom she was seated—were Sturgis saloon keepers. Later, the *Weekly Record* stated, "When informed, she took the joke good naturedly and said it made no difference, that the devil could not be routed until you got next to him."

bands—presented on Wednesday through Saturday nights—draws a younger, enthusiastic crowd. The pub is small and the music tends to be a bit loud, so don't count on intimate conversation or dancing on live-music nights. Paddy's patrons can enjoy snacks and dinners (from the adjacent Landmark Restaurant's menu); yards and half yards of any tap beer; Guinness Stout on tap and one of the largest selections of imported beers in the area; and smallbatch bourbons. You'll find the Alex Johnson Hotel in the Accommodations chapter.

i In 2006 South Dakota passed a law that will allow patrons to ride their horse under the influence of alcohol. As long as the horse isn't drinking, everything should be fine!

SILVER DOLLAR SALOON
24090 US 385 South, Hill City
(605) 574-4417
www.silverdollarsaloon.com
Newly remodeled from top to bottom, this is where the locals tend to hang out. Barn boards and rough-hewn lumber flank the walls, and bands every other weekend get

the toe tapping. For late-night pub fare (they serve until closing at 2 a.m.), diners sample a range of appetizers (homemade Funky Chicken pizza is popular) or steaks, fish, and chicken dinners. There's a full bar and a brand new deck out back, complete with picnic tables and a firepit. Open every day except Easter.

Southern Hills

AJ'S ORE CAR SALOON
537 Mount Rushmore Rd., Custer
(605) 673-3051
This small, slightly cramped bar seems like a good place to make friends, and apparently Australians think so, too. According to the owner/bartender, A.J.'s and Crazy Horse Memorial are the only two Custer listings in a US travel guide published Down Under. (He got his hearsay information from an Aussie patron who made it a point to stop in one summer.) This is a strictly casual place where 30-somethings sit and shoot the breeze while downing a few beers of the domestic variety. Happy hour, which occurs between 11 a.m. and noon on Sun in addition to weekday evenings, could be a good time to study the shelves full of slow-pitch softball trophies garnered by teams the saloon has sponsored. Having done that, you're ready to turn to the pool table, listen to the stereo, or watch sports on TV. During the summer you can sip a brew or play horseshoes in the beer garden out back. If you're looking for a pool tournament or other games, check with the bartender for the schedule.

FRONTIER BAR & GRILL
12197 US 16 West, Custer
(605) 673-8870
www.visitcuster.com/aroundtown/ restaurants/#2

The Frontier has a band once a month all year. You might dance to rock, blues, or country, depending on the night. All told, the bar is pretty quiet, though. The Frontier offers appetizers from fried gizzards to mini-tacos, and a burgers and chicken-strips menu for those wanting a meal. Check out the rib special on Thursday, the all-you-can-eat fish on Friday, and steak night on Sunday. In addition, the Frontier hosts happy hour every weeknight. This is a spacious place with a big dance floor and the entire interior was recently remodeled.

THE GOLD PAN SALOON
508 Mount Rushmore Rd., Custer
(605) 673-8850
The swinging doors and the sawdust on the floor say "Old West." The antlers, bovine skull, and cattle horns over the bar—not to mention the framed ammunition display—say "hunters' hangout." The saloon has a full bar and also offers pool tables. Happy hour is from 5:30 to 7 p.m. Mon through Fri. Though some distance from Sturgis in the Northern Hills, the Gold Pan is a popular stop for visitors to the Sturgis Rally & Races in Aug (see the Annual Events & Festivals chapter).

COFFEEHOUSES

There's nothing like watching the world go by over the rim of a steaming cup of espresso, latte, or cappuccino. You don't necessarily have to wait until nighttime either. The coffeehouses listed here open in the early morning.

Northern Hills

COMMON GROUNDS
135 East Hudson St., Spearfish
(605) 642-9066

A classy, comfortable coffeehouse in a beautiful building in Spearfish, Common Grounds entertains a mixed crowd of young people, Black Hills State University students and faculty, retired folks, and visitors. It serves great specialty coffees (including local Dark Canyon Coffee Company's blends) as well as bagels, muffins, sandwiches, soups, cookies, and biscotti, and it offers a deli bar. A popular community gathering place, Common Grounds hosts poetry readings, live music performances, and open-mic nights. It's open 7 a.m. to 7 p.m. Mon through Fri, 6 a.m. to 6 p.m. Sat and 6 a.m. to 5 p.m. on Sun.

TWO PINES ESPRESSO & GIFT SHOP
304 Main St., Spearfish
(605) 717-3636
This convenient quaint-little-house-turned-coffee-shop touts soup and sandwiches at lunch, and an outdoor garden area for dining in-season. Try the homemade desserts and pastries, prepared by owners John and Phyllis Hart, or browse the selection of gift items ranging from coffee cups and metal art to stunning photography by local artists. Drive-up service available.

NIGHTCLUBS

If there's a common element among the most popular nightlife venues in the Black Hills, it's music, whether it's boot-scootin' country or good old rock 'n' roll. If you want plenty of room for letting loose and busting a move, however, the following nightclubs are exactly what you're looking for. They all have dance floors, of course, and play music of almost any genre.

Central Hills

SPORTS ROCK AND BUDD UGLYS
321 7th St., Rapid City
(605) 388-3232
If you go into Sports Rock when it opens at 11 a.m., the place doesn't seem different from any other bar. There are spots to sit and enjoy your drink, pool tables, foosball, video lottery, and some arcade games. Hang around until 8 p.m. on Friday and Saturday nights, though, and everything will change. That's when the DJ starts to play upstairs at Budd Uglys and the dance floor fills up with a crowd ranging in age from 21 to 55. Budd Uglys plays a wide range of dance music, including classic rock and '80s and '90s music. To make dancing even more fun, the bar offers different drink specials every night. When you're hungry, you can just go downstairs to Sports Rock for some excellent oven-cooked pizza.

ROBBINSDALE LOUNGE
803 East St. Patrick St., Rapid City
(605) 342-7271
Robbinsdale Lounge promotes itself as Rapid City's music showcase. Live bands perform here Thurs, Fri, and Sat nights. The music begins at 8:30 p.m., but the lounge's 300 seats start filling up much earlier as patrons settle in with a cocktail or a beer. Two pool tables also help pass the time until the band starts playing. On Wed and Fri the bar treats its customers to snacks during happy hour. Other nights, snacks are served. A more substantial meal of burgers, hot dogs, and the like is available from the cafe in the attached bowling alley, and you can order right at the bar. Customers get to show case their own vocal cords when karaoke opens at 8:30 p.m. on Sun, Tues, and Wed. The lounge opens at 10 a.m. Mon through Fri, 9 a.m. on Sat, and 1 p.m. on Sun.

Nineteenth-Century Nightlife

On May 15, 1885, the *Black Hills Journal* reported on a meeting of Methodist ministers in Deadwood. Apparently the clergy members were concerned about nightlife in the region, and the discussion centered on which of two evils they considered to be the worse—the roller rink or the dance. Some claimed the rink at least took sinners away from the saloons, but the *Black Hills Journal* said Reverend Bartholomew insisted that "if he had a daughter old enough to go into society, he wouldn't want her associating in the rink with those who, but for the rink, would be in the saloon." Another preacher proclaimed, "The devil invented dancing when he was young. The roller rink was the product of his maturer skill, as a means of bringing the fallen elements into the midst of good society." If these reverend gentlemen came back to experience today's Black Hills nightlife, they wouldn't have to worry much about roller rinks, but we do wonder what they would think of video lottery.

TEDDY'S (FORMERLY WOODY'S AND THE BOOT)
826 Main St., Rapid City
(605) 343-1931
www.teddyssportsgrill.com
Teddy's is all about high-energy dancing and a great sports bar, and the staff pulls out all the stops to get the crowd moving. The bar is young and so is its crowd—ages range from 22 to 40. It's open every day, 3 p.m. to 2 a.m. Mon through Fri, 10 a.m. to 2 a.m. Sat and Sun. The sound system matches the energy level of the crowd, and a light show and fog amplify the whole experience. You'll hear mostly Top 40 rock and dance music. When the dancing wears you down, you can make your way through the crowd to the full bar, grab a drink, and enjoy everything else Teddy's has to offer, including a casino, pool tables, dartboards, mechanical golf, and other arcade games. Teddy's offers some munchies as well as a full menu. Check out the burgers and nachos.

SPORTS BARS

These places seem to be in competition over the number of televisions they can pack into their premises, and the benefit for you is that you can watch several favorite sporting events at once.

Northern Hills

DIAMOND LIL'S SPORTS BAR
Midnight Star
677 Main St., Deadwood
(605) 578-1555, (800) 999-6482
Televisions are all over the place here, broadcasting your favorite sports. If you get tired of watching, take a look instead at owner Kevin Costner's movie costumes and photographs on display. Barring that, you can always eat. Here you'll find sandwiches, appetizers, steaks, and other hot foods as well as video games and the popular National Trivia Network. Lil's is open every day from 11 a.m. to 10 p.m.

*OGGIE'S SPORTS BAR & EMPORIUM
The Lodge at Deadwood
100 Pine Crest, Deadwood
(605) 584-4800, (866) 290-2403
www.deadwoodlodge.com

For food, fun, fine spirits, friendly bartenders and a dozen flatscreens, Oggie's is the place to be. This spacious sports bar features bar stools, comfortable booths and high-top tables, as well as some of the best bar food we've consumed. (Insider's Tip: Sample the World Series pizza, a bold barbecued chicken delight, or order the mammoth burgers, or the buffalo meatloaf that's out of this world.)

THE STADIUM SPORTS GRILL
818 5th Ave., Belle Fourche
(605) 723-9521

This establishment gets quite a variety of customers: families, locals, and tourists. The Stadium in Belle Fourche opens at 11 a.m. for lunch and stays open until 2 a.m., although it closes a bit earlier in the winter. It has no fewer than 16 televisions, a pool table, pinball machines, dartboards, and a state-of-the-art ventilation system that whisks away cigarette and cigar smoke. The Stadium is a great place to eat (the kitchen closes at 11 p.m.), offering burgers, sandwiches, seafood, and salads, but it is best known for the specialty of the house: Stadium Beef Tips, once enthusiastically extolled by none other than the *Chicago Tribune* and the *Houston Chronicle*.

Although the Stadium in Spearfish (744 Main St., 605-642-9521) is a sports bar, it's also a family place and offers a full menu of good food served in large portions. After 5 p.m. it attracts a crowd of businesspeople; the college crowd arrives later. You can play pool, darts, video games, and the jukebox,

or watch the 13 televisions, including one large-screen TV. The Stadium in Spearfish also provides interactive fun via the satellite broadcast National Trivia Network, which is free and very popular with the bar's clientele. There's more about both Stadiums in the Restaurants chapter.

Central Hills

KELLY'S SPORTS LOUNGE
825 Jackson Blvd., Rapid City
(605) 348-1213

Satellite-style viewing of sports is the main event here—TVs are everywhere. You'll also find five pool tables, electronic darts, and other arcade games. The most popular game at Kelly's is Golden Tee, a multiplayer golf video game that's sprung up at many sports bars in the past few years. There's a full bar, and the kitchen cooks up burgers, steaks, prime rib (Wednesday only), wings, and chicken strips for a diverse crowd that ranges in age from 21 to 101.

SHOOTERS RESTAURANT
  & SPORTS BAR
2424 West Main St., Rapid City
(605) 348-3348

Shooters has more of a restaurant atmosphere, but the regulars here really love football, and a sizable crowd consistently gathers to watch professional and college games on the TVs throughout the establishment. There are a few video lottery machines in a side room. Hours are earlier than standard bar time; it's open Mon through Thurs 11 a.m. to 11 p.m., Fri and Sat 11 a.m. to midnight, and Sun 11 a.m. to 9 p.m. The setting leans toward upscale, the attitude is mellow, and the crowd is laid-back. Since it's a restaurant, everyone (from kids to seniors) is welcome, but the bar section is separate from where families sit to eat.

Shooters has a full bar and a menu that includes choice Black Angus steaks. The most famous item on the menu, however, is the outstanding hot wings. Shooters consistently wins local awards for them. Visitors are encouraged to challenge the cook to make the wings as hot as possible, but such challenges are often followed by several pitchers of ice water. Of course, the wings come in mild, medium, hot, and thermonuclear for those who want the standard range of hot wings. Read more about the food offered at Shooters in the Restaurants chapter.

VALLEY SPORTS BAR & GRILL
1865 South Valley Dr., Rapid City
(605) 343-2528
Sixteen televisions, pool tables, and darts, and a separate room for video lottery players make this establishment a favorite of sports bar enthusiasts. Sit at the big, dark-wood bar and have a brew or munch one of the popular half-pound burgers. A full menu is served seven days a week, and on Wednesday you can order sirloin steak tips, either grilled or breaded. Music is often Fri and Sat nights.

GAMING & CASINOS

When Deadwood was young, saloons were the mainstay of the town. Thousands of prospectors—many unsuccessful and disheartened—needed entertainment to lift their spirits. Spirits, in fact, were the elixirs to which many of these miners turned. But the bar and its stock of liquor was only one part of the saloon. Upstairs, ladies of the evening held court, and at the back of the building, there were the card tables.

Professional gamblers quickly followed the merchants and bar owners, hoping to play the precious metals right out of the miners' hands. In fact, if one thing bound Deadwood's early residents together, it was lust for gold: Some mined it, some traded for it, and others shuffled for it. Practiced card players could indeed walk away from a table with a profit if they stayed sober, didn't challenge other professionals, and understood the odds. Of course, the inexperienced and less clever didn't fare so well, often losing everything to an unlucky turn of a card.

Men sometimes gambled away all their money in one poker game, leaving their families destitute and struggling. It's said that one fed-up wife cured her husband's gambling problem when she stalked into the saloon (it was unheard of that a proper lady would enter such a place), raked all the money on the table into her apron, and stalked back out, followed by her humiliated husband. The woman certainly remedied her husband's compulsive gambling, if only because no one would ever play cards with him again.

OVERVIEW

When the founding fathers in the Dakota Territory were trying hard to create a state in 1889, the open gambling going on in the wild town of Deadwood was a source of embarrassment to them. A prohibition against gambling was written into the constitution of the new state of South Dakota, but it continued, although most often in the back rooms of saloons. Even Prohibition barely crimped Deadwood's style.

Slot machines arrived in the late 1930s. The one-armed bandits, technically prohibited by law, were profitable and popular. In 1947, however, the state attorney general organized a surprise raid on the gambling establishments in Deadwood. All the gambling equipment was seized and, after the trials were over, hauled to the local dump and burned. That event ended open gambling in town for many years, although, true to tradition, it continued in a few back rooms. The other back rooms were used for prostitution, which wasn't shut down until 1980.

But running both industries underground and (mostly) out of business did little to improve the economy of the town. With the closure of public gambling came the slow demise of Deadwood; the raids on prostitution in 1980 only hastened it (longtime residents will tell you that hunting season has never been the same since the brothels closed). The once-proud Victorian buildings on Main Street crumbled; those that weren't abandoned were occupied by businesses that didn't make enough of a profit to maintain them. This and other factors led to the fires of the 1980s, blazes which took as victims the Ranger Bar and Brothel, the Homestake Opera House, the oldest part of Deadwood Elementary School, and the Syndicate Building. But the more the town decayed, the more proactive residents became, until they bravely forwarded a progressive idea in the late 1980s: Legalize gambling, then take a massive percentage of the profits to use for historic preservation and visitor advertising.

Of course, this meant altering the state constitution. Fortunately for Deadwood, the lure of restoration and the idea of increasing visitors to the state was enough for the conservative voters of South Dakota. On November 1, 1989, at high noon and marked by ceremonial gunshots, Deadwood officially became the third place in the nation to legalize gambling (after Nevada and Atlantic City). In the years since, Deadwood has been returned to the glory of its golden Victorian Age, thanks entirely to this now highly regulated and strictly monitored industry.

Some two million enthusiasts now gamble in Deadwood each year, and since 1989 they have wagered more than $12.7 billion (of that, $11.5 billion was won by gamblers). From this staggering amount, many millions have funded grants and low-interest loans to restore historic buildings and landmarks, both public and private. The scale of this restoration—both in terms of funds and

number of buildings—makes Deadwood one of the largest ongoing historic preservation projects in the nation.

Gambling funds have been used to improve Deadwood's infrastructure and to repair and renovate the Adams Museum, Days of '76 rodeo grounds, the town's Carnegie Library, Mount Moriah Cemetery, Deadwood Recreation Center, and historic Main Street. Such renovations have in turn increased the wage scale and provided jobs in city and county government as well as in private businesses. In fact, there are far more jobs in Deadwood than there are residents. Though the precise figures vary from year to year, reports consistently show about 1,800 gaming-related jobs in the city. Population estimates, however, show that Deadwood has only 1,380 inhabitants.

Although modern Deadwood's gaming is somewhat controversial, and some citizens still believe the focus on gaming was an unfortunate choice, no one can argue with the positive changes in the town and the amazing improvements to both its appearance and economic outlook.

Today's Deadwood offers limited-stakes gaming, which means the maximum bet is $100 per blackjack hand, poker bet, or slot machine play. About 80 gaming establishments—few business names include the word casino—offer live poker, blackjack, Let It Ride, three-card poker, and Rainbow 21 card games, progressive and other slot machines, and video lottery machines. Most have nickel, quarter, and dollar slot machines; you may even find some dime and penny machines. Many businesses also have special events such as slot tournaments and leagues, car giveaways, cash drawings, ladies' nights, and happy hours; some offer gaming clubs for frequent visitors. Many have restaurants, bars, adjacent motel or hotel accommodations, or offer travel packages with discounts and incentives. There are several special events in Deadwood each month, ranging from a Professional Rodeo Cowboys Association rodeo and Christmas follies concert to a classic car show and two-day outdoor music festival with national recording artists. Many casinos and hotels anticipate these citywide events with their own parties or package deals; call the business and see the Annual Events & Festivals chapter for more information.

Deadwood gaming establishments line historic Main Street, but a few are on nearby Sherman Street, too. You'll find slot machines where you never expected to see them: the VFW, and even the Super 8 Motel. A walk down Main Street is nothing like a walk down the Strip in Las Vegas. Perhaps low stakes also means low-key, because you won't see building-size neon signs or chorus lines of dancing showgirls, and no football-field-size casinos or skyscraping hotels. We'd be surprised, in fact, if you heard a police car siren. As you stroll down the sidewalks that line the brick-paved streets and past the buildings restored to their former glory, you'll see gamblers hurrying from door to door. Some stop to browse in the shops, but most are looking for that slot machine with their name on it, the one that calls seductively, "You're a winner if you put just one more quarter in the slot."

Elsewhere in the Black Hills, South Dakota's state-operated video lottery—the machines that offer poker, keno, blackjack, and other electronic games—can be found in both casinos and other types of businesses in most Hills towns. In the past, video lottery has been highly controversial and has been the focus of repeal efforts in the state

legislature and at the ballot box, but the state has come to depend on the revenues from thousands of video lottery machines. Video lottery is purported to be one of the most addictive forms of gambling. A study published in the *South Dakota Medical Journal* reported that players who don't have problems with other types of gambling, and who don't display tendencies toward gambling addictions, tend to have problems with video lottery.

For this and other reasons, including government dependence on the revenue, some state legislators believe it was a mistake to institute video lottery, which was legalized in 1989. Replacing that revenue (which includes a 50 percent take on the machine's winnings, plus licensing fees and gaming taxes) will be difficult, however, especially since the most likely replacement would be a sales or income tax, an alternative that is unpopular with voters. Video lottery also generates income for the business owners and communities offering it, and they are understandably less than enthusiastic about losing that source of revenue.

Consequently, you can still play the machines, which you'll find in restaurants, bars, hotel and motel lounges, and convenience stores in addition to casinos and gaming establishments.

For fans of lottos—the kind played with paper tickets instead of electronic machines—the state offers several options. There's a Cash for Life game and a Wild Card game. One of the most popular is the South Dakota Powerball game; its large jackpots come from a pool of bets placed in several states. Several kinds of instant-win scratch tickets are available, too. You'll find them for sale at most convenience stores.

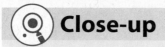

Close-up

Deadwood Booms on the Small Screen

The rough-and-tumble ways of the Old West have been portrayed in Hollywood for decades. Legends such as John Wayne, decked out in leather chaps, leather vest, and cowboy hat while toting a shiny revolver, have been permanently embedded in our imaginations. Unfortunately, these westerns have been dolled up and typically aren't the best representation of how difficult and brash life in the Old West truly was.

In the spring of 2004, the HBO cable television network debuted a rough and realistic portrayal of a small mining encampment in western South Dakota that goes by the name of Deadwood. The show began in the early years of the encampment when nearly 10,000 miners, mule skinners, and madams rushed to the gold-filled gulch in hopes of striking it rich. Whiskey was purchased with gold dust, disputes were settled with six-guns, and homes were constructed with canvas and businesses with wood. Life in those times, in that town, was difficult and, at times, deadly.

Of course, not all viewers were pleased with the show. Some called it "the *Sopranos* with six-guns," while others were taken aback by the harsh nature of some of its content—which included graphic nudity, violence, and foul language. Nonetheless, people in the small real-life Black Hills community of 1,380 were eager to strengthen ties with the program and welcomed its actors to town on several occasions.

Even three years after the series concluded,, its namesake is still reaping the rewards. According to community leaders, Deadwood had not seen that kind of boom since the gold rush that created it 130 years ago. Thanks largely to the success of the original drama, which was also shown in a half-dozen foreign countries, thousands of visitors flocked to Deadwood not only to enjoy the shopping, gambling, and scenic beauty of the Black Hills, but also to see where legends—now household names thanks largely to HBO—lived and died.

The few bingo parlors in the Hills are run by private organizations; they are listed in the Yellow Pages under Bingo Games.

Although Black Hills gaming definitely isn't Las Vegas, fans of gaming will find a great variety of lotteries, games, machines, and events (albeit low stake and mild mannered) from which to choose. Gaming is part of both the tourism and local entertainment scenes in the Black Hills and generates income for many. However, if gaming becomes a problem, you'll find the Gamblers Anonymous hotline listed in a tip in this chapter.

DEADWOOD GAMING ESTABLISHMENTS

Deadwood still has an old-time, Old West flavor. It revels in its rich history and has mined its past to create a modern-day gold rush. Enter a casino and you'll hear the metallic clinking and clanking of coins pouring out of slot machines though most have switched to paper ticket redemption systems. Twinkling lights and neon illuminate the interiors of beautifully decorated businesses, music plays over the loudspeakers, the smell of good food is in the air, and both players and employees are relaxed and friendly. Many casinos boast handsome wood trim, elegant bars, and enticing light and color, and their pleasant ambience is enhanced by the lively electronic music of gaming devices. Although we can't list all the Deadwood casinos in this chapter, here are several you may want to visit.

BULLOCK HOTEL
633 Main St., Deadwood
(605) 578-1745, (800) 336-1876
www.heartofdeadwood.com
The historic Bullock has been beautifully redecorated to exceed its original elegance, and we've written about the charming features of the hotel in the Accommodations chapter. The first floor casino has huge windows, gorgeous chandeliers, and a wide staircase that, from the bottom, seems to go up forever. It's decorated with lovely wainscoting and wallpaper, and wicker and Victorian furniture. You can eat in Bully's Restaurant, have a drink in the bar, and play the many slot machines.

CADILLAC JACK'S GAMING RESORT
360 Main St., Deadwood
(605) 578-1500, (866) 332-3966
www.cadillacjackscasino.com
About a half mile north of Deadwood's core historic district sits Cadillac Jack's. The facade makes the complex appear to be a block of a half-dozen historic brick buildings like the ones you might find farther up on Main Street; the interior, however, is one large gaming floor with slot machines, blackjack, and live poker tables. Like many of the larger casinos, Cadillac Jack's offers regular drawings, contests, and giveaways. The resort's

distinguishing features include its convention facilities, which few other hotels or casinos in Deadwood can match, and a small, sports bar on the main floor.

FIRST GOLD HOTEL & GAMING
270 Main St., Deadwood
(605) 578-9777, (800) 274-1876
www.firstgold.com
South Dakota's video lottery machines reward players with quietly printed paper tickets in lieu of cold, hard cash, a growing trend in these parts. Redeem the tickets at the establishment's counter, bar, or cash register, where the clerk or bartender will then hand over your winnings, in bills or coins. First Gold is located out where it's quieter on Lower Main Street, on the northern edge of town. ATV and pickup giveaways are often in progress inside this big building, and you can stay in the adjacent rooms and dine in the Horseshoe Restaurant on the premises. Up the hill several yards is the Terrace Hotel and Casino. Its commanding views of Deadwood Gulch and White Rocks (a mountain peak on the edge of town with bare granite spires on the summit) are among the best in town. More than half of the casino rooms at the First Gold are now smoke-free.

FOUR ACES
531 Main St., Deadwood
(605) 578-2323
www.fouracescasino.org
The Four Aces boasts lovely floral carpeting, cherry-stained woodwork, swanky chandeliers recessed into the high ceilings, and elegantly tall windows. It has a big, beautiful bar and its own restaurant. Here you can play blackjack, three-card poker, and many slot and video lottery machines.

GOLD DUST GAMING AND ENTERTAINMENT COMPLEX

688 Main St., Deadwood
(605) 578-2100, (800) 456-0533
www.golddustgaming.com

The Gold Dust is a classy place, but it lost some of its luster with several ownership changes in recent years. The floral pattern carpet is an eye-catching bright red. The walls are rose and glass, and the trim is polished brass. Small, cozy lounges are scattered throughout the complex, or you can have your drink on the upstairs balcony. If you're hungry after cranking a slot machine or studying a hand of cards, have a bite in the buffet restaurant. You can also wander over to the Gold Dust's Holiday Inn Express across the street, one of the newest structures in the core historic district. It was built in 1999 on top of a hole once occupied by the Syndicate Building, which was destroyed by fire in 1987—just after its 100th birthday. Officials say that had the December temperature been above zero, they would have lost the whole block. Ultimately the fire helped bring on legalized gambling, which in turn helped to fund the hotel's construction. Today, the only remnant of that tragic event is a large interpretive sign affixed to the yellow-brick facade near the hotel's front door.

MIDNIGHT STAR

677 Main St., Deadwood
(605) 578-1555, (800) 999-6482
www.themidnightstar.com

Actor and director Kevin Costner has said repeatedly that he has a fascination with the American West, especially the Dakotas and the Black Hills. It was that fascination which led him to star in and direct the Academy Award–winning movie *Dances with Wolves* in 1990, which was filmed primarily on the plains near Fort Pierre and in Spearfish Canyon west of Deadwood. That attraction also led him to restore Deadwood's Phoenix Building in 1991 and turn it into the Midnight Star, the tallest building on Main Street. Named for (and decorated to resemble) the saloon in Costner's 1985 *Silverado*, the establishment is lavishly adorned with etched glass, hardwood accents, plush carpet, a beautiful bar, a massive chandelier, and an imposing grand staircase with huge wooden banisters. There are dozens of slots on the main level and blackjack tables and a gift shop on the mezzanine. The second floor hosts Diamond Lil's Sports Bar (see the Nightlife chapter), while the third floor is home to Jakes, one of the best restaurants in the state (see the Restaurants chapter). Throughout the building you'll find costumes and props from some of Kevin's movies. A regular free shuttle service takes people up to Tatanka in summer (see the Attractions chapter).

i The South Dakota Commission on Gaming requires that all slot machines return at least 80 percent of the money inserted in them in the form of payouts. "Loose" slot machines return an even higher percentage, as an enticement to gamblers.

MINERAL PALACE HOTEL & GAMING

601 Main St., Deadwood
(605) 578-2036, (800) 847-2522
www.mineralpalace.com

Hotel rooms make this gaming business a perfect place to spend some time; you'll find more about them in the Accommodations chapter. The Mineral Palace has multiple gaming rooms you can stroll through, as well as small and large bars, and a cafe.

MISS KITTY'S GAMING EMPORIUM
647 Main St., Deadwood
(605) 578-1811
www.heartofdeadwood.com
Between 1876 and 1920 Deadwood was said to have had one of the largest populations of ethnic Chinese in the United States outside San Francisco. Although Chinatown was incorporated into Deadwood after the fire of 1879, it remained separate from the rest of town for several decades, even operating its own legal system and fire department. The Chinese community eventually left the Black Hills, but Miss Kitty's Gaming Emporium stands as a tribute to that part of Deadwood's history. You can play slots, blackjack, and poker inside Miss Kitty's, which occupies a number of small 1880s-era buildings just south of the original Chinatown. However, the establishment is best known for its Chinese and Mexican restaurants, the only such ethnic eateries in town (see the listings for Chinatown Cafe and the Double D bar and grill, serving outstanding Mexican food in the Restaurants chapter). The festivities surrounding Deadwood's annual Chinese New Year Celebration, which takes place in late winter, are centered here.

i The Gamblers Anonymous (Gam-Anon) hotline at (888) 781-4357 can provide a referral to a local chapter or meeting.

*OLD STYLE SALOON NO. 10
657 Main St., Deadwood
(605) 578-3346, (800) 952-9398
www.saloon10.com
Arguably the most famous establishment in Deadwood, Saloon No. 10 is the watering hole where gunslinger James Butler "Wild Bill" Hickok met his end. Shot in the back by Jack McCall in 1876, Wild Bill was playing poker when he fell over dead. The cards he was dealt also fell—revealing a pair of aces and eights, forever known as the Deadman's Hand. You'll find pictures of Wild Bill—along with photos of other famous patrons, including Calamity Jane, Poker Alice, and Potato Creek Johnny—hanging on the walls here, though they're a bit hard to find amid the other artifacts that line the walls. Once you walk the sawdust floors and gaze at the photos, game trophies, and Wild Bill's death chair hanging above you, you'll understand why they call this the only museum in the world with a bar. In fact, the bar is so crowded that come Christmas the tree has to be hung from the ceiling. Things are a bit more open at the adjacent Utter Place, named for longtime Wild Bill companion Colorado Charlie Utter. You'll find some slots here, but mostly single-deck blackjack and, of course, poker. If you happen to get a Deadman's Hand while playing here, don't get nervous; get out your wallet, because you've just won $250. The addition of the neighboring building doubled the size of the bar, added a smoke-free poker room, and gave Wild Bill Hickok more room to die, which he does five times a day to an appreciative audience.

SILVERADO GAMING ESTABLISHMENT & RESTAURANT
709 Main St., Deadwood
(605) 578-3670, (800) 584-7005
www.silveradocasino.com
Two cars a month are always up for grabs by lucky winners at the Silverado, which is appropriate because it occupies a building that was formerly an automobile showroom. This is a big, wide-open space with beautiful decor, customer-friendly staff, one of the largest restaurants in town, the better buffet,

and plenty of gaming action, both at tables and at machines.

TIN LIZZIE GAMING & GARDEN CAFÉ
555 Main St., Deadwood
(605) 578-1715, (800) 643-4490
www.tinlizzie.com
Seniors are the primary patrons here, and the Tin Lizzie works hard to get them. Visitors over age 60 get price breaks on everything from food to gaming tokens, and there are regular special events in their honor that usually feature free food and giveaways. The building is relatively small compared to other Main Street venues, though the owners have managed to pack in plenty of classic car memorabilia. There's a cafe and snack bar, as well as a small stage for occasional live entertainment. One of the more popular musical groups in Deadwood usually plays here. A tribute to the Beatles, the Abbey Road Band has a strong following in town, even among the younger crowd, and are consistently noted for their striking similarity (in sound and appearance) to the Fab Four.

THE BUFFALO-BODEGA COMPLEX
622 Main St., Deadwood
(605) 578-9993
www.buffalo-bodega.com
A century ago, the Bodega was a stage stop. But, the real action happened upstairs in the cribs where soiled doves entertained a succession of miners, mule skinners, and merchants. It's far tamer in the Bodega today with an upscale sports lounge and flat-screen TVs. But, at night, the neighboring Buffalo Saloon & Steakhouse, a substantial roadhouse with summer seating outdoors and in, can get rocking amid a festive atmosphere, great food and beverages, live music, and some of the funniest people in town. Just ask for Ole.

SHOPPING

For the folks who live in sparsely populated western South Dakota and northeastern Wyoming, the Black Hills probably look like shopping mecca. It's true that the stores and businesses do a good job of meeting the locals' material needs, and there's a lot of support for local commerce. At the same time, however, there's a limit to what a low-density area can support, and many locals head south to Denver or east to Minneapolis and the Mall of America when they can't get what they want here. So you won't find giant department stores with mind-boggling arrays of goods or streets lined with rows of specialty boutiques in the Hills. Unfortunately, you will find dozens of tacky gift stores peddling rubber tomahawks and plastic snow globes. But tucked between these tourist traps are small shops with an array of original and attractive items that you'd be hard-pressed to locate elsewhere—items that truly reflect the culture and history of the Black Hills. You'll discover these regional qualities mostly in American Indian and western art; there are more details about galleries in the Arts chapter. There are other Black Hills products to watch for, such as Black Hills Gold jewelry, items made from honey (a major South Dakota export), and custom cowboy hats, boots, and saddles. Specialty stores often keep limited hours, however, so be sure to call ahead.

ANTIQUES

If you like to browse among old things, you'll have ample opportunity at any number of places that hang out an ANTIQUES shingle. Many offer a jumble of items in raw, just-dug-out-of-the-barn condition, but other dealers are discriminating about their inventory and take pains to display their wares to best advantage.

Central Hills

ANTIQUES & ART
21424 Clover Place, Piedmont
(605) 347-5016
www.antiquesandart.com
There's a reason many of the western and Plains Indian items in this bursting-at-the-seams shop look like museum pieces: They

once were. Owners James and Peg Aplan spurn reproduction and modern artifacts, often buying museum collections in their quest for authentic Old West treasures and collectible guns. They even sell rare and out-of-print books on western Americana. There's hardly room to turn around in here, but each time you do you discover something delightful: remarkable photographs, eye-catching beadwork, stunning military uniforms, star-shaped sheriff's badges, well-worn stirrups, creaky saddles, fierce-looking branding irons, sturdy stone tools, an extraordinary Crow woman's dress decorated with elk teeth, exquisite dolls, and much more. Look up and you're likely to be startled by a mounted bison head sporting three hats. The store is open daily, so you can return as often as you like. To get there, take I-90 to exit 40.

ST. JOE ANTIQUES & GIFT MALL
615 St. Joseph St., Rapid City
(605) 341-1073
This massive downtown Rapid City fixture displays items from an eclectic array of dealers. On the bottom floor you might run across vintage Star Wars toys or comic books, while a search through the upper floor might yield weathered ranching tools or an alligator-skin purse. Of course, there is plenty of antique furniture, and much of it can be seen displayed in front of the glass windows that surround the main entry. The stock of merchandise is substantial, but it's well organized and less cluttered than in many of the smaller antiques stores you'll find in less-populated towns. You can drop by the antiques mall, which is across the street from the imposing Alex Johnson Hotel, any day of the week except Sun.

Southern Hills

SHAMAN GALLERY
405 North River St., Hot Springs
(605) 745-6602
www.shamangallery.com
Owner Linda Heath and her husband, manager Adam Heath, are justifiably proud of the Shaman Gallery, located right across from the town's waterfall in a two-story historic sandstone building. This new location has 4,000 square feet, making it the largest original gallery in the Dakotas. One transplanted California artisan said the displays were better than anything he had ever seen in California. Here you can find Native American artifacts, works by well-known Native American painters, a large collection

of western art, works by New York artists, illustration art from the 1940s and 1950s, and offerings by local artists and potters. Shaman Gallery is open each day in the summer from 10 a.m. to 6 p.m. and Mon through Sat from 10 a.m. to 5 p.m. in the winter.

BOOKSTORES

If you love books, you know how much they enrich your life. When you visit our bookstores, be sure to look over the titles of local and regional interest, especially those by local authors.

Central Hills

BORDERS BOOKS
2130 Haines Ave., Rapid City
(605) 394-5334, (800) 770-7811
www.borders.com
We don't generally list chains, but this bookstore is the place for lovers of books, coffee, magazines, music, and more, and frequently hosts Black Hills–area writers for book signings.

EVERYBODY'S BOOKSTORE
3321 West Main St., Rapid City
(605) 341-3224
Bargain-hunting bookworms can have a field day in this used-book store, which has "previously read" books, mostly in paperback editions, in just about any category you can name: arts and crafts, how-to, religion, history, romance, biography, travel, and literature. You'll find French, German, Spanish, and Norwegian titles. If you're looking for an out-of-print title and it's not on the shelves, the staff will conduct a search (ask about fees). The only new items regularly in stock are books of regional, Native American, and western interest, plus maps, including

topographic maps and globes. If you don't want to pay for your purchases, you might be able to trade for some of your old books. The store is closed on Sun.

Southern Hills

THE WILD BURRO BOOKSTORE
503 North River St., Hot Springs
(605) 745-7340
www.thewildburro.com
Featuring a small but select inventory, you're likely to be greeted by the owner's friendly golden labs on arrival at this warm and friendly bookstore. Open since 2001, you'll find bestsellers, award-winners, cookbooks, children's books, stationery, music, coffee, and gifts.

THE STORYTELLER
520 6th St., Rapid City
(605) 348-7242
Comic books rule at this storehouse of fantasy. Look for entertaining books, games, and other items with a sci-fi or comic-related focus plus nonsport trading cards and collections of old and new comic-book series. The clientele is mostly between the ages of 14 and 25, but it also includes college professors and doctors. You can shop at the Storyteller every day except Sun.

CHRISTMAS SHOP

This fun shop gets its own category. It's located in the Central Hills.

MISTLETOE RANCH
23835 US 385, Hill City
(605) 574-4197
www.misletoeranch.com
Who said you can't have Christmas every day of the year? You can if you visit Mistletoe

Ranch, where there are always more than 30 artificial trees decorated in different themes plus high-quality gifts, ornaments, and collectibles galore. The selection changes all the time, but expect any variety of traditional Saint Nicholas dolls, chubby fleece Santas, dancing reindeer, and porcelain villages, as well as all kinds of ornaments. The red plaid carpet, Christmas music, and sweet scents here could turn the grumpiest Scrooge into a right jolly old elf anytime of the year—he'd probably even want to play the antique pump organ (it really works). Believe it or not, co-owner Joan Davis said she never gets tired of Christmas, not since she stopped hearing carols in her sleep. The store, 3 miles northeast of Hill City, is open daily, and refreshments are served during open-house events each Sat and Sun Thanksgiving through Christmas.

i You can cut your own Christmas tree in the Black Hills National Forest by obtaining a $10 permit from any forest service office (see the Recreation chapter for a list of locations). You can cut up to five trees as long as you have a permit for each one. Choose from pine, spruce, or juniper.

CLOTHING

These shops feature custom western apparel and footwear.

Northern Hills

TREVINO'S LEATHERS
US 385, Deadwood
(605) 578-1271
www.trevinosleathers.com
Outside, it's a charming log cabin. Inside, it's black-leather heaven. Rhea (pronounced like

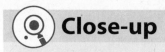 **Close-up**

Black Hills Gold and Silver

A few specks of shining gold were all it took to touch off a wild stampede to the Black Hills in 1876 (see the History chapter). The rush didn't last long—such phenomena seldom do—but a style of world-famous jewelry that dates from those turbulent days ensures that they will not soon be forgotten. Accounts vary about the origin of the yellow, green, and pink jewelry that is the signature of Black Hills Gold. Legend says the original grape-and-leaf pattern appeared to a French jeweler in a starvation-induced vision at the height of the gold rush; another variation says that early prospectors found grapes where they discovered gold. Yet another version has the motif originating in the California goldfields of 1849 and making its way east through other gold camps. We do know that Deadwood merchant S. T. Butler was making jewelry from **Black Hills Gold** here in 1878, but whether he created the design, or perhaps borrowed it from the ancient Romans, is unclear.

What matters is that the design endures today, and that Black Hills Gold is still being made by hand right here. Variations on the original pattern are the most popular, but local manufacturers are coming up with new ones all the time. They still use the lost-wax method, in which each piece is cast in a plaster mold made around a wax model. The wax is melted out and replaced by molten gold. The colored accents—leaves, grape clusters, and whatever else—are spot welded on, then "wriggled" to give them a frosted look, and finally engraved for intricate details. The different colors are made by alloying gold with copper, silver, and other metals in varying proportions; some outfits still make their own alloys.

You can see artisans handcrafting 10-, 12-, and 14-karat Black Hills Gold jewelry at several places around Rapid City. **Mount Rushmore Black Hills Gold**, 2707 Mount Rushmore Rd., (605) 343-7099, offers tours six times a day, Mon through Fri, during the summer and by request the rest of the year; call ahead to make arrangements. At **Stamper Black Hills Gold Jewelry Manufacturing Inc.**, 4 miles south of Rapid City on US 16, (605) 342-0751, and at **Landstrom Original Black Hills Gold Creations.**, 405 Canal St., (605) 343-0157, (800) 843-0009, you can watch through windows and see a video.

But does the gold in Black Hills Gold actually come from the Black Hills? Until recently, we could say an assured "yes" because Homestake Gold Mine in Lead (see the History and Area Overview chapters) used to sell gold directly to local manufacturers. Now that Homestake is closed and gold mining in the Black Hills is but a remnant of a bygone era, the metals in Black Hills Gold jewelry are assuredly from sources outside South Dakota.

You'll find many brands of Black Hills Gold and Black Hills Silver rings, bracelets, brooches, pendants, earrings, watchbands, belt buckles, money clips, and other items offered for sale in jewelry and gift stores across the country and in Europe and Asia. The tricolor gold in particular has become such a classic that it has been imitated by other manufacturers who know a good thing when they see one. However, only jewelry made right here in the Black Hills can legally carry the name "Black Hills Gold." Be sure to check before making your purchase.

Ray) Trevino has been stitching leather for a quarter century, and for most of that time he's had a steady clientele for his custom elk-hide chaps and vests. His rustic shop 6 miles south of Deadwood caters to motorcyclists with a yen for all kinds of leather garments, and the racks are hung with ready-made jackets, vests, belts, caps, and gloves. Wallets, handmade leather purses, cow-hide and buffalo rugs, and select jewelry items (yep, those rattles were once attached to real live snakes) round out the inventory, the vast majority of which is American-made. It's worth stopping here even if you're not in the market for some new leathers, because Trevino has some nice Native American artifacts displayed in glass cases. The shop is open seven days a week in summer and Mon through Sat in winter. At Trevino's it's always leather weather.

Central Hills

STAR OF THE WEST HAT COMPANY
2255 North Haines Ave., Rapid City
(605) 343-7345
www.starofthewesthats.com

Brad Montague makes custom hats with varying percentages of beaver fur and trimmings as plain or fancy as you like—and in just about any color, too. One time his stock included a dainty bone-colored bonnet shaped with a women's dress crease and adorned with a cascading ivory veil trimmed with ribbons and roses. He offers reconditioning services for hats that have been in service for a while. The average wait for a beautiful custom hat of your own is six to eight weeks. The shop is closed on Sun.

MALLS

RUSHMORE MALL
2200 North Maple Ave., Rapid City
(605) 348-3378
www.rushmoremall.com

When Black Hills locals talk about "the mall," it used to be a safe bet that they were referring to Rapid City's Rushmore Mall (www.rushmoremall.com), the area's first fully enclosed shopping center. But, no more. An explosion in Rapid City's retail sector in 2008 resulted in massive new mall developments just off I-90 on the city's northeast side and expansion was still in progress in 2011. Anchor stores at the Rushmore Mall still include national giants: Herberger's, Sears, and JCPenney. There are lots of specialty stores, too, including casual clothing stores that cater to a youthful clientele. Among them are the Buckle, Pac-Sun, Maurice's, and the Gap. Rushmore Mall is open seven days a week.

RUSHMORE CROSSING
1601 Eglin St., Rapid City
(605) 348-4480

Across I-90, construction continues at this writing on the massive new Rushmore Crossing shopping center, which developers say will eventually have 900,000 square feet of retail space. Rushmore Crossing's big anchors are Scheels, a 100,000-square-foot sporting goods superstore, Wal-Mart, Target, and a 240,000-square-foot Furniture Row, with four individual stores—Sofa Mart, Oak Express, Denver Mattress, and Bedroom Expressions. Other stores are Shoe Carnival, Gordman's, T.J. Maxx, David's Bridal, Petco, Michaels Hobby, Gordman's, Bed, Bath & Beyond, and Dress Barn.

NATIVE AMERICAN & OTHER ETHNIC ITEMS

Long revered by various Native American tribes, the Black Hills became a richly diverse melting pot with the gold rush of 1876. To enjoy the artistic expression of some of those cultures, as well as others from around the world, visit the shops listed below and find wonderful handmade decorative items, clothing, and even foods.

Northern Hills

SHANKAR ARTS
29 Deadwood St., Deadwood
(605) 578-3808
www.shankararts.com
Shankar Arts is owned by Phil Breland and his Moroccan-born wife, Georgette Ohayon. They've been traveling to the far side of the globe for more than two decades, bringing back exquisite silver and gemstone jewelry, woolen jackets, brass Buddhas, hand-knotted tribal carpets, crystals, antique ritual pieces, and other fascinating items. Their buying trips take them to North Africa, India, Thailand, Tibet, Indonesia, Nepal, and the Middle East, where they search out markets, fairs, and festivals for new folk crafts. Every piece reflects the culture from which it came, and Breland and Ohayon can tell you its story. You can buy unset gemstones here, order custom work, or have your gold and silver jewelry repaired. Shankar Arts is open daily year-round.

Central Hills

GLOBAL MARKET
617 Main St., Rapid City
(605) 343-4051
It's said that if you can remember the 1960s, you weren't part of it. Well, Global Market will transport you back to those days of head shops and clothes from the *India Imports of Rhode Island* catalog. This is the place to find imported hand-batiked clothing, garments woven from flax and other natural fibers, incense, candles, silver-filigree jewelry, South American wool sweaters, bongo and conga drums (made in New Jersey), kilim rugs, carved masks, handmade soap, baskets, books, tapes, CDs, and more. A second location is in Spearfish at 617 Main St. (605-642-9014). By the way, that's not a typo in the listing—the identical street numbers for the two stores were a cosmic coincidence. (We're convinced the owner has good karma.) Both are open daily.

HOUSE OF SCANDINAVIA
13774 US 16, Rapid City
(605) 348-3858
If you're of Scandinavian descent, you've probably been teased about lutefisk, the odoriferous Limburger of fish dishes. Well, here's a place where you can bask unabashedly in your ethnic heritage. For many decades this red-and-white chalet 9 miles south of Rapid City has stocked quintessential Northern European goods, from Norwegian sweaters (to die for) to *lefse* mix. Sweden, Norway, Denmark, Finland, Iceland, Holland, and Germany are represented here in such items as brightly painted Dalecarlian horses, needlepoint kits, delicate pewter jewelry, pretty table linens, glassware, china, funny troll dolls, kitchen utensils, food items, clogs, toys, glass Christmas ornaments, and blue delftware. The shop is open daily from May through Oct; in Nov and Dec, when co-owner Jean Watkins (she's of Swedish parentage) serves hot cider and glogg and homemade *lefse*, it's open Fri through Sun and by appointment. It's closed from the weekend before Christmas until May 1.

i Looking for a slinky little number covered in sequins or accented with spangles? See the scintillating selection of party dresses at Kathleen's, 622 Main St. in Spearfish, (605) 642-3843. This ladies' boutique also carries dressed-up casual clothes and fashionable sportswear.

THE INDIANS
141 Winter St., Keystone
(605) 666-4864, (866) 845-3426
www.theindianskeystone.com

Items on the shelves here represent the work of artisans from many tribes, and the store's Indian Arts and Crafts Association membership certificate (it's a charter member) is your guarantee of authentic Native American craftsmanship. There are works by local artists and crafters and an array of southwestern silver-and-turquoise jewelry, baskets, sand paintings, kachina dolls, and genuine Navajo rugs. Beadwork, quillwork, pottery, dance sticks, drums, moccasins, denim clothing, toys, and a great selection of books also keep you browsing. The store is open seven days a week year-round.

✳PRAIRIE EDGE TRADING CO. & GALLERIES
606 Main St., Rapid City
(605) 342-3086, (800) 541-2388
www.prairieedge.com

If you're captivated by Native American crafts and culture and you love fine handmade items, go straight to Prairie Edge. You'll know you're someplace special the instant you step into the spacious showrooms gleaming with polished-wood floors and fixtures. Set aside plenty of time for your visit, not only because there are three floors' worth of wonderful merchandise to look at, but also because the serene beauty of the displays makes you want to linger to examine each exquisite piece.

When you enter, locally made star quilts and colorful Pendleton blankets catch your eye, and cases of jewelry, beadwork, and intricate quillwork beckon. You might feel inspired to buy supplies for your own creations in the Sioux Trading Post portion of the store. The toy assortment offers games, marbles, puzzles, and many breeds of fuzzy stuffed animals. You're sure to be dazzled by the Italian Glass Bead Library, where jars upon jars hold beads in all kinds of colors and almost as many sizes—intriguingly, they're from a Venetian supplier that provided beads to 19th-century fur traders.

Most enchanting of all, perhaps, is the Plains Indian Gallery, where you'll see magnificent reproductions of traditional clothing and artifacts, including beaded cradle boards, fringed and beaded leather dresses, ceremonial garments embroidered with porcupine quills, decorative vessels, dolls, and more. From here, climb the wide staircase to browse among the fascinating books on Native American subjects, crafts, and the West, as well as a selection of tapes and CDs by Native American musicians. Finally, visit the third-floor art gallery to see works by acclaimed regional and national artists, sculptors, photographers, and craftspeople. If once is not enough, you can return seven days a week to see it all again at this 125-year-old building.

SIOUX POTTERY
1441 East St. Joseph St., Rapid City
(605) 341-3657, (800) 657-4366
www.siouxpottery.com

This isn't just a place to buy beautiful, hand-decorated pottery in muted rainbow colors.

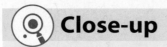

Close-up

Phoebe Apperson Hearst—and Family

Great wealth and personal popularity never went to **Phoebe Apperson Hearst**'s head. Even as a much-courted Missouri belle, the lively brunette was known for her kindheartedness and generosity, traits she continued to cultivate after becoming the wife of **George Hearst**—she was 19 and he 41 when they married in 1862. George would later become a founder of Homestake Mining Company (see the History chapter) and a US senator from California. The couple, who lived in San Francisco, occasionally visited the Black Hills city of Lead, where the Homestake Gold Mine was located.

Although the couple never made the rough-and-ready mining camp their home (George found the Black Hills a bit crude for his refined tastes), Phoebe's philanthropic efforts there earned her the admiration and affection of its citizens. In 1896 Phoebe gave Lead a public library for Christmas, and it bears her name to this day. She also came to the aid of the Lead Women's Club when financial problems threatened to shut down its free kindergarten. Her support for education spread far beyond Lead, however, as she helped found the PTA (originally the National Congress of Mothers) in 1897. That same year she became the first woman regent of the University of California, a post she held until her death in 1919.

In return for her many gifts to Lead, the citizenry and business community commissioned a Boston silversmith to create a large, ornately decorated and engraved loving cup in Phoebe's honor. No doubt the gesture pleased her, and perhaps the trophy did as well. Phoebe's love of fine things showed in her patronage of the arts and in the elegant clothes and jewels in which she posed for her portraits. The fact that she had Homestake stock issued in her own name (albeit misspelled "Phebe") hints that she was as astute in the acquisition of money as she was lavish in her dispensation of it.

Less well loved than his mother was George and Phoebe's only child, publishing tycoon and yellow journalist **William Randolph Hearst**, believed to be the model for Orson Welles's film *Citizen Kane*. William Randolph's ostentatious California home, Hearst Castle, is the setting for *Murder at San Simeon*, a book blending fact and fiction written by his granddaughter, **Patty Hearst**. The heiress made headlines of her own when she was kidnapped by the Symbionese Liberation Army in 1974 and transformed into the terrorist Tania. After her 1975 arrest and subsequent conviction for bank robbery, Patty married a prison guard, Bernard Shaw, and is reported to be living happily (and quietly) ever after.

You're also invited on a self-guided tour through the plant to ask questions and watch the craftspeople and artists at work. It's an interesting process. Clay slip, a liquid mixture of Black Hills red and Kentucky white clays and water, is poured into molds. After the edges harden, the excess slip is poured out, leaving a perfectly formed vase or other vessel. Once dry the pieces are unmolded, trimmed, sanded, painted, hand decorated, glazed, and fired. The artists use traditional geometric designs and their own imaginations in their etching and painting, which makes each piece unique. You can buy one

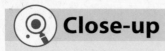 **Close-up**

Cornish Pasties

First, some clarification. We're talking here about an ethnic food called a "pasty," which rhymes with "nasty" but is really very pleasant to eat. A pasty is a turnover filled with heavy foods like meat and potatoes. The resourceful wives of tin miners in Cornwall, England, concocted pasties long ago as a sustaining meal to tuck into their hardworking husbands' lunch pails.

According to Bonnie King, who has made more than one million pasties in her hometown of Lead, the first such handheld pies had a barley crust and were filled with fish. Today's "traditional" pasty consists of a pastry crust with a steak, potato, and onion filling. When Cornish miners and their families immigrated to the Black Hills goldfields (see the History chapter), they brought their pasty recipes with them. That was fortunate for women like Bessie Richards, who lost her husband to silicosis and supported her 14 children by baking and selling pasties.

Local descendants of immigrant miners say they're not sure whether the Cornish folk imported their custom of leaving a bit of pasty crust at the mine to keep the tommyknockers from making mischief. Tommyknockers were dwarf creatures believed to live in the mines; their existence explained knocking noises miners heard while digging.

You might never get to hear a tommyknocker, but you can experience the time-honored taste of a pasty during your trip to the Black Hills. Bonnie, who made and sold traditional pasties from her grocery store in Lead when the Homestake Mine was still open, now distributes her creations to FreshStart convenience stores across the Black Hills. For custom orders you can call her at (605) 722-3875. Bonnie, who learned to make pasties from a daughter of earlyday immigrants, offers several varieties, including traditional, pizza (with a yeast crust), ham, sausage, and sausage 'n' sauerkraut.

piece or several, as well as other Native American–crafted items in the gift shop. Sioux Pottery is open daily June through Aug and weekdays the rest of the year.

NATURAL FOODS

If it tastes good it's bad for you, right? Wrong. Stock up on food from the stores listed here and you'll have everything you need for a yummy, nutritious feast. All of these stores are closed on Sun.

Northern Hills

GOOD EARTH NATURAL FOODS
638 Main St., Spearfish
(605) 642-7639

The displays here are so attractive and welcoming you feel good even before you buy any of the healthful merchandise. Along with a good selection of grains are books, nutritional supplements, bulk herbs, grooming supplies, biodegradable cleaning products, frozen and canned foods, lots of bottled and canned beverages, and many other items.

Central Hills

MAIN STREET MARKET
512 Main St., Rapid City
(605) 341-9099
www.themainstreetmarket.com
The shelves in Main Street Market are well stocked with nutritional supplements, herbs, personal-care products, books, pasta, tea, soups, condiments, and lots of other tasty, tempting goods for wholesome meals and nutritious snacks. Add the personal service and attention on which the owners pride themselves, and you will come away with a warm feeling as well as a filled market basket.

STAPLE & SPICE MARKET
601 Mount Rushmore Rd., Rapid City
(605) 343-3900
www.stapleandspice.com
Since 1921 this tried-and-true market has been able to boast the largest selection of bulk herbs and spices in South Dakota. The current confines are bursting with nutritional supplements, homeopathic remedies, personal-care products, teas, and staples for wholesome eating. Special items include free-range buffalo, chicken, turkey, and beef, whole-bean coffee, organic fruits and vegetables, and bulk honey. If the item you want isn't in stock, the staff will bend over backward to try to get it for you.

Southern Hills

EARTH GOODS NATURAL FOODS
738 Jennings Ave., Hot Springs
(605) 745-7715
Owner/herbologist Jackie Gericke offers nutritional supplements, herbs, and a generous variety of bulk dried fruits, nuts, flours, seeds, grains, and beans, plus frozen entrees

and desserts, essential oils, juices, teas, and the usual items you'd expect to find in a natural-foods store. It's all offered in a comfortable, friendly atmosphere.

Photo Supplies & Service

We've wondered how many professional photographers per square mile live in the Black Hills—we're betting it's quite a few. So it's rather baffling that we don't have a large camera store to serve them. If your photo needs are limited to basic cameras, print film, and quickie processing, you won't have any trouble finding what you're looking for. Unfortunately, you'll be more hard-pressed to find places that offer specialized services and higher-end equipment.

ROCK SHOPS

The subject of Black Hills rocks covers a wide spectrum that includes precious metals, gemstones, and fossils. To learn more about this mineral diversity, see the Natural World chapter.

Central Hills

DAKOTA STONE CO.
23863 Palmer Gulch Rd., Hill City
(605) 574-2760
www.dakotastone.net
Stones for your fireplace, patio, rock garden, or rock veneer—they're all here, along with local alabaster for the sculptor in you. Not

surprisingly, beautiful rose quartz, the South Dakota state mineral, is this store's biggest seller, and you'll find many lovely specimens from which to choose (the owners have their own quarry). Browse among the outdoor bins, where you'll see everything from milky selenite to jet-black obsidian, then do the same in the gift shop, where you'll find speckled leopard-skin rock, tumbled and polished stones, books, carvings, jewelry, and geodes—hollow rocks you can break open with a hammer to see the pretty crystals inside. The store, 3 miles north of Hill City on US 385, is open daily June through Aug but is closed on Sun the rest of the year.

SADDLES 'N' STUFF

Around here folks rely on horses for the three R's: ranching, recreation, and rodeoing.

Northern Hills

CROFT'S SADDLERY
US 385, Deadwood
(605) 578-3228
If you saw the Tom Selleck movie *Quigley Down Under*, you saw one of Jerry and Duffy Croft's saddles. Make that two—in movie work, matching pairs of everything are required for the actors and their stunt doubles. The Crofts' meticulously handcrafted saddles appeal to working cowboys as well as to filmmakers, since the saddles combine an authentic antique look with modern comfort. The Crofts, a husband-and-wife team, pride themselves on using top-quality materials and not cutting corners. They live the cowboy way of life and even raise a few buffalo on the side. Then again, corners are a Croft signature—look for the classy spot braiding in them. The Crofts do most of their business by phone, taking measurements

for both horse and rider that way. A custom saddle order takes six to eight months to fill, but other items such as chaps and bridles can be completed in two to three weeks. Croft's is open Mon through Fri.

Black Hills Farmers' Market

The **Black Hills Farmers' Market** (1529 West Omaha St., Rapid City; 605-923-4562; www.blackhills farmersmarket.com) has operated each growing season since 1989. This open-air market sets up booths two to three times a week in Rapid City from early June through the end of Oct. You'll find local meats, veggies, breads, canned goods, and artwork. Market starts at 9 a.m. the first Sat of June and continues every Sat until the end of Oct. Beginning in July, the market also is open at 9 a.m. Tues and Thurs.

Southern Hills

STOCKMAN BOOT AND SADDLERY CO.
106 South Chicago St., Hot Springs
(605) 745-6771
www.stockmanboot.com
Jim Bultsma and Monte Birdsall specialize in custom-made saddles but also do repairs and just about any other kind of leatherwork you might call for. The shop (see the listing under Clothing) stocks ready-made saddles and tack, too. Operations are in full swing Mon through Sat.

SPORTING GOODS

Central Hills

CABELA'S
3231 East Mall Dr., north of I-90 between exit 60 and 61
(605) 388-5600
www.cabelas.com
This place bills itself as the "world's foremost outfitter." A small herd of stampeding American bison realistically mounted and arranged in a prairie diorama greets guests near the 80,000-square-foot store's entrance. The bison are among the more than 350 mounted fish, elk, moose, antelope and other critters elaborately displayed inside the store. Most are arranged on Cabela's trademark "Conservation Mountain" display that dominates Cabela's indoor landscape. The Nebraska-based hunting, fishing and outdoors retailer turns each of its outlets into a wildlife museum. Cabela's is the first store of the new retail power center called The Gateway at Rapid City.

✳DAKOTA ANGLER & OUTFITTER
513 7th St., Rapid City
(605) 341-2450
www.flyfishsd.com
When you think about it, an entire store devoted to fly fishing makes sense in the Black Hills. Just ask any local fly fisher (and there are plenty of women among them). Need a float boat? No problem. Looking for fly-tying supplies? There's a whole wall full. In addition to all the practical items like rods, reels, books, magazines, and maps, there are items to keep you in the spirit even when you can't be streamside: jewelry, watches, artwork, T-shirts, dishes, and even wild rice to serve alongside your catch. For information about Dakota Angler's guide service and lessons, see the listing in the Fishing section of

the Recreation chapter. The store, which is an authorized Orvis dealer, is closed on Sun all year and on Mon during Jan and Feb.

EDGE SPORTS
619 Main St., Rapid City
(605) 716-9912
www.grabanedge.com
Edge Sports, with locations in Rapid City, Lead (11380 US 14A, 605-722-7547), and Spearfish (414 Main St., 605-722-6095) provides thrill seekers with a variety of adventure sports equipment. Their friendly and helpful staff is well trained and will assist you in finding the most suitable equipment for skiing, snowboarding, skateboarding, and rock climbing. During the winter months, they also provide the newest in ski and snowboard rentals at their Lead location, right on the way to Terry Peak and Deer Mountain ski areas. The Rapid City shop is open seven days a week all year long, and the Lead shop is open primarily from Nov to Mar. The Spearfish location is open from 10 a.m. to 6 p.m. Mon through Sat.

GRANITE SPORTS
201 Main St., Hill City
(605) 574-2121
www.granitesportsonline.com
Granite Sports offers the gear to get you there. Shoppers find climbing equipment, an assortment of camping gear, backpacks (both human and canine), hiking boots, brand-name outerwear, technical clothing, casual duds (for kids, too), and rugged sweaters.

PEAK SPORTS
1002 Jackson Blvd., Rapid City
(605) 341-5445
This shop specializes in downhill skis, snowboards, and everything you need to be

attired for playing in the snow. Personal attention is yours when you need the proper fit in a boot or a custom insole, and certified personnel are on hand to keep your skis or board in topflight condition. The store does not carry rentals. Peak Sports is open daily between Labor Day and early spring and is closed the rest of the year.

THE RUNNER'S SHOP
41 East Omaha, Rapid City
(605) 348-7866
www.sdrunnersshop.com
Lots of stores sell athletic shoes, but how many have this kind of selection, or offer the kind of knowledgeable service you find here? At last count it carried 90 styles of running shoes in stock and at least that number in other types of footwear for hiking, walking, and other activities. The staff has more than 45 years of combined experience fitting runners—and they're runners themselves, which helps. The shop specializes in modifying shoes for optimal comfort and performance to avoid problems. If it's too late for that, they'll work with you on problem resolution. You can pamper more than your feet here, though, because the shop carries the latest high-tech running wear plus accessories and books, shoe-care products, and even free maps to help you find the best trails. You can also get information about competitive and fun runs in the region. Shoppers also find custom-crafted jewelry designed specifically for runners. The store is closed on Sun.

TWO WHEELER DEALER CYCLE
& FITNESS
100 East Blvd. North, Rapid City
(605) 343-0524
www.twowheelerdealer.com

Made in the Black Hills

You'll notice lots of South Dakota–made items on the shelves in stores and gift shops. Here are some that are made in the Black Hills: the Country Caterer jellies, bread mix, and more, Belle Fourche; Dakota Delights and Homespun Naturals vegetable soaps, Custer; Dakota Gold Mustard, Spearfish; Dark Canyon Coffee, Rapid City; Daystar Candles, Custer; eggspressions! hand-decorated goose and other eggshells, Rapid City; Heart of the Earth bath products, Fruitdale; Jewelry by Waldron, including the Circle of Nations and WaterSong lines and Earth-Charms ornaments, Rapid City; and Prairie Gold Coffee Co., Rapid City. And then, of course, there is our very own Black Hills Gold.

So you want to get in shape. Now all you have to do is decide whether to buy a bicycle, treadmill, elliptical trainer, glider, strider, weight machine, or some other type of fitness equipment to help you get the job done. The decision will be much easier after you visit with the folks here, who carry all of the above and more. In bikes alone they stock mountain, road, BMX, fitness, and cruiser models. You can rent bikes also. The clothing and accessories you need for your active lifestyle are here, too, along with a full-service repair and maintenance shop. You can drop in any day of the week in Rapid City; the Spearfish location at 215A Jackson Blvd. (605-642-7545), is closed Sun.

ATTRACTIONS

The Black Hills aren't nearly as massive as some of the mountain ranges you'll find farther west, but they aren't small either. Spreading across a swath of land 125 miles long and 65 miles wide, they take up well over two million acres in South Dakota and Wyoming.

The natural wonders of this expansive region alone would provide enough activities to keep a visitor busy for weeks on end. However, the creativity and industriousness of the land's 160,000 residents continue to give travelers here more opportunities to relax and have fun.

Diversity of attractions is one of the Hills' greatest resources, yet the sheer number of things to do makes it hard to separate the activities that will capture your imagination from the ones that will make you yawn. In the following pages you'll find a selection of the best the Black Hills have to offer—but it is by no means exhaustive. If there's a specific attraction you're looking for but can't find in this book, your best bet is to ask a local. They're friendly, helpful, and willing to show off just how much they know about the area.

OVERVIEW

If you're looking for diversions geared primarily toward children, see the Kidstuff chapter. Day Trips & Weekend Getaways, Recreation, and The Badlands & Nearby are other relevant chapters to read. In these chapters, as in this one, you'll find a sampling of both major roadside attractions and out-of-the-way sights—the secluded settlements and hidden wonders known only to insiders.

Glorious Black Hills summers are the high point of the year, and most visitors come here in June, July, Aug, and Sept. Some attractions open a week or two before (or on) Memorial Day weekend and close for the winter on (or a couple of weeks after) Labor Day. Many shorten their hours and days of operation in the early and late part of the season, too. Other attractions are

family owned and operated and may be a bit casual about their operating seasons (due in part to our rather unpredictable winters). Many attractions may plan to close in November, but if the snows begin in October, they'll close early. Some may open in early May, only to find that spring rains are keeping visitors away. They may close again until later in the month or shorten their hours. South Dakotans have learned to adjust to their weather, so it always pays to call ahead before driving to an attraction.

Not only can seasons affect times of operation, but they might also affect prices, as can age makeup and group size. Many establishments have a sliding scale of rates for seniors and children. Rates for large groups may be less than for small groups.

Rates may also be less in the winter months if the establishment is even open. Again, because things can change so rapidly, call ahead.

Many places listed in this chapter have the additional benefit of being educational. You'll be entertained while you learn about geology, the history of the Wild West, the culture of old Dakota Territory, and the critters and folks who inhabit the present-day Black Hills. By the time you've worked your way through this chapter, you'll feel like a local.

Price Code

The following price ratings refer to the cost of one adult ticket; however, many places offer discounts for children, students, and seniors.

$	Less than $5
$$	$5 to $10
$$$	$10 to $20
$$$$	More than $20

CAVES

Caves lace the limestone beneath the central Black Hills. Exploration is difficult, so no one knows for sure about their depth, whether they are connected, or what natural wonders the unexplored regions may conceal. You can, however, tour the previously explored nether regions of each cave listed below. Stalactites, stalagmites, popcorn and frost crystals, cave flowers, and flowstone are just some of the fascinating geological formations you'll see.

The caverns have easy and safe walking trails, although the nature of caves makes them inaccessible to wheelchairs. Cave temperatures are in the range of 45 to 50 degrees, and they can sometimes be damp—take a jacket and wear your walking shoes (preferably with sturdy rubber soles).

The following caves are privately owned and operated and many have gift and rock shops, snack bars, hiking trails, and picnic areas. Some are open only during the summer, approximately Memorial Day to Labor Day. In planning your trip to the caverns, remember that the last tours of the day often leave sometime before the official closing hour. It's a good idea to call ahead.

You'll find the Southern Hills' Jewel Cave and Wind Cave discussed in the Parks & Nature Areas section.

Northern Hills

WONDERLAND CAVE
NATURAL PARK **$$$**
Vanocker Canyon Rd., Nemo
(605) 578-1728, (605) 343-5043
This cave is accessible from US 385 from Deadwood or via I-90, exit 32. Hours are 8 a.m. to 4 p.m. seven days a week, from May 1 through Nov 1 (or until the first snowfall, sometimes as early as Oct).

Central Hills

BEAUTIFUL RUSHMORE CAVE **$$$**
13622 SR 40, Keystone
(605) 255-4467, (605) 255-4384
www.beautifulrushmorecave.com
During its season, this cave is open seven days a week. From May 1 through Memorial Day, hours are 9 a.m. to 5 p.m. After Memorial Day and through Labor Day, hours are 8 a.m. to 8 p.m. After Labor Day until its closing on Oct 31, hours are 9 a.m. to 5 p.m.

BLACK HILLS CAVERNS **$$**
2600 Cavern Rd., SR 44 West,
Rapid City
(605) 343-0542, (800) 837-9358
www.blackhillscaverns.com

Guided tours start every 20 minutes in summer. Hours are 8 a.m. to 8 p.m. seven days a week, from mid-June through Labor Day. From May 1 to mid-June and from Labor Day until Oct 15, hours are 8:30 a.m. to 5:30 p.m., seven days a week. There's an additional fee for gold panning.

CRYSTAL CAVE PARK $$
SR 44 West, Rapid City
(605) 342-8008
Summer hours are 8 a.m. to 8 p.m. seven days a week. After Labor Day, hours are 9 a.m. to 5 p.m. on weekends only, but call ahead for fall and winter hours.

SITTING BULL CRYSTAL CAVERNS $$
US 16 South, Rapid City
(605) 342-2777
www.sittingbullcrystalcave.com
This cave is open approximately May 1 through Sept, seven days a week 8 a.m. to 8 p.m. and on weekends only in Oct 8 a.m. to 6 p.m.

STAGE BARN CRYSTAL CAVE. $$
I-90, exit 46, Piedmont
(605) 787-4505
This cave is open from Memorial Day through Labor Day; hours are 8 a.m. to 7 p.m. Open seven days a week, the cave is in beautiful, natural Stage Barn Canyon; all the flora and fauna native to South Dakota is found in this canyon. The excellent interpretive guides are prepared to lead you on the one-hour tour as you arrive; usually there is no waiting time.

HISTORIC SITES

Step back in time by visiting the places where history was made in the Black Hills.

Northern Hills

BUCKSKIN JOHNNY SPAULDING CABIN FREE
415 5th Ave., Belle Fourche
No phone
If you admire the pioneers for their courage, independence, and toughness, you should see this reconstructed cabin to understand how strong they really were. It's difficult to imagine braving a South Dakota winter in this vulnerable home. Built in 1876, the original tiny cabin sheltered pioneer and adventurer Buckskin Johnny and his sister's family, the first white settlers in the area. The cabin is now a mini-museum and an eye-opening glimpse into the primitive lives of the early settlers. Be sure to read the story on the plaque on the cabin's outside wall (or ask a volunteer) of how Johnny and his childhood sweetheart, Nettie, were separated in their youth. They were finally reunited after a 53-year hiatus and were married from 1927 until 1932, when Johnny died. The cabin is open year-round from 8 a.m. to 5 p.m. Mon through Fri. Hours may expand to include the weekends during the summer, but visitors should stop by or call the Tri-State Memorial Museum in Belle Fourche (see the listing) to be sure. Donations are appreciated.

D.C. BOOTH HISTORIC FISH HATCHERY FREE
423 Hatchery Circle, Spearfish
(605) 642-7730
www.dcbooth.fws.gov
You don't have to be a fishing enthusiast to enjoy this attraction. If you are, though, you'll find the historic hatchery and museum a delight. Trout hatchlings were once raised here to stock streams across the West. You'll learn about the hatchery process and how

it evolved as technology and knowledge improved. The fish car, an early 1900s railroad car that was equipped to transport fish all over the country on their way to new trout streams, is open for viewing.

If you're less than enthusiastic about fishing, you'll still enjoy strolling the grounds, feeding the ducks and fish, and touring the Booth home. The house was built in 1905 and is listed in the National Register of Historic Places. Furnished with period antiques and Booth family memorabilia, it is a delightful example of the attention to design and detail obvious in the gracious homes of that era. Be sure to visit the underwater viewing window near the entrance to the grounds, where the resident rainbow trout and brown trout swim by. It's a chance for a rare fish-eye view as well as a humorous glimpse from below of paddling duck feet.

The hatchery, museum, and home are open from mid-May through mid-Sept, seven days a week from 10 a.m. to 5 p.m. Donations are accepted. The hatchery and grounds are next door to the Spearfish City Park and are open from dawn until dusk.

✳MOUNT MORIAH CEMETERY (BOOT HILL) $
Lincoln Street, Deadwood
(605) 722-0837
No dedicated Deadwood visitor leaves without paying respects to those who lie at Boot Hill. Calamity Jane's and Wild Bill Hickok's graves are the main attractions, though lesser-known—but no less interesting—folks are also buried here. Pick up a walking-tour guide at the ticket booth. It will furnish the human-interest stories lacking on traditionally succinct tombstones. Take note of the nearly empty Chinese section (most bodies were eventually returned to China),

the Jewish section (where many stones are inscribed in Hebrew), and the three potter's fields. Among the colorful characters buried here are madam Dora Dufran, who is buried with her parrot, Fred, and Blanche Colman, the first woman member of the South Dakota Bar, who was self-taught.

The entire cemetery completed a three-year, $3.1 million restoration in the summer of 2003, enhancing the peace and beauty of its location overlooking the gulch. The renovations didn't alter its mountainous terrain, however, so keep in mind that some parts can be quite steep to access. Be sure to check out the new interpretive center at the base of the cemetery, which houses a small gift shop and exhibits from the collection of the Adams Museum (see the listing under Museums). Check out the stained-glass window, massive leather-bound Bible, and other artifacts from Deadwood's First and Second Methodist Churches, which were destroyed in 1885 and 2002, respectively.

The cemetery is open all year, but the ticket booth is open from May to Labor Day from 7 a.m. to 8 p.m., then from 9 a.m. to 5 p.m. for the rest of Sept, and intermittently until winter sets in. Residents and those with relatives buried here are admitted at no charge.

Central Hills

BIG THUNDER GOLD MINE $$
604 Blair St., Keystone
(605) 666-4847, (800) 314-3917
Learn about the history of Black Hills gold mining, explore an 1800s underground mine, and try panning streamside for your own specks of gleaming treasure. Guided tours begin with a 10-minute film, and each hard-hatted visitor is rewarded with a sample of gold ore at the end of the 68-foot

tunnel. If your best panning efforts fail to yield anything, you can purchase a small vial of pure, 24-carat gold leaf in the gift shop, which also carries souvenirs, books, rocks, and that great pretender, fool's gold. The mine is open May through Sept. Hours are 8 a.m. to 8 p.m. from Memorial Day through Labor Day and 9 a.m. to 5 p.m. the rest of the season. For an additional small fee, you can go gold panning, too.

Southern Hills

1881 CUSTER COUNTY COURTHOUSE MUSEUM & BOOK STORE   FREE
411 Mount Rushmore Rd., Custer
(605) 673-2443
The exhibits here provide a good overview of early life in the Custer area. Old photographs play a prominent role in telling the story, but you'll also see George Armstrong Custer's dress epaulets and antelope rifle. Rocks and minerals, native bird and animal specimens, authentic costumes, Native American artifacts, and exhibits depicting mining, lumbering, farming, and community life round out the displays. Don't miss the chilling stone jail in the basement, the courtroom on the second floor, or the buildings out back—where Custer County's only legal hanging took place. Bookstore attendants are ready to answer your questions as you browse among the reading matter. The museum, which is staffed by volunteers, is open from June 1 to Aug 31, 9 a.m. to 9 p.m. Mon through Sat and 1 to 9 p.m. Sun. Donations are appreciated.

✳MAMMOTH SITE OF HOT SPRINGS $$
1800 US 18 Bypass, Hot Springs
(605) 745-6017
www.mammothsite.com

If you think an elephant is big, wait until you meet Sinbad the mammoth. The full-size replica of a Columbian mammoth skeleton greets you at the Mammoth Site, where scientists have unearthed the fossilized remains of more than 50 of the ancient creatures that became trapped in a sinkhole and died. The find was discovered accidentally in 1974, when the ground was being excavated for housing construction. Since then, the site has provided research data about animals and the environment from thousands of years ago. It is the only *in situ* mammoth fossil display in the United States—that is, the only one in which the bones are left lying where they were found. This may be the only place you'll ever see mammoth hair on display, too. You can take a guided tour or walk through the exhibits yourself with a guidebook from the ticket counter. (The text is available in English, French, German, Dutch, Italian, and Japanese.) In the gift shop, children will find a hands-on paleontological dig. The shop features a big selection of books for all ages, in addition to other items. Mammoth Site is open daily; during the peak season, mid-May to late Aug, hours are 8 a.m. to 8 p.m., with the last tour at 7 p.m. Hours vary the rest of the year, so call ahead.

MUSEUMS

Tour restored historic homes or visit museums of mining, trains, and motorcycles. Dozens of museums offer ways to deepen your knowledge of the Black Hills and Western history.

Northern Hills

✳ADAMS HOUSE $
22 Van Buren St., Deadwood
(605) 578-3724
www.adamsmuseumandhouse.org

William Emery (known as W. E.) Adams became a successful businessman in Deadwood during the late 19th and early 20th centuries (see the Adams Museum listing below). By 1925 he and his wife were living in the finest mansion in town and awaiting the arrival of their only daughter's first baby. But by a terrible twist of fate, W. E.'s wife, daughter, and grandchild all died within a 48-hour period, each from a different cause. The once-proud Deadwood patrician was left devastated at the loss of his entire family and wondered if he'd ever find happiness again.

The details of this story, and many others relating to W. E. and the original builders of the home, Deadwood's influential Franklin family, are now a part of the regular tours through this historic house. Though there are many such historic homes scattered throughout the American West, this massive estate is different: It sat empty and unchanged for half a century. Age had taken its toll on paint and structural integrity, but all of its furnishings and decor were intact, from elegantly carved hardwood tables and handpainted frescoes to porcelain bathroom fixtures and a jar of sugar cookies in the pantry. Using gaming proceeds earmarked for historic preservation, the city of Deadwood meticulously renovated the entire house, restoring its 1892 color scheme, original stained glass, and metal shingles. When it opened as a museum in July 2000, locals agreed that it was worth every penny of the $1.5 million bill.

You can tour the home Memorial Day through Labor Day from 9 a.m. to 6 p.m. Mon through Sat and from noon to 4 p.m. on Sun. From Labor Day through Memorial Day, you can catch a tour between 10 a.m. and 3 p.m. Mon through Sat. Tours usually begin and end on the hour, but they are more frequent in summer.

i Calamity Jane, one of Deadwood's most famous citizens, passed away in 1903 in debt to the Goldberg Grocery for the sum of $7. Calamity is buried at Mount Moriah Cemetery. In recent years the grocery changed ownership and is now a casino, but the ledger book with Calamity's still-outstanding balance can be seen at the Adams Museum.

✳ADAMS MUSEUM   **FREE**
54 Sherman St., Deadwood
(605) 578-1714
www.adamsmuseumandhouse.org
W. E. Adams came to the Black Hills in 1877 as a miner and eventually became one of Deadwood's most influential and prosperous citizens. The city approached him in the 1920s about funding a museum. It was the perfect time. People were taking a keen interest in history, and many early Deadwood pioneers were still alive. Thus, the museum has many objects and collections that came straight from the collectors, their history and authenticity intact. You can view displays on Wild Bill Hickok, Calamity Jane, Potato Creek Johnny, the Chinese workers and business owners who came here for the gold rush, the ladies of the night, the gamblers and miners, the first locomotive in the Black Hills, and much more.

A skilled staff and good funding have helped to turn the once cluttered and disorganized exhibits into modern, state-of-the-art displays. Only the much larger (and far more expensive) Journey Museum in Rapid City matches the professionalism, comprehensiveness, organization, and quality you'll find at the Adams Museum.

The Adams is open during the summer (May 1 through Sept 30) from 9 a.m. to 7 p.m.

Mon through Sat and noon to 5 p.m. on Sun. Winter hours (Oct 1 through Apr 30) are 10 a.m. to 4 p.m. Mon through Sat. The museum is closed on Thanksgiving Day, Christmas Day, and New Year's Day. Admission (by the stipulation of Mr. Adams himself) is free, but a small donation is suggested.

i When the legendary Wild Bill Hickok was shot in Deadwood by the infamous Jack McCall (the first and last time Bill ever sat at cards with his back to the door), he reportedly was holding black aces and eights, known ever after as the "dead man's hand." Deadwood's Adams Museum displays what are purported to be the actual cards.

DAYS OF '76 HISTORIC MUSEUM FREE
17 Crescent Dr., Deadwood
(605) 578-2872

This museum will remind you of a rancher's attic or old barn, and with good reason: That's where many of the artifacts here came from. Less organized, more cluttered, and a bit rawer than the nearby Adams Museum (see the earlier listing), the Days of '76 Museum is literally filled with piles of Old West artifacts. There are letters, family photographs, saddles, Lakota ceremonial items, rifles, branding irons, and even some of the original bricks from Deadwood's early streets. The horsedrawn vehicle collection is extensive. You'll see real buggies, buckboards, carriages, covered wagons, three hearses, and the original Cheyenne–Deadwood Stage, which navigated wild western terrain for 11 years. In 2008, the Days of '76 Museum launched a $6 million capital campaign to

fund an impressive new museum facility, complete with upgraded interpretive displays and curatorial areas. The museum is open approximately late Apr to early Oct, from approximately 9 a.m. to 5 p.m. You'll find it off US 85/14A on Crescent Drive next to the Days of '76 rodeo grounds. Donations are accepted.

HIGH PLAINS WESTERN HERITAGE CENTER $
Heritage Drive, Spearfish
(605) 642-WEST
www.westernheritagecenter.com

The center's impressive building sits alone atop a high hill, where it is whipped by wild plains winds and overlooks the green hills beyond. If you're lucky you might get to watch a High Plains thunderstorm blow in from far away—complete with roiling black clouds and jagged lightning. The setting is perfect for a museum dedicated to High Plains life, which is greatly affected by the landscape and the weather. Inside the center you'll see many forms of western art and artifacts, including old buggies and wagons; saddles and spurs; a barbed-wire collection (old barbed wire is an art form itself); recreations of shops from the past; wood carvings; original art and photographs; and plenty more. A 17-foot-high sculpture of legendary trail boss Tennessee Vaughn astride his rearing horse is especially impressive. Outdoors, get a close-up look at grazing longhorn steers and buffalo, a one-room schoolhouse, a log cabin, and a sod dugout. Kids will love the petting farm in the summer months. The museum is open year-round seven days a week, 9 a.m. to 5 p.m. To get there, take I-90 to exit 14 south and go to Heritage Drive, 1 mile south.

OLD FORT MEADE MUSEUM & OLD
POST CEMETERY $
SR 34, Fort Meade
(605) 347-9822

Constructed in 1878 by the remnants of Custer's Seventh Cavalry, Fort Meade was designed to keep the peace between native Lakota and Cheyenne tribes and the invading white settlers. Amazingly, there is still a military presence there. Today Fort Meade includes the Veterans Administration Medical Center and the Veterans Affairs complex. The museum chronicles historic events and changes with displays chock-full of artifacts, clippings, photographs, and stories. Fort Meade was the home of Custer's Seventh Cavalry (after Little Bighorn and the death of Custer) and the Buffalo Soldiers of the 25th Infantry, Dakota Territory. It was also one of two South Dakota prison camps during World War II, housing soldiers from General Rommel's Africa Corps.

To get to the museum building, enter the grounds at the Fort Meade complex entrance and follow the blue signs. It is open daily from May 15 through Sept 15. From Memorial Day weekend through Labor Day weekend, hours are 8 a.m. to 6 p.m. Hours are 9 a.m. to 5 p.m. from May 15 until Memorial Day weekend and from Labor Day weekend until Sept 15.

The Old Post Cemetery is on a hill south of the museum, accessed by a gravel road. It's best to ask for directions at the museum before attempting to find it on your own. Soldiers, their relatives, and civilians were buried in the cemetery from 1878 until about 1948, when the Black Hills National Cemetery opened. In the tradition of the time, headstones have very little detail (some even lack dates), and the number of children

buried there may shock you. It's open all year, 24 hours a day. There is no fee for admission to the cemetery.

STURGIS MOTORCYCLE MUSEUM
& HALL OF FAME $$
**Junction and Main Streets (the Old
Post Office across the street from the
Armory), Sturgis**
(605) 347-2001
www.sturgismuseum.com

For many, Sturgis is synonymous with motorcycles. Though the first Sturgis Rally & Races was held in 1938, the event didn't gain national notoriety until the 1980s. Since then, the event has consistently attracted a crowd of around 500,000, nearly doubling the size of South Dakota and turning Sturgis into the largest city in a five-state area (read more about the Rally in the Annual Events & Festivals chapter).

This museum is a popular destination for bikers during the weeklong Rally—so popular that the museum makes enough money during that single week to support regular year-round hours, despite only a trickle of visitors during the winter months. One of the biggest draws is the collection of vintage motorcycles, including Harleys, Indians, and Triumphs. There are also a few historic photos and interpretive displays and a gift shop. As is typical of many small-town museums, the interpretive information is bland and there is little interactivity. However, the museum is run and staffed by motorcycling enthusiasts, and their inside knowledge and passion help fill in the holes left by the museum displays. Staffers especially love to talk about members of the museum's Motorcycle Hall of Fame. In general, those inducted into the Motorcycle Hall of Fame are drawn from those cyclists who support the Rally and have in some way made a substantial contribution to the sport of riding. Names in the list include entertainer Jay Leno and the late publisher Malcolm Forbes, as well as many politicians associated with motorcycling. The museum is open 9 a.m. to 5 p.m. Mon through Fri and 10:a.m. to 5p.m. Sat and Sun. It is open on weekends in both seasons, but the doors are unlocked an hour later.

TRI-STATE MEMORIAL MUSEUM FREE
415 5th Ave., Belle Fourche
(605) 892-2676, (888) 345-5859

This small and traditional museum features artifacts from ranchers and businesses in both Dakotas and Montana, giving the institution its name. There are dozens of photos depicting life around early Belle Fourche, which was once the largest livestock shipping point in the West. There are also collections of dolls and clothing that belonged to early homesteaders. For a taste of the bizarre, examine some of the 4,000 old salt and pepper shakers on display. The entire collection was reorganized in the spring of 2004 when the museum opened the doors of its new 5,000-square-foot building near the chamber of commerce. Though it is staffed by only a few part-time people and some passionate volunteers, the enthusiasm and knowledge of the museum's caretakers are more than enough to accommodate even the toughest questions from visitors. The Tri-State Museum is open 8 a.m. to 5 p.m. Mon through Fri year-round. In summer it may be open on the weekends, but interested visitors should call ahead. Donations are appreciated.

Central Hills

BLACK HILLS INSTITUTE OF
GEOLOGICAL RESEARCH $$$
217 Main St., Hill City
(605) 574-3919 (tour information)
www.bhigr.com

What this small, unassuming museum lacks in size it more than makes up for in outstanding fossil exhibits. You'll be just as impressed by the displays of smaller creatures as you are by gargantuan Stan, the mounted *Tyrannosaurus rex* skeleton. There are rocks, minerals, meteorites, and fossilized plants, too. Some of the specimens are on loan, but others belong to the Black Hills Institute of Geological Research, which has a lab in the basement (closed to the public) and a reputation for quality work. Even the gift shop, Everything Prehistoric, is a wonder world of ancient life-forms, with drawers full of specimens for sale. You'll want to linger over the fossils, minerals, cast items, books, and toys.

From May through Sept the museum is open 8:30 a.m. to 6:30 p.m. Mon through Sat and 10 a.m. to 5 p.m. Sun; the rest of the time, hours are 10 a.m. to 5 p.m. Tues through Sat. Guided tours of the paleontology lab are available by appointment for a fee.

BORGLUM HISTORICAL CENTER $$
342 Winter St., Keystone
(605) 666-4448
www.rushmoreborglum.com

Get acquainted with Mount Rushmore sculptor Gutzon Borglum before visiting the mountain he carved. A self-guided, narrated tour provides background about the artist's personal and professional history as well as the significance of the masterpiece that immortalized him. Texts of the tour are available in English, French, Spanish, German, Japanese, and Mandarin Chinese. (See

ATTRACTIONS

the Mount Rushmore listing in the Parks & Mountains chapter.) The tour, begun in 1978, includes a 25-minute newsreel compiled from old photos, news clips, and broadcasts. The gallery displays more of Borglum's work. The large museum/gift shop features artwork, books, and videos; more sculpture is displayed outside. Located in Keystone, 3 miles north of Mount Rushmore, the center is open daily May through the first week of Oct. The hours are 8 a.m. to 7 p.m. June through Aug. Call for hours in May, Sept, and Oct. Admission is discounted during Sturgis Rally & Races week each Aug.

THE JOURNEY MUSEUM $$
222 New York St., Rapid City
(605) 394-6923
www.journeymuseum.org
Housed in a spectacular building, this museum is a techno-wonder. Your own journey through it starts with a dramatic movie about the geologic and cultural history of the Black Hills. Then continue with a self-guided tour that's both educational and entertaining, thanks to hand-held sound sticks that allow you to walk, stop, and listen at your own pace. The sound sticks explain the exhibits in Lakota or English. The Journey was designed as an interactive excursion through time, beginning with the earth-shattering birth of the Hills and moving through detailed accounts of the Native American way of life, the arrival of white explorers, the gold rush, pioneer days, paleontology and archaeology, ranching and farming, and much more.

Here's a secret: When you reach the tepee, sit on the bench in front of it, hold the sound stick to your ear, and wait for the moon to come up over the tepee. You'll be treated to a holographic visit with Nellie Two

Bulls, Lakota elder. Other exhibits also "materialize" if you wait for them. The museum was designed to provide a contemplative experience; it's not to be hurried through—take your time and enjoy. We recommend you make the Journey one of your early stops: It will enhance your understanding of the rich culture of the Black Hills. The gift shop, stocked with Native-made crafts, is above average. The Journey houses two galleries, the Sioux Indian Museum Gallery, and another displaying original South Dakota and midwestern artists. The museum is open daily year-round. From Memorial Day to Labor Day, hours are 9 a.m. to 6 p.m. In winter it's open 10 a.m. to 5 p.m. Mon through Sat and 1 to 5 p.m. on Sun.

MOTION UNLIMITED MUSEUM AND
ANTIQUE CAR LOT $
6180 SR 79, Rapid City
(605) 348-7373
www.motionoldcars.com
You don't have to spend half your life under the hood of a car to appreciate the automobiles, motorcycles, and memorabilia on display here. Even the toys in glass cases look like they've been lovingly restored. The car collection spans several decades and changes over time, but you might find among the more unusual exhibits a 1926 Model T paddy wagon with bars on the rear windows, an airplane car, a 1925 Studebaker motor home, and a 1932 Ford dragster. What you see is all the more impressive when you learn that owners Bill and Peggy Napoli have done much of the restoration work themselves. They have a parking lot full of "project" cars waiting for the right owner to purchase and fix up. How about an Edsel? The museum, 2 miles south of Rapid City, is open 9 a.m. to 6 p.m. Mon through Fri and 9

a.m. to 4 p.m. Sat, Apr through Sept. There's no charge to look around the car lot, which is mostly open all year. Call ahead for winter hours.

Historic Houses

The historic houses of Lead and Deadwood appear to perch—some quite precariously—on the rocky hillsides on which the towns are built. Some houses have been beautifully renovated and others allowed to decay. Most streets are quite narrow, some are one-ways or dead ends, and you don't want to attempt them in the winter. Both Lead and Deadwood sprang up during the gold-rush days, although Lead was a camp built for the employees of the Home-stake Gold Mine. Today the mine spreads out beneath much of the town, and Lead home owners own just the surface rights to their properties. The Homestake Mine owns the rights to everything underneath—dirt, minerals, and maybe gold.

MUSEUM OF GEOLOGY   **FREE**
501 East St. Joseph St., Rapid City
(605) 394-2467,
(800) 544-8162 ext. 2467 (weekdays)
www.sdsmt.edu
Even if you're not a scientist, it's easy to spend hours among the exhibits in this museum on the Tech campus of South Dakota School of Mines and Technology. The Badlands (see the chapter called The Badlands & Nearby) and Black Hills provide a

ready supply of fossils and minerals, respectively, but you'll also see fascinating, colorful rocks from around the world on display here. There are meteorites, models of famous diamonds, gold nuggets, and a case full of South Dakota minerals. Dinosaur skeletons (including a dino leg bone you can touch), polished agates, fossilized fish, and a slice of faulted sandstone (you can see where it buckled) are other eye-catching exhibits. And here's your chance for a close-up look at boxwork, popcorn, and frostwork, which are some of the mineral formations in Wind Cave National Park (see the Parks & Mountains chapter). There's a small selection of books and minerals for sale, too.

The museum is open year-round, with summer hours 8 a.m. to 6 p.m. Mon through Sat and noon to 6 p.m. on Sun. Winter hours are slightly shorter; call for information. Donations are gratefully accepted. The museum, where students and others do research, offers several two-week paleontology digs each summer, but you have to take your own tent and sleeping bag. Call or write for information about getting college credit, which costs more.

SOUTH DAKOTA AIR AND SPACE
   MUSEUM   **FREE**
Ellsworth Air Force Base
I-90, exit 67
(605) 385-5188
www.sdairandspacemuseum.com
If you're a military or aviation history buff, or if you just love airplanes, you'll enjoy this museum. Outside displays include more than 27 planes and helicopters, including General Eisenhower's personal transport and a Mitchell B-25 bomber. Inside, explore the history of the base, tour a mock-up of a Minuteman launch control center, and see military

ATTRACTIONS

memorabilia. The South Dakota Aviation Hall of Fame is housed here, too, with tributes to pioneer aviators that are especially interesting. Read about Nellie Willhite, who—despite being deaf—became South Dakota's first licensed female pilot (see the Close-up in the Getting Here, Getting Around chapter); Clyde Ice, barnstormer, wing walker, and aerobat; and aviatrix Violet Cowden, who made her first parachute jump on her 74th birthday. Hours are 8:30 a.m. to 6 p.m. A narrated bus tour ($) is available from mid-May to mid-Sept, lasts about an hour, and includes a descent into a real Minuteman II missile silo. The museum is near the base's main gate; watch for signs and lots of parked planes.

Southern Hills

FALL RIVER COUNTY HISTORICAL MUSEUM   FREE
North Chicago Street, Hot Springs
(605) 745-5147
If taking a step back in time is one of your pleasures, this museum will delight you. The musty scent of yesterday greets you as you open the door and tread the well-worn wooden stairs of this three-story former schoolhouse. The 1893 sandstone structure, whose halls rang with the sound of youthful voices until 1961, houses extensive collections of everything imaginable, all smartly arranged in clusters and groupings. You'll find a room devoted to kitchen implements, for instance, and another filled with musical instruments and related items. There's a dentist's office well equipped enough to make you wince, and a Victorian parlor that makes you want to set a spell over tea and polite conversation. The museum is open 9 a.m. to 5 p.m. Mon through Sat from June 1 until Sept 30. The volunteer-run museum relies on donations.

NATIONAL MUSEUM OF WOODCARVING $$
US 16 West, Custer
(605) 673-4404
www.blackhills.com/woodcarving
Ignore the old saw "Don't take any wooden nickels" when you get to the National Museum of Woodcarving: You're going to need three of them to take full advantage of the displays. The museum, 2 miles west of town, features the work of Dr. Harley Niblack, a Denver chiropractor who gave up his practice at age 42 to devote his time to wood carving and animation. His talent in that area made him one of Disneyland's earliest animators, and some of his work has been displayed by the Smithsonian Institution. When you buy your ticket, you'll get enough wooden nickels to set three of the carvings in motion. But before entering the exhibit area, you'll want to watch videos in the Wooden Nickel Theater about the collection and about wood carving. The self-guided tour ends with a look at work by some of the nation's other top wood-carvers and a stop in the gallery where you can buy quality carvings. An adjacent gift shop sells snacks and souvenirs. The museum is open from May 1 until late Oct. Hours vary throughout the season, so call ahead.

MUSIC & SHOWS

Historical plays, chuck wagon supper shows, and other musical events are held evenings in spring, summer, and fall.

Central Hills

SUPPER MUSIC SHOWS $$$–$$$$
If you like beef with a little lively music on the side, you'll want to catch one of the area's nightly dinner shows. Starting times

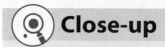 **Close-up**

Rapid City's Place in Aviation History

Think pioneer aviation and you're likely to think of Kitty Hawk, North Carolina, where the Wright brothers made a short hop in the world's first airplane in 1903. But a spot near Rapid City in the Black Hills earned a place in aviation history in 1935, when two army officers, Orvil Anderson and Albert Stevens, set an altitude record in a helium balloon launched from the Stratosphere bowl. The balloon, *Explorer II*, ascended 72,395 feet, enabling its crew to collect new data on Earth's upper atmosphere. Today the gondola that carried the men and equipment is in the National Air and Space Museum in Washington, D.C.

The **Stratobowl**, as it has come to be called, is a flat, circular field sheltered by rocky cliffs. Its unique characteristics have attracted numerous other balloonists, including millionaire adventurer Steve Fossett, who launched an unsuccessful around-the-world flight from the bowl on January 8, 1996. The bowl itself is privately owned and not open to the public, but you can look down into it from the rim. (You'll have to hike in about three quarters of a mile.) In addition to the view, the rim has a plaque commemorating the 1935 launch, which was sponsored by the National Geographic Society and the US Army Air Corps.

To get to the Stratobowl rim, look for the gate and cattle guard off US 16 about 10 miles southwest of Rapid City. Pull in and park at the gate; if you find yourself at the Black Hills National Forest overlook, you've gone too far. The rim is on USDA Forest Service land, so all agency rules and laws apply.

and prices vary for the attractions listed below. Cowboy boots and a Stetson are not required—but if you're not sure what to wear, ask.

For a cowboy-style chuck wagon supper of beef 'n' beans with all the trimmings, your choices include **Circle B Ranch Chuckwagon & Trail Rides** on US 385, (605) 348-7358, west of Rapid City, where you'll find a western town, minigolf, trail rides, gold panning, and other activities.

Or perhaps you'd like to visit **Fort Hays,** (605) 394-9653, a movie set from *Dances with Wolves,* on US 16 south of Rapid City, with continuous free showings of the four-hour version of the film. The owners offer a 99-cent cowboy breakfast from 6:30 to 11 a.m. and a chuck wagon supper beginning

at 6:30 p.m. For about $54 you can join a daylong tour starting at 9 a.m. that takes you to Mount Rushmore, Custer State Park, and the Crazy Horse Memorial. Upon your return to Fort Hays, you'll be treated to supper and a show. Fort Hays is open daily from May 12 to Oct 1.

Flying T Chuckwagon Supper and Show, (605) 342-1905, also on US 16 south of Rapid City, has provided western tradition since 1979 with a variety music and comedy show.

Southern Hills

BLACK HILLS PLAYHOUSE
SR 87, Custer State Park
(605) 255-4141, (605) 255-4242
www.blackhillsplayhouse.com

This rustic playhouse, fashioned from an abandoned 1934 Civilian Conservation Corps camp, has offered professional summer theater since 1946. Quality performances in a novel setting have made it a popular attraction for locals and tourists alike. The historic structure has been undergoing renovations so check the website for show locations before venturing down through Custer State Park solely to see a performance. For information about shows, see the Arts chapter.

MOUNTAIN MUSIC SHOW $$
US 16, Custer
(605) 673-3135

The Pee Wee Dennis family's hillbilly style of entertainment dishes up two hours of country and bluegrass music and cornball humor in an indoor theater next to Flintstones Bedrock City. Sunday is country gospel night. The show normally goes on each evening from Memorial Day weekend to Labor Day weekend, but the season may vary; call ahead to confirm. Curtain time is 8 p.m. Reservations are recommended. A free bus gets you there from any Custer motel or campground.

THE ORIGINAL SINGING
COWBOYS $$$
Heritage Village
1 Village Ave., Crazy Horse (Custer)
(605) 673-4761, (888) HAVE-FUN
www.heritage-village.com

You might call this group the South Dakota version of the Sons of the Pioneers. And indeed, one of the members of this traditional western-style band, Jim Lovell, won the Old West Trail Foundation Award for the Preservation of Western Music in 1980, an honor also bestowed on the aforementioned Sons. Lovell and fellow Cowboys

Buddy Meredith, Kenny Hamm, and Bill King sing enduring songs about enduring values, and their arrangements are so true, you just might get the urge to stretch out in a bedroll under the stars. That's especially so if you've had a filling meal from the buffet table on the main floor at Heritage Village before heading downstairs for the show in the Show Barn Theater. Performances are at 8 p.m. Tues through Sun from early May through Labor Day, and on weekends until mid-Oct. The buffet starts at 4:30 p.m. Group reservations are recommended.

i Belle Fourche claims the designation of Geographical Center of the United States. In 1959, after Alaska and Hawaii became states, the US Coast and Geodetic Survey moved the center from Kansas to a point about 20 miles north of Belle Fourche. The actual site is on inaccessible private land, but in 2008 the community of Belle Fourche dedicated a magnificent new monument on the north side of its Visitor Information Center and Tri-State Museum, 415 5th Ave.

PARKS & NATURE AREAS

These sites are among the Hills' best-known and most beloved features. We also include some lesser-known gems, perfect for an afternoon of adventure and discovery.

Northern Hills

BLACK HILLS NATIONAL
CEMETERY AND VFW
MEMORIAL CHAPEL FREE
I-90, exit 34, Sturgis
(605) 347-3830

Row upon row of gleaming white headstones framed against green grass and blue sky are an impressive sight. This is a place of tranquillity, where more than 21,000 veterans and their family members lie at rest. The cemetery opened in 1948; veterans from World War I and every war and conflict since are buried here. If you're looking for the grave of a relative, stop at the administration building by the front gate, pick up a map, and use the locator book in the foyer to find the location. While you're in the foyer, note the human-interest stories jotted in the comments column in the guest book. The cemetery is open all year and accessible 24 hours a day, although visitors are asked to restrict their visit to daylight hours. The administration building is open from 8 a.m. until 4:30 p.m. Mon through Fri, but the foyer is always unlocked.

The tiny Veterans of Foreign Wars Memorial Chapel is not part of the National Cemetery, but visitors use it as a place of contemplation before or after their visit. Take the cemetery road (which goes under the interstate) the short distance to the grounds. The chapel is usually unlocked, although it is closed in the winter and sometimes locked after occurrences of vandalism.

TATANKA: STORY OF THE BISON　$$
US 85, Deadwood
(605) 584-5678
www.storyofthebison.com
When the 19th century dawned, an estimated 30 million bison roamed the plains of central North America. A century later their number had been reduced to fewer than 1,000. But the white hunters who slaughtered the continent's largest beast by the thousands weren't just wiping out an animal—they were wiping out the only way of life known by thousands of Native tribes. This attraction serves as a memorial to the height of the buffalo culture in 1840. An interpretive center details the rise, fall, and recovery of bison; why the Lakota people were so dependent on these roaming herds; and how bison have found their place in modern culture. A small cafe serves buffalo meat. The central component, however, is a massive, heroic-scale bronze sculpture (the third largest in the world, according to the staff) depicting 14 bison being driven off a cliff by three mounted hunters. It's owned by Kevin Costner, who also owns the Midnight Star (see the Gaming & Casinos chapter) and shot some of his epic *Dances with Wolves* in nearby Spearfish Canyon. The attraction, located on Deadwood Hill less than a mile above town off US 85, is open from May to Oct, although it may be open in other months, depending on weather. Likewise, hours vary throughout the season, so it's best to call ahead. The one-time admission fee allows you to enter the attraction all season.

Central Hills

BERLIN WALL EXHIBIT　**FREE**
Memorial Park, 8th Street, Rapid City
Take a break from your busy activities and visit this quiet, thoughtful tribute to freedom. Take Mount Rushmore Road north from Omaha Street (there it becomes 8th Street) and park in the Rushmore Plaza Civic Center parking lot. These are replicas of the Berlin Wall, but the wicked-looking steel tank traps in front of the wall sections are authentic. Read the story of the Berlin Wall—how it came about, its harsh history, and how it ended—on the displays. Rapid City's sister city is Apolda, Germany, whose mayor attended the exhibit's opening in 1996. This exhibit is accessible 24 hours a day, year-round. After your visit continue your walk

through Memorial Park and explore the fantastic Rapid City park system.

CHAPEL IN THE HILLS
(STAV KIRKE CHAPEL)   FREE
3788 Chapel Lane, Rapid City
(605) 342-8281
Known in English as Chapel in the Hills, and in Norwegian as Stav Kirke, the little wooden church in the pines is a 1969 replica of the 12th-century Borgund Church in Laerdal, Norway. The ornately carved, unique structure takes its name, which means stave church, from the 12 staves around which it is built. The staves represent the 12 apostles, the foundation of the Christian church. With its wooded backdrop and broad, well-kept lawn, the chapel and its grounds impart a sense of peace and well-being. It's no wonder couples from a wide area choose to be married here. Visitors can sit on wooden benches in the chapel and listen to a continuous tape to learn more about the building's intricate features, including the dragon heads that adorn the roof. There's also a late-19th-century log cabin built by Norwegian immigrant Edward Nielsen that has been turned into a museum cozily furnished with Scandinavian antiques. The reception center/gift shop, housed in a grass-roofed stabbur (traditional pantry or granary building) imported from Norway, continues the Scandinavian motif with carvings, handcrafts, and books. In addition to its spiritual and architectural significance, Chapel in the Hills reminds visitors of the northern Europeans who immigrated to South Dakota, imbuing the state with their steadfast, vivid heritage. Chapel in the Hills is open from 7 a.m. until dusk daily, from May 1 through Sept 30. A half-hour nondenominational vespers service begins at 8 each evening from mid-June through late Aug. Weddings may

be scheduled from mid-Mar until mid-Nov. Donations to support the nonprofit operation are appreciated. To get there, take SR 44 to Chapel Lane in Rapid City and follow the signs to Stav Kirke.

Colonel Carlton's Patriotic Legacy

In 1892 Fort Meade post commander Col. Caleb Carlton and his wife discussed their idea that the United States needed a national "air." Mrs. Carlton suggested the well-known "Star-Spangled Banner" written by Francis Scott Key. Colonel Carlton commanded the melody be played at the fort's retreats, parades, and concerts. He took the opportunity to explain this new custom to the governors of South Dakota and Pennsylvania, and interest spread. Soon Secretary of War Daniel Lamont ordered that the composition be played each evening at every US Army post.

Colonel Carlton initiated the practice of standing and removing hats while the music played. The heart-stirring song and the respectful acts of patriotism accompanying its performances were so popular that in 1931 Congress declared "The Star-Spangled Banner" our national anthem.

CLEGHORN SPRINGS STATE FISH
HATCHERY   FREE
SR 44, Rapid City
(605) 394-2399 (summer only),
(605) 394-2391

No sense trying to worm your way out of it—even if you've never been caught by the lure of fishing, you're likely to get hooked on this hatchery. Besides ponds full of trout for stocking South Dakota waters, there's an aquatic center where you can learn about watersheds, fish, and fishing. There are nature programs, too, and pellets are available if you want to feed the fish. Hours are 9 a.m. to 4:30 p.m. daily from Memorial Day to the end of Aug, and you can call for information about free summer programs.

COSMOS MYSTERY AREA $$
US 16, Rapid City
(605) 343-9802, (605) 343-7278
www.cosmosmysteryarea.com
If you want to stand up straight at Cosmos, just lean forward, especially if you're standing on the wall. To learn more about this baffling place, where the laws of physics are unenforceable, see the Kidstuff chapter.

MOUNT RUSHMORE NATIONAL
** MEMORIAL**   **FREE**
SR 244, Keystone
(605) 574-2523
www.nps.gov/moru
One of South Dakota's most defining features and among the most recognizable of American icons, the massive granite faces of Mount Rushmore attract more than three million visitors from all over the globe each year. The busts of George Washington, Thomas Jefferson, Theodore Roosevelt, and Abraham Lincoln represent the events and philosophy of 150 years of American history and the lifelong dream of sculptor Gutzon Borglum. A massive restoration project in 1998 revitalized the memorial, replacing many of the outdated structures with imposing granite and glass buildings,

turning Rushmore into a world-class destination. Indeed, you're just as likely to see a family from Toulouse or Taipei as you are a couple from Cincinnati or San Francisco walking the Avenue of Flags. Of course, it's also likely that you'll see a Rocky Mountain goat lounging near the amphitheater or standing around the parking lot. These harmless creatures aren't native to the Hills, but they've been a part of the animal life that wanders the grounds at the memorial since they were introduced in 1924. The massive Lincoln Borglum Museum, set into the earth beneath the Avenue of Flags and above the amphitheater, is a must-see for any visitor. Exhibits of original carving tools, the lives of all four presidents, and Mount Rushmore in popular culture (including a clip from the *Muppet Show*) are interactive and engaging—even for kids. A more detailed description of the mountain and services available is in the Parks & Mountains chapter.

i More than 90 percent of South Dakota's land was classified as farmland in the mid-1990s.

PETRIFIED FOREST OF THE
** BLACK HILLS** $$
I-90, exit 46, Piedmont
(605) 787-4560
www.elkcreek.org/forest
Start your self-guided tour of the Petrified Forest with the informative video made by the geologist owner, Jerry Teachout. The prehistoric formation of the Hills is explained clearly, and the video will enhance your knowledge and appreciation of the area. Next, visit the museum, where you'll see displays on geologic history and collections of rocks and minerals. Then head outside to walk the property and check out the

petrified logs unearthed there. These once-wooden logs are so ancient that they pre-date the Hills themselves. In fact, they were already petrified when the slow geologic uplift that created the Black Hills exposed them, and that began 62 to 65 million years ago. Stop by the excellent rock shop at the end of your tour. (See the listing in the Shopping chapter.) The Petrified Forest is open from May 1 through Oct 15. Hours are 8 a.m. to 7 p.m. seven days a week and 9 a.m. to 5 p.m. after Labor Day.

Southern Hills

BLUE BELL LODGE AND RESORT HAYRIDE AND CHUCKWAGON COOKOUT $$$$
Custer State Park, SR 87 South
(605) 255-4531
www.custerresorts.com
An hour-long hayride with live, sing-along folk music winds through the park to Parker Canyon for a chuck wagon dinner and continued entertainment. The hay wagon is pulled by a vehicle, not by horses, but you get a complimentary cowboy hat and bandanna to take home plus your choice of steak or hamburger for supper. Plan to spend two-and-a-half to three hours relaxing and enjoying the park's splendid scenery. The lodge recommends making your reservations by 2 p.m., but walk-ins are welcome until 5 p.m. if there's space left. Rides depart at 5:30 p.m., but guests are asked to arrive by 5 p.m. Group rates are available.

✳CRAZY HORSE MEMORIAL $$
US 16 and 385, Custer
(605) 673-468l
www.crazyhorse.org
Seven years after work ceased on Mount Rushmore (see the listing above), a fifth granite face

started to emerge from another Black Hills mountaintop. This still-unfinished carving-in-the-round of Lakota Sioux leader Crazy Horse will pay homage not to US presidents but to the legacy of those who preceded them. The monument and the museum complex below it are dedicated to Native Americans of all tribes. Because no known portraits of Crazy Horse exist, sculptor Korczak Ziolkowski created one from oral reports of those who had known the chief, intending that the monument stand as a symbol of the leader's spirit rather than an exact likeness.

The project was initiated by another Lakota chief, Henry Standing Bear, who wrote to the Connecticut artist after reading that Ziolkowski's marble bust of Polish pianist-composer-statesman Ignacy Paderewski had taken top honors at the 1939 New York World's Fair. Standing Bear's now-famous invitation read, in part, "My fellow chiefs and I would like the white man to know the red man has great heroes, too." The first blast at Crazy Horse removed 10 tons of rock on June 3, 1948. Hampered by South Dakota weather and dependent entirely on private funding (at Ziolkowski's insistence), it took 50 years to complete the sculpture's nine-story-tall face. When the last bit of rock is carved away at some unknown time in the future, the head alone will be big enough to hold all four faces on Mount Rushmore. Then, Crazy Horse, who was killed at Fort Robinson, Nebraska, in 1877, will sit astride his horse for all time, his left hand pointing proudly toward home: the place where his people lived and lie buried.

Ziolkowski himself is buried near the mountain carving. Since his death in 1982, his wife, Ruth, and seven of their 10 children have continued his work. Knowing from the start that he would not live long enough to complete the 563-foot-tall memorial—taller than the Washington Monument—the self-taught sculptor drew up a detailed master plan to guide his successors.

A visit to Crazy Horse begins on the Avenue of the Chiefs, which takes you to the visitor complex where there's a model of Crazy Horse's face carved from a native pine tree, a slide show, photos depicting the work on the mountain, and many examples of Ziolkowski's *Fighting Stallions* sculpture. Continue to the Native American Educational and Cultural Center to see beadwork and prehistoric tools and to watch a documentary video. In the Indian Museum of North America, tribes from every corner of the nation are reverently represented in collections of artifacts and costumes. The sculptor's studio-home showcases more of his work. In years to come, Ziolkowski's master plan calls for a new museum, a university and medical training center for Native Americans, and other additions.

The visitor complex, where you can also buy Indian-made and South Dakota products, is open all year, with summer hours from 7 a.m. to dark and offseason hours from 8 a.m. until dark. The Laughing Water Restaurant is open from early May to late Oct. Children six and younger, Native Americans, active military personnel with ID, and Girl Scouts and Boy Scouts in uniform get into the memorial free. There are reduced rates for motorcyclists, bicyclists, walkers, and groups—call for more information.

EVANS PLUNGE $$
1145 North River St., Hot Springs
(605) 745-5165
www.evansplunge.com
Although no longer a destination point for the weak and ailing, Hot Springs still draws tens of thousands of visitors each year with its famous Evans Plunge. The original 1890 Plunge Bath came into the hands of builder Fred Evans (see the Close-up in this chapter) after the springs that feed it had traded hands several times—at one point, for a $35 horse. But legend says that long before white men claimed and bartered the renowned healing waters among themselves, Indian tribes fought each other for its exclusive use. The Sioux are said to have triumphed over the Cheyenne in a clash on Battle Mountain north of present-day Hot Springs. When white settlers took over the land, they readily added their own stories of near-miraculous cures to those handed down by the Native people. You'll find not only the world's largest natural warm-water indoor swimming pool but also a host of other recreational facilities for the entire family, including waterslides, a sauna, steam room, and fitness center. Evans Plunge is open all year; for more information, turn to the Recreation chapter.

*JEWEL CAVE
NATIONAL MONUMENT $$
US 16, Custer
(605) 673-2288, (800) 967-2283
www.nps.gov/jeca
Among the first national monuments declared by President Theodore Roosevelt, Jewel Cave is rich in geological splendor. The sparkling calcite crystal that gives the cave its name is just one of its many features, however. The cave's greatest claim to fame is probably its length. With more than 130 miles of explored passages (and perhaps another 4,900 miles to go, according to some studies), Jewel Cave is the second-longest cave in the world.

Above ground there are over 1,000 acres of ponderosa forest to explore. The diverse

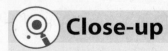 **Close-up**

Hot Springs' Sandstone Buildings

When late-19th-century white settlers discovered natural warm waters in the southern Black Hills, a health resort was the inevitable result. (See the History chapter for more information.) But enterprising developers of the day were quick to capitalize on a second treasure trove to promote Hot Springs as a premier destination. It seemed that local sandstone quarries held the perfect material to build an illustrious city, for the giant, rosy blocks that were cut and hauled to construction sites were not only enduring but also beautiful.

Present-day Hot Springs boasts 32 sandstone buildings from the late 1800s and early 1900s. They are what you notice when you arrive in town and what you remember after you've gone. Fred T. Evans, whose name resounds throughout Hot Springs today, must have had that in mind when he set about building the Minnekahta Block in 1891 and the Evans Hotel a year later. Both structures are included on a walking tour of historic buildings; you can pick up a color brochure and go on your own or make an appointment for a guided tour by calling the Hot Springs Chamber of Commerce at (605) 745-4140 or (800) 325-6991.

Your tour will take you to the sprawling, tile-roofed 1907 Veterans Administration Medical Center and the world's smallest Union Depot, built in 1891; to the 1889 State Veterans Home, the first major stone building; and to the 1932 post office, the last local building to be built from local stone. As you walk around town, look for details such as the carved face and purple accent blocks on the Petty building on Albany and Chicago Streets, and the multiple styles of tooling on City Hall. Before it got serious about preservation, the town lost some of its old beauties, and even now public opinion

ecosystem is famous for its bats (nine species) and vibrant wildflowers. A fire started by an arsonist in 2000 ripped through 90 percent of the park, destroying many of the trees, but the fallen timber has helped fuel the growth of many small shrubs, wildflowers, and ground cover. Three trails lead through the park above ground.

Several types of daily tours run through the cave itself, including a historic lantern tour and a four-hour wild caving tour. All start from the visitor center, which is open 8 a.m. to 4:30 p.m. all year, seven days a week. You'll also find interactive computer terminals and interpretive exhibits there. Extended information on Jewel Cave can be found in the Parks & Mountains chapter.

> **i** Know the difference between a national monument and a national park? A monument can be set aside for preservation by a simple presidential declaration, but it takes an act of Congress to establish a national park.

WIND CAVE NATIONAL PARK $$–$$$
US 385, Hot Springs
(605) 745-4600
www.nps.gov/wica
One of about half a dozen caves in the world to harbor honeycomb-like boxwork formations, Wind Cave offers four informative guided tours ranging from an hour to 90 minutes. Reservations are recommended for special candlelight and spelunking tours.

is divided on whether to try to save others. The 1913 Carnegie Library building, for example, was condemned and vacated in 1995 because of cracking, and at least some preservationists are unhappy about plans to raze all but the facade and build anew.

Since 1976 the city-appointed Hot Springs Historic Preservation Commission has headed up efforts to save what remains of the town's grand architectural legacy. Things got under way in 1977 when the National Trust for Historic Preservation named Hot Springs one of three pilot sites nationwide for a Main Street USA restoration project funded with matching grants. The commission has since strengthened its own ability to obtain grants for additional projects by gaining certified local government status in 1994. It's also begun stockpiling sandstone blocks from fallen buildings to use in restoration work. In addition, the local Save Our Sandstone Foundation Inc. raises money and provides labor to acquire and restore buildings. The two groups acted together to save the Evans Hotel after it was gutted by fire in 1979; it now houses 84 low-income apartments for the elderly.

The city's historic district is listed in the National Register of Historic Places, making tax credits and other advantages available for preservation work. But the high cost of restoration means that saving all the buildings, some of which are privately owned, would take many years and millions of dollars. Nonetheless, although the trains that used to puff into town four times a day have vanished along with the red carpets and bands that greeted passengers, it's nice to think that if Fred Evans arrived today he'd be able to recognize the little city he so energetically endorsed. He'd find tourists relaxing at his old Plunge Bath (now Evans Plunge), and he'd surely note with satisfaction that sandstone from his quarry still graces the streets of Hot Springs.

See the Parks & Mountains chapter for more information.

TOURS & BYWAYS

See the Black Hills through a customized tour or by traveling one of the state's remarkable scenic byways.

Northern Hills

HOMESTAKE GOLD MINE SURFACE TOURS AND VISITOR CENTER $
160 West Main St., Lead
(605) 584-3110, (888) 701-0164
www.homestaketour.com
The Homestake Gold Mine was the oldest continuously operating underground gold

mine in the world until 2001. Financial considerations, however, forced closure, and today the former mine retains only its visitor center and gift shop, which features Black Hills Gold and a deck overlooking the massive open-cut mine. Hours of operation are flexible, but count on the facility to be open from 8 a.m. to 5 p.m. daily in summer. In winter, you can visit Mon through Sat from 9 a.m. to 5 p.m. There's a charge for tours, but admission to the visitor center is free.

✳SPEARFISH RECREATION & AQUATIC CENTER $
2125 North Main St., Spearfish
(605) 722-1430
www.spearfishparksandrec.com

New in 2009, this former Wal-Mart was converted to an immense indoor and outdoor rec center. Locals and travelers find a complete indoor athletic and exercise facility with a double-court gymnasium, suspended three-lane walking and jogging track, open fitness area, and aerobic room. The newest attraction in Spearfish, the outdoor Aquatic Waterpark has a splash pad with interactive play features, zero depth entry pool with geyser spray, lazy river with sprays and bridge, 25 yard, three-lane pool with wheelchair access, double flume slides, drop slide, climbing wall, floating adventure walk, and bubble pit vortex. Fill up at the snack shop. Hours are 5:30 a.m. to 9 p.m. Mon through Fri, 8 a.m. to 6 p.m. Sat, and 1 to 6 p.m. Sun.

✻SPEARFISH CANYON STATE
SCENIC BYWAY
US 14A
www.spearfishcanyon.com

One of the glories of South Dakota is the amazing diversity of scenery: mountains, prairie, badlands, forest, high plains. But nothing quite compares to Spearfish Canyon. The canyon—six times older than Grand Canyon—is so spectacular, in fact, that it is a State Scenic Byway, a designation that acknowledges its famous beauty. US 14A is a 19-mile winding paved road that ends at Cheyenne Crossing and US 85 at its south end and at the Spearfish city limits at its north end.

The byway is often a bit crowded, especially in summer and also in fall, when the aspens burst into autumn color framed by deep green spruce and pine. The highway follows Spearfish Creek through towering limestone cliffs and thick forests and goes past Bridal Veil Falls, Roughlock Falls, and the mighty Spearfish Falls, restored after nearly a century of diversion by the now-defunct Homestake Mine. The shoulders of the highway are wide enough for bicycles (the grade is a comfortable 3 percent), and there are picnic areas and pullovers so you can safely stop and take photographs.

Allow enough time to hike into the woods or an adjoining canyon. The creek is known for its trout. You can find plenty of listings for nearby places to dine or spend the night in the Restaurants and Accommodations chapters. Be sure to allot enough time for a relaxed drive through the idyllic canyon. Your only concern should be the other drivers, who are gazing around in awe as much as you are.

Central Hills

BLACK HILLS CENTRAL RAILROAD/
THE 1880 TRAIN $$$
222 Railroad Ave., Hill City
(605) 574-2222
www.1880train.com

A favorite among visitors, this attraction features vintage railroad cars pulled by a steam locomotive that chugs along the original Chicago, Burlington & Quincy route that served Hill City and Keystone more than a century ago. Before or after your ride you can dine at the Highliner snack shop, where seating is available on the deck or in a railcar decorated with railroad memorabilia. In the gift shop you'll find train-related videos, books, and other items. After Memorial Day and before Labor Day, the train pulls out from Hill City at 7:15 a.m., 9:45 a.m., 1:15 p.m., and 4 p.m. Mon through Fri. From Keystone the train pulls out at 8:30 a.m., 11 a.m., and 2:30 p.m. Before Memorial Day and after Labor Day, the schedule is limited. Reservations are recommended because space for the two-hour rides is limited. A restricted timetable is in effect from mid-May to mid-June and after Labor Day until early Oct; call for information. You also need to call if you want to board at the Keystone junction or to find out about special evening rides during July and Aug.

PETER NORBECK NATIONAL SCENIC BYWAY

This 66-mile loop, named for the late nature-loving South Dakota governor and US senator Peter Norbeck, takes in some of the most rugged scenery in the Black Hills. The byway will take you into the Norbeck Wildlife Preserve, the Black Hills National Forest, and Custer State Park when you travel the Needles Highway (SR 87), Iron Mountain Road (US 16A), Horse Thief Lake Road (SR 244), and Sylvan Lake Road (SR 89). Norbeck laid out portions of the route himself on foot and horseback.

Along the way you'll encounter switchbacks, looping "pigtail" bridges, narrow 1930s tunnels that open onto breathtaking views (look for Mount Rushmore and the Needles Eye, an aptly named granite spire) and Sylvan Lake, so be sure to have your camera ready. There are historic sites, too, such as the spot along US 16A that served as a base camp for Lt. Col. George Custer's 1874 expedition to the Black Hills, when reports of gold set off a human stampede to the area.

The Needles Highway is in the Custer State Park fee area, so you'll need to buy a park entrance license if you go that way. You'll also need a license if you plan to tour or stop in the park. See our Parks & Mountains chapters for information about park features and license fees. Parts of Iron Mountain Road and the Needles Highway are closed during the winter.

RUSHMORE AERIAL TRAMWAY $$
US 16A, Keystone
(605) 666-4478
www.rushmoretramway.com
Trams depart about every five minutes for a short ride to an observation deck where you can look out over a scenic valley to Mount Rushmore, about a mile and a half away. Trails lead to other overlooks, and you can pack a picnic and stay as long as you like before returning to the gift shop to browse for souvenirs. The tramway runs 9 a.m. to 6 p.m. or later, weather permitting, from late May through mid- to late-Sept.

Southern Hills

BLACK HILLS AERIAL ADVENTURES $$$–$$$$
US 385, Custer
(605) 673-2163
www.coptertours.com
The Black Hills are breathtaking any way you view them, but few are the individuals who get to look down upon their pine-covered slopes. Black Hills Aerial Adventures hopes to change that with some help from their Bell 47 helicopter. Resembling a giant one-eyed dragonfly, this helicopter with its large glass cockpit provides passengers with incredible views of the Black Hills' more famous locations, including Crazy Horse Memorial, Mount Rushmore National Monument, and the Needles. Tours range from a quick 8 minute ride to longer 30-minute excursions, although pilots are happy to create custom tours on request. Prices vary depending on the length of your tour but start at $20 per person and go all the way up to $189 per passenger. The well-marked helipad is located 1 mile north of Custer on US 385.

WILDLIFE EXHIBITS

Learn about the Hills' animals—including bison, elk, fish, wild horses, reptiles, and more—at these sanctuaries and exhibits.

Northern Hills

SPIRIT OF THE HILLS WILDLIFE SANCTUARY $
500 North Tinton Rd., Spearfish
(605) 642-2907
www.wildlifesanctuary.net

This nonprofit animal rescue facility is dedicated to animal welfare and advocacy and features a variety of animals in natural settings, including lions, white tigers, panthers and pumas, camels, llamas, and bears. Reservations are recommended in the off-season, but generally tours occur at 10 a.m., noon, and 2 p.m. in summer. Group tours available.

Central Hills

*BEAR COUNTRY U.S.A. $$$
13820 South US 16, Rapid City
(605) 343-2290
www.bearcountryusa.com

It's not every day you have to brake for a big, burly bruin or a gaggle of geese, but at Bear Country you can count on it. Here it seems natural for the animals to roam about while the people are confined to their cars with the windows up. Besides bears you'll see elk, reindeer, mountain goats, bighorn sheep, wolves, bison, mountain lions, and other species as you drive through the 200-acre park on paved roads. After your drive you'll be able to get out and walk through the Wildlife Center and Baby Land for a (relatively) close look at bear cubs and other small animals. The youngest visitors can take a few turns around the pony pen. (Pony rides are $1.) You'll find more critters,

though not live ones, in the Bear's Den gift shop and gallery, where collectibles, clothing, and other items are for sale. There's also a snack bar and picnic area for hungry folks and brownbaggers. Bear Country, 8 miles south of Rapid City, is open from early May to late Nov, weather permitting. During peak season, mid-June to mid-Aug, hours are 8 a.m. to 7:30 p.m. daily; the rest of the time it's roughly 8 a.m. to 5 p.m., but it would be wise to call ahead. Plan to spend at least an hour and a half once you get there.

*REPTILE GARDENS $$–$$
US 16, Rapid City
(605) 342-5873, (800) 335-0275
www.reptilegardens.com

Everyone from lizard lovers to flower fanciers will be enchanted by the displays and plantings at Reptile Gardens. This award-winning attraction—the building capped by the Sky Dome 6 miles south of Rapid City—claims the world's largest reptile collection, as well as the largest variety of venomous species on exhibit anywhere. You'll be entranced by Maniac, at 15-foot, 10 inches and 1,200 pounds, the largest saltwater crocodile in North America, and Methusela, a 500-pound Galapagos tortoise born in 1881. But if creepy, crawly creatures make you cringe, you can soothe your nerves with an extravagant indoor orchid display or the more than 50,000 bedding plants in the outdoor gardens. Reptile Gardens offers educational 20-minute shows featuring alligators, snakes, and birds. The shows promote conservation and understanding of the important role animals play in our world. Millions have toured Reptile Gardens since it opened in 1937 after a local man, the late Earl Brockelsby, found that visitors enjoyed meeting the pet rattlesnake he kept under his hat. Along with your self-guided tour, you can have a light meal or snack in the Green Parrot Cafe and shop for jungle- and rainforest-related items, New Guinea tribal art, and other treasures in the gift shop. The complex is open from Apr 1 to Oct 31. Hours are 8 a.m. to 7 p.m. from Memorial Day through Labor Day and 9 a.m. to 4 p.m. the rest of the season. During the summer, shows run throughout the day, with the last one starting at 7 p.m.

TROUT HAVEN   **$–$$**
US 385, Rapid City
(605) 341-4440
Here you can catch a trout (all fishing gear furnished), have it cleaned and fried up fresh, and you won't even get your hands dirty. It's a family place, and you can read all about it in the Kidstuff chapter.

Southern Hills

BLACK HILLS WILD
   HORSE SANCTUARY   **$$$**
Rocky Ford Road, Hot Springs
(605) 745-5955, (800) 252-6652
www.wildmustangs.com
The drive to Black Hills Wild Horse Sanctuary is worth every dusty mile (the last 5.5 are on gravel roads), for the preserve is a place of tranquility and wild beauty. Two-hour bus tours through the 11,000-acre sanctuary stop for unforgettable views of the Cheyenne River, an intact set from the TV movie *Crazy Horse,* ancient petroglyphs, sacred caves, and, of course, free-roaming horses. Along the way you'll learn about the area's natural and human history, and whether you're a novice or an expert equestrian, you'll have plenty of opportunity to talk horses with your fellow passengers. Author, rancher, and conservationist Dayton O. Hyde established the sanctuary in 1988 as a haven for unadoptable wild horses. The grounds support 350 mares and their foals; stud colts are sold to help support the nonprofit operation. Registered Cheyenne River paints also are for sale. If you're interested in helping out with work around the place, call for information about the volunteer program. You can also inquire about sponsorships. Tours leave at 9 a.m., 10 a.m., 11 a.m., 1 p.m., and 3 p.m. Apr through Oct. Call for information about group rates or to make special arrangements for off-season tours. The sanctuary is 14 miles west of Hot Springs; to find it, follow SR 71 south and turn right after the Cheyenne River Bridge.

KIDSTUFF

The Black Hills attract people from all walks of life, but two groups travel the highways and walk the streets here more than others: retired couples and young families. As a result, you'll find many attractions that cater especially to older crowds or children. In this chapter, we discuss an extensive list of places designed for the latter.

Though there are plenty of developed sights and fun parks for kids, the natural beauty and expansiveness of the Black Hills is a great asset for parents. Kids are free to roam (and hopefully tire themselves out) in the national parks, forests, and grasslands while remaining free from the dangers found in the wilder parts of Wyoming, Montana, or Colorado. There are no bears or wolves and few big cats, though poison ivy and snakes can be a nuisance. Check with park or forest service personnel if you have questions specific to an area, and read the Natural World chapter.

Price Code

The following price code ratings refer to the cost of one child's ticket or admission fee.

$	Less than $5
$$	$5 to $10
$$$	$10 to $20
$$$$	More than $20

FUN PARKS

Get wet, get wild—there are plenty of fun parks in the Hills where youngsters (and their parents) can burn off energy and have good, clean fun.

Northern Hills

GULCHES OF FUN FAMILY FUN PARK $-$$$$
US 85 South, Deadwood
(605) 578-3386, (800) 961-3096
www.gulchesoffun.com
Ride the bumper boats and go-karts, play through the 18-hole miniature golf course, play every arcade game, and fill up at the snack bar. For little kids, there are kiddie go-karts and rides. This place does birthday parties (with pizza), too. Gulches of Fun is open from Memorial Day through Labor Day but may be open earlier and later in the season if weather permits. Each activity at the park requires one or more tickets, which are $1.75 each. All-day wristbands are available for $18 and $30 and are more cost-effective. Gulches of Fun is on Deadwood's south side, on the way to Lead.

SPEARFISH RECREATION & AQUATIC CENTER $$
2125 N Main St., Spearfish
(605) 722-1430
www.spearfishparksandrec.com
This immense recreation center houses a complete indoor athletic and exercise facility with a double-court gymnasium, suspended three-lane walking and jogging track, open fitness area and aerobic room. Aerobic fitness classes are available year-round. The

outdoor Aquatic Waterpark, open June through August, has a zero depth entry pool with geyser spray, lazy river with sprays and bridge, splash pad with interactive play features, double flume slides, drop slide, climbing wall, 25-yard, three-lane pool with wheelchair access, floating adventure walk, and bubble pit vortex. Hours are 5:30 a.m. to 9 p.m. Mon through Fri, 8 a.m. to 6 p.m. Sat, and noon to 6 p.m. Sun.

Central Hills

BLACK HILLS MAZE & AMUSEMENTS $$
6400 South US 16, Rapid City
(605) 343-5439
www.blackhillsmaze.com
If you like puzzles you'll love this bilevel, ever-changing maze with more than a mile of mind-boggling paths. Time yourself to see how quickly you can find your way out of the fortresslike network of towers, bridges, stairs, and sharp corners. There's also Bankshot Basketball and Water Wars with water balloons, a climbing wall, a zipline, and scooterlike Roller-Racers. Worn out yet? Take a break at the snack bar and pick up a South Dakota souvenir at the gift shop. The maze, 3 miles south of Rapid City, is open 8:30 a.m. to 9 p.m. daily from Memorial Day through Labor Day, except on Flashlight Fridays, when it's open an hour later and the lights go out. During Sept and Oct it's open Fri through Sun on a varying schedule, so call ahead for times.

FLAGS AND WHEELS $–$$$
405 12th St., Rapid City
(605) 341-2186
www.flagsandwheels.com
If you want to go fast, get excited, and let off some steam, this is the place. Also known as

Flags of Fun, this 47,000-square-foot fun park is one of the largest indoor racing facilities in the region. There are small go-karts and an arcade area for younger children, but the primary attractions here are for the bigger "kids." Biz-Karts, high-speed competitive racers built in England, are available for anyone over 16 (although the average age of racers is probably twice that). The indoor urban paintball is open to anyone (kids and parents sign a waiver form), but it's usually the domain of kids in their 20s and 30s. There are also batting cages, a snack bar, and some small party rooms. Flags and Wheels is open all year. Hours are 4 to 10 p.m. Mon through Sat and noon to 6 p.m. Sun. From Labor Day to Memorial Day hours are Mon through Sat noon to 10 p.m., and noon to 6 p.m. Sun. Prices range from 75 cents for a few pitches in the batting cage to $19.75 for a round of paintball.

i The Black Hills, Badlands, and Lakes Association (a nonprofit promotion group) publishes an annual list of Family Approved Attractions. While not all of the businesses on the list are specifically designed for children, they are appropriate for any age group. Many businesses have joined the listing system and display the pine tree logo with bright yellow and red lettering.

GIGGLEBEES $
937 East North St., Rapid City
(605) 399-1494
The name of this pizza arcade says it all. There's enough to do to keep you giggling for hours. Check out the kiddie rides, video games, Skee-Ball, pinball, and the play space. The restaurant—specializing in kid food—will help you keep up your energy for play.

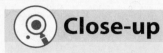 **Close-up**

Laura Ingalls Wilder

Laura Ingalls Wilder gently drew the curtain on her *Little House* books in DeSmet, the "little town on the prairie" in eastern South Dakota. But several characters from her enduring tales of pioneer childhood went west and left their imprint on the Black Hills. Laura's younger sister Carrie pursued a newspaper career that took her to Keystone in 1911. There she married a widower with two children, David Swanzey (who played a part in naming Mount Rushmore), and lived there until her death on June 2, 1946. Mary, the blind sister of the stories, died at Carrie's house on October 17, 1928; both sisters are buried with Ma and Pa in DeSmet. Laura's Uncle Henry and Aunt Polly, from the Big Woods of Wisconsin, also came to the Black Hills and are buried with their daughter, Ruby, in Harney Cemetery east of Keystone. Laura herself traveled to Keystone with her husband, Almanzo, to visit Carrie and see the sights.

But long before any of that, when Laura, Mary, and Carrie were still little girls on the banks of Plum Creek and before sister Grace was even born, their Uncle Tom Quiner, Ma's brother, ventured to the Hills in search of gold with the Gordon Party. (See the History chapter for more.) Years later, Uncle Tom visited Laura and her family in DeSmet and told them about his adventure; much later still, when Laura was in her 70s, she recalled Uncle Tom's story and wrote it down in *These Happy Golden Years*.

Gigglebees hosts birthday parties, too, with cakes, game tokens, even hats. Gigglebees is open year-round; its hours are 11 a.m. to 10 p.m. Mon through Thurs, 11 a.m. to 11 p.m. Fri, and 10:30 a.m. to 11 p.m. on Sat. There is no admission fee, but all games and rides require one or more tokens that cost 25 cents each. Token specials are often available.

THE RANCH AMUSEMENT
PARK   **$$–$$$$**
6303 South US 16, Rapid City
(605) 342-3321, (877) 302-3321
http://ranchamusementpark.com
This modest facility doesn't hold a candle to big-city amusement parks, but it does seem to have attractions for all ages. The go-karts are by far the favorite for both kids and adults.

The slick track is fairly long (three-quarters of a mile) and well designed, and the slow pace of the go-karts will make it safe and fun for younger drivers. The bumper boats, inflatable jumping castle, and two 18-hole miniature golf courses with a Wild West theme are also popular with the younger crowd. The climbing wall and arcade cater to the older kids, but everyone seems to appreciate the small snack bar after a round of golf or few laps in a go-kart. On the downside, the park is expensive when compared to many Black Hills attractions. Two laps on the go-kart track (which take a little over five minutes to complete) are $5. Repeated activities quickly add up, so wristbands, from $13 to $30, are usually the way to go. The staffers here don't go out of their way to be friendly—a rarity in the Black Hills, where hospitality is the major industry.

The Ranch is open 10 a.m. to 10 p.m., from Memorial Day to mid-Aug. Hours vary from Apr to May and from mid-Aug to Sept, so it's best to call ahead. While you're on the phone, ask about the weather—thunderstorms shut down most attractions here. "Wacky Wednesday" is especially busy, since all visitors receive $5 off the price of a wristband. Call ahead for group rates and schedules.

i South Dakota law prohibits fireworks of any kind, including firecrackers, in the Black Hills Forest Fire Protection District, except within the incorporated boundaries of municipalities. The district encompasses pretty much all of the Hills from Spearfish to Edgemont and Rapid City to the Wyoming border.

RUSHMORE WATERSLIDE
PARK $$–$$$
1715 US 16 Bypass (Catron Boulevard), Rapid City
(605) 348-8962
www.rushmorewaterslide.com
In the mood for some liquid refreshment? Make a splash at the waterslides, where you can take your pick of the super-speedy Bonzai or something slightly more sedate. In addition to the two steep slides, there are four 400-foot descents, an inner-tube river ride, a short ramp, and a kiddie slide. You'll also find volleyball, basketball, and horseshoe courts. If constant motion isn't your mode of operation, you can soak in the 30-foot hot spa, take shelter in the shaded picnic area, mosey along the minigolf course, sneak over to the snack bar, or browse among the beach accessories in the gift shop. The park, which is 3 miles south of Rapid City, is open early June to the end of Aug, 10 a.m. to 7 p.m., depending on the weather. Call ahead if it's questionable. Coin-operated lockers and hot showers are available, as are swimsuit, life-preserver, and towel rentals. There's even a fenced area to keep your dog safe while you play.

Southern Hills

EVANS PLUNGE $$
1145 North River St., Hot Springs
(605) 745-5165
www.evansplunge.com
Take your pick of the waterslides before taking the plunge into a swimming pool heated with naturally warm water. For information about other things to do at Evans Plunge, see the Recreation chapter.

FLINTSTONES BEDROCK CITY $$
US 16 West, Custer
(605) 673-4079
www.flintstonesbedrockcity.com
Fred, Wilma, and the gang are ready to welcome kids of all ages to Bedrock City. Enter the Stone Age and see the faces of Mount Rockmore, ride the Flintmobile and the Iron Horse train, and zip down the Slideasaurus. Then get your strength back with a Brontoburger or Dino Dog at the Drive-In, and check out the licensed Flintstones items in the gift shop. Bedrock City, at the west end of town, is open from mid-May through Labor Day. From early June to mid-Aug, hours are 9 a.m. to 8 p.m.; call for times the rest of the season. For information about the park's campground, see the Campgrounds chapter.

HISTORIC SITES & MUSEUMS

History comes alive at these sites and museums. Each has an emphasis or special feature that appeals to kids.

Northern Hills

BROKEN BOOT GOLD MINE $
US 14A, Deadwood
(605) 578-9997
www.brokenbootgoldmine.com

So you think you might strike it rich here? It could happen, but, more likely you'll get rich quick in historical knowledge. The Broken Boot is a real gold mine, abandoned and closed for about 50 years, then reopened in 1954 for tours. When modern-day engineers explored the mine, they found a miner's boot that had been abandoned half a century before; hence the name. Today you can follow a tour guide 840 feet back and deep into the hillside. You'll learn about the way early miners looked for gold and about the history of the Black Hills gold rush. Mining is hard work, but this tour isn't, and you should have enough energy left over for gold panning. The Broken Boot will provide the pans and other supplies, show you how to look for gold in the panning troughs, and let you keep the shiny stuff if you find some.

The mine is at the intersection of Upper Main Street and US 14A, at the south end of Deadwood. It is open mid-May through mid-Sept, 9 a.m. to 5 p.m. seven days a week. Tours leave every 30 minutes during those hours. The mine is not wheelchair accessible. There's an additional charge for gold panning but you are guaranteed to find some "color."

TRIAL OF JACK MCCALL $
715 Main St., Deadwood
(605) 578-1876

Deadwood may have been only a few months old in the summer of 1876, but the illegal gold camp already claimed 5,000 inhabitants—mostly prospectors, gamblers, and opportunists of dubious origin. Wild Bill Hickok, a legendary lawman and gunslinger, was one of them. It was no secret that he was in Deadwood to profit at the card table, which is what he was trying to do on August 2, 1876, when he walked into Saloon No. 10 on Main Street. After failing to convince fellow gambler Charlie Rich to give up his stool, Wild Bill reluctantly took the only open seat and joined the game. Forsaking years of cautious habit in a moment of greed, the gunman sat with his back to the door. The decision would prove fatal when drifter Jack McCall sidled through the door. Hickok, distracted by his losses to another player ("The old duffer, he broke me on the hand," he was muttering), didn't notice when McCall finally walked up to the table, gun drawn. "Damn you! Take that!" McCall shouted, discharging the death-dealing round into Hickok's head. Hickok's murder happens four times a day, seven nights a week, in summer at the Old Style Saloon No. 10 (657 Main St.; more in the Nightlife chapter), subsequently followed by McCall's brief escape and capture farther up the street. The last performance at 7 p.m. is followed by McCall's trial in the Masonic Temple's theater at 715 Main St.

Southern Hills

FOUR MILE OLD WEST TOWN $
US 16, Custer
(605) 673-3905
www.fourmilesd.com

A talking outhouse with a sense of humor? That's just the beginning of your self-guided trek through the Old West at its most rustic. More than 50 wooden shacks house artifacts from days gone by, and there are plenty of witticisms sprinkled in with the history lesson—for instance, the proprietress of the seamstress shop is Mrs. Hattie Coates. But only the worthy may enter through the front door. A sign outside admonishes, TINHORNS, GAMBLERS AND LAYABOUTS, USE THE BACK DOOR. There is even a rebuilt stockade. Stagecoaches used to stop here to water their horses at Four Mile Spring, and the town of Moss City was located here more than a century ago. The owners offer lots of hands-on activities for the kids. The present-day tourist complex 4 miles west of Custer has regular tours 8 a.m. to 5 p.m. Mon through Sat and 9:30 a.m. to 7 p.m. on Sun, May through Sept, and by appointment or chance during the winter.

MAMMOTH SITE OF
HOT SPRINGS $$
US 18 Bypass, Hot Springs
(605) 745-6017
www.mammothsite.com
How is an elephant's ear like an air conditioner? Find out at Mammoth Site, where you can touch an elephant's ear, see the giant (and sometimes tiny) bones of ancient animals that died here, and "dig" for fossils. To find out more, see the Attractions chapter.

i Kids younger than 21 are welcome in Deadwood gaming halls if they come with a parent or guardian. But according to state law, they are not allowed to touch or play the gaming machines or handle money used for gambling, and they must stay 3 feet behind any player.

PARKS & NATURE AREAS

Playgrounds, open space, and fresh-air activities are found in these parks and nature areas.

Northern Hills

SPEARFISH CITY PARK   FREE
Canyon Street, Spearfish
The playground here isn't just another collection of swings and slides. Local kids worked with an architect to design it, and it was built by local volunteers, including kids, in 1996. You'll find an area with a sandbox and smaller equipment just for tots as well as swings, slides, monkey bars, a tire swing, and other fun equipment for older children. A wooden fence encloses the entire playground. When you're played out, soak your feet in Spearfish Creek, which runs along the west side of the park. City Park is on the south end of town.

Central Hills

COSMOS MYSTERY AREA $$
US 16, Rapid City
(605) 343-9802, (605) 343-7278
www.cosmosmysteryarea.com
You'll be confounded by the Cosmos, where balls roll uphill, people get shorter, and the laws of physics are unenforceable. What's more, your guide on a half-hour tour will do everything possible to confuse you. Don't expect to get an explanation for the odd things that occur here; according to the staff, even scientists can't agree on what causes folks to feel off-balance at the Cosmos. It's been a tourist attraction since 1952, when two college boys discovered the area known as "the strangest location in the Black Hills." The Cosmos is open 7 a.m. to dusk daily, June 1 to Labor Day; and from 9 a.m. to 5 p.m. Mon through Fri during Apr, May, Sept, and Oct. Cosmos is 18 miles south of Rapid City; look for signs pointing to the turnoff.

The South Dakota Triceratops

The South Dakota state fossil is the *Triceratops,* one of the last dinosaurs to live in North America. The word *Triceratops* means "three-horned face." This 30-foot-long, 12-ton dino had a head more than 6 feet long, protected by those three fierce horns. His neck was topped by a bony plate and beaked snout. A heavy, pointed tail made him well armed against his predator, the much larger *Tyrannosaurus.*

The South Dakota *Triceratops*'s skull was discovered in Harding County in 1927 and is on display at the Museum of Geology, but his concrete likeness can be seen at Dinosaur Park. Both are in Rapid City.

DINOSAUR PARK   FREE
Skyline Drive, Rapid City
(605) 343-8687

It's not every kid who gets to slide down the face of a dinosaur. That's because most towns don't have a special park full of the green monsters. The seven concrete giants aren't very detailed, and they look a bit out of place (perhaps even tacky) atop a giant hill that overlooks the city, but it's their symbolism—not their appearance—that matters. Built in the depths of the Depression by the Works Progress Administration, the bright green dinos represent a determination to survive in tough times, even by very creative means. Among the first roadside dinosaurs ever constructed, they are listed on the National Register of Historic Places, and Rapid City park officials continue to tend them with pride. The giant *Brontosaurus* (as the *Apatosaurus* was known in 1936) is the only structure visible from both the east and west sides of town. He's usually lit up at night, and he marks the holiday season with a big red bow that hangs from his neck.

Dinosaur Park is open 6 a.m. to 10 p.m. year-round. A gift shop and snack bar are open 8 a.m. to 8 p.m. daily, June through Aug, and 9 a.m. to 5 p.m. in May, Sept, and Oct. It's closed from Nov through Apr. From Quincy Street in Rapid City, follow the signs west to Dinosaur Park. It's seven-tenths of a narrow, twisting mile up Skyline Drive.

MOUNT RUSHMORE NATIONAL MEMORIAL   FREE
SR 244, Keystone
(605) 574-2523
www.nps.gov/moru

Youngsters ages 5 to 12 can do much more than tag along with Mom and Dad when the family visits Mount Rushmore. Kids who participate in the park's learn-and-earn Junior Ranger Program pick up a booklet at the information center and fill it out as they gather information about the monument by watching a video, taking a tour, or doing other activities. When they're done an hour or so later, a park ranger will sign their book, entitling them to a certificate. Those who wish to may also buy a patch for a small charge to sew on their hat or coat. The park's children's program offers age-appropriate talks on a variety of topics related to Mount Rushmore. Talks are offered once each afternoon and last about 30 minutes; call ahead for the schedule or check at the information center when you arrive. Take US 16 south from Rapid City or US 16A south from

Keystone and follow the signs to SR 244 and Mount Rushmore. For more information about the memorial, see the Parks & Mountains chapter.

STORYBOOK ISLAND   FREE
1301 Sheridan Lake Rd., Rapid City
(605) 342-6357
www.storybookisland.org
Nursery rhymes are the theme at Storybook Island, where tykes and grown-ups enter the world of characters from some of the best-known children's stories. Cinderella and her pumpkin coach are here, along with Dorothy and Toto, the Crooked Man, and many others. The Storybook Island Theatre Troupe performs all season; call for the schedule. The park is open 9 a.m. to 8 p.m. daily from Memorial Day weekend through Labor Day. It reopens on weekends from the day after Thanksgiving through Christmas, when miles and miles of lights deck the trees and displays, and special events are planned. Call for more details. The Rapid City and Rushmore Rotary Clubs support Storybook Island. However, donations are always welcome.

i The American Lung Association of South Dakota offers the Children's Fun Pass that gives youngsters ages 6 to 12 free or reduced rates on admission, games, and food at more than 40 Black Hills area attractions (and others across South Dakota). The pass costs $15 but is valued at more than $250. Call (800) 873-5864 for more information.

WILDLIFE PARKS
Northern Hills

SPIRIT OF THE HILLS WILDLIFE SANCTUARY $
500 North Tinton Rd., Spearfish
(605) 642-2907
www.wildlifesanctuary.net
This nonprofit animal rescue facility is dedicated to animal welfare and advocacy, features a variety of animals in natural settings, including lions, white tigers, panthers and pumas, camels, llamas, and bears. Reservations are recommended in the off-season, but generally tours occur at 10 a.m., noon, and 2 p.m. in summer. Group tours available.

Central Hills

BEAR COUNTRY U.S.A. $$$
13820 South US 16, Rapid City
(605) 343-2290
www.bearcountryusa.com
Lions and reindeer and bears, oh my! Look who's looking at you, kid, as you drive through this wildlife park. Here, you're in a "cage" and the animals get to wander around. For more about Bear Country, turn to the Attractions chapter.

REPTILE GARDENS $$–$$$
US 16, Rapid City
(605) 342-5873
www.reptilegardens.com
Like rattlesnakes? How about tropical flowers? Either way, you'll find what you're looking for at Reptile Gardens. Plus, you'll get to know more about alligators, birds, and other animals. See the Attractions chapter for a more complete description of one of the Black Hills' most popular stops.

TROUT HAVEN $-$$
US 385, Rapid City
(605) 341-4440

This place is quite a catch. It's your chance to hook a trout, and you won't have to stand in the middle of a stream and get cold water in your waders to do it. It's also your chance to tell a big fish story. Trout Haven furnishes poles and bait, encouragement and advice. When you've got that big one, they'll clean it and either fry it up in the restaurant or pack it in ice. If you and your family are traveling for a while, they'll even keep your filleted and frozen fish until you return.

Trout Haven is open from approximately Memorial Day to late Sept, but call ahead to be sure. Hours are 8 a.m. to 6 p.m. seven days a week during the summer. Your big catch will cost you 50 cents an inch, or $4.95 for a meal that supplements your fish with french fries, Texas toast, and coleslaw. Breakfast is also served (and if you've never tried fresh trout for breakfast, you're in for a treat). Other items are available on the restaurant's menu if you don't like fish. Trout Haven is 19 miles west of Rapid City, 20 minutes south of Deadwood on US 385. There are plenty of signs on the highway to guide you.

ANNUAL EVENTS & FESTIVALS

Black Hills residents have always known how to have a good time. Since the land was settled, festivals and special events have been important here. Out on the range the ranchers learned to plan cowboy-style rodeos and fairs, while the more rowdy miners and mountain men deeper in the Hills threw wild parties and street dances. To this day you'll find a great series of events out on the plains, but the closer you get to the ancient mining towns of the Hills, the more spirited and more frequent the festivals become. Deadwood, for example, has more special events than any other town in the region. There's always something cookin' there, and the town really knows how to throw a party—often rolling the shindigs, which usually include live music, dancing, and open containers, right out onto the streets.

Because some events change dates from year to year, only approximate dates are listed here. Call ahead or check the local papers or visitor guides for firm dates. The information here is not meant to be exhaustive—many events change, new events are added, and those decreasing in popularity fall by the wayside. You'll notice a minimum of events in Jan, Feb, Mar, and Apr. Blame it on South Dakota winters and wet springs, which make getting out and about a bit difficult and undesirable. If you're visiting during those months, you'll still find plenty to do, but don't expect the variety of festivals you'll find in the summer. Our festivals and events are your chance to get in on some local celebrations and festivities. Have fun!

JANUARY

Central Hills

✳BLACK HILLS STOCK SHOW AND RODEO
Rushmore Plaza Civic Center
444 Mount Rushmore Rd., Rapid City
(605) 394-4115
www.bhssf.com
Begun in 1958, the Black Hills Stock Show and Rodeo is the third-largest stock show in the country. This annually anticipated event is a place for ranchers to show, buy, and sell cattle and horses, and a great community get-together. If you've never been to a stock show, you'll find that they're highly educational and a great way to learn about the trials, tribulations, and rewards of the South Dakota ranching life. You may even learn to tell the difference between one breed of cow and another. There are plenty of other things to look at, too: art, clothing, gifts, and food. The show is held in late Jan or early Feb and runs for about 10 days. Admission to the stock show is free, but tickets must be purchased for the rodeo and a few other events.

ℹ️ According to the *Guinness Book of World Records,* on January 22, 1943, the temperature in Spearfish rose 49 degrees in just two minutes! A thermometer disc marked the 7:30 a.m. temperature at -4 degrees; at 7:32 a.m., a temperature of 45 degrees was recorded. This astounding change was the result of a chinook, and the sudden change from frigid to mild cracked windows around town.

FEBRUARY
Northern Hills

CHINESE NEW YEAR CELEBRATION
Miss Kitty's Casino
647 Main St., Deadwood
(605) 578-7777, (605) 578-1811
www.deadwood.com

Since Chinese New Year is a lunar holiday, it's hard to pin down the exact date of this celebration, which takes place in early Feb. Deadwood history has a fascinating chapter on the Chinese immigrants and business-people who joined in the glory days of the gold rush. The city celebrates that culture on Chinese New Year with lion dancers, a parade, firecrackers (which drive away evil spirits that threaten the coming year), and a display of photographs and artifacts from the Adams House and Adams Museum. Miss Kitty's also has a buffet for the event.

MARDI GRAS CELEBRATION
Main Street, Deadwood
(605) 578-1876, (800) 999-1876
www.deadwood.com

It's the Mardi Gras of the West, with costumes, a night parade, a Cajun-food cook-off, and all the trappings (well, most of them) of New Orleans. But this one also has gaming and the charming amenities and atmosphere of Deadwood, South Dakota—something New Orleans can't claim. Mardi Gras takes place in late Feb or early Mar, and it's an outrageous party you won't soon forget, done up Deadwood-style.

Central Hills

BLACK HILLS COMMUNITY THEATRE SEASON
Dahl Fine Arts Center
713 7th St., Rapid City
(605) 394-1786, (605) 394-6091
www.bhct.org

The community theater presents five quality performances—a good mix of drama, comedy, and music—throughout the year, with the first scheduled for Feb. Performances are professionally staged by dedicated local actors in the theater at the Dahl. Ticket prices vary and season tickets are available, so call ahead to check prices and reserve seats. The Black Hills Community Theatre also conducts classes and workshops and presents plays for children. You can read all about it in the Arts chapter.

MARCH
Northern Hills

BLACK HILLS BOX SLED CHAMPIONSHIPS
Mystic Mountain Ski Area
US 85, Lead
(605) 584-3230
www.skimystic.com

Yes, the sleds are literally boxes. Kids of all ages are welcome to build a cardboard box sled using tape, glue, and imagination. Sharks, Vikings, and Model Ts have all plowed through the snow in the past. And, if their sleds actually stay together (there are quite a few wrecks at this race), competitors have a chance to win! There are all kinds of prizes, including best of show and best costume. The entry fee is $15. Mystic Mountain has several other fun events and also serious competitions. Check its website for the latest dates. The Chuckwagon Hour (finger food) begins at 6 p.m., and the show starts at 7 p.m. Admission is $5.

ST. PATRICK'S DAY CELEBRATION
Downtown Deadwood
(605) 578-1876, (800) 999-1876
www.deadwood.com

Show your colors (as long as they're green) at St. Paddy's parade and celebration in Deadwood. There are usually Irish bands, great food, green beer, a parade that tosses out money, and special events taking place in the casinos and restaurants on Main Street.

Central Hills

COUNTRY FAIR ARTS AND CRAFTS SHOWS
Various locations in Rapid City
(605) 342-3694, (605) 343-8783

Six shows are held each year, beginning in late Mar (with others held in July, early Oct, mid- and late Nov, and Dec). Most are at the Rushmore Plaza Civic Center, but the mid-July show takes place outdoors in pretty Canyon Lake Park. Crafters come from all over the country, and local and regional artisans participate. This is the largest indoor craft show in the area, and it's been a popular annual event for more than 20 years. Sometimes there is informal musical entertainment, and homemade baked goods and candy are available from vendors. You'll find the newest craft and gift trends here, as well as old favorites. Admission is free for the summer shows, $1 for benefit at the other shows, and vendors pay for their booth space.

APRIL

EASTER EGG HUNTS AND FESTIVITIES
Various locations throughout the Hills

Many Black Hills towns celebrate Easter and the pending arrival of spring weather with Easter egg hunts and other activities. Most are small community celebrations and, thus, aren't planned as organized annual events, but we mention them here because they're fun, especially for children. Check local papers and visitor publications for current information.

MAY

BLACK HILLS MOONWALKS
Various locations throughout the Hills
(605) 343-1567

Moonwalks take place one day each month, May through Oct (usually the Saturday nearest the full moon), and each is held at a different park or recreation area. They are sponsored by the Black Hills National Forest and the Black Hills Parks and Forests Association and conducted by people who can tell you a lot about each place. The moonwalks take participants to a certain destination where an expert in a field related to the hike's location gives a 30-minute presentation. Past talks have focused on wildlife such as bats and coyotes, archaeology in the Deadwood area, the Battle Creek forest fire, and the history of the Williams Ranch near Pringle. The moonwalks begin in the evening (between 7 and 9) and are usually 1- to 3-mile round-trips that last two to three hours. There is no charge, and you can call any of the forest service offices in the area to request current information. Bring your binoculars, something to drink, sturdy shoes, and layers of clothing (it can be chilly at night). Check with the Mystic Ranger District office (at the number above, or visit 803 Soo San Dr., Rapid City) or see local newspaper listings for details and directions.

i Elvis Presley performed one of his final concerts at Rapid City's Rushmore Plaza Civic Center on June 21, 1977, less than two months before his death on August 16 at the age of 42. And, no, he hasn't been seen in Rapid City since.

SPRING OPEN HOUSE AND FREE FISHING WEEKEND
Various locations throughout the Hills
(605) 773-3391
www.state.sd.us/gfp
This is a very special event held at all 38 South Dakota state parks and recreation areas. It's a sort of visitor appreciation weekend, a way of inviting visitors back to the parks in the spring. The open house is held the weekend before Memorial Day, and from Saturday morning through Sunday evening there is no charge for park entrance, and fishing licenses are not required. Each park and recreation area offers entertainment, naturalist programs for kids, fishing tournaments, and presentations. For more information call the South Dakota Parks and Recreation Department in Pierre at the above number.

JUNE
Northern Hills

JOHANNA MEIER OPERA THEATRE INSTITUTE
Black Hills State University
1200 University St., Spearfish
(605) 642-6420
www.about-arts.com
In June, Black Hills State University sponsors this competitive program that not only benefits the participants but the community as well. Students 17 and older from across the nation and around the world audition to study with international opera star Johanna Meier and other professors, and the students present at least two performances for the public. The educational program is called the Vocal Arts and Opera Theatre School, which is the main part of the Summer Institute of the Arts. The focus is on vocal, opera, and theater performance. The programs' events (which also include classes and lectures) most often take place in BHSU's recital hall, that has been named in Meier's family's honor. Meier Hall is small (280 capacity), but the design is beautiful and created especially for music performances.

The performances are open to the public, but you need to buy tickets. An opening performance by the students includes a reception; admission is $5 for adults, $2.50 for children under 15 and seniors. At the final performance, A Night at the Opera, students and teachers present a selection of opera scenes and arias; admission is $10 for adults, $5 for children and seniors, with a reception afterward. There is also a pre-performance dinner and lecture for an additional $15, but you need to make reservations the day before.

CENTER OF THE NATION ALL CAR RALLY
Herrmann Park
Off 8th Street, Belle Fourche
(605) 892-2676, (888) 345-JULY
www.bellefourche.org
Collectible cars and trucks from across the nation show up here to show off. Owners can participate in the show-and-shine

competition, and the event runs in conjunction with the South Dakota State Chili Cook-off, which is open to the public for spicy sampling and bears a cash prize for the winner. Most types of collectible cars and trucks are welcome, but call ahead to learn if there are restrictions. There's a registration fee for vehicle owners, but spectators and those who just want to ooh and aah don't have to pay. The All Car Rally is held the second weekend of June on Fri, Sat, and Sun.

STURGIS CAVALRY DAYS
**Various locations in Sturgis and
at Fort Meade
(605) 347-2556
www.sturgis-sd.org**
Honoring the history of the West, and Sturgis's part in it, this mid-June event takes place at different locations and offers some interesting western-style activities. Past ones have included an arts festival, horse and carriage rides, living-history and cavalry reenactments, a buffalo feed, a trial of Lt. Col. George Custer by real-life modern-day lawyers, a military ball, and a trader rendezvous.

WILD BILL DAYS
**Downtown Deadwood
(605) 578-1876, (800) 999-1876
www.deadwood.com**
Deadwood celebrates history in June by remembering one of its most famous permanent residents: James Butler "Wild Bill" Hickok. You'll see reenactments of Wild Bill's famous murder and the carousing of his friends Calamity Jane and Charlie Utter, and you'll also see these characters at the parade. If that's not enough excitement for you, the fast-draw and gunspinning competitions are sure to get your heart racing. The activities are free and include two free concerts by

national recording artists on Main Street (past performers have included Loverboy, Blackhawk, and Big & Rich).

Central Hills

MUSIC IN THE PARK MEMORIAL PARK
**5th and Omaha Streets, Rapid City
(605) 343-5176**
Free outdoor concerts are presented each summer at the Memorial Park band shell, and indoor winter concerts are held at coffeehouses or the Dahl Fine Arts Center. Read about Music in the Park, listed under Backroom Productions, in the Arts chapter.

FAMILY CRUISER NIGHT
**Various locations in Rapid City
(605) 394-4133
www.rcgov.org**
On one hand, this is a chance for proud car owners to parade down Mount Rushmore Road, then display their shiny vehicles at the Rushmore Plaza Civic Center parking lot or downtown. It's also a chance to participate in the long-standing pastime of cruising. But it's really an evening for families—an opportunity for parents to cruise with their kids and to spend time together. Spectators have great fun, too, watching the streams of beautifully restored, well-cared-for, and customized cars, from classic '57 Chevys and antique Model As to snazzy low-riders with fuzzy dice dangling from their rearview mirrors. With good weather, Cruiser Night will get as many as 500 cars.

The event starts and ends at the civic center, next to Memorial Park, and is sponsored by the Rapid City Police Department. There's usually music downtown or at the band shell, plus public-safety displays and demonstrations that show what's new in law enforcement. Food and T-shirt sales benefit the DARE program. Family Cruiser Night is held on a Friday evening in mid-June, but it is sometimes canceled because of rain, so call ahead.

WEST BOULEVARD SUMMER FESTIVAL
Wilson Park
Mount Rushmore Road, Rapid City
(605) 348-9439, (605) 343-1744
A very popular community arts-and-crafts festival, this one is held in pretty Wilson Park, just a block from historic West Boulevard, in mid-June. You'll enjoy shopping for creative arts and crafts, listening to the musical performances, and sampling a variety of ethnic food. Then stroll over to West Boulevard and take a look at the beautiful historic houses. Vendors pay a fee for their booth space, but browsers are admitted free.

BLACK HILLS BLUEGRASS FESTIVAL
Mystery Mountain Resort
US 16, Rapid City
(605) 394-4101
It's a weekend of toe-tapping, feel-good bluegrass and acoustic music. For more than 20 years, the festival has taken place on the last full weekend in June, starting Friday night and ending Sunday morning with a gospel show. The festival is a warm and homey event, with concerts by nationally known entertainers, workshops, informal jam sessions, food, and plenty of music. The organizers describe it as a big family reunion because so many people come back year after year. The price for a single show is $10; a ticket for all day Saturday is $20; a weekend ticket is $30. Discounts are available for advance purchases, and children under 12 are admitted free. The resort offers special camping rates for the bluegrass event. Call the resort at (605) 342-5368 or (800) 658-2267.

Southern Hills

BLACK HILLS PLAYHOUSE
Custer State Park, Custer
(605) 255-4141, (605) 255-4242
www.blackhillsplayhouse.com
A visit to the playhouse is a perfect chance to tour beautiful Custer State Park and catch a great stage performance, too. The summer season runs from June through Aug each year. You'll need a South Dakota state park sticker to access the park. You'll find detailed information about the playhouse in the Arts chapter. The historic Playhouse buildings have been undergoing extensive renovations so check before making the trip into the park for a performance for actual show locations.

CRAZY HORSE VOLKSMARCH
Crazy Horse Memorial
US 16/385, Custer
(605) 673-4681
www.crazyhorse.org
Just once each year, participants are allowed to walk right up to the huge carved face of Crazy Horse and view the work in progress close-up. (You can read about Crazy Horse Memorial in the Attractions chapter.) In recent years, between 10,000 and 14,000 hardy folks have made this 6.2-mile trek. The Crazy Horse Volksmarch, the largest Volksmarch in the country, is held on Saturday and Sunday during the first full weekend of June and costs just $2 per person. To receive official credit for your Volksmarch, you must pay $2; to receive the "Volksmarch Crazy Horse" medal, you must pay $7.

JULY

FOURTH OF JULY CELEBRATIONS
Various locations throughout the Hills

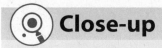

Close-up

Mattie Goff Newcombe

From the time she was a teenager, **Mattie Goff Newcombe** had a reputation. She was known as the fastest trick rider on the fastest horse in rodeo.

Even when she was a little girl, Mattie knew she was born to ride. When she sat astride a horse for the first time, she was just three years old. Luckily, growing up on her family's Meade County ranch gave her plenty of opportunity to break wild horses and become a skillful rider, and at 14 she entered her first rodeo. Back then, in 1921, not many women competed in rodeo, and Mattie helped pave the way for other talented riders of her sex.

Weighing only 100 pounds, Mattie was an agile woman who wore a wide-brim hat atop her smiling face and fancy boots on her tiny feet. She quickly earned fame for performing exciting stunts with names like "the slick saddle liberty stand," "spin the horn," "under the neck," "under the belly" and, most dangerous of all, "the suicide drag." She loved to square-dance on horseback in a quadrille made up of four couples. And no one could beat her at relay racing—she was that fast and that good at leaping from horse to horse without touching the ground.

Mattie was fearless. The only time she felt nervous was just before she performed for President Calvin Coolidge in 1927. But once she got on her horse, her jitters faded. She later reported, with some disappointment, that Silent Cal had talked to her and wasn't silent after all.

She never intended to retire, but Mattie married Maynard Newcombe in 1927 and discovered, as she often said, "You can't run a ranch and rodeo, too." So she came home to South Dakota and a life of hard work but no regrets. She stayed active, and 60 years after she entered her last rodeo she could still fit into her trick-riding costume.

In 1961 Mattie became a charter member of the National Cowboy Hall of Fame, and for more than 30 years after that she continued to accumulate honors. In 1989 she was inducted into the South Dakota Hall of Fame, and three years later Mattie was named South Dakota Rodeo Personality of the Past by the Casey Tibbs Foundation. Local sculptor T. R. (Tony) Chytka cast a small bronze statue of Mattie that's on display in First Western Bank in Sturgis, where she settled after her husband died. A life-size version will go in the Casey Tibbs South Dakota Rodeo Center in Fort Pierre, in central South Dakota. In 1994 Mattie became a Cowgirl Honoree in the National Cowgirl Museum and Hall of Fame.

Most Black Hills towns and cities hold their own Fourth of July celebrations, patriotic community events that may include parades, picnics, barbecues, street dances, craft fairs, special events for children, and, of course, fireworks after dark. Check local papers and visitor publications for details.

Northern Hills

BLACK HILLS ROUNDUP
Roundup Grounds
Roundup Street, Belle Fourche
(605) 892-2643, (888) 345-JULY
www.bellefourche.org

The first roundup in 1918 was a Red Cross benefit. This long-standing and entertaining event still takes place over five days around the Fourth of July, and there's a lot to see and do. You can enjoy carnival rides, a free barbecue, roundup and horsemanship performances, a 10K run, a parade, and the Miss Rodeo South Dakota Pageant. The roundup itself is a Professional Rodeo Cowboys Association (PRCA) event, with traditional rodeo competition and entertainment. Brothers Marvin and Mark Garrett, Belle Fourche's world-champion riders, usually attend and compete as well. Ticket prices for the rodeo range from $9 to $16 for adults, depending on seating selection, with discounts for children. Most other roundup events are free. The Roundup Grounds are 1.5 blocks west off US 85 (5th Street).

FAMILY CREEK FAIR
D.C. Booth Historic Fish Hatchery
423 Hatchery Circle, Spearfish
(605) 642-7730
www.dcbooth.fws.gov
The fair is held on Father's Day on the lovely grounds of the hatchery. It's designed as a family event, a day when dads, moms, kids, and extended families can be together in a beautiful setting and have fun. Besides children's activities, there's brunch in Mrs. Ruby Booth's garden at the historic house. Parents can watch the demonstrations on fishing and wildlife, and everyone will enjoy feeding the trout and ducks and touring the hatchery museum. It's all free, except for the brunch (advance reservations are required). Read more about the D.C. Booth Fish Hatchery in the Attractions chapter.

FESTIVAL IN THE PARK
Spearfish City Park, Spearfish
(605) 642-7973

The Festival in the Park, held on the third full weekend in July, is a huge, popular event with more than 300 vendors. Arts and crafts of every variety, having passed the jury's discriminating eye, are presented in booths for the public's pleasure and purchase. In addition, there's a wonderful variety of food, jazz bands, dancing, music, and children's events and performances. These entertainments run all day long, so you can rest and snack, then walk around and look some more. The vendors pay a fee to display their work, but the festival is free to everyone else, except for the first night, when there is a $5 charge which helps to fund the Spearfish Arts Council.

> **i** Casey Tibbs, from rural Fort Pierre, South Dakota, was the youngest cowboy to win the national saddle bronc riding championship (he has won six of them!), plus a bareback championship and two all-round cowboy championships. His record is still unequaled in the Professional Rodeo Cowboys Association.

BLACK HILLS CORVETTE CLASSIC
Various locations in Spearfish
(605) 929-1100
www.blackhillscorvetteclassic.com
In 1971 the Sioux Falls Corvette Club (which consisted of seven couples and their cars) took a vacation together in the Black Hills. The event took on a life of its own, and hundreds of people and their Corvettes have been having fun together ever since. In recent years, some 1,700 people and 800 cars from 40 states have attended. The Corvette Classic takes place on the third full weekend of July (Thurs through Sun). On

Thursday, the group caravans from Sioux Falls to Spearfish, and everyone is welcome to tag along (not just club members, and not just Corvette owners). On the way home Sunday morning, everyone takes a detour to Mount Rushmore.

The main event is "Vette Street USA," when all those cars park on Main Street for a giant car show. Music, food, and merriment abound, plus competitions, touring and side trips, autocross, and drag races. The base registration fee is $165 per couple or $145 for one person, and participants can preregister by July 1. You can also register on-site at the Holiday Inn of the Northern Hills. The fee includes entrance to all the parties. If you just want to wander and browse through all that gleaming, curvy steel (no drooling on the cars!), there's no charge.

DAYS OF '76
Various locations in Deadwood
(605) 578-1876, (800) 999-1876
www.deadwood.com
This is rightfully billed as "the best rodeo in the hills—no bull." To prove it, the rodeo holds ten consecutive awards from the Professional Rodeo Cowboy Association (PRCA) for the best rodeo in its class. This action-packed event runs for five days and includes the rodeo, three nights of street dances, and two historic parades on Main Street in downtown Deadwood. The traditional parade is 3 miles long and mostly horse powered. The PRCA rodeo events attract enthusiastic crowds, and sometimes the Budweiser Clydesdales show up. President Coolidge attended the Days of '76 in 1927. It's a real (and real entertaining) tradition around Deadwood.

Central Hills

INDEPENDENCE DAY CELEBRATION
Mount Rushmore National Memorial
SR 244, Keystone
(605) 574-2523, (605) 574-3171
www.nps.gov/moru
Largely considered one of the top-10 fireworks displays in the nation, the Independence Day Celebration at Mount Rushmore is one of the more extravagant annual festivals held in the Black Hills. Besides the incredible pyrotechnics show, produced by internationally famous Zambelli Fireworks, there are live bands from local organizations and all branches of the military; flybys of F-16 fighters, Black Hawk helicopters, and B-1 bombers by Air National Guard and US Air Force personnel; and daylong entertainment from comedians, professional presidential impersonators, and others.

The main event, of course, is the explosive fireworks display directly above the four presidential heads, which occurs on the evening of July 3. In 2010 the National Park Service canceled the show due to extreme fire danger so if you are considering a trip to view this event, check before you leave home to be sure you will still witness fireworks. If you want one of the coveted places in the memorial's amphitheater, plan to arrive no later than mid-morning on the day of the display. On the other hand, if you can't handle the crowds, which number into the tens of thousands, the show is televised by local stations, South Dakota Public Broadcasting, and by some national news networks.

GEM AND MINERAL SHOW
Rushmore Plaza Civic Center
444 Mount Rushmore Rd., Rapid City
(605) 394-4115

This is a great show for rock hounds, gem and mineral fans, and folks shopping for interesting gifts and treasures. Vendors come from all over the country to sell, buy, swap, and exhibit their collections. You can find jewelry, rough rock, fossils, and specimens here and enjoy demonstrations, educational programs, and the silent auction. It's sponsored by the Western Dakota Gem and Mineral Society and held on the third weekend in July.

BLACK HILLS JAZZ AND BLUES FESTIVAL
Memorial Park, Civic Center Grounds, Off Mount Rushmore Road, Rapid City (605) 787-6619

This is a very special event for jazz and blues lovers. Each year on the last Saturday in July, five nationally and regionally known performers make Memorial Park come alive with the sound of their music. It starts at noon and lasts until 10:30 p.m., and it's a great family day spent in a beautiful setting, with music all around. Food is available; bring lawn chairs and blankets for seating. Wristbands, which cost $10, enable you to come and go as you like, skipping one performance and reentering the grounds for another. Discounts are available for children, too (please inquire).

AUGUST

Northern Hills

RUBY'S GARDEN PARTY
D.C. Booth Historic Fish Hatchery
423 Hatchery Circle, Spearfish
(605) 642-7730
www.dcbooth.fws.gov

The elegantly beautiful D.C. Booth home and gardens on the fish hatchery grounds are the setting for Ruby's Garden Party. Mrs. Ruby Booth, a charming hostess, loved to entertain; this party is named in her honor and is patterned after her gracious style and evokes the charm of the early 1900s. This lovely, dressy affair is held in mid-Aug in the garden behind the home and includes a champagne dinner with musical accompaniment. Advance registration is required. Proceeds from the party help the D.C. Booth Society maintain the historic home and grounds.

> **i** If you want to tie the knot while attending the Sturgis Rally & Races (which many couples do each year), there are rules. Both persons must be present, older than 18, and carry identification. The license is $40, and neither waiting period nor blood test is required. You can get the license at the Meade County Register of Deeds in the courthouse at 1425 Sherman St., Sturgis.

✴STURGIS MOTORCYCLE RALLY
Sturgis and other locations around the Hills
(605) 347-9190
www.sturgismotorcyclerally.com

The Sturgis Motorcycle Rally, South Dakota's largest special event, began in 1938. The little town of Sturgis, South Dakota (normal population about 7,000), swells to a temporary population of about 400,000 to 500,000 each year during the event. How this happens is a sort of motorcycling miracle. (For more about the history and idiosyncrasies of the Rally, see the Close-up in this chapter.)

The Rally officially runs from Mon through Sun the first full week of Aug, but bikers begin to descend on the Hills weeks early, and some stay just as long after the

Rally ends. For about two weeks each summer, the Black Hills vibrate constantly to the thunderous music only hundreds of thousands of motorcycles can make. After you're here for a couple of days, you can even sleep right through it.

So many events of vast and amazing variety are held during Rally week that it's impossible to describe them all. Official events include motorcycle auctions and displays, demonstration rides, concerts, parties, motorcycle jumps and hill climbs, races and ride-ins, guided tours of the Hills, exhibits, and poker runs. Four blocks of Main Street are closed to all vehicles except bikes, and you haven't seen anything until you've viewed thousands of shiny motorcycles parked perpendicular to the curbs, and in a double row down the middle, stretching as far as the eye can see.

Almost every downtown storefront is occupied by someone selling nearly every type of food you can imagine, or T-shirts, leather clothing, bandannas, cigars, motorcycle parts and accessories, and souvenirs.

Other Black Hills towns throw their own parties for bikers, and Rapid City's Rushmore Plaza Civic Center hosts the free Harley-Davidson show, with vendors, seminars, competitions, and demonstrations, plus a major concert (past performers have included ZZ Top, Willie Nelson, Lynyrd Skynyrd, and Def Leppard). You must purchase tickets to the concert. Deadwood is sometimes as crowded as Sturgis, since most casinos have weeklong activities planned for the biker crowd. Expect rowdy concerts, custom-bike giveaways, and celebrity appearances by people such as G. Gordon Liddy and *Playboy* centerfolds.

Call the number or browse the website listed in the heading for information and schedules, to register, and for help in finding accommodations (which you should book months, maybe even a year, in advance). You aren't required to officially register (and there's no charge for doing so), but you can stop at Rally Headquarters in the Armory building on Main Street to enter your name in the guest book and put a pin in the US or world maps to mark where you're from.

i Need accommodations for your trip to the Sturgis Rally in August? Check the Campgrounds and Accommodations chapters. Or call Sturgis Rally & Events, Inc., at (605) 347-9190 or the Sturgis Area Chamber of Commerce at (605) 347-2556 and request accommodations information. Better yet, go online at www.sturgis motorcyclerally.com.

BLACK HILLS STEAM AND GAS THRESHING BEE
Hereford Road, Sturgis
(605) 347-2556
www.sturgis.sd.us

Elders remember the farming equipment you'll see at this show: early steam- and gas-powered machinery that (in those days) made work easier. At least it was easier than doing it by hand and with horses. The Threshing Bee marked its 40th year in 2008. That's an indication of how popular it is, and how the old equipment still strikes a chord in the heart. More than 200 pieces of antique equipment are exhibited. The Threshing Bee will transport you back to a simpler, but more strenuous, time. It may even be a chance for elders to share their stories and heritage with those who are younger. You'll see antique tractors, threshing machines, sawmills, steam engines, miniature engines, blacksmithing, a

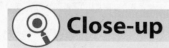

Close-up

The Sturgis Motorcycle Rally

Every year, during the first full week of August, tens of thousands of black-leather-clad folks ride their roaring steeds into Sturgis, South Dakota. They take over the town, park in every available parking space, fill the restaurants, crowd the sidewalks, and stay up half the night partying. The air is filled with the thundering sound of their steel horses, and normal conversation is downright impossible.

Why don't the good citizens of Sturgis do something about this intrusion, you ask? Don't they resent this yearly invasion of their peace and quiet, of their quaint little town? Heck, no! They invited these invaders, and they even gave the event a name: Sturgis Rally & Races.

It all started in 1938 when J. C. "Pappy" Hoel (who owned the local motorcycle shop) and his friends organized a race. Nineteen people showed up, and it was so much fun that they formed the Jackpine Gypsies Motorcycle Club and started an annual tour of the Hills. Events and activities were added each year; attendance grew, and the whole thing snowballed.

Now, most of the businesses on Main Street and neighboring blocks clear out and make way for hundreds of vendors, including custom-bike builders such as West Coast Choppers (owner Jessie James, a devout biker, usually rides his chopper all the way up from California). Bikers still race and tour the Hills, but there are also Motorcycle Hall of Fame inductions (Jay Leno and Peter Fonda are members), rock 'n' roll concerts, fighting competitions. . . . One thing's for sure, you'll never be bored at the Rally.

Nearly everyone attending the Rally takes the opportunity to show off in some way. You'll see incredibly creative custom bikes and paint jobs, wild headgear, bikers with parrots, bikers with snakes, bikers with dogs in sidecars, Christian bikers and unregen-

one-room schoolhouse, and more. There are plenty of demonstrations, threshing, and hay binding in the field next door, tractor races, and a daily parade. Music is provided by the Grimm Reapers (would anyone else be more appropriate?). The bee takes place on Fri, Sat, and Sun of the third weekend in Aug, on the grounds owned by the Western Dakota Antique Club, a half mile east of the Sturgis Airport, off SR 34. Admission is $5 per day for anyone 13 and older.

✳**KOOL DEADWOOD NITES**
Various locations in Deadwood
(605) 578-1876, (800) 999-1876
www.deadwood.com

It's the finest kind of retro concert 'cause you get to pretend you're back in the '50s and '60s again. It's held on Fri, Sat, and Sun in late Aug. You can dance at the sock hop or attend the parade and show and shines. Typically over 700 classic cars are displayed, and prizes are awarded for beauty. Don't miss the Sunday morning Show & Shine that packs Main Street with vintage vehicles. The "prom," complete with authentic music, is on Saturday night, and everyone is encouraged to dress up in style. In the past, music has been provided by the Turtles, Dion, and Chubby Checker.

erate ones, tattoos that cover more square inches of skin than clothing, piercing on every conceivable body part, and rude (but funny) T-shirts.

Although "biker" might sound a bit scary—conjuring up visions of burly, mean, criminal types—most bikers aren't like that at all. Few rally-goers are hardcore bikers anymore; very rarely will you see someone who might belong to an infamous biker gang. The vast majority are middle-aged professionals (doctors and lawyers especially) from the East and West Coast who don black leather and grow their beards out or abandon the makeup bag for a week. For them, the Rally is time to let loose in a way that isn't ordinarily possible.

But while the adults reign, you'll notice a fair share of kids at the event, too. It's not uncommon to see a toddler on a bike in a leather jacket or kids as young as six geared up with helmet and pads, ready to race on bikes just their size. Many locals and visitors like to make the Rally a family event. Others stay clear of the event altogether, citing stories of licentiousness and rowdy behavior. True enough, some venues can get a bit shady and family unfriendly during the week, but they're clearly identifiable (and carry age restrictions to boot). And admittedly, no matter where you are it's not uncommon to hear a little rough talk or see some bare skin.

Regardless of how rough, scraggly, or naked bikers may look, they all have an interesting story to tell, and most are pretty sociable if you can get up the nerve to talk to them. If you need an icebreaker, just ask about their bikes; whether they built them themselves or just bought them yesterday—all bikers take pride in their steel beast. It will probably be a Harley-Davidson, which is the official bike of the Rally. Other brands, such as Kawasaki and Honda, are minorities and may even get a few laughs. Unless, of course, the owner sports a studded leather jacket and outweighs everyone by 100 pounds.

Central Hills

ELLSWORTH AIR FORCE BASE OPEN HOUSE

I-90, exits 63 and 67, Ellsworth
(605) 385-4414
www.ellsworth.af.mil

"There's always a plane in the air during this exciting open house," say the organizers, and if you like planes, you'll get your fill of them here. You can watch aerial demonstrations, fly-bys, and parachute jumps and see both vintage and modern combat aircraft. The Golden Knights army parachute team has appeared, and attendees have been treated to aerobatic stunts and air rescue demonstrations.

CENTRAL STATES FAIR & RODEO

Central States Fairgrounds, Rapid City
(605) 355-3861
www.centralstatesfair.com

This is a traditional fair with those familiar events that make country fairs so much fun. You can browse 4-H and agricultural exhibits, sit in on classes and demonstrations on cooking and crafts, walk through the livestock barns, pet an exotic critter at the petting zoo, ride the carnival rides, catch a horse show or parade, and stuff yourself with cotton candy and caramel apples. Or sit back in the grandstand and be entertained by famous musical talent (past performers include the Nitty Gritty Dirt Band and Creedence Clearwater

Revival). If you'd rather sit on the edge of your seat, try the Professional Rodeo Cowboys Association rodeo instead. So many things go on at this eight-day fair that you'll have trouble finding time to enjoy them all, so check local newspapers and sort out each day's events. The Central States Fair takes place in mid- to late Aug.

SEPTEMBER

Northern Hills

BLACK HILLS AIRPORT FLY-IN
Black Hills Airport, Spearfish
(605) 642-4112, (605) 642-0277
Pilots and aviation buffs alike love this annual event, which takes place on a Saturday in September. Seventy-some planes have been displayed, including vintage warbirds as well as experimental planes, ultralights, and helicopters. Pilots can fly their planes in, and spectators can take rides and enjoy the displays. Demonstrations and food are offered, too. You can watch the South Dakota Aviation Hall of Fame induction ceremony, a very special event. The fly-in is free to everyone, pilots and spectators alike.

DEADWOOD JAM
Downtown Deadwood
(605) 578-1102, (800) 999-1876
www.deadwoodjam.com
The "Jam" has become one of the largest musical festivals in the Black Hills, and if you're a music fan you won't want to miss it. It's held in mid-Sept each year, outdoors. Advanced ticket prices are as low as $15, slightly more at the gate. Food and alcohol are available by vendors. George Clinton and the Parliament Funkadelics, Big Head Todd & The Monsters, Collective Soul, Spin Doctors, Inner Circle, and Tonic have performed in the past.

HARVEST FEST
Main Street, Spearfish
(605) 642-5421
www.spearfish.sd.us/dba
Two blocks of Main Street are blocked off for the annual Harvest Fest. Enjoy crafts, kids' entertainment, apple pie–baking contests, music, displays, puppet shows, a quilt show, and more, all free. A new addition to this event is the Fiddle Fest, the only sanctioned fiddling contest in South Dakota. Everyone is welcome to compete in this toe-tappin' hoedown—the first performance in 2003 drew musicians from the entire midwest region. Impressive talent vies for a sponsored ride to the national competition. There is an entry fee to compete, but the public can watch for free.

i Autumn is a great time to visit the Hills. The weather is usually fine, traffic is lighter, leaves are turning gold, and most attractions are open. For a brochure on the "Autumn Expedition," annual events and festivals from mid-Sept to early Oct, call the Black Hills Visitor Information Center in Rapid City at (605) 355-3700 or stop by (exit 61 off I-90).

TASTE OF SPEARFISH
Spearfish Park Pavilion
115 S Canyon St., Spearfish
(605) 642-2626
www.spearfishchamber.org
This city-park event, generally on the third Thursday of the month, features more than a dozen local restaurants boasting their signature dishes in a fun, family-friendly atmosphere. $1 admission and a family can generally eat for under $20.

Central Hills

ANNUAL DAKOTA POLKA FESTIVAL
Canyon Lake Viking Hall
2900 Canyon Lake Dr., Rapid City
(605) 787-5584

Admit it: You've always wanted to polka. This is your chance. This festival takes place on a September weekend, and all kinds of dance steps are performed, not just polka. Live bands provide the music, and the Friday and Saturday night dancing goes on until 11 p.m. If you don't polka, you can observe, or ask one of the friendly enthusiasts to teach you on the 5,400-square-foot floor. Homemade food and RV parking are available at the center. A two-day pass is $15 per person, a Friday-night pass is $6 per person, and a Saturday-night pass is $10 per person. Smoking and alcohol are not permitted.

Southern Hills

CRAZY HORSE NIGHT BLAST
Crazy Horse Memorial, Custer
(605) 673-4681
www.crazyhorsememorial.org

This ceremonial blast on the mountain takes place each year in early June and on Sept 6. (You can learn about the Crazy Horse Memorial in the Attractions chapter.) The latter date commemorates both Crazy Horse's untimely death in 1877 and the late sculptor Korczak Ziolkowski's birthday. The blast takes place after dark for spectacular effect, and it's free with your entrance fee. An open house, during which you can tour the visitor complex and exhibits, is held on Labor Day weekend.

BADGER CLARK HOMETOWN COWBOY POETRY GATHERING
The Mueller Center
801 South 6th St., Hot Springs
(605) 745-3446
www.hotsprings-sd.com

Locally and regionally famous cowboy poets tell their tales and play their music in this late September event. It's designed to pay tribute to both Badger Clark, South Dakota's "Poet Laureate," and the art of cowboy poetry. In addition to the performances, there are symposiums, displays of western gear, jam sessions, open sessions where amateur poets can give tale telling a try, and more cowboy boots in the audience than you can shake a stick at.

OCTOBER
Northern Hills

OKTOBERFEST
Downtown Deadwood
(605) 578-1876, (800) 999-1876
www.deadwood.com

This is a German celebration, presented Deadwood-style. It takes place over several days in early Oct. You can enjoy German and other music, clog dancing, a microbrew expo, a German cook-off and food tasting, accordion music, a lederhosen contest, and a home-brewers beer contest. German folk band the Sauerkrauts usually provides the music. It all takes place on Deadwood's Main Street, though most downtown casinos, restaurants, and hotels also have something special to offer. The entertainment and events are free.

DEADWEIRD
Downtown Deadwood
(605) 578-1876, (800) 999-1876
www.deadwood.com
Don't miss out on this spooky event, because it happens only once each year—on Halloween night. It's a citywide bash, with trick-or-treating for the kids and a costume contest (for big kids older than 21) that rewards winners with cash. Since Deadwood is haunted by such illustrious ghosts as Calamity Jane, Seth Bullock, and Wild Bill Hickok, this event is perfectly appropriate. It's doubly appropriate because Deadwood also is haunted by some very odd—and very alive—people who seem to descend into the town from their mountain homes only for Halloween. Despite the colorful crowds, Deadwood (and Deadweird) is safe and family friendly.

Central Hills

BLACK HILLS CHAMBER MUSIC SOCIETY
First Congregational Church
1200 Clark St., Rapid City
(605) 718-5666
www.rapidcityweb.com
The society's five-performance series begins in Oct (and runs through Apr) and always boasts outstanding performances. We've included more information in the Arts chapter.

MOUNT RUSHMORE INTERNATIONAL MARATHON
Various locations, Rapid City
(605) 348-7866, (605) 721-1251
www.mtrushmoremarathon.com
The annual marathon takes place on a Sun in early Oct. The route winds through the scenic Black Hills and ends in Rapid City,

and for the entry fee ($40) you can compete and enjoy the scenery at the same time. A marathon relay is run in conjunction with the marathon itself (cost is $70 per group), and a pasta buffet at Mount Rushmore is on the schedule, too.

RAPID CITY CONCERT ASSOCIATION
Rushmore Plaza Civic Center Theater
444 Mount Rushmore Rd., Rapid City
(605) 394-4101
www.rapidcitycvb.com
The annual six-concert series begins in Oct (and ends in Apr) and presents fun and exciting musical performances. You can read more about them in our chapter on the Arts.

BLACK HILLS POW WOW AND ART EXPO
Rushmore Plaza Civic Center
444 Mount Rushmore Rd., Rapid City
(605) 343-5718
www.rapidcitycvb.com
Powwows are spectacular events and a rich opportunity to learn about Native American culture and tradition. To participants, powwows are a spiritual experience, a celebration of culture, a chance to dance together and to renew old friendships and make new ones. The steady drumbeats accompanying the dancers represent the heartbeat of the people, a powerful emotional experience. The Black Hills Pow Wow and Art Expo take place in mid-Oct and last for three days. Call for exact dates. Traditional and contemporary art is on display and for sale, and in past years there have been storytellers, flute players, dance and drumming performances, educational activities for children, and a Native American fashion show. Pre-powwow programs are held at the Journey Museum (see the Attractions chapter) several days

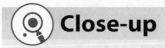

Close-up

Fall Color Heralds Bison Roundup

In the Black Hills, fall is a time when managers at Custer State Park reduce bison numbers to be compatible with the land's carrying capacity. The time is right, for the blood of the bison has cooled following the intensity of their summer ardor. Now, as the Black Hills begin to turn gold, bison plod along like patriarchs of old, at least that is until the roundup begins. Then, their blood is anything but cool.

Game Lodge campground is conveniently located for the roundup, which the park holds the first Monday after the last weekend in September as one of their fall interpretive programs. Set against the plains that thread throughout the hills and the ponderosa pine, the roundup has a splendid fall backdrop. The herd thunders over hills, finally charging through the coulees and ravines, urged on by riders. Once the bison are in motion, the direction is easy to sustain, for as managers say, "A moving herd is easier to contain than a stationary one."

After the herd is contained in a huge holding area, biologists begin the process of reduction. Bison are herded into various chutes according to age and sex. Culled animals are then auctioned off to the highest bidders. After the roundup, the much-reduced herd of about 950 is returned to roam the park, where it joins those that eluded the riders. The two-day event is one of the most dramatic in the Black Hills, and it's made even more spectacular as it coincides with a time when the Black Hills turn gold.

prior to the event. There is a charge for daily sessions and three-day passes.

Be sure to watch the Grand Entry, an event that is repeated on all three days of the powwow. Observers, who are expected to respectfully stand during the entry, are treated to a stunning visual and auditory display of finery, drums, dancing, and passionate musical voices. The participants enter the arena in a line, singing and dancing as they go, accompanied by drumbeats and preceded by the sacred eagle staff and tribal and US flags. Hundreds of dancers fill the arena in a sacred circle, winding round and round, until the floor is a whirl of movement, color, and sound. It's a spectacular sight, especially from the civic center's seats high above the arena.

SKI FOR LIGHT SKI SWAP
Rushmore Plaza Civic Center
444 Mount Rushmore Rd., Rapid City
(605) 394-4115, (605) 381-1172
www.rapidcitycvb.com

The Black Hills Regional Ski for Light organization holds its annual fund-raiser in late Oct or early Nov. It's an equipment consignment swap, where 20 percent of the sale price goes to the nonprofit organization to fund programs that help the visually impaired ski, camp, canoe, and enjoy the outdoors. This is your chance to pick up some great used equipment at a fair price and help support the Ski for Light programs, too. There is no entrance fee to shop at the swap. For information on outdoor and recreational programs for the visually impaired (including a January ski event at Deer Mountain, near

Lead, which draws participants from all over the country), call Ski for Light at the second number above.

Southern Hills

*ANNUAL BUFFALO ROUNDUP AND ARTS FESTIVAL
Custer State Park, Custer
(605) 255-4515
www.custerstatepark.info
Organizers have called this event "Feel the Thunder." You can't quite understand why until you've seen, heard, and felt 1,500 buffalo running across the plains, herded by cowboys, cowgirls, and park rangers (riding pickups and horses) into corrals. It's really something to experience. The roundup is held on a Mon in late Sept or early Oct in the corral area south of the State Game Lodge on Wildlife Loop Road. You can watch the critters being branded and vaccinated (but you need to arrive between 6:30 and 7:30 a.m. and stay until the "all clear" signal is given). The buffalo not returned to the park for the winter are sold at auction in Nov.

Plenty of less dramatic (but equally interesting) events take place during roundup weekend, on the Saturday and Sunday before the roundup itself. The arts festival is staged near the State Game Lodge, and you'll find great collectibles and gifts in the booths. There's also terrific entertainment: Native American dancers, cowboy poets, cloggers, fast-draw competitions, and western music. You can enter the Buffalo Wallow Chili Cook-off, or just sample the entries, and enjoy a pancake feed and chuck wagon cookout, too. It's all free, except for the food.

For convenience, you can stay at the Custer State Park campgrounds (see the Campgrounds chapter) or resorts (see the Accommodations chapter). Visitors also will discover 50 new camping cabins located in at the State Game Lodge, Blue Bell, Stockade South and French Creek Horse Camp campgrounds, all at $45 per night.

NATIVE AMERICAN DAY OBSERVANCES
Crazy Horse Memorial
US 16/385, Custer
(605) 673-4681
www.crazyhorsememorial.org
A special program and events are held each Oct at Crazy Horse Memorial to commemorate the struggles, triumphs, heritage, and legacies of Native Americans. You can enjoy lectures and demonstrations, drumming, singing, dancing, and storytelling. Tour the Indian Museum of North America and the Native American Cultural Center; both are housed on the grounds. A special day blast is planned on the mountain (see more about the sculpture in the Attractions chapter), and there's a buffalo stew feed at noon. It's all free with your admission to the memorial.

NOVEMBER

In November, holiday home tours, craft shows, "festival of lights" parades, and Christmas tree decorating festivals are popular. Check a local newspaper for details.

Central Hills

BLACK HILLS SYMPHONY ORCHESTRA
Rushmore Plaza Civic Center Theater
444 Mount Rushmore Rd., Rapid City
(605) 348-HORN (season tickets),
(605) 394-4111 (individual performance tickets)
Six fine concerts are presented by our very own symphony orchestra each season. Read about these great events in the Arts chapter.

Southern Hills

BUFFALO AUCTION
Custer State Park, Custer
(605) 255-4515
www.custerstatepark.info
Read about the Annual Buffalo Roundup and Arts Festival that takes place in Custer State Park in September's listing (Southern Hills) or in the Parks & Mountains chapter. The surplus animals culled from the herd along with the park's surplus burros are sold at this auction held on the third Saturday of November annually, which helps support the park's operations. It's an interesting event to watch, even if you're not inclined to take a buffalo or burro home.

DECEMBER

Northern Hills

ADAMS FAMILY CHRISTMAS
Adams Museum and Adams House
54 Sherman St., Deadwood
(605) 578-3724
www.adamsmuseumandhouse.org
The Adams Museum and Adams House always celebrate Christmas in Victorian style, and one of their favorite events each December is *An Adams Family Christmas Carol*, an original play written for the organization that is based not on the Dickens classic but on Deadwood's historic Adams family during the 1920s. Performances usually take place at the house, not the museum (read about these two sites in the Attractions chapter). Enjoy Christmas readings, a masquerade, dramatic musical presentations, and special exhibits (the events change from year to year).

CHRISTMAS STROLL
Downtown Spearfish
(605) 559-0359
www.spearfish.sd.us
This lovely community event takes place on a weekend afternoon in early December, on Spearfish's charming Main Street. With a little luck, you can bask in the sunshine of a Black Hills winter day, or at least listen to music and carolers, shop for crafts, enjoy the food, and take a horsedrawn wagon ride. The fun is free, although there is a charge for food. This old-fashioned Christmas is a fun event for all ages. Adults can enjoy chestnuts roasted on an open fire, and children can have their pictures taken with Santa, the Mystery Snowman, or the Snow Queen.

FESTIVAL OF TREES
Spearfish Park Pavilion
5th Street, Spearfish
(605) 642-2761
Beautifully decorated Christmas trees are on display for about four days in early December; you can view them without charge, but a donation of a can of food is appreciated. The festival is sponsored by the businesswomen's community service organization, Zonta. At the end of the display period, the trees are auctioned at a gala event, and proceeds go to charity. You can take home a decorated tree and help out those less fortunate at the same time.

HATCHERY HOLIDAYS
D.C. Booth Historic Fish Hatchery
423 Hatchery Circle, Spearfish
(605) 642-7730
www.dcbooth.fws.gov
The hatchery grounds and D.C. Booth historic home are lovely places and the perfect backdrop for a Christmas event. The house

is decorated in the finery of a long-ago Victorian Christmas, and the many trees on the grounds are draped in finery of their own. You can take a tour of the house and museum and enjoy the special displays and events. It's all free and a charming way to spend a holiday Sunday in early December.

NEW YEAR'S EVE CELEBRATION
Main Street, Deadwood
(605) 578-1876
www.deadwood.com
Deadwood has been a party town since the first rowdy prospectors descended upon the gulch in 1876. Though the gold is now gone, residents still throw some wild celebrations here, and with the possible exception of Mardi Gras, New Year's Eve is Deadwood's wildest shindig. People come from all over the Dakotas, Nebraska, Wyoming, Montana, and beyond to usher in the new year in Deadwood. The casinos have parties and special giveaways, the saloons bring in bands that play all night long, and the hotels fill up fast. If you'd like to join in the festivities, be sure to reserve a room well in advance.

Southern Hills

CHRISTMAS IN THE HILLS
Various locations in Hot Springs
(605) 745-5642
The folks in Hot Springs—who work hard to present this event—are rightfully proud of this old-fashioned festival, which goes back more than two decades. Traditions include a children's procession and living nativity, an arts-and-crafts fair, music, art shows, community dinners and chili suppers, a tour of local homes, and appearances by Mrs. Santa Claus. There is also a parade of lights, a tree lighting ceremony, and open house at downtown businesses. It takes place during the first weekend of December and attracts visitors from surrounding states as well as residents and folks coming home for Christmas.

THE ARTS

Many people don't associate the American West with fine art. True, there are no world-class ballet companies based here, nor are there any internationally famous art museums. But art imitates life—and there is plenty of life in the Black Hills. The landscape, with its physical and spiritual wonder, has triggered the imagination of countless artists. Anyone who spends time in the Hills will quickly see that art runs strong here, especially on the local front. Photographers, composers, poets, painters, singers, writers, and sculptors of all backgrounds and ages practice their craft and form the broad base of the area's cultural community.

You'll find art on display and for sale at many events (see the Annual Events & Festivals chapter). Especially worthy of note are the Black Hills Pow Wow and Art Expo, the Black Hills Heritage Festival, even the Black Hills Stock Show and Rodeo, all in Rapid City, and the Festival in the Park in Spearfish.

The rich traditions of this area also have an influence. Western themes and traditional Native American art predominate, although some visual artists choose other themes or abstract forms, and a growing number of Native American artists are exploring contemporary paths. Literary arts run from cowboy poetry and stories of western life to work that transcends the sense of place that defines the Black Hills.

OVERVIEW

As the Black Hills cultural community is strong, so are the organizations that support and fund them. **Rapid City's Allied Arts Fund Drive,** (605) 394-4106, is responsible for sponsoring many of the performances, concerts, exhibits, and readings that happen in the Rapid City area; several occur at the Dahl Fine Arts Center, which is owned by the city and administered by the independent **Rapid City Arts Council,** (605) 394-4101. The organizations continue to consolidate and work more closely with one another. They recently completed a $6.5 million renovation and expansion, paid for only partly by city taxes (see the Galleries and Exhibit Spaces section of this chapter for more information).

The state government and nearly every town in the Hills support the arts. The **South Dakota Arts Council,** (605) 773-3131, is part of the state's Department of Education and Cultural Affairs. It funds residencies and grants to help local artists share their work with schoolchildren, who experience poetry, Lakota dance and flute music, stories, photography, mural painting, rodeo clowns, puppets, classical guitar, and more through the program.

The Sturgis Area Arts Council sponsors theater performances, Art for Lunch Bunch discussions, book signings, a juried art show, and the Community Sculpture Garden. The **Spearfish Center for the Arts and**

Humanities, (605) 642-7973, helped restore the town's Historic Matthews Opera House, now a performing arts center, and sponsors art shows and an annual foreign-film series.

The **Historic Deadwood-Lead Arts Council,** (605) 584-1461, sponsors exhibitions in the under-renovation Historic Homestake Opera House. The recent addition of an innovative floor heating system now allows for winter performances. **South Dakotans for the Arts,** (605) 578-1783, based in Lead, is an arts advocacy, service, and education organization that sponsors the US West Artists in Rural Schools program, the five-state Art Beyond Boundaries Conference, and much more.

Hill City prides itself on a growing reputation as an art community. The **Hill City Area Arts Council,** (605) 574-2890, supports exhibits and demonstrations, including June's Heart of the Hills Art Show. The **Hot Springs Area Arts Council,** (605) 745-4225, manages the Main Street Arts and Crafts Festival (more than 20 years old) and children's programs and scholarships. **Southern Hills Arts and Humanities,** (605) 745-6473, promotes all types of arts activities, including a summer music series.

We encourage you to learn about the arts in the Black Hills in this chapter—then watch, listen, participate, and enjoy.

DANCE

One venue specializes in dance, including performances, workshops, and master classes.

Central Hills

BLACK HILLS DANCE THEATRE
4939 Spring Tree Court, Rapid City
(605) 342-1564
www.bhdancetheatre.org

This dance theater is managed by an all-volunteer board, a sure sign of community commitment. It sponsors two professional dance performances each year, one in the spring and another in the fall, with master classes and school activities coinciding. In recent years, the Kothi modern dance group has performed, as has Kim Robards's modern dance company from Denver, the Joffrey Ballet from New York, and Spectrum, a jazz company from Seattle. The theater performs the *Nutcracker* ballet biennially, bringing in a professional performer to complement local talent, and also offers weeklong summer dance workshops for both children and adults. Ticket prices vary for each performance but range between $7 and $20.

FILM & CINEMA

Choose from classic and foreign films or contemporary blockbusters that may one day become cinema classics.

Northern Hills

THE FOREIGN FILM FESTIVAL
Northern Hills Cinema
1830 North Main St., Spearfish
(605) 642-7973
The Spearfish Center for the Arts and Humanities sponsors this tribute to films from other nations. Four are shown on alternate weekends in Sept and Oct, and each is run twice, on Sun afternoon and Mon evening. Season passes are available for $20, or tickets are $8 each. Those planning the event choose a variety of film subjects but often include one in English and three in other languages, with English subtitles.

NORTHERN HILLS CINEMA 4
1830 North Main St., Spearfish
(605) 642-4212
The six theaters in this cinema show first-run movies, and tickets are $9.50 for adults and $6.50 for children ages 3 to 11 and seniors age 65 or older. Matinee tickets are $6.50. The Northern Hills Cinema hosts a foreign film festival sponsored by the Spearfish Center for the Arts and Humanities.

Central Hills

ELKS THEATRE
512 6th St., Rapid City
(605) 341-4149, (605) 343-7888
(reserved seating)
www.elkstheatre.com
If you missed that blockbuster the first time it came to town, you're likely to get a second chance at the Elks. You might wait a few weeks, but think of the savings: Seats are just $4. When you consider that this historic theater boasts the biggest screen in South Dakota—a whopping 48 feet wide by 22 feet tall—it's even more of a bargain. And an eight-channel digital sound system means you won't miss any all-important movie dialogue no matter which of the 605 comfortable seats you choose, even if it's in the balcony.

The more intimate Screening Room features a 10-by-20-foot screen and seating for 100. The Screening Room is on the third floor, above the balcony, in what was once the Elks Club's elegant ballroom.

The theater building dates back to the early 1900s, when the Elks hosted live vaudeville shows and, later, motion pictures. In fact, this is one of the oldest movie theaters in the nation. So think of it as carrying on tradition when you catch any of the daily or nightly shows. You'll find some services here that are reminiscent of the days when businesses catered to the public as a matter of course. Thursday is BYOB night—bring your own bag and get three free scoops of popcorn. And you can request reserved seating for any show by calling up to a week in advance.

The Elks also shows classic movies and local independent films from time to time; there's even an after-school movie program for kids. Call for more information.

FRIENDS OF THE DEVEREAUX LIBRARY FILM SERIES
Elks Theatre
512 6th St., Rapid City
(605) 394-1262
The Friends of the Devereaux Library, at South Dakota School of Mines and Technology, sponsor this annual film series, a fund-raiser for the library. Ten classic films are presented, one each Sunday evening from mid-Jan through mid-Mar. Previous showings have included *Rear Window, Meet Me in St. Louis,* and *North by Northwest.* The cozy, historic theater has a great old-fashioned balcony and a huge screen. You can purchase season tickets for about $30.

RUSHMORE 7
350 East Disk Dr., Rapid City
(605) 341-7021, (605) 341-6960
The seven theaters in this modern cinema boast chairs that rival those in your living room. Comfortably seated, you can see first-run movies, with matinees (before 6 p.m.) costing $6.50 for both children and adults. After 6 p.m., tickets for children younger than 12 and seniors 55 and older are $6.50; others pay $9.25.

Southern Hills

HOT SPRINGS THEATRE
241 North River St., Hot Springs
(605) 745-4169

This circa-1912 theater features first-run movies now instead of the vaudeville acts of old. Showtime is at 7 p.m. Fri, Sat, and Sun as well as 2 p.m. Sun; the theater is closed on other days. Ticket prices are $7 for adults, $5 for children ages 2 through 11 and seniors 60 and older.

GALLERIES & EXHIBIT SPACES

We've included galleries that carry original art (for display, for sale, or both), although many also offer prints, custom framing, art supplies, and gifts. All are great places to see what's being created in artists' studios around South Dakota or to purchase a work of art. Some galleries close for the winter or shorten their operating hours, so call ahead.

Northern Hills

FOCUS WEST GALLERY
939 Colorado Blvd., Spearfish
(605) 722-0708
www.focuswestgallery.com

Features powerful nature photography of the Black Hills, Badlands, and classic destinations in the western US, as well as custom framing, photo gift products, coffee mugs, greeting cards, books, and coasters. All the exceptional photography in the gallery was taken by owner Les Voorhis.

THE PHOTOGRAPHER'S GALLERY
Black Hills State University
1200 University St., Spearfish
(605) 642-6769, (605) 642-6062

Interest in photography is growing in the Black Hills, and BHSU has responded by dedicating a small display area to photographers. Exhibits are shown in the newly remodeled basement of Jonas Academic Hall in a long hallway next to the darkroom and studio, and you can check out the display anytime the building is open. Students often show their new work toward the end of each semester, and established local photographers, such as Ray Tysdal, are invited to fill the hall at other times. Known in the area for his abstract black-and-white pictures of Black Hills animals (especially buffalo), Tysdal displays his traditional work alongside sepia-tone prints of African wildlife. Other local artists to grace the gallery's first year of exhibits included multimedia artist Bob Miller, who displayed interesting Polaroid prints, and photojournalist and nature photographer Dick Kettlewell.

RUDDELL GALLERY OF ART
Black Hills State University
1200 University St., Spearfish
(605) 642-6852, (605) 642-6104

A small gallery tucked away on the second level of the student union, the Ruddell is a pleasant space with some fine exhibitions. A wide variety of work circulates through this gallery, including artistry by young and old alike. Students have two shows each year, one for photography and one for other visual arts, and alumni also have an annual display. In addition, the Ruddell makes room for four or five other artists each year, with work in many media. In recent years the gallery has hosted the South Dakota Health Care Association's Dakota Master Works exhibit, a touring show of work by artists age 60 and up. Toward the beginning of the schools' second semester, the Ruddell puts on an educational program show that deals with social issues through art. The displays often coincide with speakers. Past shows have included topics such as threats to democracy (which displayed war art from 1960 to 1975) and abused women and children. Displays usually last about a month, and the gallery is open year-round during regular campus hours.

TERMESPHERE GALLERY
Christensen Drive, Spearfish
(605) 642-4805
www.termesphere.com
Dick Termes has become internationally known for his six-point perspective spherical paintings, known as Termespheres. When you step across the threshold of his geodesic-dome gallery, you enter a magical room filled with so many colorful spheres and mobiles twirling from the ceiling that you'll be browsing in awe for an hour. If you're lucky, Termes himself may explain his complicated techniques for making these unique works of art. One-of-a-kind originals, reproductions, and limited editions are on display and for sale. In addition to spheres, you'll see cubes, tetrahedrons, polyhedrons, icosahedrons, and dodecahedrons. Each gives you the sense of standing in the center of the environment that is the subject of each piece, yet—at the same time—you are viewing it from the outside. Call ahead for directions. The gallery is on Christensen Drive, in the countryside south of Spearfish.

Central Hills

APEX GALLERY
South Dakota School of Mines and Technology
501 East St. Joseph St., Rapid City
(605) 394-1254, (605) 394-2481

The fact that "Tech" encourages art studies (there's not yet a formal art program) impresses us; that outside-the-lines thinking shows in the quality of exhibitions at this gallery. There's more about Tech in the Education chapter. As part of the School of Mines, the Apex welcomes exhibits not only by contemporary artists but also by scientists, many of whom are nationally and internationally recognized. The gallery often aims for educational enrichment in its exhibits and has included work that relies on interactivity. For example, installation artist Sandy Skoglund worked with art history students in 2001 to create a surreal environment. Exhibits are usually shown for six to eight weeks and often are launched with an opening reception. Even though you'll have to park in the main lot and walk a bit to reach the gallery in the Classroom Building, it's well worth a visit.

BLACK HILLS GLASS BLOWERS
901 Old Hill City Rd., Keystone
(605) 666-4542
www.blackhillsglassblowers.com
This is the working studio of glass artists Gail Damin and Pete Hopkins. You can watch them create their glass art but, they stress, only when they're working, which is not all the time. It's best to call ahead if you want to see a glass artist in action, or in the winter months to make sure the studio is open. Gail and Pete do both lamp (or flame) working and offhand (or traditional) glassblowing. They make figurines, such as unicorns and dragons, and colorful art glass, including vases and bowls.

DAHL FINE ARTS CENTER
713 7th St., Rapid City
(605) 394-4101
www.thedahl.org

Plan to spend some time at the Dahl. The Ruth Brennan Gallery has six to eight exhibitions every year, each with an opening reception. Themes vary widely, from Mexican folk art and impressionistic oils to photography and Black Hills landscapes. The gallery focuses on education—and this includes regional, national, and international work, and traveling exhibits. The center has a 170-seat theater and offices and serves as the hub for several arts organizations in Rapid City. It's open 10 a.m. to 5 p.m. Tues through Sat and 1 to 5 p.m. Sun.

Adjoining the Ruth Brennan Gallery is the Central Gallery, which focuses on community work and involvement. Artwork, often from local schools or organizations, is displayed in three- to six-week-long shows. Art classes are offered for both children and adults, and the subject matter varies. Local artists regularly give talks and presentations. The *Cyclorama* mural by Bernard Thomas is in a room adjacent to the Central Gallery. It is a representation of 200 years of American history from an economic perspective (it was commissioned by the Dahl's founder, a banker). Ask a staff member to turn on the taped narrative and lighting system to accompany your look at the mural. You'll find South Dakota Public Radio at 89.3 FM in Rapid City; 88.1 FM in Belle Fourche and Hot Springs; 99.1 FM in Spearfish; and 91.9 FM in Lead.

i The Northern Plains Watercolor Society sponsors a juried exhibition of watercolors each fall. The show includes the work of its members and is open to watercolorists from other states. The exhibition is usually held in November at Prairie Edge Art Gallery, Sixth and Main Streets, Rapid City. For information go to www.prairieedge.com.

DAKOTA ART GALLERY
632½ St. Joseph St., Rapid City
(605) 394-4108
This lively gallery in downtown Rapid City is operated by the Dakota Artists Guild. Each month the gallery features either a solo or group display by regional artists. Work on continuing display includes jewelry, paintings, pottery, and glasswork. The guild offers classes for adults and children in drawing, painting, pottery, and other art forms, plus some odd-but-fun classes for the kids, such as 3-D and sidewalk art, paper-bag puppets, and papier-mâché. And for even more of a learning experience, the guild offers workshops with visiting artists. Another unique program put on by the gallery is the occasional lunch and art series, where an artist is invited to speak or give a demonstration while participants kick back with a packed lunch or food available at the gallery. Call for information on upcoming events.

JON CRANE WATERCOLORS
336 Main St., Hill City
(605) 574-4440
www.joncranewatercolors.com
"Art That Takes You Home," this gallery's motto, perfectly describes the work of nationally known watercolorist Jon Crane. His subjects are often the rural landscapes of isolated farms and aging homesteads, lovely forests and trout streams, and heartwarming scenes that remind the viewer of home. Even the titles are nostalgic: *Home for Hot Chocolate, A Great Day to Be a Kid, Heartland Legacy,* and *Almost Christmas* are among the many works you'll see here. The pleasantly decorated gallery carries original work, framed and unframed open-edition miniature prints, and limited-edition prints and note cards. Custom framing is offered.

THE PERFECT HANGING GALLERY
520 Kansas City St., Rapid City
(605) 348-7761

The Perfect Hanging is a display space for prints by South Dakotan and internationally known artists. The gallery has Jon Crane watercolors and paintings by Terry Redlin and Gene Stocks. It also carries artist giftware, including music boxes, pins, sculptures, and mugs. If the Perfect Hanging doesn't have what you want in stock, the staff can order any print available and dress it up with custom matting and framing. They specialize in conservation and museum-quality mounting and framing.

PRAIRIE EDGE TRADING CO. & GALLERIES
606 Main St., Rapid City
(605) 342-3086
www.prairieedge.com

Prairie Edge is a local landmark. It's a great place to shop (more about that in the Shopping chapter), and the restored building's stunning architecture alone is worth a visit. The second-floor fine art gallery is a gem in the Prairie Edge crown. Here, basking in the light from the huge old windows, you may see the amazing photographs of Robert Wong of Rapid City and the contemporary Native American work of Don Montileaux, or the work of local artists Paul Goble, Loy Allen, Jim Whartman, and James Van Nuys. Changing exhibits feature the art of many artists, but the astounding cast-paper art of Allen and Patty Eckman is on permanent exhibit, so be sure to have a look.

RIMROCK ART & FRAME COMPANY
1108 Jackson Blvd., Rapid City
(605) 342-7263, (888) 849-8485

The oldest frame shop in Rapid City, Rimrock Art & Frame is also an artists' gallery that displays original work and prints of regional artists, including the oils of Jan Wiedmeier, the original lithographs of Russell Chatham, and the fantasy art of John Backlund. Jon Crane's prints (both current and secondary-market editions) are here, as is the work of Kay Williams and Ron Holyfield, longtime summer artists-in-residence at Custer State Park. The owners, Mike and Debbie McLane, are fine artists themselves: Mike, a certified professional framer, produces great watercolors, and Debbie is a talented photographer.

SIOUX INDIAN MUSEUM GALLERY
The Journey Museum
222 New York St., Rapid City
(605) 394-2381
www.journeymuseum.org

This small gallery is devoted to Native American art. It is inside the Journey Museum, near the gift shop, and your Journey ticket will admit you at no additional charge. The gallery has shown delightful and colorful contemporary Sioux quilts from the Journey's permanent collection; the paintings and three-dimensional art of Jim Yellowhawk of Rapid City; the beading, pottery, and batik of Linda Szabo of Mission; the acrylics and oils of Del Iron Cloud, also of Rapid City; and the sculptures of Tom Red Bear of Hot Springs.

STANFORD ADELSTEIN GALLERY
The Journey Museum
222 New York St., Rapid City
(605) 394-6923
www.journeymuseum.org

We've written about the Journey Museum in the Attractions chapter, but the adjacent Changing Exhibition Gallery is separate from the museum and has its own exhibitions.

In fact, visitors can tour the gallery without paying the museum's fee. Each exhibit is launched with a reception, often held in the evening. Exhibitions are accompanied by educational programs for children and gallery talks by experts. One of the more popular programs is the Storyteller's Series every Sun from 2 to 3 p.m. (cost is $3). This event complements the display in the gallery at that time and may be geared toward children and adults. For one session, the mayor of Rapid City read stories to children while they sat with treats and drinks. The shows usually change monthly and range widely in topic. For example, they once held a World War II exhibit in which Black Hills residents contributed personal artifacts, such as a Japanese parachute and a German flag. A theme show during Aug is held in conjunction with the Sturgis Rally & Races.

*WARRIORS WORK STUDIO AND BEN WEST GALLERY
310 Main St., Hill City
(605) 574-4954
www.leatherframegallery.com
The smell of leather greets you as you open the door to this gallery. Artist Randy Berger creates deerskin-wrapped frames, each individually designed, hand cut, and handcrafted according to his IDT ("I Don't Tell") method. Each is an original work of art, although some are limited editions of two to seven.

The studio carries the work of several artists, including Jim Yellowhawk, Ryan Burr, Frank Howell, Peggy Detmer, Kirby Sattler, Ben Wright, Joe Geshick, and Mike Larsen. You'll find pencil and pen-and-ink drawings, original lithographs, serigraphs, giclée prints, and much more. A recent addition to the Warriors Work Studio is the Ben West Gallery,

which shows contemporary work. The displays, always different and unique, have included wood turnings and tables by Craig Richardson, watercolors by Sarah Rogers; black-and-white animal and landscape photography by Ray Tysdal, and stone sculptures by Cheston Turnbull.

As for Berger's frames themselves, they sometimes have a symbolic message or tell a story related to the picture inside. He knows most of the artists and creates his frames as an extension of the spirit of their work. Some frames are inlaid with colorful beads or other decorative or symbolic items. Each takes from two days to more than a week to complete. One of Berger's favorite tools for detailed leatherwork is his pocket knife's bottle opener, a humble apparatus that helps create his exquisitely beautiful art.

Southern Hills

CABIN FEVER
444 Mount Rushmore Rd., Custer
(605) 673-2525
This downtown Custer gallery is a pleasant space that displays art all the way up to the high ceiling. You'll see Brenda Bruckner's pencil drawings of horses and the ranching life, silver handcrafted jewelry, photographs and pottery, as well as gifts and prints. Take note of the antler carvings by Custer resident Tony Ramer, a nationally known artist whose work graces the White House. Also represented are works by Tim Cox and Merle Locke, both local artists. Cabin Fever carries tack, blouses, and leather and suede jackets, among other offerings.

LITERARY ARTS

If you're a fan of reading, you'll be happy to know that a fair number of book signings, readings, and discussions take place here. In Rapid City, signings often are held at Prairie Edge Trading Company and Galleries, and Borders (discussed in the Shopping chapter). In smaller towns, you might find events at bookstores (most of which have sections dedicated to local authors), art galleries, libraries (see the Relocation chapter), or community centers. Check the local newspapers for announcements; book signings are great opportunities to meet local authors.

BLACK HILLS WRITERS GROUP
(605) 341-3224
Founded in 1956 by local author Laura Bower Van Nuys, this group meets at the Rapid City City Hall and School Administration Center, 300 6th St., on the fourth Tuesday of each month (except December). Members plan events, read their work, critique, and conduct impromptu writing assignments. The group sponsors the Black Hills Writers Conference in the fall of odd-numbered years, and the Laura Bower Van Nuys Writing Contest in even-numbered years. The contest, which receives entries from writers all over the United States and from other countries, is named for the author of *The Family Band*, a history of Van Nuys's family that was made into the Disney movie *The One and Only Genuine, Original Family Band*. The contest accepts fiction and nonfiction entries, has an Apr 15 deadline, and is judged by professional writers. Call (605) 341-3224 to request guidelines.

MUSIC

Concerts, both indoors and out, are offered year-round and enrich life in the Black Hills.

Northern Hills

BLACK HILLS AREA MUSIC TEACHERS
(605) 642-6241, (605) 722-8033
The Music Teachers' Association is a professional group that works to make music education prevalent in the Hills. This private organization consists of teachers from the entire Black Hills area. Concerts are free and presented year-round. The association sponsors several student recitals and competitions throughout the Hills, and teachers join students for an annual performance in May at the Rushmore Mall in Rapid City. Performances are often held at Black Hills State University in Spearfish at the new Meier Recital Hall.

i The *Rapid City Journal* publishes an Arts Calendar each Sunday in its Life & Style section. It's a one-stop source to learn about upcoming events you won't want to miss.

Central Hills

BACKROOM PRODUCTIONS
(605) 341-5940, (605) 348-6295
www.backroomevents.com
These guys have something going on every month, and then some. The main event is Music in the Park, a series of 8 to 10 free concerts at Memorial Park in Rapid City during the summer. Concerts may include jazz, country, rock, big band, bluegrass, or Native American music and dance. Additionally, Backroom annually hosts the Guitar Masters, an all-acoustic concert in March at the Journey Museum in Rapid City, and the Black Hills Sun Writers Workshop in June at Nemo Guest Ranch. The workshop invites participants to spend a weekend learning music, usually for guitar and keyboards, and holds

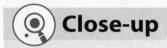

Close-up

Ambrose Bierce

Ambrose Bierce was never happy. And after trying his hand at gold mining in the Black Hills, he was more miserable than ever.

Born in 1842 into a large, pious family, Bierce was a gloomy, withdrawn child. As a young man he distinguished himself during the Civil War but questioned the Union cause for which he fought. Later he became a renowned journalist but was contemptuous of the press. Even his wife, Mollie, and their three children didn't please him.

Settling in San Francisco after the war, "Bitter Bierce" became famous for his scathing "Town Crier" and "Prattle" newspaper columns. But at age 38, perhaps suffering from a midlife crisis (or trying to run away from himself), and hoping to quit journalism for good, Bierce resigned from his job and left home to become general agent for the Black Hills Placer Mining Company in Rockerville, in Dakota Territory. One of his assignments was to complete a 17-mile wooden flume to carry water from Spring Creek to Rockerville. That was in 1880, and today you can hike along the Flume Trail and see remnants of his work (see the Recreation chapter for more information). To protect the company's assets, Bierce hired a famous gunslinger named Boone May and listed him on the payroll as "Boone May, Murderer."

The mine proved unsuccessful, though, and Bierce returned to San Francisco within a few months, broke, depressed, and jobless. He soon was offered editorship of the *Wasp,* a satirical journal, and revived his "Prattle" column. Readers noticed he was more bitter than ever, hurling savage verbal attacks at seemingly every person and institution in sight. He later became chief editorial columnist for the *San Francisco Examiner* under William Randolph Hearst, and then Washington correspondent for Hearst newspapers. He wrote for *Cosmopolitan* and put together a collection of his works.

Bierce never "mined" his experiences in the Black Hills for his writing, and biographers speculate that he simply couldn't bear to admit failure, even though it wasn't his fault. His most enduring work is a short story, "An Occurrence at Owl Creek Bridge," that influenced many later writers, including Stephen Crane and Ernest Hemingway.

In 1913, when he was 71 years old, Ambrose Bierce disappeared. Many people think he went to Mexico and died in Pancho Villa's revolution. But some think he took his own life in Grand Canyon. In any case, he got his last, bitter wish—that no one would ever find his bones.

concerts at the end. Sign up for the workshop or find out more information about each event online.

BLACK HILLS CHAMBER MUSIC SOCIETY
(605) 718-5666, (605) 342-8480

The society's series runs from Oct to May, and most performances are held at the First Congregational Church, 1200 Clark St., Rapid City. The Dakota String Quartet has performed, as well as the Black Hills Chamber Orchestra, Nebraska Brass, the Rawlins Piano Trio, and the Dakota Woodwind Quintet. The Chamber

Music Society has outreach programs for children and seniors, including performances in schools, local nursing homes, and rehabilitation centers. Ticket prices range from $30 to $35 for season tickets and $10 to $15 for individual performances.

BLACK HILLS SYMPHONY ORCHESTRA
(605) 348-HORN (season tickets),
(605) 394-4111 (individual performances)

Rapid City may be a small city, but it has a symphony with big-city quality. The orchestra was founded in 1932, and current conductor Jack Knowles has been with the group since 1972. Six concerts are scheduled each season, and all take place at the Rushmore Plaza Civic Center. Ticket prices for adults range from $11 to $22 for individual performances; season tickets are available.

CATHEDRAL CONCERTS
520 Cathedral Dr., Rapid City
(605) 342-0507
www.cathedralolph.org

The Cathedral of Our Lady of Perpetual Help boasts the largest pipe organ in a five-state region, a 62-rank Casavant. The Fifth and Broadway Dessert Theater, featuring Broadway tunes, is presented each June in the cathedral. And each December the South Dakota School of Mines and Technology choir presents two free concerts.

DAKOTA CHORAL UNION
(605) 394-4111 (tickets)

The Dakota Choral Union is composed of more than 100 vocalists from the South Dakota School of Mines and Technology and the Black Hills community. It includes several choral ensembles and is the official chorus provider to the Black Hills Symphony

Orchestra. Performances are held at varying locations around the Black Hills, including the Rushmore Plaza Civic Center. Ticket prices for adults are $12 for individual concerts and $35 for season tickets. Four to five concerts are presented each season.

i The Black Hills Symphony League supports the symphony orchestra, the Black Hills Chamber Music Society, the Music in the Schools program, and the Young Artists' competition. It also awards music lesson scholarships to children. This organization sponsors a Homes for the Holidays fund-raiser each year in early Nov; tickets can be purchased at the Dahl Fine Arts Center, (605) 394-4101.

RAPID CITY CHILDREN'S CHORUS
(605) 341-5304, (605) 394-2564

Children in grades three through eight audition to join the Children's Chorus, which has been performing since 1986. Most concerts feature classical choral music, but some include ethnic, jazz, and gospel. The chorus presents concerts the first Sun of each May and Dec at Dakota Middle School, 615 Columbus St., and travels around the country to perform as well. Tickets are $5 for adults and $12 for families.

RAPID CITY CONCERT ASSOCIATION SERIES
(605) 721-3914

The volunteer Rapid City Concert Association plans and schedules five concerts each year, presenting national touring artists who perform at the Rushmore Plaza Civic Center. Past performances have featured pianist Valentina Lisitsa, Czech Boys Choir Boni Pueri, and the brass group Side Street Strutters. The series runs from Sept through May. Ticket prices are $25 for students, $50 for adults, and $110 for families.

Southern Hills

HOT SPRINGS AREA CONCERT ASSOCIATION
801 South 6th St., Hot Springs
(605) 745-3886, (605) 745-4140
Four concerts are presented each season, and admission is by membership only (that is, only season tickets are sold). Ticket prices are $10 for students, $25 for adults, and $60 for families. Tickets include reciprocity to concerts in Newcastle, Wyoming, Belle Fourche, and Rapid City. Concerts are family-oriented music that can be instrumental or vocal. One of the association's goals is to pull in entertainment that appeals to all age groups in the area.

PUBLIC ART

You may want to make some side trips to see our noteworthy public art. In addition, two fine works of art grace the lobby of the Radisson Hotel at 445 Mount Rushmore Rd., Rapid City. Both are mosaics; one is a landscape of the Black Hills, and the other, a depiction of Mount Rushmore. These are not public art (they're owned by the hotel), but they are worth a visit.

i Tickets—both season and individual performance—to many events can be purchased through the Rushmore Plaza Civic Center's box office. The toll-free number is (800) GOT-MINE, and the local number is (605) 394-4111.

Northern Hills

Bust of Wild Bill Hickok, Korczak Ziolkowski, Custer. Granite sculpture. Sherman Street Park, Deadwood.

Generation, Jim Maher, Belle Fourche. Bronze sculpture. D.C. Booth Historic Fish Hatchery, 423 Hatchery Circle, Spearfish.

Gold, Tony Chytka, Spearfish. Entrance to Days of '76 rodeo grounds, Crescent Drive, Deadwood.

Kinship, Dale Lamphere, Sturgis. Bronze sculpture. Community Sculpture Garden, 1401 Lazelle St., Sturgis.

Lasting Legacy, Tony Chytka, Spearfish. Bronze sculpture. Centennial Park, US 85 and National Street, Belle Fourche.

Peace Memorial, Dale Lamphere, Sturgis. Bronze and granite sculpture. Visitor center, 415 5th Ave., Belle Fourche.

Spherefish, Dick Termes, Spearfish. Termesphere. Spearfish City Hall, 625 5th St., Spearfish.

Wild Bill Hickok, James Borglum and Monique Ziolkowski, Custer. Bronze sculpture. Four Aces Casino, 531 Main St., Deadwood.

Central Hills

Bluestem Woman, Dale Lamphere, Sturgis. Metal and found objects sculpture. Rapid City Public Library, 610 Quincy St., Rapid City.

Cyclorama, Bernard Preston Thomas, Florida. Oil on canvas. Dahl Fine Arts Center, 713 7th St., Rapid City.

Endless Horizon, Dick Termes, Spearfish. Termesphere. Rushmore Plaza Civic Center, 444 Mount Rushmore Rd., Rapid City.

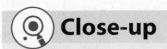 **Close-up**

The City of Presidents

Since tourists began arriving here en masse in the 1930s, Rapid City has been known as the gateway to South Dakota's legendary Black Hills, where the towering stone portraits of four of America's great presidents were carved from a pine-clad cliff. But, visitors to the community today are encountering presidents on virtually every street corner. Rapid City has literally become **"The City of Presidents"** where 39 of the nation's leaders have now been immortalized with life-sized bronze statues manning downtown.

"We've witnessed the incredible patriotism that has been created by Mount Rushmore National Memorial," said Dallerie Davis, co-founder of the City of Presidents project. "It's become iconic, a symbol of our country, our patriotism and who we hope to be and what we hope to accomplish as a nation. We trust that these presidential statues will be a continuation of that dream."

Since its inception in 2000, as many as four presidential sculptures have been placed within the city's historic district each year—two from the early years of the presidency and two from more recent administrations. By 2011, organizers expect to have all of the country's leaders greeting visitors to Rapid City.

"On Mount Rushmore, we see four great presidents," Davis said. "On Main Street, you'll be able to see all of our presidents. When you see these leaders, you realize that some were great and others were not so exceptional. But, it's all a part of the process, a democratic ideal we must respect. Seeing each of the presidents will remind us of this democracy, which is, in the history of the world, an extremely unique process."

The work of five South Dakota artists—Lee Leuning, John Lopez, James Michael Maher, Edward Hlavka, and James VanNuys—each of the $50,000 sculptures has been created with the support of local benefactors or businesses. More impressive, each of the presidents is depicted in the context of their time. JFK is shown walking with John Jr., holding one of his son's toy airplanes. FDR firmly grips a podium to steady himself against the affects of his polio as he addresses the nation. Nixon is posed in a Chinese-style chair, his hands projecting a power posture as he negotiates with Mao Tse-tung.

To date, the presidential likenesses have weathered sun, rain, and snow well, although President Harry Truman had a run-in with a Ford in 2007. According to Rapid City police, an officer was pursuing a suspected intoxicated man driving a 1999 Ford Taurus in the early morning hours of March 2, 2007. When the Ford's driver failed to negotiate a turn at a downtown intersection, his car slid into the statue of Truman, who was proudly holding the newspaper carrying the erroneous headline, DEWEY DEFEATS TRUMAN. The impact sheared Truman's statue from its stainless steel mounting pegs, and the president suffered minor scrapes and a damaged lapel. The Ford was totaled. Its driver, who attempted to flee on foot, was apprehended by police a short time later and was charged with third-offense DUI, reckless driving, aggravated eluding, driving under revocation, hit and run, and no insurance. After an extended hospital stay and treatment that included sandblasting, polishing, and a re-patina, Truman resumed his pose on Mount Rushmore Road later that summer.

City of Presidents—302 Main St., Rapid City: Offers information and a self-guided walking tour brochure. Open 12 p.m. to 9 p.m. each day, June through Sept. For more information, call (605) 490-4001.

He Is, They Are, Glenna Goodacre, New Mexico. Bronze sculpture. Prairie Edge Trading Company and Galleries, 606 Main St., Rapid City.

Iron Eagle, Vic Runnels, Aberdeen. Metal and wood sculpture. Central High School, 433 Mount Rushmore Rd., Rapid City.

Legacy, Dale Lamphere, Sturgis. Bronze and concrete sculpture. Memorial Park, Omaha and 6th Streets, Rapid City.

Mitakuye Oyasin (All My Relatives), Richard UnderBaggage, Rapid City, and Dale Lamphere, Sturgis. Bronze sculpture. Southwest corner of 6th and Main Streets, Rapid City.

Monolith, Fiorenzo Berardozzi, Rapid City. Western Dakota Technical Institute, 800 Mickelson Dr., Rapid City.

Pinocchio, John Eng, Hill City. Wood sculpture. Rapid City Public Library, 610 Quincy St., Rapid City.

Rapid Trout, Martin Wanserski, Vermillion. Concrete sculpture. Founders Park, Omaha Street near 12th Street, Rapid City.

St. Thomas More Mural, Fr. Peter Wilke and Julia Poage, Rapid City. Porcelain tile mural. St. Thomas More High School, 300 Fairmont Blvd., Rapid City.

Spirit of Healing, Dale Lamphere, Sturgis. Bronze sculpture. Rapid City Regional Hospital, 353 Fairmont Blvd., Rapid City.

The Ingalls Family, Harvey Hultquist, Minneapolis. Wood carving. Rapid City Public Library, 610 Quincy St., Rapid City.

Toth, Andrew Leicester, Minneapolis. Timber, concrete, and steel sculpture on a hill above South Dakota School of Mines and Technology, 501 East St. Joseph St., Rapid City.

Untitled, student artists under the direction of artist Vic Runnels. Painted mural. At the railroad overpass, East Boulevard near New York Street, Rapid City.

Vigilance, Peggy Detmer, Rapid City. Bronze sculpture. Memorial Park, Rapid City.

i Learn what's going on in the world of South Dakota fine arts by listening to the *Arts Advocate* on South Dakota Public Radio. The Weekly Arts Calendar is broadcast Monday at 5:25 p.m. (mountain time). Hear the Daily Arts Calendar Tues through Fri at 6:50 a.m. and 7:50 a.m. *Arts Advocate Report* is broadcast Tues through Fri at 7:30 a.m. and 5:25 p.m.

THEATER
Northern Hills

HISTORIC MATTHEWS OPERA HOUSE
614 Main St., Spearfish
(605) 642-7973

A working performing arts center, the renovated opera house (where operas are not performed) was built in that wonderful turn-of-the-20th-century western style that walks the line between ornate and practical. Year-round community theater productions, events, and exhibits are held here; it is also the home of the Spearfish Center for the Arts and Humanities. Community theater performances run during Mar, May, Aug, Oct, and Dec for three weekends each month. Past plays have included *M.A.S.H.,* the musical *Annie,* and *Cowgirls.* Ticket prices are $12.50 for adults and $6.50 for children. You can sometimes purchase tickets at the door, but it's best to call ahead and reserve them. Year-round Mon through Fri, you can tour the opera house. When plays are scheduled, you can visit until the plays begin at 7:30 p.m. Call ahead to ask about visiting during the remainder of the year. Staff members are available to answer questions during your visit, and there is no admission charge.

i Black Hills Community Theatre is justifiably proud of Friends of the Theatre, its volunteer action group that claims some 350 local volunteers. These enthusiastic people help with everything from fund-raising and ticket sales to ushering and painting sets. The Friends can be reached through the theater's office at (605) 394-1787.

Central Hills

BLACK HILLS COMMUNITY THEATRE
713 7th St., Rapid City
(605) 394-1787, (605) 394-1786
www.bhct.org

This community theater was established in 1968. Its five-performance series runs from Sept to May; each play runs three weeks, with both a Sunday matinee and evening presentations. Professionally staged performances are presented by dedicated local actors, and most take place in the Dahl Fine Arts Center's theater, but larger productions and musicals may be held at the Rushmore Plaza Civic Center. Past performances included *Guys and Dolls, Great Expectations, Little Shop of Horrors, Dial M for Murder,* and a January dinner theater fund-raiser. Season ticket prices range from $40 to $65. Tickets for single performances go on sale at the Dahl's box office a few days before each performance begins. Black Hills Community Theatre presents plays for both children and adults and offers theater workshops and classes. A children's troupe gives at least two performances each year.

Southern Hills

BLACK HILLS PLAYHOUSE
Custer State Park, Custer
(605) 394-7797, (605) 255-4242, seasonal
www.blackhillsplayhouse.com

The playhouse is inside Custer State Park, which provides a beautiful setting for this professional theater. Summer season begins in June and continues through Aug. Each play runs two to three weeks and has matinee and evening performances. Past performances have included *I Hate Hamlet, Brigadoon, Crimes of the Heart, Steel Magnolias,* and *Cat on a Hot Tin Roof.* Ticket prices range from $18 to $28. Discounts are available for groups of 12 or more. Reservations should be made at least 48 hours in advance. You must purchase a park entrance license, since you'll be accessing the park to reach the playhouse (for license fees, see the Custer State Park listing in the Parks & Mountains chapter). Take advantage of the opportunity: Come early, and visit the park before having dinner and enjoying the play. The historic Playhouse buildings have been undergoing extensive renovations. The shows, however must still go on. So please check for the location of the show you would like to see before heading down into the park.

VENUES

You'll find several venues mentioned in this chapter: the Dahl Fine Arts Center's intimate theater, the Historic Matthews Opera House's restored stage, the band shell at Rapid City's Memorial Park, and various churches, schools, and community centers where the acoustics and size lend themselves to performances. But the largest and most versatile venue in the Black Hills is the Rushmore Plaza Civic Center, listed at right.

Central Hills

RUSHMORE PLAZA CIVIC CENTER
444 Mount Rushmore Rd., Rapid City
(605) 394-4115, (800) GOT-MINE (tickets)
www.gotmine.com
The civic center is the major venue in the Black Hills. It has hosted ice shows, the Black Hills Stock Show and Rodeo on the last weekend in Jan, monster truck rallies, ballet and Broadway performances, theater troupes, concerts, powwows, art and antiques shows, and conventions. Its grand-opening concert in 1976 was one of Elvis's final performances. The center boasts 150,000 square feet of exhibit space, a 10,000-seat arena, a 5,000-seat ice arena, the 1,779-seat Fine Arts Theater, two large halls (La Croix and Rushmore), 27 meeting rooms, and 3,000 free parking spaces. It's set on nine acres adjacent to Rapid City's Memorial Park and is fewer than 100 steps away from the Rushmore Plaza Holiday Inn. Among the many events here is the Broadway Play series, which recently included touring productions of *Cats, My Cousin's Wedding, The Music Man*, and *Saturday Night Fever.* Ticket prices for performances range from $25 to $60; season tickets are available.

PARKS & MOUNTAINS

When it comes to finding places to play outdoors, the Black Hills can't be beat—and the numbers prove it. The region claims the highest concentration of national parks, memorials, and monuments in the country: Mount Rushmore National Memorial, Jewel Cave National Monument, Wind Cave National Park, Devils Tower National Monument (just a few miles across the Wyoming border), Badlands National Park (see The Badlands & Nearby chapter for in-depth park information), and the Minuteman Missile National Historic Site, which opened to the public in 2005. Add to that four state parks and recreation areas (Bear Butte State Park, Custer State Park, Angostura Recreation Area, and the Mickelson Trail), and you'll start to see the essence of the region. Don't forget that the 1.2-million-acre Black Hills National Forest sprawls over the whole area, with Buffalo Gap National Grasslands almost touching its southern and eastern borders and the Thunder Basin National Grasslands only a few miles to the west in Wyoming.

Most of these places are also listed in the Attractions or Recreation chapters, but four of the most striking mountain parks in the Black Hills are detailed below. Even though many of these areas are located near each other (for instance, Wind Cave and Custer share borders), each has its own distinctive features. Indeed, some places in these parks will seem like worlds unto themselves.

NORTHERN HILLS

BEAR BUTTE STATE PARK
Off SR 79, north of Sturgis
(605) 347-5240
www.state.sd.us/gfp

As you drive into the area around Sturgis, you'll see Bear Butte blue-gray in the distance. Isolated from the rest of the Black Hills by a mile or more, the mountain looks out of place, rising up from an otherwise unbroken stretch of prairie. That makes its distinctive silhouette (that of a bear sleeping on the plains) easy to spot from a distance. In fact, the peak has been guiding people to the Black Hills for millennia.

This is Mato Paha, Lakota for "bear mountain." The Cheyenne call it Noavosse ("good mountain"). For centuries it has been a place of worship, a powerful site from which to contact the holy, and a Native American landmark. Cheyenne legend tells that the prophet Sweet Medicine received four sacred arrows here and four commandments for his people to live by.

It appears that Bear Butte has always been sacred. Artifacts 10,000 years old and an ancient ceremonial site have been unearthed here. Today Native Americans still climb the mountain to pray and fast, leaving medicine bundles, tobacco offerings, and ribbons as physical manifestations of their prayers. Please respect this holy site and don't disturb the privacy of worshipers or the offerings, including rocks placed in the forks of branches, which are the traditional markers of someone's visit.

The mountain will offer you incredible views, both out over the plains and toward the Black Hills. Take all the scenic photographs you like, but do not photograph the ceremonial items, offerings, or worshipers. The signs at the trailhead ask that you walk quietly and reverently and speak in low tones. Use the same respect you would feel when touring a cathedral where the worship service is in progress, for that is what Bear Butte is.

The first white men to see the mountain, and the Black Hills, were probably the Verendrye brothers, François and Louis-Joseph, French explorers who climbed Bear Butte in 1743. They called it Montagne des Gens des Cheveaux, the "Mountain of the Horse People," because the inhabitants there (unlike some tribes of that era) had horses.

In 1855 Dr. Ferdinand Hayden, a geologist, climbed Bear Butte and discovered, 600 feet up, a previously unknown flower, *Anemone patens,* the pasqueflower. You may find it sprouting up through melting snow. It later was designated South Dakota's state flower. For more on this flower, see the Natural World chapter.

The Teton Sioux held a great council at Bear Butte in the summer of 1857. Men from Custer's 1874 expedition climbed it while the troops camped nearby, resting for the last leg of their trip back to Fort Lincoln. In 1880 Rev. George Pelton traveled through the area on his way to Deadwood and reported in his journal that it took "nearly three hours" to get around the mountain with horse and wagon.

A pioneer's landmark because it could be seen at such great distances, Bear Butte eventually overlooked three goldrush roads, a stage line, and Fort Meade, the military post of the Seventh Cavalry.

Bear Butte State Park was created in 1961, and the mountain was named a Registered Natural Landmark in 1965. It was entered into the National Register of Historic Places in 1973, under the National Preservation Act, because of its spiritual significance to Native Americans and its importance as a landmark to early pioneers.

Geologically speaking, the mountain (which is not really a butte) is a laccolith, a dome of molten lava that expanded and bulged upward through the overlying surface rock, which slowly eroded away. Basically, it's a volcano that didn't erupt. From a distance Bear Butte looks almost touchable and soft. Rising more than 4,400 feet above sea level, more than 1,200 feet above the surrounding plains, it is mostly bare rock, but some trees and vegetation are scattered on its sides.

History books cite eyewitness accounts of fires on Bear Butte in the 1800s and claim that it was once more heavily forested than in recent decades. Until recently ponderosa pine was the predominant species at the higher elevations, and elm, cottonwood, hawthorn, juniper, chokecherry, and native grasses dominated the middle and lower regions.

In August 1996 an out-of-control ceremonial fire burned much of Bear Butte in a spectacular blaze that lasted two days. Between 80 and 90 percent of the ponderosa pines died, and it will be decades before they reestablish themselves. Ceremonial fires are permitted for Native American

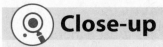

Close-up

Peter Norbeck

The name of **Peter Norbeck** is one you encounter often as you travel around the Black Hills and Badlands. That's because Norbeck—art lover, conservationist, South Dakota governor, and US senator—did so much for the area. Therefore it seems only fitting that an overlook, a wildlife preserve, a visitor center, and a scenic byway, all in or close to Custer State Park, as well as a pass through Badlands National Park, are among the places named in his honor.

Norbeck loved the outdoors and played a major role in the establishment of both parks. His efforts to set aside a game preserve and map out a scenic route through rugged, virgin Black Hills terrain also bore fruit. And he answered the call when South Dakota's state historian, Doane Robinson, sought his help in promoting and funding the carving of Mount Rushmore National Memorial.

His influence extended well beyond the borders of his home state, however, when he left his mark on the creation of Wyoming's Grand Teton National Park and passage of the federal Migratory Bird Conservation Act.

Born to Norwegian immigrant parents on a Clay County homestead in southeastern South Dakota on August 27, 1870, Norbeck learned early the value of hard work. Unwilling to become a farmer himself, however, he accumulated a modest fortune with a well-drilling business and Wyoming oil interests. His prominence in the private domain helped propel him to positions of leadership in public life.

Nicknamed "the benevolent buffalo," the 225-pound Norbeck inspired confidence and loyalty in his supporters with his honesty and can-do enthusiasm. Yet he had a stormy relationship with Mount Rushmore sculptor Gutzon Borglum, whom Norbeck deemed a poor businessman.

The two were still at odds when Norbeck, suffering from cancer, died at his home in Redfield on December 20, 1936. Fifteen years later, a decade after Borglum's own passing, they made a sort of posthumous peace when the sculptor's bronze bust of his most ardent backer, Norbeck, was placed in the state capitol building in Pierre.

ceremonies only (inquire at the visitor center). Campfires are not allowed.

Today Bear Butte's environment is making a comeback. For nearly a year the National Hiking Trail that climbs the summit was closed for repairs and to protect the mountain from erosion caused by the lack of vegetation and tree canopy. The summit trail reopened with new wooden steps and erosion edging, the lumber for which was airlifted to the top by National Guard helicopters. The trail is rocky but is only moderately difficult. The north end of the Centennial Trail starts at the summit of Bear Butte. Read more about the Centennial Trail in the Recreation chapter.

The state park is open year-round. At the visitor center (open 9 a.m. to 5 p.m., seven days a week, from May to early Sept only), you can learn about the geologic and cultural history of Bear Butte and the park. The center contains a museum and presents educational videos. The entrance fee is $6 per car per day. There is no charge for children 11 and younger. A Custer State Park entrance license or annual state park pass will admit you without charge.

Bear Butte State Park is a low-key entertain-yourself park. Organized activities are few, but summer programs for groups can be arranged with the staff naturalist, who will give presentations on history and natural history and conduct hiking tours. Special programs need to be arranged in advance. No concessions are available in the park, but the town of Sturgis is just 5 miles away.

You can also watch the park's buffalo herd, fish (by state permit—see the Recreation chapter), swim in the lake, camp in the campground (see the Campgrounds chapter), and hike. Try photographing the mountain at different times of day, when it changes color and texture in the light of sunrise and sunset, thunderstorm and snow.

You can sit at its base and stare at it, mesmerized by its powerful beauty. Or you can climb it and look out over the plains and hills (which you can see stretching into Nebraska or North Dakota), imagining Custer and his men marching by, or the Verendrye brothers climbing up beside you, or Sitting Bull waiting patiently for the mountain to speak.

i If you'd like to support educational programs and research in Black Hills forests and parks, join the Black Hills Parks and Forests Association, which publishes books and educational materials and funds research and intern programs. Membership includes a semiannual newsletter and a discount on books, maps, and posters at their sales outlets (Custer State Park, Wind Cave, and Jewel Cave) and most national park bookstores. Call (605) 745-7020.

CENTRAL HILLS

MOUNT RUSHMORE NATIONAL MEMORIAL
SR 244, Keystone
(605) 574-2523
www.nps.gov/moru

Egypt has the pyramids, England has Stonehenge. But ancient artisans were not the last to create world-class stone monuments, for a modern-day example is found in the Black Hills at Mount Rushmore. One of the nation's most recognizable landmarks, the towering busts of four US presidents—George Washington, Thomas Jefferson, Abraham Lincoln, and Theodore Roosevelt—stand in tribute to the American ideals of freedom and progress. But the carving by American sculptor Gutzon Borglum can't help inspiring awe as an impressive feat of engineering and an extraordinary work of art as well.

Flamboyant, patriotic, and hugely talented, Borglum, the son of Danish immigrants, believed a great nation deserved public art as big as all outdoors. So when he was invited to Georgia in the 1920s to create a Confederate soldiers' memorial, he envisioned giant likenesses of Dixie leaders carved onto the granite face of Stone Mountain. With the work under way, a bitter quarrel with his sponsors led to Borglum's dismissal—and an invitation to start over in South Dakota.

Borglum was 60 years old in 1927 when he started work on Mount Rushmore, hiring nearly 400 workers to drill, blast, and chisel rock off the mountainside. They were almost done when the sculptor died on March 6, 1941, leaving his son, Lincoln, to oversee the job's completion. Ever since then there have been suggestions (some serious, most not) to add more faces. However, Gutzon Borglum was very clear in expressing his vision of just four presidential sculptures. Washington was chosen for his leadership in the Revolutionary War and as the first president, roles that signify the independence and establishment of the Republic. Jefferson was selected not so much for the Declaration of Independence but for the acquisition of the Louisiana Territory in 1803, effectively doubling the size of the country. As such, Jefferson represents western expansion. Lincoln symbolizes the permanent union of the nation and equality for all its citizens. And Roosevelt, who had been dead for only eight years when Borglum started work on the mountain, was chosen by the sculptor because he completed the Panama Canal, allowing the United States to exert its influence worldwide. The National Park Service is dedicated to preserving Borglum's choices and preserving the monument as it stands. Besides, there's no more rock suitable for carving.

Newsweek columnist George F. Will called Mount Rushmore "an agreeable example of American excess," and indeed, more than three million people from around the world visit the Shrine of Democracy each year. Before viewing the 60-foot-tall faces, you'll want to stop in the information center to learn about the memorial and the 1,240-acre park's other features and free activities. For starters, you can see original tools, models, and other relics in the Sculptor's Studio, and the wheelchair-accessible Presidential Trail will take you to the talus slope along the base of the mountain. The park service offers guided walks and talks daily throughout the summer, and those in the 5- to 12-year-old crowd have their own activities that make learning about Mount Rushmore fun. Parents can help their youngsters earn a certificate through the Junior Ranger Program or

Photographing Mount Rushmore

Visitors like to photograph Mount Rushmore through the tunnels on Iron Mountain Road, and that requires tricking your camera. The darkness of the stone is a high contrast to the light on the tunnel's other end. Your camera's meter will read the darker stone, overexpose the shot, and, when your photos are developed, the great faces will be washed out. The trick is to ignore your camera's meter reading. "Stop down," or close down, the lens aperture to let in less light. You'll need to use F8, F11, F16, and maybe F22, and you should also match (or approximate) the shutter speed to the film speed. Another method to photograph Mount Rushmore from the nearby tunnels is to move to the mouth of the tunnel, point the camera directly at the faces and set your exposure by the meter reading you get. Then move back and photograph, ignoring the metering changes your camera wants you to make. Don't forget, too, that Mount Rushmore's southeastern exposure makes morning the best time to take pictures of the faces.

have them take part in a 30-minute ranger-led program. (Turn to the Kidstuff chapter for more details.)

There's also an interpretive center/museum complex with 5,000 square feet of exhibit space and two theaters for viewing an informational video. It's just one of numerous recent improvements that include the pergola, or grand entryway, the information center and restroom complex, the amphitheater, a new Avenue of Flags, a spacious gift shop, and a food-service facility with two snack bars and a cafeteria.

Most of these additions are the product of a nearly $25 million fund-raising campaign by the Mount Rushmore National Memorial Society, an organization Borglum himself helped form in 1930. Contributions poured in from dozens of South Dakota communities, all 50 states, and about 20 foreign countries. Private donors have included descendants of New York attorney Charles Rushmore, who was visiting the Hills on behalf of mining interests when the mountain was named for him, partly in jest, in 1885.

The campaign also made possible the completion of the Hall of Records. One of Borglum's greatest fears was that future civilizations would have no idea why these four faces graced a mountain in the middle of the continent. It was always his intent to construct a cavernous hall on top of the sculpture, hidden behind the heads, into which would be placed copies of the Constitution and its Bill of Rights, documents explaining the carving of the mountain, and busts of famous Americans. However, dwindling funds and the onset of World War II forced him to abandon the project. The hall remained unfinished until the 1998 renovations, when officials finally decided to complete Borglum's dream. Today, a vault chiseled into the Hall of Records' floor contains porcelain tablets etched with the documents Borglum requested, encased in titanium and sealed with a half-ton block of solid granite. Though not completed on

"Buffalo Are Dangerous. Do Not Approach."

You'll see this and similar signs in Custer State Park and Wind Cave National Park. But the animals we call "buffalo" are not buffalo. That species includes African cape buffalo and water buffalo, which are not native to North America. The big, shaggy creatures of the West are North American bison, but most people just call them buffalo. Their Lakota name is *tatanka*.

These big creatures may look docile, but they are not livestock, nor are they domesticated. Bison are wild, can run at 35 mph or faster and turn on a dime, and are equipped with sharp horns, which they use to make their point when they feel threatened. People have been gored and attacked when they got too close or harassed bison. Cows with calves are especially prickly tempered.

Males (standing 5 to 6 feet high at the shoulder and weighing 2,000 pounds) keep to themselves or live in bachelor groups, while cows and calves stay in a herd. The rut (breeding season) begins in July and lasts through Sept. Bulls fight for females, and you may hear their roars or witness fierce battles. The bison are temperamental at this important season, so don't leave your car to get a better look. Don't approach the buffalo!

the scale Borglum had envisioned, the Hall of Records serves its original purpose: to protect and preserve the ideals of the nation led by the men carved into the giant granite mountainside.

Of course, preserving the sculpture is important, too. Thus, restoration and maintenance efforts are a major priority here. Every fall hairline cracks in the faces are painstakingly sealed by hand with silicone caulk, ensuring that generations will have an opportunity to see the sculptor's dream.

One of the best ways to share Borglum's vision is to attend the lighting ceremony that begins with a talk and a film at 9 in the amphitheater each summer evening. Lights illuminate the faces at 9:30 p.m. (Everything begins an hour earlier between Labor Day and mid-Sept.) Weather-related cancellations are rare, but call ahead if in doubt. Even during the off-season, the faces are bathed in light for an hour or two each evening, beginning shortly after dusk. It's a tradition that at least some local people take seriously—a temporary federal government shutdown in 1996 left Mount Rushmore in the dark, so Keystone rancher Art Oakes dug into his own pocket and took up a collection to pay the light bill.

Mount Rushmore is open 24 hours a day all year except Christmas Day. The information center is open from 8 a.m. to 10 p.m. during the summer and from 8 a.m. to 5 p.m. for the winter. The season for special activities is May 15 to Sept 30.

You can park for free if you don't mind climbing 60 or more steps from the parking lot. Otherwise, parking in the new trilevel ramp just outside the grand entryway costs $10 per passenger vehicle for as many visits as you care to make in a single calendar year.

(Buses pay $25 every time they enter.) The parking fees were established to pay off an $18 million loan to the Mount Rushmore Society for the parking ramp and related roadways. So although admission to the actual park grounds is free, your Golden Eagle, Golden Age, or Golden Access pass won't be honored at the parking ramp.

SOUTHERN HILLS

CUSTER STATE PARK
SR 87 South or North, SR 36 West, or US 16/16A East
(605) 255-4464, (605) 255-4515, (888) 875-0001
www.state.sd.us/gfp

One word defines all of Custer State Park: big. With 71,000 acres of ponderosa forest, towering granite peaks (including North America's tallest mountain east of the Rockies, the 7,242-foot Harney Peak), and grassy prairie, Custer is one of the largest state parks in the country. And then there are the bison, the largest land mammals on the continent. Custer State Park has about 1,500 of the animals in one of the largest free-roaming herds of bison in the world. It's fitting that these great one-ton reflections of nature's might reside here, for only a group of such powerful animals would suit such a powerful mountain landscape.

Custer State Park was the idea of Peter Norbeck, a popular US senator and the governor of South Dakota from 1916 to 1920. Originally from eastern South Dakota, Norbeck visited the Black Hills in 1905 and conceived the idea of establishing a wild game park in Custer County. Legislation was passed in 1913.

A practical man, Norbeck planned that timber production and resource

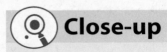

Close-up

Badger Clark, Poet Laureate

South Dakota once had a Poet Lariat.

In reality, **Badger Clark** was named the first poet laureate in 1939, but many people—including the poet—preferred the humorous cowboy title of honor, a tribute to his western heritage, a larger-than-life designation for a colorful, larger-than-life man.

Charles Badger Clark was born in Iowa in 1883. His family moved to the Dakota Territory when he was three months old. Just months shy of being born a Dakotan, he nevertheless is considered a native son and our own beloved poet.

When Clark was 15, his mother died. Several years later, his frontier-minister father married a strong woman with an interest in writing, a woman Clark loved and admired enough to call Mother Anna. She would push him along the paths of poetry, prodding him to write, to submit his work to publications, and to publish books.

As a boy, Clark spent vacations at his uncle's Wyoming ranch and developed a taste for the wide-open, romantic West and cowboy life. In 1903, having given up on college and not knowing what he wanted for his future, he accompanied a party hoping to colonize Cuba. The expedition was a failure, but Clark stayed on, seeking adventure. After Cuba he came home, joined a Badlands surveying party, tried (and failed at) business, and got a taste of the writing life at the lead newspaper.

Then near-tragedy struck: Clark was diagnosed with tuberculosis. On his doctor's advice, he moved to Arizona and found an ideal job on a Tombstone ranch, tending cattle and enjoying time to write and think. The dry air and rest sent his tuberculosis into remission. And when he mailed his stepmother a poem and she sent it on to a magazine that published it, a surprised new poet was born. Later he wrote one of his most famous poems, "The Cowboy's Prayer," in which he captured the souls of the men of the West:

> Oh Lord, I've never lived where
> churches grow.
> I love creation better as it stood
> That day You finished it so long
> ago . . .
> I know that others find You in the
> light

management would help keep the park self-sustaining. Today camping fees, revenue from buffalo sales, entrance fees, concession revenue, and timber sales generate the multiple-use funds that maintain the park and its facilities. Custer State Park is self-funded on a day-to-day operational basis, although major deferred maintenance projects are sometimes funded by tax dollars.

If you'd like to stay in the park, you have your choice of four resorts: the State Game Lodge (where President Calvin Coolidge stayed during his 1927 summer vacation), Legion Lake Resort, Blue Bell Lodge, and Sylvan Lake Resort. Both Legion Lake and Sylvan Lake resorts rent boats, kayaks, and hydrobikes, and you can reserve a mountain bike at Legion Lake. Each resort in the park has dining

That's sifted down through tinted
    window panes,
And yet I seem to feel You near
    tonight
In this dim, quiet starlight on the
    plains.

Clark, a bachelor, spent years in Hot Springs, then moved to a cabin he built in Custer State Park. Although a friendly, popular man, he craved the solitude and independence only a rustic cabin in the woods could provide. In the 30 years he lived there, he wrote and read, answered fan mail, fed pancakes to the deer, received intrigued visitors, and gave poetry readings.

His two cabins still stand. The first he lived in while building the larger home, which is just as he left it in September 1957 when he went to his nephew's Rapid City home three weeks before dying of lung cancer. His fans still visit Badger Hole, the property and the cabins. There you can delight in his fine library—the comfortable spot where he wrote late into the night—and his kitchen, still stocked with staples and utensils.

As any legendary character does, Clark always wore a trademark outfit: high riding boots and breeches and an officer's coat and hat. His boots still stand in his bedroom, and his jackets hang on their pegs, seemingly awaiting their owner's return.

You can walk the Badger Clark Historic Trail, which winds up the hill behind the cabin and down again. Carry a brochure (available at the cabin) with some of his many poems, and stop at the markers and read a verse that commemorates that spot. When you reach this one, pay closer attention. It's called "I Must Come Back":

No, when the waning heartbeat fails
I ask no heaven but leave to wend,
Unseen but seeing, my old trails,
With deathless years to
    comprehend . . .

Badger Clark is buried in Hot Springs, but his spirit lingers in Custer State Park.

facilities and a store or gift shop where you can purchase food or a souvenir. Read about these resorts in the Accommodations chapter.

There are also seven modern campgrounds, two primitive and two group campsites, and the French Creek horse camp, which has corral space. You can read about these facilities in the Campgrounds chapter.

At Custer State Park you can cross-country ski, fish, hike, and climb the rocks. Scale Mount Coolidge to its 6,023-foot peak and get a look at the Badlands 90 miles away. Or travel back in history at the re-created Gordon Stockade, where, in the summer, you can watch daily activities as they were carried out in 1874 by gold-seeking pioneers. Both Mount Coolidge and the Gordon

Stockade are on the west side of the park. We recommend you pick up maps and brochures at the visitor centers or the park entrances, which will make everything easy to find.

When you're ready for a break from your own activities, there's plenty of daily organized entertainment in the park (summers only, though). You can enjoy educational programs, slides and films, guided nature and historic walks, informal lectures, and fishing demonstrations. Some great programs for kids are offered, too, including a Junior Naturalist Program that teaches children about nature. Call the Norbeck Visitor Center for more information about these programs.

i Some state parks use prescribed burns to mimic the work of wild prairie fires: The destruction of vegetation and subsequent rejuvenation of the land help restore the natural balance between grasslands and pine forests. While traveling through a park, you may come across fire personnel monitoring the blazes, smoke, and wind direction. No need to worry, and it's fine to watch and learn.

At Blue Bell stables you can sign up for trail rides or overnight pack trips (see the Recreation chapter) or go on the Old-Fashioned Hay Ride and Chuck Wagon Cookout (with cowboy fixin's). If motorized transportation is more your speed, try the Buffalo Safari Jeep Tour and Chuck Wagon Cookout Adventure, which start at the State Game Lodge. These activities are daily summer happenings. Each attraction and resort area is well marked with highway signs and easy to find on park maps. Some activities require advance reservations; call the general information number to inquire about hours and fees.

The State Game Lodge has a rotating artist-in-residence program for wildlife and western artists. In the gallery off the lobby, you can watch artists create, browse through their displayed work, and take home an original work of art.

Theater lovers will want to take in a summer theater performance at the Black Hills Playhouse (see the Arts chapter). Poetry buffs will enjoy a pilgrimage to Badger Hole, the carefully preserved cabin that was the home of Badger Clark, South Dakota's first poet laureate. It's open in the summer from 10 a.m. to 5 p.m. Memorial Day to Labor Day. Admission is free with your park entrance license.

You can take a scenic drive along the Needles Highway (14 miles), which wanders through the Needles formations, granite spires that point to the sky. The Needles Highway is closed in the winter (approximately Nov 1 to Apr 1, depending on the weather).

Or try Iron Mountain Road, which winds between the intersection of US 16A and SR 36 and Mount Rushmore. Along that route you'll see the marvelous pigtail bridges, artistically engineered creations designed by Governor Norbeck that switchback up steep hills. The 70-mile Peter Norbeck National Scenic Byway is another great drive; there's more information about it in the Attractions chapter.

A drive on the Wildlife Loop is a must. Its 18 miles go directly through the areas most often frequented by the park's wildlife. Try it in the early mornings and evenings when you're likely to spot white-tailed and mule deer, pronghorn antelope, mountain goats, bighorn sheep, wild turkeys, and prairie dogs. You're less likely to see the elk and coyotes, but you might get lucky. You'll see many birds, including—quite possibly—hawks and golden eagles as well as small mammals such as squirrels, chipmunks, and skunks. You might even see a snake or two.

Coolidge General Store

The **Coolidge General Store** at Custer State Park has a most amazing ceiling. It was built to resemble the hull of a ship (turned upside down, above you), and it's beautifully constructed of native ponderosa pine. It is said to have 11,000 angle cuts (the cuts made in the boards to make them all fit perfectly together). Virtually every board meets the adjoining board or beam at an angle, in a stunning display of fancy crafts-manship. If you try to count all those angles, however, you'll get a crick in your neck for your efforts. The ceiling was crafted in 1927 by shipbuilders from Minnesota, who built the general store and other buildings to accommodate Presi-dent Coolidge and his entourage during their summer vacation at Custer State Park.

These roads were designed as scenic drives. Take your time, enjoy the scenery, and don't travel too fast. As Governor Norbeck himself said about the scenic byway, "You're not supposed to drive here at 60 miles an hour. To do the scenery half justice, people should drive 20 or under. To do it full justice, they should get out and walk."

While driving on the Wildlife Loop and Iron Mountain Road, you'll eventually be slowed by a wily burro (or two, or several). Do be careful and watch out for them. Attempted escape is not recommended, sometimes not even possible. These guys will simply stand in front of your vehicle and solicit handouts. Or they'll poke their big heads in your window and stay there awhile, keeping you effectively trapped. The burros are not indigenous; they are the descendants of those brought to the park in 1927 to take visitors to Harney Peak. The park management discourages feeding the critters. Roll up your windows and enjoy watching them until they become bored and let you pass.

The 1,500-head bison herd is the park's main attraction. You may find the animals standing in the road, too, or grazing along-side. In the spring the little red calves are born. They are shy, and their mothers are protective, but (from your car) you can get some good pictures. In Oct the herd is rounded up, corralled, vaccinated, and sorted during the Buffalo Roundup (more about this in the Annual Events chapter). Of these, about 950 are returned to the park to winter (that's the amount the range can sup-port), and the rest are auctioned in Nov. The sale provides income for the park and helps control the herd population.

Custer State Park is open year-round, and you must purchase an entrance license to enjoy it. An annual license is $28, and a second license for another of your vehicles is $14. You can also purchase a temporary license good for up to seven days for $6 per person (six and older) or $15 per vehicle. Your entrance license allows you to enter any state park or state recreation area during the term of the license.

Narrow Tunnels

Three scenic roads within Custer State Park have tunnels that are great fun to drive through unless you're steering a big RV, camping trailer, or bus! Few of the tunnels have a bypass, so your overlarge vehicle will have to turn around, which may not be an easy task. These roads, and their pulloffs, are narrow. Plan ahead! Iron Mountain Road (US 16A North) has three tunnels, as narrow as 12 feet 2 inches high and 13 feet 2 inches wide. The narrowest tunnel on the Needles Highway (SR 87/89) is 12 feet high and 8 feet 4 inches wide.

JEWEL CAVE NATIONAL MONUMENT
US 16, Custer
(605) 673-2288, (800) 967-2283
www.nps.gov/jeca

The narrow, winding road to Jewel Cave primes travelers for a voyage into the mysterious depths of the earth. Rich in history and natural wonders, if not in actual gems, this cave 13 miles west of Custer was discovered by prospectors Frank and Albert Michaud and Charles Bush in 1900. Mistaking a sparkling layer of calcium carbonate (also called calcite crystal) for diamonds, the men staked a mining claim but failed either to extract anything of value or to mine tourists by turning the cave into an attraction. Yet Jewel Cave's vast chambers hold a treasury of stalactites, stalagmites, and other marvels, and in 1908 President Theodore Roosevelt declared it a national monument.

Continued exploration has established Jewel as the second-longest cave in the world, with more than 150 miles of mapped passages (outdone only by Kentucky's 346.20-mile Mammoth Cave, the world's longest). However, some cavers and scientists have forwarded the theory that Jewel Cave is connected to nearby Wind Cave (the fourth longest in the world; see the Wind Cave National Park listing in this chapter). If true, that would make the cave system the longest on the planet. Of course, that's assuming that there are very few passages left to explore. Air-volume studies show the opposite. In fact, regardless of whether the two caves are linked, research suggests that less than 10 percent of the cave system has been explored, and park rangers guess that there may be a total of 5,000 miles of passages.

But there's more to the monument than the cave itself. Above ground there are 1,274 acres of ponderosa forest and prairie grassland that are host to an array of native creatures. There are deer, coyotes, 9 species of bat, 120 species of birds, and a plethora of wildflowers that bloom in a colorful show of glory each spring. Three trails (two accessible from the visitor center, one beginning on the park's western boundary off US 16) cut through the terrain and offer visitors an up-close look at the flora, fauna, and geology of the south-central Black Hills.

Of course, there are plenty of options for hiking the cave, too. Half-mile guided tours that depart from the visitor center last 80 minutes and incorporate 723 stairs—the equivalent of 40 flights, but it's mostly downhill. Sturdy, rubber-soled shoes and a light jacket are de rigueur.

Tours leave every 15 to 30 minutes beginning at 8:30 a.m. Tickets are sold on a first-come, first-served basis, so your best bet is to arrive during the morning. Historic lantern tours begin daily on a varied schedule, mid-June to mid-Aug, at the cave's natural entrance in Hell Canyon, a mile west of the visitor center. Prices are the same as for the regular tours, but children younger than six are not permitted on these tours, which last one hour and 45 minutes and cover a half mile. Call ahead for the tour schedule. The last tour is at 6 p.m.

Reservations are required for the two-thirds-mile, four-hour spelunking tours in the cave's undeveloped areas, where groups of five begin their adventure at 12:30 p.m. daily from mid-June to mid-Aug. Hard hats and headlamps are complimentary, but you're required to bring ankle-height, lace-up, lug-sole boots, gloves, and soft knee pads. Be prepared to crawl through a concrete-block tunnel to qualify for this tour, which is off-limits to anyone age 16 or younger. Those age 16 or 17 must have their parent's or guardian's written consent.

It's OK to take your camera but not your tripod on any of the tours. Touching any part of the cave's interior is prohibited, since skin oils and general wear and tear will damage the fragile formations. Anyone who's been recently hospitalized or who has respiratory or circulatory problems is advised to consult a park ranger before embarking on any cave tour. Jewel Cave is open all year except Thanksgiving, Christmas, and New Year's Day. The visitor center is open 8 a.m. to 4:30 p.m. year-round. Hours occasionally change, especially in summer months; call for information.

i Never feed a wild animal, even those that seem tame. The animal may suddenly bite, kick, scratch, or attack you. Moreover, park officials will be forced to kill wild animals that have sickened after eating human food. Animals that are hand-fed also lose their natural fear and are at greater risk of being struck by a vehicle or abused.

WIND CAVE NATIONAL PARK
SR 87 South or US 385
East or North, Hot Springs
(605) 745-4600 (visitor center)
www.nps.gov/wica

This park has as much to offer below ground as above. Adjacent to Custer State Park (directly south), it is a wildlife park as well, set on 28,000 acres. It has similar rolling prairie hills and pine-forest vistas, and it also boasts pronghorns, a bison herd, prairie dogs, deer, elk, coyotes, and more.

But this park has one feature Custer State Park lacks: Wind Cave, one of the most complex caves in the world. Its explored maze today totals more than 132 miles, all within 1 square mile of land area. But there's more down there; scientists estimate that only 5 percent of the cave has been explored. An early adventurer, Alvin McDonald, wrote in 1891, "Have given up the idea of finding the end of Wind Cave." Fortunately, explorers who came after McDonald didn't give up, and the cave is still being explored and mapped.

Wind Cave became the nation's seventh national park in 1903. It was also the first cave to become a national park and is the world's fourth-longest cave. More than 100,000 people tour the cave each year.

Wind Cave's natural opening is a (barely) adult-size hole in the ground. It was discovered in 1881 by two hunters, one of whom was Tom Bingham. When Bingham bent down for a look, the wind escaping from the hole blew his hat off his head. He excitedly went to tell his friends and brought them back to the opening. When he leaned down to show them, the wind sucked his hat inside.

Today we know that Wind Cave is a breathing cave; that is, the wind escaping or entering the cave is controlled by the atmospheric pressure outside. When the pressure rises, air is drawn inside the cave; when the atmospheric pressure lowers, the air blows out. You can stand outside the natural entrance today and experience the same phenomenon.

Wind Cave has beautiful and delicate subterranean formations such as flowstone, frostwork, popcorn, and helictites, but it is best known for a rare formation called boxwork. The cave has more boxwork than any other in the world. Millions of years ago, when the area was covered by ocean, limestone formations were created below the waters. Later the ocean receded, and over millions of years other waters seeped in and out, the limestone slowly dissolved, and passageways began to form. About 62 million to 65 million years ago, the slow geologic uplift that formed the Black Hills also caused the limestone to shift and crack, and more passages were opened.

Acid-laden water filled the cracks in the underground limestone. As the limestone dissolved in the slowly seeping water, hardened calcite boxwork formations were left behind. They are delicate and fragile, thin honeycombs clinging to the walls and ceilings of the cave.

Wind Cave Lint

No one would accuse Wind Cave of being dirty, but it does have a lint problem. Every visitor impacts the cave in the same way: by leaving behind microscopic skin cells, some hair, some clothing fibers.

It all adds up to lint! And with 100,000 visitors each year, lint is a big problem.

How do you clean a cave? Wind Cave National Park organizes lint cleaning camps, where volunteers carefully brush and vacuum sections of the cave and its trails, then remove bag after bag of lint. Wind Cave National Park management strives for a balance between public enjoyment of the cave and protecting it from the impact of all those intrigued visitors.

Although early explorers and owners used the cave for commercial tours and blasted caverns and paved walkways, today it is carefully protected. Its vital signs (humidity, temperature, and water quality) are constantly monitored to spot environmental problems early.

This living, breathing cave is constantly changing, but the temperature inside is always around 53 degrees. Wear a jacket and sturdy, rubber-sole walking shoes, and remember that some of the ceilings are low and some paths are wet. It's fine to take flash photographs and video shots, but tripods are prohibited. It's also forbidden to touch the cave walls, disturb the formations in any way, or smoke, eat, chew gum, or leave litter behind. There are no restrooms underground either, so plan ahead.

Wind Cave and the visitor center are open year-round (the center does close on Thanksgiving, Christmas, and New Year's Day), but tour hours vary by season. You can take your choice of different walking tours, which during the summer season leave every 20 minutes or so. Each is led by a well-informed park ranger. The tours are popular, and in the summer you may have to wait. Try the morning tours, which aren't as crowded.

Children younger than six can participate free of charge in the first three tours listed. Golden Age discounts apply for each tour (you must show your Golden Age Passport).

The Natural Entrance Tour lasts 75 minutes. You will navigate 300 stairs, most of which go down, and exit the cave by elevator. Prices range from $4.50 for children 6 to 16 to $9 for adults 17 and older.

The Garden of Eden Tour lasts one hour and is the least strenuous (you will navigate only 150 stairs and enter and leave by elevator). Prices are $3.50 to $7. It is the only tour offered in winter.

The Fairgrounds Tour lasts 90 minutes and navigates 450 stairs. You'll enter and exit by elevator. Prices are $4.50 to $9.

The Candlelight Tour is conducted entirely by candlelight in an unlighted part of the cave. It's the longest tour: It lasts two hours and covers a mile of strenuous trails.

You must make reservations (sometimes a month in advance), and children must be eight or older to participate. Prices are $4.50 to $9.

The Caving Tour is for the most adventurous types. It's a three- to four-hour tour with a beginning course in spelunking on trails the other tours don't cover. You'll be crawling quite a lot, so wear old clothes, long pants and sleeves, sturdy shoes, and gloves. The park will provide the hard hats and lights. Only those 16 and older may participate, and reservations are required. The cost is $23.

You can make reservations for tours by contacting Wind Cave National Park at (605) 745-4600.

There are also summer-only activities held outside the cave. Discovery programs are held three times each day (ask at the visitor center), a two-hour prairie hike takes place once a day, and evening campfire programs are presented at Elk Mountain Campground. You can stay at the campground or in the backcountry (inquire at the visitor center for free permits), hike cross-country or on the trails, and bicycle on the roads (offroad biking is not allowed). You can also ride horseback.

Whether your preference is for the above-ground or below-ground sights and scenery, you'll thoroughly enjoy Wind Cave National Park, a South Dakota natural treasure.

RECREATION

The Black Hills are relatively isolated in the center of North America, separated from the nearest major population centers (Sioux Falls, Billings, and Denver) by several hundred miles. While that means that there's very little urban culture here, there are also very few urban problems—overcrowding, traffic jams, pollution, and high crime rates are unheard of. Unfortunately, good paychecks are also rare. The average salary in South Dakota is among the lowest in the nation, and Black Hills residents take bigger hits to their pay stubs than their counterparts east of the Missouri. So why do people continue to make the Black Hills their home?

Because people who choose to live and work here are content to take some of their pay in trees. They consider the 1.2-million-acre national forest in their backyard, and all the recreational opportunities that come with it, as part of their salary—a fringe benefit, perhaps. Locals spend their weekends hunting out new trails and mountain streams, getting acquainted with hidden forest service roads, and fishing or cross-country skiing in that beautiful, isolated spot passed on by a friend or family member. They never get bored, since there's always something new: National parks annex more land, new hiking trails are developed, new attractions open and others rebuild, and once-developed property is reclaimed, reforested, and returned to the Black Hills.

Hiking, biking, horseback riding, skiing, and snowmobiling on the hundreds of miles of trails that belong to the Hills are probably the area's most popular activities. You'll find some of them listed in this book, but the list is by no means exhaustive. For more information and detailed maps, check with forest and park service officials at any ranger station or visitor center, and look for any number of specialized books at local book and gift stores.

OVERVIEW

If staying on dry land isn't your idea of a good time, turn to the Boating and Fishing sections in this chapter for a preview of recreational waters. There are more than a dozen lakes, all of them man-made, and more than 300 miles of streams at your disposal. You'll find information about licensing regulations in the appropriate sections.

With additional sections on ballooning, climbing, golf, horseback riding (including commercial trail rides), hunting, jeep tours, skiing, swimming, and even skydiving, you might conclude (correctly) that this chapter is heavily weighted toward outdoor activities. However, notice the sections on bowling, roller-skating, and organized sports and other indoor recreation possibilities. And be sure to check the Spectator Sports chapter to find out where to see others competing in the games you love to watch.

We've provided information about where and how to get rental equipment for many of the activities listed here. Some rentals have to be reserved ahead of time. Even when it's not necessary, though, it's a good idea to call in advance so you have a better chance of getting what you need. Refer to the Shopping chapter if you've arrived minus some vital piece of gear or clothing.

Many activities on public land have their own set of regulations; before heading out, reference the appropriate recreation or park section in this book, or contact the park or ranger station that applies to your plans. However, there are a few all-inclusive guidelines to keep in mind before engaging in any outdoor pastime in the Black Hills.

- Fires are allowed only in grates in designated campgrounds; if the year has been really dry, there may be a ban on even those fires (check with the forest service for information). Violations aren't taken lightly, especially after the rash of western wildfires in the late 1990s and early 2000s, which included major blazes that threatened Lead, Deadwood, Jewel Cave National Park, and the Black Elk Wilderness Area.
- Watch for wildlife wherever you are, and keep your distance. Be especially watchful for bison. They are unpredictable animals, particularly during the rut, or mating season, and the only difference between being hit by a one-ton pickup going 35 mph and a bison is that the truck doesn't have two horns.
- The weather in the Black Hills and Badlands is wildly unpredictable. Snow can fall in any month, although summer afternoons are more likely to yield thunderstorms that can produce high winds, lightning, flash floods, and softball-size

hailstones. Snowfall in the northern hills averages 150 inches a year. Temperatures can vary by 40 degrees or more on a single day, due partly to an elevation range of 3,200 feet to 7,200 feet. Wear layers, and be prepared.

- The rules in the Black Elk Wilderness Area are especially strict. No motorized equipment or transportation, and anything packed in must be taken out. It's a good idea to follow the latter rule no matter where you are. If we all practice zero-impact principles, the beauty of the Black Hills will endure for generations to come.

BALLOONING

What could be prettier than sunrise over the Black Hills? And what finer way to experience it than at a leisurely pace in a hot-air balloon? Most people choose this activity during the summer, but in winter you have the advantage of beating the windchill factor as you travel at the same speed as the breeze. Whatever time of year you go ballooning, dress in layers so you can make adjustments. And plan to be up before dawn—balloons fly mostly during the calm of early morning.

Southern Hills

BLACK HILLS BALLOONS
US 16 West, Custer
(605) 673-2520, (800) 568-5320
www.blackhillsballoons.com
Gain a new perspective as you leave Earth and drift at altitudes of 7,500 feet (2,100 feet above the ground) or more, for an hour or longer. Seen from aloft, pine-clad peaks, bison herds, elk, deer, Mount Rushmore, or Crazy Horse Memorial will leave an indelible impression. Any way the wind blows, your hot-air balloon ride will be an unforgettable

experience—and since no two flights are identical, the owners guarantee that yours will be unique. When you touch down you'll follow tradition and mark the occasion with champagne, croissants, muffins, and cheeses. Plan on three hours to accommodate launch preparations, flight time, and the return van ride. Flights with experienced, licensed balloon pilots are available daily (weather permitting) between early May and the end of Sept and during the rest of the year by special arrangement. Five balloons with leather and wicker gondolas are available to carry 2 to 12 passengers, but reservations are needed for all flights. The fare is $195 per child 12 and under and $245 per adult. Black Hills Balloons is just outside the Custer city limits across from Pizza Hut, but riders meet their pilot at Flintstone Village.

BOATING

For a region with no natural lakes, we have an astonishing number of places to launch boats. Most popular are motorized pleasure boats and personal watercraft, but you'll also see sailboats, catamarans, fishing boats, paddleboats, canoes, kayaks, and rowboats.

Power boaters, water-skiers, sailers, and riders of personal watercraft are drawn to our largest lakes, all of which are accessible from US 385: **Pactola Reservoir** west of Rapid City, **Sheridan Lake** southwest of Rapid City, and **Angostura Reservoir** southeast of Hot Springs. All three have marinas where you can rent boats and buy supplies (see below).

Many smaller lakes are set aside for no-wake boating (less than 5 mph) to heighten the enjoyment of trollers, canoeists, and others seeking a slowerpaced, more contemplative experience. Among them is popular **Deerfield Lake,** which is off FR 17 northwest of Hill City.

Motors are allowed on **Bear Butte Lake,** near Sturgis off SR 79, but they have to be less than 25 horsepower. Electric motors are allowed at **Cold Brook and Cottonwood Springs Reservoirs** west of Hot Springs, as well as **Sylvan and Legion Lakes** in Custer State Park. At CSP's **Center and Stockade Lakes,** all motors are allowed with some wake restrictions at Center Lake.

This list is not exhaustive; for more information call the forest supervisor's office at (605) 673-2251 or the state Game, Fish & Parks Department at (605) 394-2391. The department's annual *South Dakota Fishing Handbook* also contains information about boating regulations.

The **Cheyenne River** offers limited canoeing, although the water level is often too low during the summer and fall. There are no designated access points, but the lower end of **Angostura Reservoir** is a convenient launch site. Angostura itself is popular among sailboarders and sail boaters. The large surface area, consistently powerful winds, and two marinas make the lake one of the only appropriate venues for these sports in the state.

Any boat more than 12 feet long and all motorboats must be registered either in South Dakota or your home state. If you dock here, you need a South Dakota license, which is available from any county treasurer's office or the licensing office of the state Division of Motor Vehicles, 118 West Capitol Ave., Pierre, SD 57501. Boats can be licensed for one to three years, and license fees range from $11 to $81.

Life jackets are mandatory, as are proper lights between sunset and sunrise. The following locations rent boats to the public.

Central Hills

PACTOLA PINES MARINA
23060 Custer Gulch Rd., Rapid City
(605) 343-4283

Pontoon boats can be rented for two hours or a full day. Rates depend on the size of the boat and day of the week; generally they range from $75 to $250. Fishing boats with six-horsepower motors are also available for rent, either hourly or daily; the rates range from $30 to $70. Life jackets and instruction are included. A snack bar at the marina serves chicken, ice cream, and beverages. The marina rents its 200-plus boat slips mostly by the season, but overnights can sometimes be accommodated with advance notice. Prices vary, so call for information. The marina is on Pactola Reservoir's south shore. To get there, turn right off US 385 at the Black Hills National Forest Visitor Center.

SHERIDAN LAKE MARINA
16451 Sheridan Lake Rd., Rapid City
(605) 574-2169
www.sheridanlakemarina.com

Boats and recreational equipment can be rented here. Canoes that accommodate three to four people rent for $8 for the first hour, $5 an hour thereafter. Fourteen-foot, four-passenger aluminum fishing boats with outboard motors cost $25 for two hours, with reduced rates for additional time. Pontoons that can hold 8 to 10 people start at $70 for two hours. All rentals include fuel, life jackets, and other mandatory safety equipment. Call for age limits to rent various boats. The marina offers ice fishing in the winter. About 4 of the approximately 70 boat slips are available for short-term rental at $10 a night; other prices vary, so call. The marina store with boat and equipment rentals is at

the North Recreation Area, which is accessible from Sheridan Lake Road or US 385. The marina is closed in Mar and Oct.

i When it was built in 1927, the Custer Community Building at 644 Crook St. in Custer was reported to be the largest all-log building in the United States. Paid for with money raised by the Custer Women's Civic Club, it was dedicated by first lady Grace Coolidge. Now known as the Grace Coolidge Memorial Log Building, it is owned by the city and occupied by the Custer YMCA.

Southern Hills

COMMON CENTS MARINA
Angostura Reservoir
Off US 385, Hot Springs
(605) 745-6665

A 16-foot fishing boat and pontoons in two sizes can be rented here. Boat rental costs $100 per day. An 18-foot pontoon rents for $150 per day, while a 20-footer goes for $200. Life jackets and safety equipment are included, but you pay for your own gas. The minimum age for all rentals is 21. Boat slips are available by the day, week, month, or season. Daily rates are $10; call for other rates. The marina is at the north end of the reservoir.

CUSTER STATE PARK
Custer
(605) 255-4772, (888) 875-0001
www.state.sd.us/gfp

Paddleboats, rowboats, and one-person kayaks can be rented at Sylvan Lake and Legion Lake Lodges. Call for prices.

BOWLING

Bowling is a serious sport for many Black Hills residents. Most of the bowling opportunities are in the Northern and Central Hills, and we've listed some.

Northern Hills

BEDROCK LANES
145 Glendale Dr., Lead
(605) 584-9013

There's a strong emphasis on youth league bowling here, but the 12 lanes of tenpins are open to everyone. Hours are noon to about 9 or 10 p.m. all week in winter and 6 to around 9:30 p.m. Mon through Fri in summer, and reservations usually are not needed. An arcade room, a pro shop selling equipment, a snack bar, a bar serving beer and wine coolers, and party facilities add to the amenities. You can bowl for $3.75 per game and rent shoes for $1.25. Lessons from a certified coach are available.

BUFFALO BILL'S BOWLING
910 1st St., Sturgis
(605) 347-2741

Buffalo Bill's, formerly Key City Lanes, is a popular venue for Northern Hills league bowlers. Since league traffic can be heavy or light depending on the day of the week, it's a good idea to call ahead and ask how many of the 12 lanes are open at a given time. Friday nights will always be open, however, for Rockin' Bowl, a teen-oriented event that begins around 9 p.m. and lasts until midnight. There is a full bar that serves snacks and a video game room. The lanes open around noon and close whenever demand tapers off, usually around 10 p.m. Games are $3 for adults and $2 for children under 15. Likewise, shoe rentals will cost grown-ups

$1.25 a pair, while those 14 and younger pay half that much. Rockin' Bowl costs $8 for the 3-hour event.

LUCKY STRIKE LANES
1740 Ryan Rd., Spearfish
(605) 642-7367
luckystrikelanesandgolf.com

League play is heavy at this six-lane bowling alley, especially in winter, so call ahead to check for available space. Your best bets for open bowling are Sun from noon to 6 p.m. and Sat from noon to 10 p.m. Fri from 7 to 11 p.m. is Club Bowling, popular among the younger crowd for its neon lights and loud music. There are midweek student specials from Tues through Thurs from 9 p.m. until closing—call for details. Hours vary, but generally Lucky Strike is open from noon to 10 p.m. daily. Rates vary, too, but during the times of heaviest play (after 6 p.m. and on weekends) games cost $2.50 and shoes cost 75 cents. Senior and student rates are available.

Central Hills

MEADOWOOD LANES
3809 Sturgis Rd., Rapid City
(605) 343-5985

Meadowood is the Black Hills' busiest bowling venue. Its 36 lanes are packed all hours of the day, nearly every day of the year. In fact, the bowling alley used to be open 365 days a year, although it now may close for Christmas and Thanksgiving, depending on demand. Every other day of the year Meadowood is open from 9 a.m. to midnight. Leagues play from 5 to 9 p.m. almost every day of the week, and you can forget about open bowling anytime on Wednesday, Saturday morning and evening, and Sunday evening. The lanes are taken over late Friday and Saturday (sometime between 10 p.m. and 2 a.m.) by teenagers for Cosmic Bowling, an event marked by flashing neon and loud music. The event costs $15 per person and covers shoe rental and as many games as you can play. A regular game will run $3.50 per person, and shoes cost $2.25. Facilities here include a lounge with a full bar, a full-service restaurant, pool tables, video games, and video lottery machines. For the serious bowler, the pro shop sells the accessories you need for your game, and there's an expert on hand to answer questions and make sure you get the right equipment.

Southern Hills

WINNERS CIRCLE LANES AND GAMES
733 Jensen Dr. (US 385 North), Hot Springs
(605) 745-5414

This medium-size facility claims some of the newest bowling equipment of any alley in the Black Hills. However, its primary distinguishing feature is that all 12 lanes are non-smoking (smoking is only allowed at the full bar in the lounge, which is separated from the open public areas). A modest pro shop keeps bowling enthusiasts content, but the majority of patrons come to appreciate the full restaurant (which serves dishes like sirloin and prime rib), video game arcade, video lottery casino, and banquet room. Few visitors find their way here, so the staff can be a bit wary of strangers at first. Once they get to know you, however, they can be very hospitable. Fees vary depending on events, ages, season, and times of day, but a game of open bowling will run $2.75 per person, kids are $1.50, and shoe rentals are $1. League action can be heavy in fall and winter, so call ahead to be sure there's a lane available. The facility opens at 9 a.m. It closes at midnight

on Fri and Sat and 10 p.m. every other night. Cosmic Bowling, complete with thumping music and neon, runs from 10 p.m. to midnight on Fri and from 8 to 10 p.m. on Sat. The $10 admission covers all the bowling you can do in two hours.

CLIMBING AREAS

You'll find world-class rock climbing among our granite peaks and limestone outcroppings, and listed below are the areas most highly recommended by local climbers. There are specific guidebooks for some areas; a few of the titles are listed below.

Be aware that helicopter tours operate in the Hills during the summer (see the Attractions chapter), and climbers say the noise sometimes interferes with their communication. This is particularly true in the Cathedral Spires area of the Needles.

A growing number of rock climbers looking to expand their abilities are turning to ice climbing these days. Opportunities are limited here, but Spearfish Canyon (Bridal Veil Falls in particular) in the Northern Hills offers short, grade 1 climbs that are close to the road. The back side of Harney Peak, in the Black Elk Wilderness Area, develops 130-foot floes, but the area is hard to reach and you have to snowshoe in when the snow is deep. Also, there are no comprehensive guidebooks to tell you where to ice climb, so the best way to get information is to contact local climbing shops.

Northern Hills

SPEARFISH CANYON
US 14A, Spearfish
Spearfish Canyon's limestone palisades are becoming increasingly popular with climbers. These routes are primarily bolted sport

climbs, requiring little in the way of your own hardware. No maps or guidebooks are available for this area, so you'll have to contact a climbing shop for information.

Central Hills

FALLING ROCK
SR 44, Rapid City
Another bolted sport climbing area on a limestone ridge, Falling Rock is 3.1 miles west of Rapid City. Turn left (if you're coming from town) off SR 44 onto Falling Rock Road, a dirt road where you'll find two parking areas a short distance apart, both on your left. Trails leading from the first parking area will take you to the top of the limestone cliff, and those leading from the second one go to the cliff base. Contact local climbing shops for information about routes.

MOUNT RUSHMORE CLIMBING AREA
SR 244, Keystone
The area northwest of the four famous faces has become increasingly popular among climbers. The routes along the granite here tend to be bolted. You can learn more about them in the Mount Rushmore National Memorial Climber's Guide by Vernon Phinney, which is widely available. You can park along the highway in any of several pulloffs between Horse Thief Lake (on SR 244) and the monument. Recommended classic routes include Waves (5.6), Stardancer (5.8), Baba Cool (5.9), and Mr. Critical (5.11).

Southern Hills

✳THE NEEDLES
SR 87, Custer State Park
Climbers popularized the granite spires along the Needles Highway (SR 87) in the 1940s and 1950s, and this well-known area still offers traditional climbing as well as bolted routes. On many of them you'll have to pack various forms of hardware and place your own protection. The Needles area is recommended for more experienced climbers. Newer routes are not included in Paul Piana's comprehensive *Touch the Sky,* which was published in 1983; other titles include *Recommended Climbing Routes in the Needles of Custer State Park,* by John Page; *Black Hills Needles: Selected Free Climbs,* by Dingus McGee, and *Classic Rock Climbs No. 7 Devils Tower/Black Hills,* by John Harlin. This area is within the boundaries of Custer State Park, and you'll need a park entrance license if you drive in. Parking is available along the highway from Sylvan Lake to the spires. Classic routes include Riddle (5.7), Tricouni Nail (5.8), and Nantucket Sleighride (5.10).

Wyoming

DEVILS TOWER NATIONAL MONUMENT
US 24, Devils Tower
(307) 467-5283, (800) 354-6316
You'll find a wealth of information about Devils Tower in our Day Trips & Weekend Getaways chapter, but we include it here because it's one of North America's premier crack-climbing areas. *Devils Tower National Monument Climbing Handbook,* by Guilmette, Carrier, and Gardiner, lists more than 200 routes. Among the most popular are Durrance (5.7), Soler (5.7), Walt Bailey Memorial (5.9), and Matador (5.11). Climbers are asked to refrain from climbing here in June out of respect for Native American religious observances. However, many guide services ignore the voluntary ban.

CLIMBING LESSONS, EQUIPMENT & GUIDE SERVICES

If you need books, maps, gear, or information, don't hesitate to stop in at our local climbing shops, which are listed here. We also tell you where you can find lessons and guide services.

Central Hills

GRANITE SPORTS
201 Main St., Hill City
(605) 574-2121
www.granitesportsonline.com
The helpful staff here is made up of experienced hikers and climbers who know their way around the area, as well as purveyors of great outdoor apparel.

✳SYLVAN ROCKS CLIMBING SCHOOL & GUIDE SERVICE
Custer
(605) 484-7585
www.sylvanrocks.com
Sylvan Rocks offers courses from entry level through advanced. With solo rates from $70 to $290, guide Daryl Stisser provides all of the equipment and instruction necessary to conquer your summit, and arguably will be one of the nicest people you meet in the Black Hills. Reservations are strongly recommended. Guide service, including guiding at the Tower, is available for climbers with solid technical skills who want to make optimal use of their climbing time.

CROSS-COUNTRY SKIING

The Black Hills' moderate altitudes and temperatures, combined with plenty of dry, powdery snow, provide just the right conditions for a satisfying, invigorating workout in a beautiful alpine setting. If you're feeling brave, you can strike out on your own and break trail in the Black Hills National Forest. The trails listed below are in the Northern Hills, where the snow is deepest and most dependable.

Northern Hills

BIG HILL
Spearfish Ranger District
2014 Main St., Spearfish
(605) 642-4622, (800) 445-3474
Beginners and experts alike will find something to match their skills on 16 miles of mostly groomed trails that wind through groves of aspen, pine, and spruce 8 miles south of Spearfish. The area is on forest service land but is maintained for skiing through an agreement with the Northern Hills Cross-Country Ski Club, which pays for the grooming. The donation box at the trailhead is for that purpose. The popular Loop A1 is recommended for beginners; other trails are more challenging. The demanding Loops C and D cover a lot of ground and appeal mostly to accomplished skiers. C has the best overlooks, with views of dazzling Spearfish Canyon; a casual tour with time out for stops can easily take three hours. Maps are available at forest service ranger stations and at the trailhead. To get to Big Hill, take Jackson Boulevard in Spearfish west, turn north onto Jonas Boulevard, and then turn west onto Oliver Street. Pass Pope & Talbot sawmill, turn south onto FR 134, and go about 8 miles to the trailhead.

✳EAGLE CLIFF
Spearfish Ranger District
2014 Main St., Spearfish
(605) 642-4622, (800) 445-3474

Approximately 23 miles of marked, ung-roomed trails southwest of Cheyenne Crossing offer some of the finest skiing in the Hills. (Cheyenne Crossing is at the junction of US Highways 85 and 14A on the south end of Spearfish Canyon.) The closest trail, Dead Ox, is about 4 miles from the crossing, with the nearest official trailhead (Bratwurst) and parking area another 3 miles down the road. Most of these trails are easy to moderately difficult, but steep canyons and twisting turns test your mettle. If you're lucky enough to have two cars, you can park each in a different lot and enjoy a nice long trek without having to retrace a single glide of your skis. But the trails interconnect so that you can make a loop and wind up back at your starting point. Sunny Meadow and Bratwurst are good trails for beginners and those with single vehicles. Eagle Cliff is a fairly easy trail, as well; Roller Coaster, Deep Snow, and Wipeout are more demanding. Dead Ox, the most popular trail in the system, gets twisty and steep, and Lily Park can be downright scary. The forest service has made Eagle Cliff an official ski area, making it easier to maintain the trails and keep roadside parking areas plowed. Maps are available at forest service ranger stations, the Cheyenne Crossing Store, and the Bratwurst trailhead.

MYSTIC MOUNTAIN SKI AREA
US 85, Lead
(605) 584-3230, (888) 265-2197
www.skimystic.com
About 10 miles (15 kilometers) of gently sloping, groomed trails wind through the woods, beginning near the base of the downhill slopes. You can ski from 9 a.m. until dark. You can also rent skis, poles, and boots at the ski lodge. Mystic Mountain is open from approximately late Nov until about the end of Mar. It's closed Mon and Tues except during the Christmas season.

CROSS-COUNTRY SKI RENTALS
Northern Hills

SKI CROSS COUNTRY
701 North 3rd St., Spearfish
(605) 722-3851
All sorts of cross-country skiing equipment and clothing is for sale or rent here. Rental times and rates are flexible depending on your needs—call ahead for more information, or work out a deal with the operators when you arrive in town.

i It's against the law to damage, destroy, disturb, or remove any natural feature of the Black Hills National Forest. That means you can't take prehistoric artifacts home, collect wildflowers for commercial use without a permit, and so on. A good rule of thumb is, "Leave what you find."

CYCLING

Many communities have recreational paths that are ideal for riding a bicycle, whether for fun or transportation. They're easy to spot, because they're almost always in use by cyclists, joggers, and walkers. If you're a mountain biker with a yen for the backcountry, keep reading: We've listed some local favorites. Don't bypass our back roads and cross-country ski trails (see the Cross-country Skiing section), which offer excellent riding, too.

CENTENNIAL TRAIL (NO. 89)
Created in celebration of South Dakota's 100th birthday in 1989, the Centennial Trail

stretches 111 miles down the length of the Black Hills, from Bear Butte State Park to Wind Cave National Park. Bikes are forbidden only on the sections in the Black Elk Wilderness and Wind Cave (see the Parks & Mountains chapter.) Alternate routes are available around the Black Elk Wilderness that add just a few miles to your trip—a trail map will help you choose your path.

Centennial Trail ends (or begins) in Wind Cave park, so avoiding the 6-mile stretch there is simply a matter of ending or beginning your trek at the park boundary. Along the trail you'll see lakes, streams, grasslands, dramatic rock outcroppings, and wildlife. There are more than two dozen well-marked trailheads and access points, some with night parking for extended trips. For complete information, consult the *Centennial Trail User's Guide,* which is widely available wherever you find brochures in the area.

Its length and accessibility make the Centennial Trail ideal for any style of trip—it's really just a matter of deciding where you want to start and where you want to end up. One section we recommend is the 10-mile stretch between Pactola Reservoir and Sheridan Lake. Start at the Rapid Creek trailhead at Pactola. From SR 44 west of Rapid City go 2.1 miles south on US 385, turn left onto gravel Pactola Basin Road, then go one half-mile to a four-way intersection, turn left, and park at the trailhead. Drop a second vehicle at Dakota Point trailhead by taking US 385; go east 1.6 miles on Sheridan Lake Road southwest of Rapid City, turn right onto gravel Dakota Point Road (FR 434), and go another 0.3 mile to the trailhead, which will be on your left. You can do this route in reverse if you want to.

CUSTER STATE PARK
Custer
(605) 255-4515
www.custerstatepark.info

The park has trails that range from moderately difficult to difficult. The shortest goes through the 3-mile Grace Coolidge Walk-in Fishing Area, which runs between Center Lake and Grace Coolidge Campground, with a trailhead at either end. Three other trailheads—Iron Creek, Badger Hole, and French Creek—provide access to the 22 miles of Centennial Trail that thread through the park. The most difficult section, from Badger Hole to French Creek, is also the shortest at 4.2 miles. Less strenuous are the 7.3 miles between Iron Creek and Badger Hole, and the 10.3 miles from French Creek to the Wind Cave National Park border. Big Tree Robbers Roost Draw Trail makes a 10.5-mile loop that begins and ends at French Creek trailhead. Maps are available at Custer State Park visitor centers, but you can also ride on any trail or logging road in the park that isn't posted as closed. Cycling in the park's Sylvan Lake watershed is prohibited. See listings under Cycling—Tours and Rentals for information about where to find bicycles.

DEERFIELD LAKE LOOP TRAIL (NO. 40L)

This easy 10-mile trail circles Deerfield Lake, which is not only scenic but gives you the added advantage of a place to take a cooling dip after, or during, your ride. Three campgrounds are a short distance from the trail—Dutchman, Whitetail, and Custer Trails—where you can refill your water bottle en route during the summer. Access points with free parking are Gold Run and Hilltop trailheads on the south side of the lake off FR 17 (also called Deerfield Road, which runs northwest from Hill City), and North Shore trailhead on the northwest side (follow F.S. 17 to FR 461 and turn south). You can access the trail from Custer Trails Campground, too, but during the summer you'll pay a user or camping fee to leave your car there. The trail offers varied scenery from pine forest on the south side of the lake to an open meadow, known as Reynolds Prairie, on the north.

✳GEORGE S. MICKELSON TRAIL (NO. 104)
www.mickelsontrail.com
Named for the South Dakota governor who championed it and then met an untimely death in a 1993 plane crash, the Mickelson Trail is an abandoned railroad bed that has undergone a rails-to-trails transformation through the joint efforts of government agencies and local volunteers. Completed in 1998, the 10-foot-wide trail offers 114 miles of scenic beauty and gentle grades for non-motorized recreation between Deadwood and Edgemont. Restored tunnels, trestles, and the ruins of section houses along the Rochford-to-Mystic stretch speak to its railroading past.

The Mickelson Trail is easily the most popular trail in the Black Hills, and with good reason. First off, it's accessible: There are 14 trailheads, each with parking and trail-pass vending machines, and all but one (White Elephant, between Custer and Pringle) have tables and vault toilets. Several trailheads are within the towns of Deadwood, Lead, Rochford, Hill City, Custer, Pringle, and Edgemont, giving riders and hikers access to food, water, lodging, entertainment, and bike equipment rentals. The trail is relatively easy. Since it was built on top of old railroad tracks, the grade is never steeper than 2 percent. And then there's the crown jewel of the trail: the

landscape. The natural wonder of the land along the trail is spectacular, giving riders unparalleled views of bizarre granite rock formations, waterfalls, alpine meadows, wild berry patches, and vistas that stretch for miles. There's plenty of historical wonder, too. Telegraph poles, roundhouses, railroad signs, tunnels, rock bridges, stagecoach stops, ghost towns, abandoned lumber mills, and ancient gold camps, some dating from the 1870s, are all easily visible from the trail. While some sites are off-limits on private land, other places can be explored on public property. Interpretive signs along the trail explain the sites' histories.

This trail relies on small user fees to help with its upkeep. Those 12 and older are required to buy a daily ($2) or annual ($10) trail pass. Fees are payable at self-registration boxes and some businesses along the trail. No fee is required within city limits. Check out the website for great information and registration for the annual fall trail ride.

CYCLING—TOURS & RENTALS

These Black Hills bike shops rent equipment and can direct you to nearby trails for memorable rides. Some offer guided tours.

Northern Hills

✳LATCHSTRING VILLAGE ALL SEASON SPORTS CENTER
US 14A, Spearfish Canyon
(605) 584-2207, (800) 439-8544
www.spfcanyon.com
Mountain bikes and helmets can be rented here for a half or full day. Trails depart from the premises of Spearfish Canyon Resort. They really mean "All Season" here—snowmobiles can be rented for a half or full day,

Organized Sports & Recreation Resources

Black Hills communities do a good job of providing organized sports for youths and adults, often thanks to the work of volunteers. Activities may include team sports such as baseball, softball, basketball, soccer, and volleyball. If you enjoy individual sports such as racquetball, swimming, tennis, running, and walking, you're likely to find free and low-cost indoor and outdoor facilities wherever you are. To help you get involved and find what you need, we've compiled the addresses and phone numbers of information and recreation centers for most of our communities.

Northern Hills

**Belle Fourche Area
Community Center**
1111 National St., Belle Fourche
(605) 892-2467

Deadwood Recreation Center
105 Sherman St., Deadwood
(605) 578-3729

Northern Hills YMCA
845 Miners Ave., Lead
(605) 584-1113

**Spearfish Parks, Recreation
and Forestry (Public Works
Department)**
625 5th St., Spearfish
(605) 642-1333

Sturgis Community Center
1401 Lazelle St., Sturgis
(605) 347-6513

Young Sports & Fitness Center
1200 University St., Spearfish
(605) 642-6098

Central Hills

Hill City City Hall
324 Main St., Hill City
(605) 574-2300

Hill City Youth Center
111 McGregor St., Hill City
(605) 574-2010

Rapid City Recreation Department
235 Waterloo St., Rapid City
(605) 394-4168

Rapid City YMCA
815 Kansas City St., Rapid City
(605) 342-8538

Southern Hills
Custer City Pool
Crook and 3rd Streets, Custer
(605) 673-3935 (summer)

Custer YMCA
644 Crook St., Custer
(605) 673-3154 (school year)

Hot Springs City Hall
303 North River St., Hot Springs
(605) 745-3135

too, and Latchstring is *the* place to go for everything you need before hitting the trails. Trails depart from the premises of Spearfish Canyon Resort, and head west through scenic Spearfish Canyon. The lobby and lounge in the spacious Spearfish Canyon Lodge provide the ideal place to relax with a warm toddy after hitting the trails.

Central Hills

TWO WHEELER DEALER CYCLE & FITNESS
100 East Blvd. North, Rapid City
(605) 343-0524
www.twowheelerdealer.com
Here you can rent mountain bikes, kiddie carts, tandems, and car racks. Helmets are included with bike rentals; call for daily or extended rates.

Southern Hills

CUSTER STATE PARK
Custer
(605) 255-4515
www.custerstatepark.info
You can rent mountain bikes by the day or hour for use in the park at Legion Lake Lodge, (605) 255-4521, and the Game Lodge (605) 255-4541) during the summer. Reservations are recommended.

FISHING

Around here, angling is a year-round activity. There are enough lakes and streams to satisfy all enthusiasts, whether they prefer to fish while standing on shore, sitting in a boat, crouched over a hole in the ice, tucked into a float tube, or slogging up to their wader tops in midstream.

Although trout aren't native to this area (having arrived by wagon in the 1880s),

they're the main attraction for Black Hills anglers, along with walleye and large-mouth bass. Most of our trout—brookies, browns, rainbows, and a brook-lake cross called splake found in Deerfield Lake—are spawned in our fish hatcheries. Nevertheless, some native reproduction is taking place, particularly among brook trout.

Walleye fishers tend to gravitate toward the warm waters of Angostura Reservoir near Hot Springs. Sheridan Lake southwest of Rapid City is a good place to cast for perch and northern pike. Colorful rainbow trout bite in Custer State Park's Sylvan Lake and in Spearfish Creek up north. And you'll find bass swimming in Pactola Reservoir west of Rapid City.

These are just a few of our excellent fishing holes. For a complete rundown, pick up a free copy of the Game, Fish & Parks Department's *South Dakota Guide to Public Fishing Waters,* which is available through license agents.

Speaking of licenses, you'll need one unless you're fishing at an attraction or campground where it's not required—you'll find those places listed in their respective chapters in this book. Licenses are available at sporting goods stores, convenience stores, and other businesses as well as at some county treasurers' offices. And don't forget about entrance fees at state parks and user fees at some lakes.

Daily and possession limits for trout have gotten stricter since a survey of local anglers showed they want to catch bigger fish. (Raising bigger fish in hatcheries means raising fewer of them.) Thus, the daily trout limit is five, with just one of those being 14 inches or longer. You're allowed to have no more than ten trout in your possession—and that includes the ones back home in your freezer or packed in ice at your campsite—at any one time.

Limits are higher for other species, and you'll find all that information, along with regulations for organic bait, catch-and-release areas, and so forth, in the yearly *South Dakota Fishing Handbook* issued by Game, Fish & Parks. Make sure you get the current copy, which comes out around the first of the year.

Wheelchair-accessible fishing is available at Pactola Reservoir and at Strawberry Lake, which is off US 385 south of Deadwood.

ℹ️ The Black Hills National Forest Visitor Center at Pactola Reservoir features outstanding natural history and cultural exhibits and offers educational programs between Memorial Day and Labor Day weekends. Plus, the center is in a scenic spot overlooking the lake.

FISHING GUIDE SERVICES

Lessons and guided trips treat anglers to some of the best fly fishing in the region.

Northern Hills

CUSTOM CASTER
21207 Thunder Lane, Lead
(605) 584-2217
http://members.mato.com/bhangler
This one-man operation is locally known for custom rods, although the shop carries professionally manufactured rods, reels, flies, and tying accessories. Owner Dale Peters, a 40-year fishing veteran, performs repair work, and he conducts half-day or full-day guided fishing trips.

Central Hills

DAKOTA ANGLER & OUTFITTER
516 7th St., Rapid City
(605) 341-2450, (888) 319-3474
www.flyfishsd.com
Everything here is geared toward fly fishing. The shop offers guided half- and full-day trips as well as fishing and fly-tying lessons. Trips cost from $165 to $275 and include transportation and lunch or a snack. Reservations are required. The cost for lessons varies, so call for information. The shop sells equipment, clothing, gifts, and even artwork. You can rent a fly rod, reel, and waders.

GOLF

The beautiful landscape of the Black Hills has inspired countless outdoor enthusiasts, and golfers are no exception. Despite the brevity of summer, most Black Hills communities have their own small course, and Rapid City claims seven. And it's not unusual to see a few brave souls teeing off in Dec or Jan if warm chinooks have melted the snow and ice from the fairway. All the courses below have pro shops, motorized and pull carts, club rentals, and grass greens. Most have policies about spikes and attire (which is usually pretty casual), so ask when you reserve your tee time. This list isn't exhaustive, but local parks departments (find their information in the gray box at the end of the chapter) can help you locate other courses.

Northern Hills

SPEARFISH CANYON COUNTRY CLUB
Intersection of US 14 and 14A
Spearfish
(605) 642-7156
www.spearfishcanyoncountryclub.com

The only 18-hole golf course in the northern Black Hills has a lot to recommend it, not the least of which is the historical integrity of its original nine holes (the front nine). You can play them today the same way golfers did in pre-heavy-equipment 1922, when the natural lay of the land dictated the design of greens and fairways. The views are beautiful, and at the eighth hole (par 3), which is situated on a ridge looking into the mouth of Spearfish Canyon, you're required to aim the ball through a narrow lane of tall pine trees. Tee times are requested for the par 71, semi-private course. You'll find bent-grass greens and a wide variety of elevation changes, plus an outdoor driving range, a Professional Golf Association (PGA) pro and teaching pro on staff, a full-service bar and restaurant, and a swimming pool. During the week, a round of 9 holes will run $27 and a round of 18 will cost $48. On weekends, fees jump to $30 and $53, respectively. A golf cart will cost $10 for a round of nine and $16 for the whole course per rider, irrespective of season. Rates will be higher on weekends and holidays, but there are twilight discounts for golfers who tee off after 4 p.m.

TOMAHAWK COUNTRY CLUB
US 385 South, Deadwood
(605) 578-9979, (605) 578-2080
www.tomahawkgolf.com
You'll play on a true mountain course here, where five tee boxes are elevated to compensate for the rolling terrain. Two creeks run through the picturesque ninehole course, making your game more challenging in spite of wide fairways. There are two par 5 holes for men and one for women, with a total par 36 for the 3,300-yard course. A practice range, full bar, and grill take care of your needs off the course. Open play means there's no need to reserve a tee time, but you do have to abide by the rules governing ladies' day, which begins at 2 p.m. on Wednesday, and men's day, which starts at 2 p.m. on Thursday. The course opens as early as possible in the spring but for sure by May 1. It closes Oct 31. Hours are 7 a.m. until dark. Greens fees are $18 for 9 holes and $30 for 18. Carts are $14 for 9 holes, $22 for 18. Tomahawk is 8 miles south of Deadwood.

Central Hills

HART RANCH GOLF COURSE
23759 Arena Dr., Rapid City
(605) 341-5703
www.hartranch.com
Bring your A game, not your B game, advises resident PGA pro Craig Hatch. This challenging 18-hole course is for veteran golfers who can play around Spring Creek where it winds through the 6,285-yard, par 72 course. Lessons and a complete practice facility are available, and there's a snack shop. Alcohol is not served and is not allowed on this well-manicured course. The course is open daily from sometime in Mar through Nov, depending on the weather. Starting time varies with the season, but tee times can be requested before 5 a.m. in summer. At all times, the course closes at dark. Greens fees vary by season, but the peak summer rates are $44 for 18 holes and $26 for 9 holes. Cart rentals are $30 per person and $18 per person, respectively. To reach Hart Ranch Golf Course from Rapid City, take US 16 south for 8 miles, turn left onto Neck Yoke Road across from Reptile Gardens, and left again at Spring Creek Road, then go 1.5 miles to the entrance

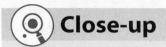

Close-up

A Tribute to Last the Ages

There is a little-known park just two and a half miles from Deadwood, hidden atop a forested hill, up a dusty gravel road. The park was constructed in 1919, but the story behind it begins with an unlikely meeting between a Harvard-educated New York politician and a Canadian-born lawman and rancher.

In 1844, while riding the range on his Belle Fourche ranch, US Marshal and former Deadwood sheriff Seth Bullock came across three men. One of these three frontiersmen was current deputy sheriff and future US president Theodore Roosevelt, who along with another deputy was transferring a prisoner he had just captured. Despite their differences in background, Roosevelt and Bullock hit it off immediately. Over the next 30 years, the two men formed a friendship that has truly lasted through the ages.

Following Roosevelt's death in January 1919, Bullock was deeply saddened and immediately enlisted the help of the Black Hills pioneers to erect a monument to the former president on what is now known as **Mount Roosevelt**. Dedicated on July 4, 1919, it was the first monument in the nation dedicated to the trust-busting conservationist president. The stone tower sits just above Deadwood, with views that stretch miles across the plains into Roosevelt's ranch country in North Dakota.

Bullock died a few months after the dedication, secure in the knowledge that he had paid proper tribute to his longtime friend. In accordance with his wishes, Bullock was buried high above Deadwood near White Rocks, where those visiting his isolated grave site could cast their gaze across the gold-filled gulch toward Mount Roosevelt.

Today, Mount Roosevelt is maintained by the Black Hills National Forest. The park can be difficult to find, but visitor information centers in Deadwood will provide directions. There is a designated parking lot below the tower, with a well-marked, half-mile trail leading to the summit. A brisk hike can get you to the tower in about 10 minutes, although those with smaller children or who have trouble walking will need to take periodic rests. Several markers with information about the views along the way make for convenient stopping places.

Although visitors could once ascend stone stairs to the top of the tower, it has since been closed due to public safety concerns. While the tower's reopening remains uncertain, one thing is clear—the monument that was built to honor a friendship has stood the test of time and remains an enduring reminder of two frontiersmen who helped tame the West.

MEADOWBROOK MUNICIPAL GOLF COURSE
3625 Jackson Blvd., Rapid City
(605) 394-4191 (advance reservations),
(605) 394-4192 (same-day reservations)
www.golfatmeadowbrook.com

This city-operated, scenic course rates high with golfers who like a challenging game. It also rates high on *GolfWeek* magazine's list of the top-50 public courses in the country. Open daylight to dark whenever the weather permits, the 6,520-yard, par 72 course has 18 holes with bent-grass greens.

A driving range, PGA pro, and lessons are at your disposal, and beer and snacks are available. Greens fees are determined by age, residency, season, and day of the week. Moreover, the entire rate system changes almost yearly, usually increasing across the board by about 5 percent. Count on paying $17 to $24 for a round of 9 holes in summer, $27 to $38 for 18, and about $17 or $27 for cart rental on 9 or 18 holes, respectively.

Southern Hills

ROCKY KNOLLS GOLF COURSE
US 16 West, Custer
(605) 673-4481

Curious deer and marmots might be watching while you tee off at this tree-lined, nine-hole course, which borders West Dam and French Creek. Following the contour of the land, the 3,001-yard, par 36 course features rock outcroppings, bent-grass greens, and outstanding views of the Black Hills. Off the course, you'll find a grill, a full bar, and a putting green. Tee times are by reservation. Greens fees in summer are $18 for a round of 9 and $28 for 18. There is a $3 reduction in price from Sept through May. Golf cart rentals are steady at $15 for each round of 9 holes. You can tee off almost anytime during daylight hours, provided the fairways aren't too snowy.

✳SOUTHERN HILLS MUNICIPAL GOLF COURSE
West US 18, Hot Springs
(605) 745-6400
www.southernhillsmunicipal
golfcourse.com

These seemingly modest city-owned links are actually part of one of the most-praised golf courses in the country. Consistently recognized in golf journals for its stunning beauty

and design, the course was honored at the start of the millennium by *Golf Digest* magazine for being the best 9-hole public course in North America. It will never get that honor again: In 2006, the course opened its back nine, making it eligible for an 18-hole award.

The fairways here wind among abundant ponderosa pine trees, and most tee boxes are set on cliffs where you're required to shoot over canyons to the bent-grass greens. Most golfers play 18 holes, making the 5,700-yard course par 70. Riding is recommended because of the steepness, but walkers are welcome. Lessons and a driving range are available, and snacks and beer are served. Reservations are recommended but not required for tee times.

The well-groomed course is open from early Mar to Oct 31, weather permitting; summer hours are 7 a.m. to 7 p.m. Greens fees for 18 holes are $33 weekdays and $37 on weekends, Cart rentals are $27. Group rates are available. The golf course is about one half mile west of town.

HIKING & BACKPACKING

Trails in the Black Hills National Forest range from easy (see the George S. Mickelson Trail listing under Cycling) to steep (Crow Peak and Harney Peak, below). That means everyone from small children to veteran trekkers can ramble at his or her own pace. There are scores of scenic hiking opportunities not covered in this chapter; you'll find at least some of them in your wanderings, including those in state and national parks.

Regardless of the length of your hike, make sure you take a good supply of drinking water, because in all likelihood you won't find any on the trail. And if you need water bottles or other equipment, see the listings of sporting goods stores in the Shopping chapter.

Of special interest are four wheelchair-accessible trails. In the Northern Hills the mile-long Roughlock Trail begins in the parking lot at Spearfish Canyon Lodge (see the Accommodations chapter) and goes to Roughlock Falls; take US 14A through the canyon to the resort and turn onto FR 222. In the Central Hills are Veterans Point Trail (No. 56—see the Close-up in this chapter), at the north end of Pactola Dam at Pactola Reservoir, the trail at Norbeck Overlook on US 16A south of Keystone, and the Presidential Trail at Mount Rushmore.

CENTENNIAL TRAIL (NO. 89)

All 111 miles of the Centennial Trail are open to hiking, and if you've brought your tent along, you can set it up either in a designated campground or in the wilderness. If you want to camp in Wind Cave National Park's backcountry zone in the northwest section of the park, you need a free permit that's available at the park's visitor center or at either end of the Wind Cave portion of the trail. You must stay 100 feet from the trail or any water source and out of sight of the road while camping. If you camp in Custer State Park, you must stay in one of the designated camping areas. (See the Campgrounds chapter for information about reserving campsites in the park.) Many of the trailheads have long-term parking space, but if you plan to leave your car overnight or longer in Fort Meade National Recreation Area, Bear Butte State Park, or Wind Cave National Park, be sure to notify a ranger.

Northern Hills

CROW PEAK TRAILS (NO. 64)

This hike is rated difficult, but you'll be glad you made the effort once you reach the summit of this historic landmark. Crow Peak takes its name from the Sioux *Paha Karitukat-eyapi,* "the hill where the Crows were killed" in a long-ago battle. After gaining 1,600 feet of elevation (to 5,800 feet) in a little more than 3 miles, you'll have a 360-degree view of South Dakota (including Bear Butte, which you can read about in the Parks & Mountains chapter) as well as parts of Montana and Wyoming. To reach the trailhead, which is southwest of Spearfish, take Utah Boulevard west out of town to Higgins Gulch Road (FR 214), turn south, and go 4 miles.

DEVIL'S BATHTUB TRAIL

This is a popular hike in summer, but most of the people who ascend this rocky canyon are locals. Either visitors don't know about it, they can't find it, or they'd rather not get their feet wet. And wet they will get, unless you are a deft acrobat and attempt hiking the creek bed during a very dry Aug or Sept, when the Devil's Bathtub is least impressive. Of course, most hikers appreciate the clear, icy waters when they make the climb in the heat of summer. The Bathtub itself, a massive boulder eroded into a smooth pool about 25 feet in diameter, used to hold water 4 or 5 feet deep. However, erosion and concerned forest officials have filled in much of the pool with small pebbles. It's still a good place for wading, and many visitors slide down the smooth rock waterfalls when the creek runs fast. To reach the Bathtub, you'll hike about 45 minutes up a narrow, heavily wooded canyon. When the trail disappears, you must walk in the creek. To find the trailhead, travel north on US 14A through Spearfish Canyon. A few miles north of Savoy, turn right onto Cleopatra Place, which is marked by a blue street sign. Almost immediately you'll find yourself in a small parking area at the confluence of Spearfish and Squaw Creeks. The trail to Devil's Bathtub leads up the smaller creek branch.

i Dogs are welcome on national forest hiking trails, but they must be on a leash or under voice control at all times.

Central Hills

FLUME TRAIL (NO. 50)

This National Recreation Trail is reserved for hikers and with good reason: Along it are fragile historic artifacts and tunnels from 1880s gold mines that relied on the Rockerville Flume to carry water from Spring Creek to their operations. Read the trailside signs to learn more about that, and see the History chapter for information about the Black Hills gold rush.

Trailheads are located at the east end of Sheridan Lake, which is off US 385 southwest of Rapid City; at Coon Hollow, off CR 233 about ¼ mile west of the intersection with US 16 in Rockerville (which is south of Rapid City); and at points in between. A trail map will help you locate them.

The Upper Spring Creek trailhead is closest to the two tunnels; it's about a mile west of the Spring Creek picnic area on Sheridan Lake Road southwest of Rapid City. You can leave the 11-mile-long trail for the 3-mile Spring Creek Loop at the north end or to ascend the trail to 5,331-foot Boulder Hill, whose summit provides awesome views of the Black Hills, Badlands, and prairies. The 1.5-mile stretch along the southeast shore of Sheridan Lake from the Calumet trailhead is flat and doable for young children. You'll have to pay the $2 daily fee to park at Sheridan Lake Southside Campground where the trailhead is. Turn east off US 385 at the lake

Forest Service Ranger Stations

Here is a list of USDA Forest Service Ranger Stations where you can get information about the Black Hills National Forest. For general information, contact the Forest Supervisor's Headquarters at R.R. 2, Box 200, Custer, SD 57730, or call (605) 673-2251.

Northern Hills
Spearfish/Nemo Ranger District
2014 North Main St., Spearfish
(605) 642-4622
US 14A, Deadwood
(605) 578-2744

Central Hills
Pactola/Harney Ranger District
803 Soo San Dr., Rapid City
(605) 343-1567
23939 US 385, Hill City
(605) 574-2534

Southern Hills
Custer/Elk Mountain Ranger Districts
330 Mount Rushmore Rd., Custer
(605) 673-4853

onto Calumet Road and follow the signs for the campground.

HARNEY PEAK (MULTIPLE TRAILS)

To the Lakota of the Black Hills, Harney Peak was a mystical mountain. Black Elk, a prominent medicine man among the Oglala people, considered Harney Peak the center of the world. For him it was a place for vision quests and spiritual rejuvenation. In addition to the mountain's spiritual embodiments, Harney Peak is a significant mountain because it is North America's highest peak east of the Rocky Mountains.

Harney Peak was named after Gen. William S. Harney, the commanding officer of Lt. G. K. Warren, who mapped the peak during a military expedition to the Black Hills in 1857. Valentine McGillycuddy also climbed the peak in the 19th century, completing the ascent in 1875 at the age of 26. McGillycuddy mapped the peak and photographed it. Later he served as an agent on the Pine Ridge Reservation and as the first president of the South Dakota School of Mines. When he died in 1940, his remains were cremated and placed at the base of a fire tower that had been constructed on Harney Peak. A bronze plaque is cemented in the base of the stairway to the tower containing an inscription that reads, in part, Wasicu Wakan. In Lakota, the words mean "holy white man."

The stone fire tower was constructed in 1938 and 1939 by the Civilian Conservation Corps (CCC). The CCC also constructed stone steps leading to the tower, steps that hikers still ascend today. The peak's importance for detecting fires had long been recognized. From 1911, the tower had made the life of a fire lookout here a little less extreme. In 1967, more modern techniques of spotting fires took over, and today the tower stands in mute testimony to the lonely life spotters led on the peak.

You'll find moderate or challenging hikes to the top of the Hills' tallest peak, depending on where you start. The easier—and more popular—hikes begin at Sylvan Lake in Custer State Park; the round-trip is about 7 miles. On the north side, Willow Creek/Harney Peak Trail (No. 9 North) ascends from just outside Willow Creek Horse Camp (off SR 244, 3 miles east of US 16) and is considerably more strenuous, somewhat longer (about 11 miles round-trip) and less populous. Either way, your reward for reaching the 7,242-foot summit is a spectacular, 60-mile view from the stone lookout tower, now listed in the National Register of Historic Places.

From the tower, hikers have distant panoramic views of South Dakota, Nebraska, Wyoming, and Montana, as well as close-up vantage points of the granite formations and cliffs of the Black Elk Wilderness Area. One caveat: Sylvan Lake/Harney Peak Trail (No. 9 South), gets extremely heavy use during the summer, and the forest service is asking hikers to use alternate routes to the summit whenever possible. The most likely choices for hikers are No. 9 North and Cathedral Spires Trail (No. 4), which departs from Sylvan Lake and heads east, then picks up No. 9 South near the summit.

Southern Hills

HELL CANYON TRAIL (NO. 32)

This 5.5-mile loop starts out steep, but after a half mile the going is easy along fairly level grades. The trail winds along the base of the limestone plateau for about 2 miles, and the last 2 miles take you along the canyon floor, which is especially pretty in the fall when hardwood trees in riparian areas show their colors. Note the ruins of a Civilian Conservation Corps camp along the bottom of the trail. The trailhead is about 1 mile west of the entrance to Jewel Cave National Monument and 11 miles west of Custer on US 16.

HORSEBACK RIDING

Horses are practically synonymous with the West, and they continue to occupy an

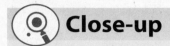

Close-up

National Forest Trails

To build or to maintain—that is the question foresters face each year when presented with their limited trail budgets.

The Black Hills National Forest trail system consists of some 360 miles of track for hiking, horseback riding, bicycling, and cross-country skiing. The heavy use those trails receive shows how important they are. But in recent years, tighter purse strings in Washington, D.C., have meant tough choices about whether to build new trails to keep up with demand or maintain existing trails. Frequently, the choice is painfully obvious.

"When things start to deteriorate, they accelerate. You've got water coming down a trail and you've got to take care of it," said Rusty Wilder, a civil engineer at the forest supervisor's office in Custer.

The USDA Forest Service gets some very welcome help from volunteers who clear downed trees, clean drainage structures, work on trail surface maintenance, repair and replace trail markers and signs, and perform heavy tasks such as bridge repair. There's an Adopt-a-Trail program that allows a volunteer group or individual to assume official responsibility for maintenance of a trail, or portion of a trail, under specific guidelines.

First, of course, trails have to be planned for and built, and both processes are more complex than you might expect.

The first step is to identify a need and the type of users looking for new trails. Foresters survey potential sites—often old roads—by walking the area and examining aerial photos and topographic maps to ensure that a new trail will meet specifications for grade and varied terrain. Then a decision is made about whether to do the work themselves or hire a contractor.

important place in the local culture and economy. The trails listed below are a tip of the hat to our equine tradition. See the Campgrounds chapter for more horseback-riding opportunities. And, of course, you're free to ride almost anywhere in the Black Hills National Forest. Just be sure to avoid private land or get permission before you cross it.

CENTENNIAL TRAIL (NO. 89)

See the Cycling and the Hiking & Backpacking sections earlier in this chapter for basic information about this trail. Note that horses are not allowed on the Wind Cave National Park section (although a free horse-riding permit from the park's visitor center allows you to ride alongside the trail or anywhere else in the park). Horses aren't allowed in the eastern portion of Bear Butte State Park, where the Centennial Trail begins (or ends, if you're coming from the south).

Central Hills

NORBECK WILDLIFE PRESERVE & BLACK ELK WILDERNESS AREA

The forest service's two horse camps, Willow Creek on SR 244 between Hill City and Mount Rushmore and Iron Creek off US 16A east of Custer, are the starting points for a dozen

Wolfgang Schmidt of Nemo is one contractor who has worked for the forest service. In one instance, Schmidt said, he used a shovel and hand tools to build a trail in an area where heavy equipment couldn't be used.

"For me, to build one just by hand was quite a challenge," said Schmidt. "I like the hard work and being outside in nature. It's been a wonderful experience."

Loren Poppert, a recreation forester in the Custer/Elk Mountain Ranger District, also finds satisfaction in the hard labor of trail building. He helped cut trees, move rocks, dig out trail tread on a side slope, and build retaining walls for the Hell Canyon Trail. Especially gratifying, he said, is the positive feedback, "hearing the comments about how nice of a trail it is and the number of people who love to hike it."

Doing things the old-fashioned way extends to hauling materials on pack mules into the Black Elk Wilderness, where federal regulations prohibit the use of mechanized equipment of any kind. Most years, local officials import a 10-mule pack string from Colorado for the beast-of-burden duties.

Most trail work is not so romantic, however. Without the help of present-day dirt-moving equipment, many of the trails we enjoy would not be so readily accessible.

But the human spirit can be just as powerful as any big machine. Thanks to a cooperative effort between the forest service and the Rapid City chapter of Disabled American Veterans (DAV), a paved trail at the north end of Pactola Reservoir allows people with disabilities to enjoy the outdoors in new ways. The DAV raised money to help with initial construction of the Veterans Point Trail, where anglers can fish from wooden piers.

So the next time you set booted foot, waxed ski, or nubby tire on a Black Hills recreational trail, we're certain you'll appreciate the hard work that's gone into making it available for you to enjoy.

pathways in the 50-mile Harney Range Trail System in this protected area. All of these forested trails provide lots of opportunities to see wildlife, but we call your attention to other interesting features. The rugged Grizzly Bear Creek Trail (No. 7) will take you to beaver ponds and old-growth vegetation; Lost Cabin Trail, one of three National Recreation Trails in the national forest, passes near two old mining sites. This area has the highest concentration of trails in the Hills; any comprehensive trail map can help you sort them out. You can contact the forest service for information about the trails and about riding as well as horse camping in the backcountry.

Southern Hills

CUSTER STATE PARK
Custer
(605) 255-4515
www.custerstatepark.com

A favorite riding place with abundant wildlife, the park gives almost free rein to equestrians. Horses aren't allowed in the Sylvan Lake watershed area or the walk-in fishing area that links Grace Coolidge and Center Lake Campgrounds (both areas are posted), but otherwise you're free to ride to your heart's content through this fabulous park. If you want to follow marked trails, you have options for both long and short rides ranging from 45 minutes to seven-hour loops. Maps and detailed information about these and other trails are available at the park or by calling (605) 255-4464 or (605) 255-4515.

HORSEBACK TRAIL RIDES AND PACK TRIPS

Summer trail rides are plentiful, and a number of roadside corrals offer one- to two-hour rides. Those we've listed are a bit more off the beaten path or offer unusual opportunities. Some require reservations.

i The South Dakota Professional Guides and Outfitters Association issues a free publication, *Directory of Hunting, Fishing and Horseback Services,* that you can obtain by calling (605) 945-2928.

Central Hills

GUNSEL HORSE ADVENTURES
P.O. Box 1575, Rapid City, SD 57709
(605) 343-7608
www.gunselhorseadventures.com
Take a real Old West–style pack trip of 4 to 10 days (or longer), camping along the way. No modern amenities are found along the trail, just plenty of fabulous scenery and folksy song and poetry entertainment at night. Trip choices include riding the length of the Centennial Trail, Fort Meade, the Badlands, or a ride to Deadwood's historic Main Street. Trips are available from mid-Apr through Sept or Oct, weather permitting. Bob Lantis, proprietor of Gunsel, is one of the oldest (since 1968) outfitters in Yellowstone National Park. For hearty souls, Bob offers a bison roundup trip, a cattle roundup, and a spring turkey hunt. Call, write, or use the website for more information, including prices.

HIGH COUNTRY GUEST RANCH
12172 Deerfield Rd., Hill City
(605) 574-9003
www.highcountryranch.com
Ride for one to three hours, sheltered in seclusion in the Black Hills National Forest. Even the shortest ride treats you to a view of Harney Peak, and the longest takes you to an abandoned gold mine. If you feel like riding longer, call and ask about a custom trip. Riders must be at least six years old to go on the trail, but little people can take a pony ride around the ranch as long as their parents accompany them on foot. You can ride from mid-May to mid-Sept here. Rates depend on the length of your ride and the season; call for more information. To get here, look for the little covered wagon 4 miles west of town. The guest ranch has 17 cabins for rent.

Southern Hills

BLUE BELL STABLES
Custer State Park
SR 87 South, Custer
(605) 255-4700
There are many fine ways to view the natural wonders of Custer State Park, but sitting astride a horse has to be one of the best. On a one- or two-hour guided trail ride departing from the stables at Blue Bell Lodge and Resort, you can expect to come upon wildlife and learn about the park itself from your guide. The rides are extremely popular, and reservations are recommended; they're required for half-day and full-day pack trips. Children must ride alone and be four or older. Rides are available daily from 8 a.m. until 4:30 p.m., mid-May until mid-Sept. Fees start at $28 for adults and $22 for children 11 and younger; ask about the special rate for groups of 10 or more. Other rides range from $40 to $190 per person.

HUNTING

South Dakota boasts some of the best hunting in the nation, due in no small part to the species diversity found in the Black Hills. Among the animals with hunting seasons are pheasant, grouse, partridge, deer, turkey, duck, geese, antelope, and coyote. It's even legal to hunt bison, elk, mountain goats, and bighorn sheep, although these exceptionally rare opportunities are usually open only to residents and, even for them, often once in a lifetime.

Licenses for big game are issued through a state-run lottery system. Applications are available at many hardware, sporting goods, and convenience stores; county treasurers' offices; and the state Game, Fish & Parks Department's Wildlife Division regional office, 3305 West South St., Rapid City, (605) 394-2391. Or contact the department's main office at 523 East Capitol Ave., Pierre, (605) 773-3485.

The seasons and prices for deer, turkey, and waterfowl are long and varied. For details, visit www.state.sd.us/gfp, or call one of the phone numbers above.

The list of licenses, prices, and other details for hunting grouse, rabbits, and other animals is also long and complex, so inquire for the information you need. Nonresidents are not allowed to trap predators and fur-bearers at all in South Dakota and are not allowed to take mink, beavers, bobcats, and certain other species by any other means either; those privileges are reserved for state residents.

With a mishmash of public and private land, you need to know where you are and who owns what before you begin hunting. Make sure you have permission before you enter private property. Atlases and maps are available from Game, Fish & Parks and from the USDA Forest Service, R.R. 2, Box 200,

Black Elk

Most people think of John G. Neihardt's classic book when they hear the name of **Black Elk**. First published in 1932 and still in print, *Black Elk Speaks: Being the Life Story of a Holy Man of the Oglala Sioux* recounted Black Elk's visions so powerfully and affected readers so profoundly that it has been credited with planting the seed not only for the 1960s cultural revolution but for the ongoing revival of Native American cultural and spiritual life.

Born in 1863, Black Elk participated in the ghost dance movement and rescued an infant from the carnage at Wounded Knee (see the Day Trips & Weekend Getaways chapter for information about the Wounded Knee Massacre). He also toured with Buffalo Bill's Wild West show.

In later life, he converted to Catholicism but also used the Red Road/Black Road (good actions/ evil actions) approach in his tribal ministry. In the wrenching conclusion to *Black Elk Speaks,* he climbed Harney Peak with Neihardt and cried, "O make my people live!" Now, thousands of people each year visit Harney Peak in the protected Black Elk Wilderness Area, and Black Elk's people are finding renewed strength and identity in the old ways.

Custer, 57730, (605) 673-2251. Game, Fish & Parks also issues an annual hunting handbook with all the latest regulations, including restrictions in state parks—be sure to get the current copy (which comes out around Labor Day) when you buy your license or pick up your application. Knowing the rules is your responsibility.

i If you know about poaching or other wildlife law violations, you can make an anonymous report by calling the South Dakota Turn In Poachers (TIPs) hotline at (800) 592-5522.

And one more thing: Uncased .22 caliber rimfire firearms are prohibited at all times in state parks and recreation areas and on the George S. Mickelson Trail. Further, firearms and bows may not be discharged on or across the Mickelson Trail right-of-way.

Custer State Park sponsors its own buffalo hunt from Nov through Jan. A trophy bull license is the most sought for, but the rarest: Fewer than 10 are issued each year. Since 2003 the park has made available three or four dozen cow and nontrophy licenses. None of the licenses are cheap or quick to obtain, as fees run from $1,200 to $5,000 and hunters may wait for two years before their name is drawn. The upsides are that nonresidents are welcome to apply, and the fee pays for a guide to accompany you on your hunting trip for up to three days. For an application or more information, call the park at (605) 255-4515.

JEEP TOURS

Southern Hills

BUFFALO SAFARI JEEP RIDES
Custer State Park
Wildlife Loop Road, Custer
(605) 255-4541
www.custerresorts.com

Feel the wind in your hair as you head out in an open-air jeep in search of wildlife and scenic splendor. Guided trips of about two hours take you through rolling hills and into the backcountry while your driver tells you about the park. To prolong the experience, you can join an evening chuck wagon cookout (see the Blue Bell Lodge and Resort Hayride & Chuck Wagon Cookout listing in the Attractions chapter) with live folk music. Rides are available from 8 a.m. to 6 p.m. daily, from Mother's Day until the weekend before the roundup in late Sept. Prices range from $25 to $35 per person, with a minimum of $115 per jeep. Group rates for 10 or more are available. Reservations are recommended. The cookout ride departs at 4:30 p.m. and returns by 8:30 p.m. The price is $70 for those older than 12 and $50 for children. Reservations are required by 2 p.m.

SKATING

All forms of skating are popular in the Black Hills, but ice-skating is especially big. In addition to the indoor rink listed below, Rapid City has four outdoor skating areas, at Wilson Park, Sioux Park, College Park, and near the fish hatchery on the west side of town. Outdoor rinks can also be found in Belle Fourche (Weyler Park) and Spearfish (the City of Spearfish Campground). There is a skateboarding park in Rapid City (at 221 New York St.), a snow-skate park at Deer Mountain Ski Area near Lead (see the Skiing and Snowboarding section in this chapter), and an old-fashioned roller-skating rink in Rapid City (listed below). If you plan on roller-skating or skateboarding in city limits, be sure to check at the city hall or police station for local ordinances.

Central Hills

RAPID SKATE
2302 East St. Andrew St., Rapid City
(605) 342-8944
A popular place for roller-skating parties, Rapid Skate has a special party room and a snack bar in addition to a skating rink. Summer hours vary, so call for information. Winter hours also vary, but Rapid Skate is usually open Wed, Fri, Sat, and Sun. Hours on other days change weekly. Rates include skates; speed skates and in-line skates are extra. Lessons, including artistic dance skating, are available. Call for rates and times.

ROOSEVELT PARK INDOOR ICE ARENA
235 Waterloo St., Rapid City
(605) 394-6161
www.rcgov.org/Parks-and-Recreation/ice-arena.html
Forest service ranger district offices are open Mon through Fri year-round and are excellent places to get maps, brochures, information, and directions. They also sell Christmas tree- and firewood-cutting permits. Check outdoor racks for maps and brochures if the doors are locked. This indoor complex receives heavy use by hockey leagues in winter, but there are plenty of opportunities for public skating, too—just call ahead. Times are set aside for public hockey and curling. If you're interested in either sport, call the arena for more information. If public skating isn't available, you can always come in to watch the leagues play or the figure skaters practice. Getting out on the ice for a day will cost $4.75 for adults and $3.75 for children 18 and under. Skate rentals are available for $3.25.

SKIING & SNOWBOARDING

The Black Hills aren't capped by sheer granite peaks in the same way that the Rockies are, but the beautifully forested landscape and gentle intimacy of the Hills make them a great place for downhill skiing.

Northern Hills

MYSTIC MOUNTAIN SKI AREA
1000 Mountain Rd., Lead
(605) 584-3230, (605) 717-0422, (888) 636-0626
www.skimystic.com
Natural snow, night skiing, and groomed cross-country trails (which we've covered in the Cross-country Skiing section of this chapter) are hallmarks of Mystic Mountain. At an elevation of approximately 6,800 feet, with a 750-foot vertical drop, Mystic Mountain offers downhill slopes for all skill levels—Meadow and Snow Bowl for beginners, Racers' Cliff or the Chute for hotdoggers. A 3,000-foot triple chairlift and two other lifts serve the trails, which get plenty of use between 4 and 9 p.m. Fri and Sat, when the area is lighted for night skiing. Snowboarders have their own territory in the regulation-size half-pipe and a terrain park with tabletops and jumps. Even tubers have a trail all to themselves. When it's time to come in from the cold, patrons head for the cafeteria and full-service bar in the lodge. Lessons, equipment rentals, and a ski shop round out the amenities.

Lift ticket prices range from $5 to $41. Call for information about season passes and group rates. A half day of tubing costs $10, with tube rental included. Ski rentals are $20 for adults, and $15 for kids. Snowboards are $20 a day. Poles and boots are included. Mystic Mountain is closed on Mon and Tues except from about mid-Dec to early Jan, when the lifts run seven days a week. Hours are 9 a.m. to 4 p.m. Wed, Thurs, and Sun, and 9 a.m. to 9 p.m. Fri and Sat. To get there, go 3 miles west of Lead on US 85/14A and watch for the well-marked turnoff to the ski area.

TERRY PEAK SKI AREA
Nevada Gulch, Lead
(605) 584-2165, (800) 456-0524
www.terrypeak.com

Our largest and tallest ski area (7,076 feet, with 1,052 feet of vertical drop), Terry Peak also sets itself apart with its high-tech, computerized snowmaking machinery. Five chairlifts, including a high-speed detachable quad chair, serve more than 20 miles of slopes for all skill levels. Stewart Slope and River Run offer beginners a gentle start, while Ben Hur and Holy Terror give advanced skiers a run for their money.

Snowboarders will find a terrain park on the Snowstorm trail. Stewart Lodge has a cafeteria, lounge, ski shop, and rentals. Nevada Gulch Base Lodge has a cafeteria, ski shop, and the adjacent Dark Horse Saloon. Lessons are available through the certified ski school. All-area day passes cost $43 for adults ages 13 to 69 and $33 for juniors 6 to 12. Passes are free for children 5 and younger and seniors 70 and older. Reduced rates are available for limited access and for half days. Call for information about that and season passes as well as group rates. Complete ski sets (skis, boots, and poles) rent for $21 for adults and $16 for juniors. Snowboards with boots are $23, and snowblades are $18. Traditionally, Terry Peak opens the day after Thanksgiving, assuming there's enough snow, and operates on weekends until mid-Dec, when it's open seven days a week.

Hours are 9 a.m. to 4 p.m. To reach the ski area, turn off US 85/14A at the Terry Peak billboard west of Lead.

SNOWMOBILING

The Black Hills are consistently ranked by enthusiasts as one of the best places on the continent to snowmobile. More than 350 miles of groomed trails, regular snowfalls, and more than two million acres of creek-carved canyons and ponderosa-covered hillsides make the Hills a favorite destination for sledders from all over North America.

Restrictions are few; just be sure you avoid logging areas, plowed roads, private land, cross-country ski trails, and wildlife winter ranges. Ski trails and winter range are defined on the South Dakota Snowmobile Trails Map, which is available at no charge at trailside businesses and other locations around the Hills, by calling the state tourism department at (800) 732-5682, or logging on to www.travelsd.com. Call (800) 445-3474 for current conditions.

Snowmobiles must be licensed (a valid out-of-state license is acceptable); if your machine isn't, you can purchase a five-day license for $10 at trailside businesses and other locations. A state license costs $20 for two years and is available at county treasurers' offices.

You can legally snowmobile in the national forest whenever there's enough snow, but the agreements on which the trail map is based (and which make it valid) are in effect only between Dec 1 and Mar 31. Trail grooming doesn't begin until Dec 15. If you snowmobile before then, be sure you sled on land that isn't off-limits, and watch for hunting parties.

The Northern Hills and the Deerfield area in the Central Hills tend to get more snow and colder temperatures than elsewhere, and those are two places we recommend; the O'Neill Pass area along US 85 near the Wyoming border is especially consistent in the quality of its snow. The trail system, however, rambles through the western portion of the Hills from Spearfish practically to Custer, a stretch of almost 80 miles. And when the Needles Highway in Custer State Park is snow covered, it becomes a paradise of switchbacks, tunnels, and spectacular scenery for snowmobilers.

Parking is provided along the state trail system, and the map will show you where the lots are. Some trailside businesses also have space for your road vehicle, but it doesn't hurt to ask permission before you take to the trails.

SNOWMOBILE RENTALS

Here we've listed rental outlets that are close to popular trails and areas that get heavy snow. But you'll find rentals at other places, too, and several are listed on the snowmobile trail map mentioned previously.

Northern Hills

LATCHSTRING VILLAGE ALL SEASON SPORTS CENTER
US 14A, Spearfish Canyon
(605) 584-2207, (800) 439-8544
www.spfcanyon.com
Single-seat sleds are $140 for a full-day rental on weekends and $110 on a weekday. Half-day rentals are $100 on weekends and $80 on weekdays. Double-seater sleds and other equipment are extra. Excellent package deals

are available for guests of Spearfish Canyon Lodge, where the sports center is located. Call early for reservations—the machines are popular.

RECREATIONAL SPRINGS LODGE
US 85 South, Lead
(877) 584-1228
www.recsprings.com
Located just a few miles southwest of Lead, "Rec Springs" rents a variety of performance snowmobiles. Rates depend on the make and model of the sled, but they range from $85 to $100 for a half day and from $135 to $150 for a full day. There are modest accommodations here, as well as a restaurant, repair shop, and some clothing rentals. Before December the lodge is the domain of hunters.

TRAILSHEAD LODGE
US 85 South, Lead
(605) 584-3464
www.lead.sd.us/trailshead
Single sleds rent for $135 a day Mon through Thurs and $159 Fri through Sun. Doubles are $145 and $169, respectively. Half-day rates start at $99. Prices include a helmet, but there is a $12 oil and gas charge. A full set of outerwear rents for $15, with varied prices for individual pieces. The lodge is 21 miles southwest of Lead.

SWIMMING

Here we've listed some of the most popular indoor swimming venues in the Black Hills. But don't forget about our lakes and reservoirs, some of which are mentioned in the Boating and Fishing sections.

RECREATION

Northern Hills

DEADWOOD RECREATION CENTER
105 Sherman St., Deadwood
(605) 578-3729
Built in 1912 by the Deadwood Business Club as the city auditorium, this beautiful brick facility fell into disuse and decayed with the rest of Deadwood over the years. However, historic preservation money from gambling proceeds has helped renovate and restore the structure. Today, after a $6 million renovation and new addition, the building holds a massive indoor pool with a special area for kids, changing rooms, elevated running track, exercise equipment, and basketball courts (indoor and outdoor). Few towns with populations of less than 1,500 sport such a facility, and Deadwood residents know it; the building gets used frequently all year, especially in the afternoons after school. There is a daily use fee of $2.75 for adults, but prices are reduced for families, seniors, children, and high school students. Hours vary, but the center is usually open 5 a.m. to 9 p.m. weekdays, 1 to 9 p.m. Sat, but closed on Sun.

Central Hills

ROOSEVELT PARK INDOOR AQUATIC CENTER
235 Waterloo St., Rapid City
(605) 394-4168
Rapid City's antiquated public swimming pools went through a massive rebuilding project in the late 1990s and early 2000s, and the Roosevelt Aquatic Center is the pool system's crown jewel. The massive indoor structure, which opened in 2004 next door to the Roosevelt Indoor Ice Arena (see the Skating section), has a shallow play pool, a mock river for tubing, a giant waterslide, spray toys, a 25-yard racing pool with diving boards, a hot tub, and a "vortex area," a small pool that resembles a toilet flushing. The center hours vary depending upon programming, but it is generally open year-round, 6 a.m. to 10 p.m. Mon through Fri, 8 a.m. to 10 p.m. Sat, and noon to 8 p.m. Sun.

There are two other modern outdoor swimming areas, at Sioux Park, 1000 Sheridan Lake Rd., (605) 394-1894, and at Parkview Pool, 4221 Parkview Dr., (605) 394-1892. The Horace Mann Pool, 818 Anamosa St., (605) 394-1891, has yet to be renovated. Admission at all pools is $4.50 for adults, $3.50 for children under 18, and $3 for seniors over 60.

The outdoor pools are heated, have full-time lifeguards, and offer lockers and showers. They generally open Memorial Day weekend and close, one by one, between mid-Aug and Labor Day. Hours are 1 to 8 p.m.

Southern Hills

EVANS PLUNGE
1145 North River St., Hot Springs
(605) 745-5165
www.evansplunge.com
The warm mineral waters that made Hot Springs a turn-of-the-20th-century health resort still feed the swimming pools at Evans Plunge. Inside, a long, twisting waterslide and a short, zippy one will dump you into the 87-degree water in the 200-by-50-foot pool, touted as the "world's largest natural warm-water indoor swimming pool." Outside, you can speed slide into a smaller pool when the summer sun warms the water even more. Added attractions include giant

tubes for paddling or floating, Tarzan rings for the strong of bicep, water basketball and volleyball, a 3-foot kiddie pool with tyke-size slide, spas, a steam room and sauna, weight and exercise rooms, a snack bar, and a gift shop.

Evans Plunge is open from 5:30 a.m. to 10 p.m. during the summer and from 5:30 a.m. to 8 p.m. in the spring, fall, and winter. Daily rates are $11 for ages 13 and older, $9 for children 3 through 12, and free for those 2 and younger. Use of the spa and fitness center costs $2.50 extra, or $7.50 if you don't swim. Inquire about group discounts and membership rates. Forgot your suit and towel? You can rent those here, along with life jackets and lockers. For your safety, lifeguards are on duty; children younger than 13 are not allowed in the weight room and exercise area.

SPECTATOR SPORTS

Physical activity is common in the Black Hills, and with good reason. The pine-covered bluffs and creek-carved canyons of this region are an incredibly beautiful backdrop for any number of recreational pursuits. Because of this, local residents usually prefer being in the thick of the action to being anchored on the sidelines.

There are a handful of venues for spectator sports, but not many. It isn't for a lack of trying, either; Rapid City has hosted several semiprofessional teams since the last decades of the 20th century, but few have lasted. The city had a fantastic semiprofessional basketball team in the 1980s, but attendance numbers dwindled, and the franchise packed up and left. A replacement team failed to keep local attention. Officials decided residents needed a change of pace, so they established an indoor football league in 2000. The Rapid City Flying Aces played several seasons but folded in 2007. The newest edition to the semipro sports saga began in late 2008, with the addition of the Rapid City Rush, a Central Hockey League team playing in the Rushmore Plaza Civic Center's new $20-million-plus, 5,000-seat ice arena.

College and high school sports attract a more passionate group of fans than any regional pro franchise. Rapid City's two American Legion teams—Post 22 and Post 320—are especially popular, and each maintains high national rankings. Other Black Hills communities sponsor teams. Since the local American Legion officials change regularly, the best way to obtain information is to check the local newspapers. You can find out more on school-sponsored sports in the Education chapter.

There are three universities in the Black Hills: Black Hills State in Spearfish, South Dakota School of Mines and Technology in Rapid City, and National American University in Rapid City. Each has a smattering of sports teams, and you'll find some information on the teams below. However, since each school is relatively small, sports teams are formed and disbanded depending on student and local interest. A phone call or a quick look on the sports page is your best bet for updated information.

BASKETBALL

BLACK HILLS STATE UNIVERSITY
1200 University Station, Spearfish
(605) 642-6882
www.bhsu.edu/athletics
The BHSU men's and women's basketball season runs from Nov until Mar. Yellow Jackets home games are at the Donald E. Young Sports and Fitness Center on campus. Tickets are sold on-site; prices are $6 for adults and $3 for students of all ages.

SOUTH DAKOTA SCHOOL OF MINES AND TECHNOLOGY
501 East St. Joseph St., Rapid City
(605) 394-2601
www.sdsmt.edu/athletics

The men's and women's basketball season begins in early Nov and continues until mid-Mar. Home games are in Goodell Gymnasium (called the New Gym) on the Tech campus. Women's games generally begin at 5:30 p.m. and men's at 7:30 p.m. Tickets are available at the gym; prices are $6 for adults, $4 for youths 10 to 18, and free for those 9 and younger. The Lady Hardrockers have appeared in the Division II national championships eight times since 1994, and they reached the final four twice. The men's team has also done well, competing multiple times in the national championships since 1997.

i Rapid City hosts a boys' high school basketball tournament each year in March, alternating between Class A and Class AA.

CROSS-COUNTRY

BLACK HILLS STATE UNIVERSITY
1200 University Station, Spearfish
(605) 642-6882
www.bhsu.edu/athletics
Men's and women's cross-country running events take place from Sept to Nov at Spearfish Canyon Country Club, (605) 642-7156, at the intersection of US Highways 14 and 14A. Admission is free. Both men's and women's teams maintain high national rankings, and members have earned All-American honors in recent years. The men's team earned conference championships in 2002, and 2005 through 2008, while the women's team finished third overall in the country in 2002, and garnered conference championships from 2005 through 2009.

SOUTH DAKOTA SCHOOL OF MINES AND TECHNOLOGY
501 East St. Joseph St., Rapid City
(605) 394-2601
www.sdsmt.edu/athletics
Men's and women's cross-country events generally take place on Saturday during the fall. Each year a meet featuring regional teams is held in conjunction with the school's homecoming events. The meet is open to the public at no charge, but since the location varies you'll need to call for information.

FOOTBALL

BLACK HILLS STATE UNIVERSITY
1200 University Station, Spearfish
(605) 642-6882
www.bhsu.edu/athletics
Football season for the BHSU Yellow Jackets runs from early Sept until the first week of Nov. Home games are played at 1:30 p.m. on Sat at Lyle Hare Field on the university campus. Ticket prices are $6 for adults and $3 for students of all ages. Tickets are sold at the stadium at game time.

SOUTH DAKOTA SCHOOL OF MINES AND TECHNOLOGY
501 East St. Joseph St., Rapid City
(605) 394-2601
www.sdsmt.edu/athletics
The Hardrockers' season begins around the first part of Sept and goes until early Nov. Home games are usually at 1 p.m. on Sat at O'Harra Field on the Tech campus. Tickets are available at the stadium, and prices are $7 for adults, $4 for ages 10 to 18, and free for anyone 9 or younger.

ℹ Most Black Hills residents share a common trait: We spend time on sports—participating, watching, or both.

of the biggest names in the Professional Rodeo Cowboys Association. More information on these competitions can be found in the Annual Events & Festivals chapter.

HOCKEY

RAPID CITY RUSH
Rushmore Plaza Civic Center
444 Mount Rushmore Rd., Rapid City
(605) 394-4115; (605) 716-PUCK (7825)
www.rapidcityrush.com
In late Nov 2008, the Rapid City Rush played its first home game in an impressive new home—the Rushmore Plaza Civic Center's expanded $20 million ice arena, complete with 5,002 seats and 13 sky boxes, called suites. The Rush play in the Northwest Division of the Central Hockey League, formed in 1992. The league hosts an all-star game in Jan, and a four-round playoff series in late Mar for the Ray Miron President's Cup Trophy. General admission tickets range from $18 to $28. Season tickets are $100 to $956 per seat.

RODEO

Organized rodeo teams used to exist at the institutions of higher learning in the Black Hills, but as the region has become more metropolitan and the universities attract more out-of-state students, interest in the sport has waned. There are still informal rodeo groups at the colleges, but there are no regular events open to the general public. Your best bet for ridin' and ropin' action is going to be one of the many annual rodeo events that happen in the Black Hills. **The Days of '76** in Deadwood, **Black Hills Roundup** in Belle Fourche, and **Black Hills Stock Show and Rodeo** in Rapid City are among the most popular and attract some

TRACK & FIELD

BLACK HILLS STATE UNIVERSITY
1200 University Station, Spearfish
(605) 642-6882
www.bhsu.edu/athletics
The men's and women's indoor season is in Jan and Feb, with Yellow Jackets events at the Donald E. Young Sports and Fitness Center on the BHSU campus. Outdoor events take place from late Mar through May at Lyle Hare Field on the campus. There is no cost to attend.

SOUTH DAKOTA SCHOOL OF MINES AND TECHNOLOGY
501 East St. Joseph St., Rapid City
(605) 394-2601
www.sdsmt.edu/athletics
Men and women hold indoor track competition during Jan and Feb. Outdoor events for the Hardrockers are generally on Sat from late Mar through late Apr at O'Harra Field on the Tech campus, with one regional meet each year open to the public at no charge, usually at 10 a.m. on the first Saturday of April.

VOLLEYBALL

BLACK HILLS STATE UNIVERSITY
1200 University Station, Spearfish
(605) 642-6882
www.bhsu.edu/athletics
South Dakota–Iowa Conference champions in 1997, 2008 and 2009, the women's Yellow Jacket team plays from Aug through Nov, with home games in the Donald E.

Young Sports and Fitness Center on campus. Admission is free.

SOUTH DAKOTA SCHOOL OF MINES AND TECHNOLOGY
501 East St. Joseph St., Rapid City
(605) 394-2601
www.sdsmt.edu/athletics
Women's volleyball competition takes place from early Sept through mid-Nov. The Lady Hardrockers' home games are in Goodell Gymnasium (the New Gym) on the school campus, but you'll need to call for the schedule. Tickets are sold at the door and cost $6 for adults and $3 for ages 10 to 18. Admission is free for those ages 9 and younger. When the parking lot at Rushmore Plaza Civic Center in Rapid City fills up, locals drive across Mount Rushmore Road and park at Central High School.

DAY TRIPS & WEEKEND GETAWAYS

The Black Hills have often been described as an island of emerald forests in a sea of prairie. It's also true that the Hills are an island of people in a sea of relatively unpopulated land. There are about 200,000 hardy souls in the Black Hills, but the hundreds of miles of short-grass prairie that surrounds them are decidedly less peopled. The nearest towns with more than a few thousand people are Casper, Wyoming, and Billings, Montana, nearly 300 miles away to the west. If you travel 350 miles east you'll find Sioux Falls; 400 miles south and you'll come across Denver. In between is a stretch of vast and empty country, dotted only with cattle and bison ranches, a few tough cowboys, and a handful of small and dying towns.

Without a doubt, the Black Hills are gorgeous. Yet the wide tracts of prairie and clear skies beyond its foothills have a timeless beauty all their own. Inhabited by the descendants of resilient American pioneers, this land represents the nation's last great frontier. But the population grows older every day, and many towns and ranches are hanging on by a thread. In 2003, South Dakota Governor Mike Rounds suggested that unless circumstances change, the state could have fewer than 20 populated towns by 2025. Our neighbors Montana, Wyoming, Nebraska, and North Dakota might share the same fate.

The very emptiness of the land is what brought pioneers in the first place, and it's what continues to attract visitors today. There are few places in the country where the sky is wider, the air fresher, or the stars brighter. In this chapter you'll find destinations and attractions listed in most of the states mentioned above. For some attractions, the nearest town is several miles distant and claims only a couple hundred residents. Others are located in the middle of larger towns. Cafes and restaurants show up almost anywhere, but your best bet for accommodations is going to be the larger cities. As you watch your gas gauge, keep in mind that distances between service stations are usually several dozen miles or greater. However, none of the places listed below will require driving more than four hours from the Black Hills.

NORTH OF THE BLACK HILLS

Northwestern South Dakota

The **Sioux Ranger District** of Custer National Forest, (605) 797-4432, maintains Camp Crook and two National Natural Landmarks: Capital Rock (west of Buffalo, just across the Montana border) and Castles in Harding County (east of Buffalo, on SR 20). These are mixed-use and mixed-landscape areas, with buttes, grasslands, and pine forests, where you can hike, hunt, watch wildlife, and camp (limited facilities only) at no charge, year-round. It's best to get a map because the district's land units are not always contiguous or easy to find. To get there, take US 85 north from Belle Fourche for about 70 miles until you reach the junction with SR 20. Follow SR 20 east to the Castles, and west to Camp Crook. You'll cross into Montana to get to Capital Rock, but it's only a few miles across the border.

Grand River National Grassland, (605) 374-3592, is on 197,000 acres on the North Dakota and South Dakota border. It's a primitive place without developed facilities (except fishing ponds) and, like most grasslands, is broken up into blocks of federal, state, and private land. Call ahead for a map. It's open year-round, and there are no entrance fees. The Shadehill Reservoir Recreation Area is within the grassland, near the town of Shadehill. To get to the grasslands, take SR 79 north from Sturgis. At Newell, turn onto US 212 and follow it northeast to the outskirts of Faith. There, turn north onto SR 73, which will take you into the grasslands and past Shadehill Reservoir. The trip is about 190 miles one-way. For more information on northwestern South Dakota, call the South Dakota Office of Tourism at (605) 773-3301 or (800) S-DAKOTA, or, better yet, log on to South Dakota's website, www.travelsd.com.

North Dakota

The 19th-largest state, North Dakota is a huge expanse of prairie, farm, and ranch land that is quietly and understatedly beautiful. The state is rich in history and historical sites. Teddy Roosevelt, Sitting Bull, Custer, Lewis and Clark, and Sacagawea all left their mark there. Roosevelt said, "My experience when I lived and worked in North Dakota with my fellow ranchmen, on what was then the frontier, was the most important educational asset of my life." Outsiders often snicker when they hear the words "North Dakota," but that just makes it obvious they've never been there. The state is still relatively undiscovered, and that fact alone makes it a special place.

US 85 from Belle Fourche is the fastest way to reach North Dakota from the Black Hills. Follow it until you reach I-94, which you can take west to get to **Theodore Roosevelt National Park,** one of the best reasons to visit North Dakota. The only national park named for a person, it encompasses North Dakota's Badlands, where Roosevelt rode and hunted in 1883. Teddy called the area "the romance of my life" and went on to work to preserve such beautiful places as national parks and monuments. The South Unit, (701) 623-4466 (on mountain time), is near Medora, and I-94 cuts through it. The North Unit, (701) 842-2333 (70 miles away and on central time), is near Watford City, off US 85. The Little Missouri River flows through both, and the North Unit is more rugged and heavily forested. Views at both are glorious, and you can mountain bike, hike, ride horses, camp, or take a scenic drive and watch buffalo, wild horses, deer, and prairie dogs.

The **Little Missouri National Grassland,** (701) 225-5151, has one million acres that surround Theodore Roosevelt National Park. It's open year-round, and there are no entrance fees. It's primitive, although there are some established camping sites and hiking trails. It's a great (and great big) place to view wildlife, birds, and butterflies, or to fish and hunt and just get away from it all. Call ahead for a map.

Historic **Medora,** (800) 633-6721, (701) 623-4444, near the south entrance to the South Unit of Theodore Roosevelt National Park, is a 3-block-long restored Old West

A Bogus Banner

North Dakota and South Dakota were admitted to the Union at the same time, as the 39th and 40th states. When President Benjamin Harrison signed the statehood act on November 2, 1889, he intentionally shuffled the papers so neither state could claim admittance before the other. The Fort Meade Museum, near Sturgis, South Dakota, displays an old flag with 39 stars, but it's a bogus banner, for the United States never had only 39 states, having gone directly from 38 to 40, thanks to North and South Dakota.

town owned almost entirely by the Theodore Roosevelt Medora Foundation. To get there, take I-94 to exit 27 (westbound) or exit 24 (eastbound). Walk on the boardwalks along gaslighted streets, visit the museums and galleries, and have a meal of beef or buffalo. Tour the 28-room Chateau de Mores, the historic 1880s home once owned by the Marquis de Mores, a local rancher, and his wife, Medora. Other attractions include the Doll House (antique dolls and toys), the Rough Rider Time Machine (a free multimedia presentation), and the Museum of the Badlands. Medora attractions operate from about Memorial Day through Labor Day.

The *Medora Musical* (call phone numbers for Medora above) is performed outdoors in the 2,750-seat Burning Hills Amphitheater on a bluff outside town (there's no official address, but there are plenty of signs). It has a nifty reversible outdoor escalator. The rollicking musical is a boot-stomping salute to Teddy Roosevelt and the American spirit. It is held nightly at 8:30 from early June through early Sept; ticket prices are $30–$34 for adults, $14–$16 for students (grades 1 through 12), and free for preschoolers and those younger. We recommend that you order tickets in advance. The trip from the Black Hills to Medora and the nearby Theodore Roosevelt National Park and Little Missouri National Grassland is about 200 miles one-way.

From Medora you can take I-94 35 miles east to Dickinson and the **Dakota Dinosaur Museum,** (701) 225-DINO, 200 Museum Dr., exit 61 off I-94. Here you can look at more than 12,000 fossils, rocks, minerals, shells, and re-created dinosaurs. The museum has educational activities for kids, including a once-daily Dino Dig (Memorial Day through Labor Day, kindergarten through sixth grade students only). The museum is closed Sept to May; however, groups of 20 or more can make advance arrangements to visit during that time. From May 1 until Memorial Day, hours are 9 a.m. to 4 p.m. Mon through Sat, and 11 a.m. to 4 p.m. Sun. From Memorial Day through Labor Day, hours are 9 a.m. to 6 p.m. seven days a week. Admission prices are $7 for adults, $6 for seniors, $4 for children under 13, and $6 for the Dino Dig. While you're there, visit the other museums on the grounds. The Joachim Regional Museum (local artifacts and displays) is open year-round. The Pioneer Machinery Museum and Prairie Outpost Park operate from Memorial Day through Labor Day.

Request a visitor packet from the North Dakota Tourism Office by calling (800) 453-5663, or log on to the website at www.ndtourism.com.

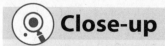

Close-up

Black Hills' Time Zones

Until the 1880s, the United States had no time zones. Each town simply operated on its own "local time," which for farmers was nature's time, clocked by the sun's movement. As railroads became the most popular means of travel and transportation, "railroad time" was instituted to make timetables simpler. But eventually there were 100 different railroad times, and it became quite confusing. Travelers found themselves arriving at a station before they'd left the previous station—according to the timetable, that is.

In 1883 the railroads in the United States and Canada established four time zones to alleviate the problem. On November 18, the newly coordinated times were telegraphed to cities all over the country, and everyone—even farmers—adjusted his or her schedule to the newfangled way. It is said that a Mr. Sears, agent at the Minneapolis and St. Louis railroad station in Minnesota, made a tidy sum selling pocket watches to people who had never needed them before. And it wasn't long before he moved to Chicago and started a new business called Sears, Roebuck and Company.

The time zone system was so successful that Congress made it official in 1918. The dividing line between the central and mountain standard time zones runs through the Great Plains, but the railroads chose its exact route. Thus, the line meanders and jogs, apparently for the convenience of the railroads and their scheduled stops. You'll find some towns, even the mighty Missouri River, divided by the line and neighbors on central time living next door to folks on mountain time.

NORTHWEST OF THE BLACK HILLS

Montana

The landscape of the fourth-largest state is striking and gorgeous, and it makes a great backdrop for the places you'll visit there. Best of all, Montana—despite its size—has fewer than a million residents, which means you can find lots of elbow room. In fact, population in some parts of eastern Montana is measured in square miles per person, and in many counties the cattle outnumber the human inhabitants.

Cross into Montana from Belle Fourche on US 212. The first town you'll come to is Alzada, in ranching country. Enjoy the empty scenery until you come to Broadus, about 100 miles from Belle Fourche, where you can visit the free **Powder River Historical Museum,** www.mcdd.net/museum, on the town square, and see the old county jail, a chuck wagon, artifacts, antique cars, and a collection of 200,000 seashells. The **Powder River Wagon Train and Cattle Drive** is an annual midsummer event in Broadus, and you can participate on horseback or by wagon. Call (406) 436-2388 or (800) 492-8835 to sign up.

Continue on US 212 for 50 miles and you'll come to Ashland and Lame Deer, on the Northern Cheyenne Reservation. Custer's last camp before his troops began the Battle of the Little Bighorn was in the area. The free **Cheyenne Indian Museum** is in Ashland, (406) 784-2746, on the St. Labre Indian

School campus. There's no street address—Ashland is a small town—but you can't miss it. It's open year-round. The **Ashland Pow Wow** is held each year on Labor Day weekend, and the **Northern Cheyenne Pow Wow** is on the Fourth of July weekend. For information about the powwows, call the tribal offices at (406) 477-6284.

Fifty miles west of Lame Deer you'll reach the junction with I-90, where the **Little Bighorn Battlefield National Monument,** (406) 638-2623, is located. For more than a century the only monuments here were to the battle's losers (in fact, up until 1991 it was called the Custer Battlefield), but in 2003 an elaborate memorial was finally erected to honor the Sioux, Cheyenne, Crow, and other Native American warriors who lost their lives here. You'll also find an interactive interpretive center and a national cemetery.

If you're feeling adventurous, you can follow I-90 60 miles west to Billings, Montana's largest city. In the middle of a metropolitan area claiming more than 120,000 people, you can enjoy fine restaurants, museums, and parks, including the **Yellowstone Art Museum,** (406) 256-6804, and **ZooMontana,** (406) 652-8100 This would be a long day trip, however, since Billings is 270 miles from Belle Fourche (you can make the same trip via I-90, but it will take you through Wyoming and add about 60 miles to the journey). Fortunately, Billings also has a number of good hotels.

You can get to Miles City by traveling northeast on I-94 150 miles from Billings, or by taking SR 59 north for 80 miles from Broadus. Miles City is home of the annual **Jaycee Bucking Horse Sale,** (406) 232-2890, held downtown on the third weekend in May. You can watch as the horses run down Main Street, and there's a parade, good

western home cooking at the steak fry and pancake breakfast, and more fun events. The annual **Western Art Roundup,** (406) 232-2890, is held in conjunction with the Bucking Horse Sale. At nearby **Pirogue Island State Park,** (406) 232-0900, Kinsey Highway, you can hunt for agates.

Don't miss the free **Custer County Art Center,** (406) 232-0635, Water Plant Road, which features work by local and regional artists. The **Range Riders Museum,** (406) 232-6146, just west of town and across the Tongue River on SR 10, displays the town's original Main Street, a heritage center, and exhibits devoted to local history. There is an admission charge; call ahead for hours.

From Miles City head northeast to Terry, also on the Yellowstone River. The **Prairie County Museum,** (406) 635-4040, is located in the town's 1906 bank building and displays a collection of historical artifacts related to the community. It also has a 19th-century caboose, a steam-heated brick outhouse, a reconstructed homesteader cabin, and a collection of photographs taken by British pioneer women who arrived in the area in the late 1800s. It's open Memorial Day through Labor Day every day except Tues.

i The *Anatosaurus,* or duck-billed dinosaur, is the Montana state fossil, and the mighty ponderosa pine is the state tree.

Seventy-five miles farther northeast is Glendive, home of the free **Frontier Gateway Museum,** (406) 365-8168, Belle Prairie Road, a collection of Plains Indian, ranch, and farm artifacts that's open only in the summer. You'll also want to visit **Makoshika State Park,** (406) 365-6256, Snyder Avenue, where erosion has created some spectacular rock formations on 8,800 acres that also contain fossils, including those of the amazing *Triceratops,* whose skull is on display in the visitor center (open year-round). A Montana state park license is required to enter the park; the license is $5 daily per car or $30 annually and admits you to any state park in Montana. A complement to the strange natural wonders of Makoshika, Montana's largest state park, is **Buzzard Days,** an annual spring celebration dedicated to the return of the turkey vultures to the park. Call for the exact date; it varies each year. You can take a birdwatching tour, participate in the 10K run, and enjoy breakfasts and barbecues. The park's entrance fee is waived during the celebration.

Thirty miles to the east of Glendive on I-94 (and 35 miles west of Medora; see the previous section on North Dakota) is the town of **Wibaux,** named for cattleman Pierre Wibaux, who owned the Roubaix Mine and the 777 Ranch in South Dakota's Black Hills. The town is also the home of **St. Peter's Catholic Church,** downtown, built in 1885, which has an unusual lava-rock facade and beautiful stained glass. You can't tour the church, and there's no telephone, but you can take a look at the outside of the structure. At the free **Pierre Wibaux Museum Complex,** (406) 795-9969, Orgain Street, you'll learn about eastern Montana through the exhibits and by touring Wibaux's 1892 home and offices as well as the other historic buildings in the complex, which is open only in the summer. The Wibaux County Fair is held in late Aug.

Drive 70 miles south and you'll come to **Medicine Rocks State Park,** (406) 232-0900, off SR 7, 10 miles north of Ekalaka, where it is said Native American hunting parties found magical spirits. The sandstone rocks there

do indeed have strange and mystical forms. Ekalaka has an almost-complete *anatosaurus* (duckbilled dino) skeleton that awaits you in the downtown **Carter County Museum,** (406) 775-6686. It has been consistently rated one of the best county museums in the nation, despite being located in a town that, according to the 2000 census, claimed only 410 hardy souls. Another famous community landmark is the **Old Stand Saloon,** (406) 775-6661, Main Street, which is immortalized in town legend. The story claims that buffalo hunter Claude Carter was on his way to build a saloon on the railroad tracks in Montana Territory during the late 1880s when his wagon got stuck (or his horses refused to budge, depending on whom you ask) near the border with Dakota Territory. Carter stood up on his wagon full of logs, scanned the surrounding country, and spat, "Hell, anywhere in Montana is a good place for a saloon." Not only did the saloon thrive in its remote location, but it grew its own small town.

A bit farther south are the Chalk Buttes and Custer National Forest, but SR 7 is unpaved after it leaves Ekalaka, so you may want to turn back to town and choose another route to your desired destination.

For a Montana travel packet, call Travel Montana's Custer Country offices at (406) 665-1671 or (800) 346-1876, ext. 6. You can also call Travel Montana's Helena office at (406) 444-2654 or (800) VISITMT, or log on to the Travel Montana website at www.visitmt.com.

SOUTH OF THE BLACK HILLS

Nebraska

Nebraska, like North Dakota, is an "undiscovered" state, often believed to be just an uninteresting, flat expanse of rangeland. Although parts of the state are indeed flat and plain, western Nebraska—known as the Panhandle—may surprise you. This is a varied landscape of rocky geological wonders, grasslands, rolling hills, and the fabled, mysterious sandhills. The western counties of Box Butte, Sioux, and Dawes hold a wealth of sightseeing adventures, especially for the traveler interested in history and natural wonders.

US 385 from Hot Springs will take you 55 miles to the town of Chadron, Nebraska. The **Chadron State College** Administration Building's second floor, (308) 432-5276, Main Street, has local author Mari Sandoz memorabilia and archives as well as a Sandhills library.

Chadron State Park, (308) 432-5167, 8 miles south of Chadron off US 385, is set in the spectacular Pine Ridge cliffs and buttes of the Nebraska National Forest. You can camp, hike, swim, cross-county ski, and trail ride, and planned activities such as cookouts and demonstrations are offered in the summer. Cabins are available from mid-Apr through mid-Nov. A Nebraska state park entrance license is $4 daily per car or $20 for the season. The northern section of the park closes in the winter.

The fascinating **Museum of the Fur Trade,** (308) 432-3843, east of Chadron on US 20, will give you insight into how the trade helped develop western Nebraska. It is open only from Memorial Day through Labor Day, 8 a.m. to 5 p.m. Fur Trade Days are held in Chadron on the second weekend of July each year.

Twenty-five miles southwest of Chadron is Nebraska's largest state park. The 22,000-acre **Fort Robinson State Historical Park,** (308) 665-2900, US 20 near Crawford, is both

the site of the 1874 fort where Crazy Horse was murdered and a recreation area. It's open year-round for hiking, cross-country skiing, and mountain biking. The **Fort Robinson Museum,** (308) 665-2919, and the **Trailside Museum,** (308) 665-2929, are also on the grounds and are open Memorial Day through Labor Day. Cabins and the lodge are open mid-Apr through mid-Nov. You must purchase a state park entrance license to enjoy this or any other Nebraska state park. The annual **Western Art Show** is held at the fort over the Fourth of July weekend.

i Wyoming and Montana are on mountain standard time, but the line between the central standard and mountain standard time zones runs through North Dakota, South Dakota, and Nebraska—and the dividing line takes a wild westward swing in northern North Dakota. Time zone lines are marked on most maps and on telephone directory maps, too.

This is also the region of the Nebraska Badlands, with some spooky natural scenery. Visit strange **Toadstool Geologic Park,** (308) 432-0300, Toadstool Road, off SR 2/71, a National Geologic Site that has hiking trails and picnic facilities. It's located 20 miles northwest of Crawford.

Drive 25 miles west of Crawford to get to Harrison, then take SR 29 south for about 20 miles to reach the **Agate Fossil Beds National Monument,** (308) 668-2318. Here you'll see fossil beds 19 million years old and paleontology exhibits in the visitor center. The free center is open year-round, 8 a.m. to 7 p.m. daily during the summer and 8 a.m. to 4 p.m. during the winter months.

For more sightseeing, return to Chadron. Then, as you journey south on US 385, you will cross the **Niobrara River,** ranked among the top-10 canoeing rivers in the country. Then turn east (60 miles south of Chadron at Alliance) on SR 2, and you will come to the **Sandhills,** once called the Great American Desert. Wildlife refuges and tiny lakes are scattered over this area; to learn more about them, call the Nebraska Game and Parks Commission at (402) 471-0641.

Check out the town of **Alliance,** the Coal Capital of Nebraska and a railroad town since the late 1800s. The town's **Central Park** encompasses the **Sunken Gardens, Sallows Conservatory and Arboretum,** and the **Central Park Fountain,** a WPA project listed on the National Register of Historic Places. The free **Knight Museum,** (308) 762-2384, 908 Yellowstone Ave., has cavalry and Native American artifacts and is open May 1 through Labor Day weekend.

i Nebraska, the Cornhusker State, became a state in 1887. Arbor Day originated in Nebraska, the 16th-largest state.

Somewhat less elegant, but equally fascinating, is Alliance's **Carhenge,** (308) 762-4954 or (308) 762-1520, 2.5 miles north of Alliance on US 385, which replicates England's Stonehenge using old cars instead of stone. The satiric display was created in 1987 using Stone Age construction methods: lots of people pushing and pulling, and probably muttering and groaning. Although the state Department of Roads insisted it was a junkyard and tried to have it removed, it is still maintained by the Friends of Carhenge, which accepts donations for its upkeep (admission is free). Sculptures on the

grounds are also made of car parts. Some 80,000 people visit this pseudo-mystical shrine to used transportation each year.

Forty miles south of Alliance, near Bridgeport, are **Courthouse Rock, Jailhouse Rock,** and **Chimney Rock National Historic Site,** (308) 586-2581, impressive geologic formations that were milestones for pioneers traveling the Oregon and Mormon Trails. **Scotts Bluff National Monument,** near Gering, (308) 436-4340, is another great landmark, with a fine visitor center. To the pioneers, these formations were signs that they had made it through the vast prairie and were about to embark on the difficult trails through the mountains. History buffs will want to tour the **North Platte Valley Museum** in Gering, (308) 436-5411, where Nebraska pioneer history is lovingly preserved.

The Nebraska Division of Tourism can give you more information about the state on their website at www.visitnebraska.org.

SOUTHEAST OF THE BLACK HILLS
South Central South Dakota

South and east of the Black Hills lies the 11,000-square-mile **Pine Ridge Indian Reservation,** the second largest reservation in the country. Follow US 18 from Hot Springs east across the reservation. Pine Ridge is home to the Oglala Lakota people, many species of wildlife, and some beautiful, expansive landscape. The Oglala tribe is one of the seven that make up the Great Lakota (Sioux) Nation. Famous leaders Crazy Horse, Red Cloud, and American Horse were Oglala Lakota.

For a taste of Lakota culture, time your visit with the **Oglala Nation Powwow,** (605)

867-5821, which is held each Aug. You can take scenic drives across the reservation, too, watching for spectacular geological formations with romantic names such as Yellow Bear Canyon, Slim Buttes, and Wolf Table. Some bus and van tour companies offer sightseeing tours of the reservation; these are listed in the Getting Here, Getting Around chapter. For information about Pine Ridge scenic drives, events, and tourism, call the Oglala Sioux Tribe's Office of Tourism at (605) 867-5301.

If you'd like to try your money-winning luck, your first stop as you enter the reservation could be the **Prairie Wind Casino,** (605) 867-6300, (800) 705-WIND, off US 18, near the town of Oglala about 50 miles east of Hot Springs. The casino is open 24 hours a day.

Just west of Pine Ridge (about 15 miles south of Oglala) is the **Red Cloud Indian School,** (605) 867-1105, off US 18, founded in 1887 when Chief Red Cloud asked the Jesuits to teach his people. The **Holy Rosary Church,** completed in 1898, was the first brick church west of the Missouri River.

In the original building on the Red Cloud campus (built in 1888), you can tour the **Heritage Center,** (605) 867-5491. The center houses a rich Native American art collection, with paintings, traditional artifacts, sculptures, beadwork and quillwork, and a gift shop. The **Red Cloud Indian Art Show** is sponsored annually by the school, from the first Sunday in June through the third Sunday in Aug. It is the largest juried show of its kind for Native American art in the country and is attended by collectors from all over the world. Other pieces remain on permanent display at the Heritage Center. Ask at the administrative offices (adjacent to the Heritage Center) for a tour of the

cemetery atop the hill, where the grave of the venerable Red Cloud is located. The great chief, who died in 1910, possessed admirable foresight about the education of the children of his people. Many others are buried in the historic cemetery, both Native American and white, including nuns and priests who served at the school.

Next you'll come to the town of **Pine Ridge,** headquarters of Oglala tribal government. And at the intersection of Bureau of Indian Affairs (BIA) Route 27 and US 18, where a sign points to the town of **Wounded Knee,** you'll see a cemetery and church on the hill. Look for a cement block and iron arch at the entrance—it is not otherwise marked. This is the site of the 1890 Wounded Knee Massacre. You can look around without charge, but please don't disturb the offerings you see on the graves. The cemetery is open year-round all day long; if you need information, call the Oglala Tribe's Office of Tourism at (605) 867-5301. A large sign across the highway tells the story; note where the word "Battle" has been corrected to read "Massacre."

EAST OF THE BLACK HILLS
West Central South Dakota

As you head east on I-90, you'll pass some interesting and quaint farming towns. The Badlands and Wall area east of the Black Hills are in their own chapter in this book (see The Badlands & Nearby).

Stop at **Murdo,** 135 miles east of Rapid City, where the line that separates the mountain standard time and central standard time zones is just to the west of the town limits—don't forget to reset your watch! Murdo is the home of the **Pioneer Auto Show and Antique Town,** (605) 669-2691, I-90, exit

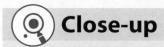

Close-up

The Massacre at Wounded Knee

The **Wounded Knee Massacre** site, on a windswept hill sloping down to a valley and ravines, is a powerful place that marks a shameful incident. Here, in 1890, 14 years after their comrades and commander Lt. Col. George Custer were wiped out at Little Bighorn, and still nursing a grudge, the Seventh Cavalry opened fire on men, women, children, and elderly Lakota of Chief Big Foot's band, including the chief himself, who was dying of pneumonia.

Although the massacre started when an accidental rifle shot panicked the soldiers, eyewitness accounts say the cavalry then methodically hunted down the fleeing people. Bodies—including those of mothers with babies and small children—were found as far as 3 miles away, and many had been shot at close range. Although the military immediately began an investigation, charges against officers were soon dropped, and several soldiers received the Congressional Medal of Honor for their part in the massacre.

It is estimated that 100 to 300 Lakota died that day, or later, from their wounds. Many were found by their kin, taken to camps to die, and buried elsewhere. Of the cavalrymen, 25 died then and 39 were wounded, some of whom died later. Eyewitnesses' and researchers' accounts conflict. Some believe the Lakota were unarmed; others believe that despite being disarmed, a few warriors had hidden guns. Some historians think that many soldiers were killed by their comrades' panicky cross fire. Whatever the historical truth, that night, four days after Christmas, a number of survivors were taken to the nearby Episcopal mission where, it is said, a festive holiday banner still hung. Ironically, it read: "Peace on earth, good will to men."

On the night of the massacre, a blizzard hit, with raging winds and minus 40-degree temperatures. By the time the storm passed and a burial detail arrived, three days had gone by. A 60-foot-long trench was dug at the top of the hill, and frozen Lakota bodies were laid in it, after first being stripped of clothing and possessions, which were sold as artifacts. This grave is now fenced and marked by a monument at the Wounded Knee Cemetery, which is still in use.

Near the mass grave is the burial site of Lost Bird, who, just four months old, miraculously survived frigid temperatures for three days before being discovered beneath her mother's body. Her tragic story is told in *Lost Bird of Wounded Knee* by Renee Sansom Flood. Lost Bird died in 1920 at age 29 in California. In 1991 her remains were returned to Wounded Knee and reburied with her own people.

192, with the country's largest private collection of vehicles. Elvis Presley's motorcycle is there, as are 250 other classics. There are also collections of minerals, antique tractors, old china and crystal, antique clothing, organs and music boxes, and antique toys. The exhibits are housed in 39 buildings on 10 acres that also include a restored town. You can lunch at the food court and shop for gifts and antiques, too. The Pioneer Auto Show is open year-round. Call ahead for current hours and admission charges.

To take a side trip to South Dakota's capital, **Pierre** (pronounced "Peer"), turn off I-90 at exit 212; Pierre is about 35 miles farther north on US 83, and you'll pass through the Fort Pierre National Grassland on your way. The elegant **State Capitol,** (605) 773-3765, in the Capitol Complex between 4th Street and Capitol Avenue, is worth a visit. Built in 1910 with a South Dakota granite foundation and solid copper dome, the building has been restored to its early-1900s glory. Free tours are conducted from 8 a.m. to 5 p.m. Mon through Fri, and must be scheduled in advance at the visitor information center in the capitol.

While you're at the complex, visit Capitol Lake, which hundreds of migrating Canada geese use as a stopover in the fall. You'll also want to see the memorial dedicated to the victims of a 1993 Iowa plane crash that took the life of popular South Dakota governor George S. Mickelson. The centerpiece is a replica of the *Fighting Stallions,* a piece designed by Crazy Horse Memorial sculptor Korczak Ziolkowski in 1935.

Pierre celebrates its visiting Canada geese with the annual **Goosefest** in late Sept. Festivities have included a wine tasting, arts-and-crafts displays, concerts, and the Honker 5K and 10K runs. Call the Pierre Area Chamber of Commerce, (605) 224-7361 or (800) 962-2034, for information about the annual event.

The **Museum of the South Dakota State Historical Society** and the **Cultural Heritage Center,** (605) 775-3458, are also on the Capitol Complex grounds, north of the capitol building. You'll find exhibits on cultural, pioneer, and Native American history, the State Archives (which the public can use for genealogical research), an observation gallery with views of the capitol grounds and Pierre, and a gift shop that carries South Dakota–made products. Admission for those

19 and older is $4; those 18 and younger are admitted free. Hours are 9 a.m. to 4:30 p.m. Mon through Fri, and 1 to 4:30 p.m. Sat and Sun (it's closed for Thanksgiving, Christmas, and New Year's Day).

Kids will enjoy the **South Dakota Discovery Center and Aquarium,** (605) 224-8295, 805 West Sioux, Pierre. It has more than 60 hands-on activities, planetarium shows, and several aquariums with fish from the local aquatic environment (no dolphins or performing sea lions). After Labor Day until Memorial Day, it's open 1 to 5 p.m. Sun through Fri, and 10 a.m. to 5 p.m. Sat. From Memorial Day through Labor Day, it's open from 10 a.m. to 5 p.m. Mon through Sat, and 1 to 5 p.m. Sun. Admission is $4 for those 13 and older, $3 for children 3 to 12, and free for kids younger than 3.

i Just beyond the Black Hills lie prairie flatlands, the Pine Ridge Indian Reservation, the state capital, the broad Missouri River, and numerous pioneer-turned-tourist towns. Neighboring states beckon with attractions, too.

The 231-mile-long **Lake Oahe** reservoir, created from the great Missouri River, stretches from Pierre to Bismarck, North Dakota, and is the fourth largest manmade reservoir in the country. One of the state's greatest recreational treasures, Lake Oahe has more than 2,200 miles of shoreline (nearly twice that of California) and 900 square miles of water. It's a great place to fish for walleye, salmon, bass, and trout or to sail, ski, and windsurf. The Pierre Area Chamber of Commerce, (605) 224-7361 or (800) 962-2034, has more information.

Lake Sharp is another great fishing and recreation waterway, south of Lake Oahe, off SR 47 on the way to Chamberlain. If you're there in the summer, you can also visit nearby **Lower Brule and Crow Creek Indian Reservations** and watch the annual powwows. Or try your luck at the tribes' casinos; the Crow Creek tribe operates the **Lode Star,** (605) 245-6000, and the Lower Brule tribe operates the **Golden Buffalo,** (605) 473-5577. For information about visiting the reservations, call the Crow Creek Sioux Tribal Office at (605) 245-2221 or the Lower Brule Sioux Tribe Office at (605) 473-5399.

Back on I-90, continue to Chamberlain (about 2 miles from exit 263), home of the **Akta Lakota Museum and Cultural Center,** (605) 734-3452 or (800) 798-3452 (there's no address, but you'll see it as you drive through Chamberlain). On the grounds of St. Joseph's Indian School, the museum has been amassing a rich collection of Lakota art and artifacts since the school was founded in 1927. Admission is free, but donations are appreciated. Both a gift shop and a gallery of original art are part of the museum. From May 1 through Sept 30, hours are 8 a.m. to 6 p.m. Mon through Sat and 9 a.m. to 5 p.m. Sun. From Oct 1 through Apr 30, hours are 8 a.m. to 5 p.m. Mon through Fri only.

WEST OF THE BLACK HILLS

Wyoming

Our neighbor to the west is Wyoming. A very small portion of the Black Hills creeps into Wyoming, but the terrain quickly flattens out until you reach the Bighorn Mountains, the start of the Rockies, more than 150 miles to the west. In reality, northeastern Wyoming and western South Dakota are very much alike—not just in geography, but in economy and the attitudes of their residents. It's not unusual for people to live in Wyoming and work in Spearfish or Deadwood, or for Rapid City businesses to serve clients in Gillette and Sheridan.

For your day trip, try the tiny town of **Aladdin** first. Take SR 34 west for about 20 miles from Belle Fourche (SR 34 becomes SR 24 in Wyoming). Just east of town, you'll come to the free **Aladdin Historic Interpretive Park,** site of the coal mine that sustained the town. Only about 15 people live in Aladdin now, and its main attraction is the big old **Aladdin General Store** and post office, (307) 896-2226, right off the highway. It was built in 1896 and still operates both as a supplier to area ranchers and as a tourist draw. The funky store has groceries, gifts, and crafts, and there's a great antiques shop and boutique in the deteriorating, but charming, upstairs. The store is open every day, although hours are shortened a bit in the winter. The **Hard Buck Cafe** next door is a fun place to eat for adventurous visitors who aren't afraid of a casual cleaning philosophy. Ask about the homemade pies.

ℹ Wyoming is affectionately called "The Cowboy State." Ranching is one of the state's most important industries, and the cowboys who make ranching possible are among the state's most beloved assets. A cowboy's likeness is even on Wyoming's license plates.

Then journey on to **Hulett,** (307) 467-5430, where Devils Tower National Monument will appear on the horizon as you approach. You'll be passing through the Bear Lodge district of the Black Hills National Forest and the Bear Lodge Mountains. Hulett

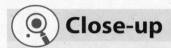

Close-up

Devils Tower National Monument

There is no word for "devil" in the Lakota language. How, then, did **Devils Tower** get its name?

The massive landmark was christened by Col. Richard Dodge in 1875. Dodge and his army troops accompanied the Jenney-Newton expedition, a scientific team ostensibly studying the Black Hills region (although they were also looking for gold). The expedition was in violation of the Fort Laramie Treaty of 1868, which had ceded the Hills to the plains tribes.

Dodge wrote that when he asked Native American scouts about the Black Hills, they responded with what he called "studied silence." Perhaps they hoped the intruders would give up in disappointment and go away. If so, it didn't work. The scouts did say that the enormous tower's name was "bad god's tower," and again, this may have been an attempt to frighten the explorers, whose curiosity was then only more intensely piqued. Dodge decided the proper translation of the tower's name was "Devils Tower."

For centuries, Native people have had great respect for the mystical tower. It was the site of the ancient Sun Dance and is still a place of great power that plays a consecrated part in seasonal rites. The Lakota call it *mato tipi la paha,* "the hill of the bear's lodge." Other tribes revere the tower, too, and have their own names for it.

Several tribes share a legend about its origin: It is said that seven little girls, playing outside their camp, were chased by a huge bear. Frightened, they jumped atop a rock and prayed for help. Hearing their pleas, the rock began to rise, higher and higher above the bear. The angry bear clawed at the rock as it rose, straining to reach its prey until the rock was so high that it had to give up. The little girls were pushed upward into the sky, where they became a group of seven stars, *wicincala sakowin,* the constellation Pleiades. The bear's claw marks are still there on the tower's sides, a legendary reminder, perhaps, of nature's power to aid respectful believers.

is a western logging town with interesting buildings and shops, and the town hosts a rodeo on the second weekend in June.

Nine miles south of Hulett on SR 24 looms **Devils Tower,** (307) 467-5283, which entered into pop culture via the Steven Spielberg film *Close Encounters of the Third Kind.* The formation has another reason for fame, however: it was the first national monument, having received that designation from President Theodore Roosevelt in 1906. The product of ancient volcanic activity, the spectacular tower is 865 feet high, 1,000 feet in diameter at the base, and 1,267 feet

above the Belle Fourche River valley below. The 1.3-mile Tower Trail meanders around the base and past huge granite columns that have fallen from the tower. The 3-mile Red Beds Trail circles the tower and explores the nearby forest and river valley.

Devils Tower National Monument is open year-round, 24 hours a day. You can stay at the campground there from Apr through Oct. The visitor center is open daily 8 a.m. to 8 p.m. May through Oct only, and it has a museum and natural history exhibits. Daily programs and demonstrations on geology, wildlife, history, climbing, and more are

Those less interested in mystical nature and ancient legend offer a scientific explanation: Some 60 million years ago, molten volcanic magma forced its way upward through rock layers but did not break the surface, instead cooling and hardening below. This cooling process caused the volcanic rock to fracture into the huge columns on the tower's sides. Over millions of succeeding years, the softer rock above and around the core eroded away, and the tower rose higher as the rock around it disappeared. The sides of Devils Tower are nearly vertical, all the way to the slightly sloped top, which is about the size of a football field and covered in grasses, sagebrush, and cactus. Small animals—chipmunks, wood rats, snakes—live on the top, having apparently climbed there.

Since 1893 people have climbed the tower, too. That year, two entrepreneurs were first (it's not known if Native Americans climbed the tower), and many thousands followed. In recent decades climbers began to interfere with Native American religious observances still held at the age-old place of worship, creating controversy. In 1995 the National Park Service proposed a plan to curtail climbing during June's traditional summer solstice observances. The 1995 NPS voluntary closure plan was evaluated in 1999, found to be the best solution, and instituted as part of the monument's final management plan. Since the policy went into effect, the number of June climbs each year has held steady at about 250. (By comparison, there are nearly 5,000 climbs at Devils Tower each year, almost entirely between Apr and Oct.) Park officials estimate that 8 out of 10 climbers comply with the ban and refrain from ascending the mountain in June.

Devils Tower National Monument offers many opportunities, recreational and spiritual, for Americans both native and newcomer. The tower itself, however, is above it all. It is simply there, a place of power and wonder, reverence and beauty.

conducted by staff in the summer. The park entrance fee is $10 per vehicle. You can find refreshments at the **Devils Tower Trading Post,** (307) 467-5295, at the entrance to the monument. For more on Devils Tower, see the Close-up in this chapter.

Drive 30 miles down US 14 to Sundance (where the Sundance Kid got his name) and visit the free **Crook County Museum and Art Gallery,** (307) 283-3666, in the courthouse basement at 309 Cleveland. Kids love the exhibits about the Kid, who was tried for horse stealing in town. The museum has the original court records, even the "Wanted"

posters, plus western artifacts and an exhibit devoted to the nearby Vore Buffalo Jump. Each month a local artist exhibits work at the museum, too. It's open year-round, Mon through Fri, 8 a.m. to 8 p.m. in the summer and 8 a.m. to 5 p.m. in the winter.

A visit to the **Vore Buffalo Jump** is a must. Exit I-90 at Beulah and drive 2.5 miles west on the frontage road. Pull off the road at the sign, stop at the new visitor center, walk down the trail, and read the interpretive display there. Over a period of 300 years (beginning in the 1500s), Native American hunters drove 20,000 stampeding bison into a natural sinkhole to their deaths. There the animals were butchered (nearly every part was used) and their bones were left in the hole to slowly compress and be filled in with earth. The Vore site is one of the largest and best-preserved sites of its kind in the world.

The layers of bones (along with tools that were left behind) are some 20 feet deep and can be counted and studied, much like tree rings, to learn about ancient weather and ecological conditions. In the summer you can look over the shoulders of University of Wyoming archaeologists and students as they work. For information about excavation schedules, call (307) 766-5136, (307) 766-2208, or (307) 283-1192. The Vore Buffalo Jump Foundation and the university have raised funds to construct a visitor center, so donations are appreciated.

For more exploring, backtrack 50 miles west on I-90 to Moorcroft, where the Old Texas Trail crosses the Belle Fourche River, and Pine Haven. Nearby **Keyhole State Park and Reservoir,** (307) 756-3596, 353 McKean Rd., has mountain biking, camping in primitive sites and the backcountry, boating and swimming, fishing, and cross-country skiing.

Thirty miles west of Moorcroft is the very wealthy town of **Gillette,** Energy Capital of the Nation, and the **Rockpile Museum,** (307) 682-5723, US 14/16, open all year. Gillette, founded in 1891 and originally a ranching town, is now the largest coal-producing city in the country. In fact, if Gillette and surrounding Campbell County were its own country, it would be the third-largest coal-producing nation in the world. Not bad for a town of fewer than 20,000 people. You can take a tour of one of the 16 mines in the area (summers only). Reserve your place by calling (307) 686-0040.

About 100 miles northwest of Gillette on I-90, a few miles from the Montana border, is the town of **Sheridan.** Only slightly smaller than Gillette, Sheridan sits on the edge of the Bighorn Mountains, a small range of the Rockies that are much taller, younger, and less developed than the Black Hills. You'll find a few modest ski slopes and snowmobile lodges outside town, and some good restaurants and museums, including the **Trail End Historic Site,** (307) 674-4589, and the **Sheridan Inn,** (307) 674-5440. The trip is about 200 miles from Spearfish via I-90, so if you plan on seeing much, you might want to consider making this an overnight trip.

Backtrack east on I-90 to Moorcroft and head south on US 16 to see the towns of Upton and Newcastle. Newcastle (about 50 miles south of Moorcroft, or 40 miles west of Custer) is the home of the free **Anna Miller Museum,** (307) 746-4188, Delaware Washington Park, off US 16, which has local artifacts, fossils, dinosaur bones, dolls, an original stone cavalry barn, treasures from nearby Cambria ghost town, a re-created country store, and old pioneer buildings. The museum is open year-round, Mon through Fri 9 a.m. to 5 p.m. Sat hours (9 a.m. to noon) are added in the summer, but the museum is always closed on Sun. The annual Sagebrush Festival is held in late June in Newcastle; it features cowboy poetry, arts and crafts, and parades.

The Wyoming Division of Tourism, (307) 777-7777 or (800) 225-5996, can provide more information and send you a visitor packet. Or, log on to the tourism website at www.wyomingtourism.org.

THE BADLANDS & NEARBY

Your first glimpse of Badlands National Park might well prompt comparison to a giant, mythological beast or bring to mind a bleak lunar surface. With its stony face and jutting spine, parched soil, and eroded, barren peaks, the Badlands give many visitors the impression of a place long ago forsaken.

Yet this eerie world is very much alive. Get acquainted with it, and you might find yourself warming to those thirsty slopes and windy plains that, like patient teachers, show us how to look beyond the surface. All they ask is that we take time to notice and marvel at their splendor. The more time you spend in the Badlands, the more familiar and precious its features become.

Badlands National Park is a place for meandering and making frequent stops, whether you are traveling by car or on foot. The scene changes minute by minute. The time of day and weather patterns constantly alter the way the Badlands appear. A winter sunset casts over the snow-covered peaks and white, frozen canyons a cloak of orange and gold, while a summer sunrise over the sandy buttes paints the landscape in shades of pink and red. One minute you'll think you're on the moon, and the next you'll imagine that you're on Mars. Perhaps that's why the Badlands have been the set for a few science-fiction movies, including the 1997 flick *Starship Troopers*.

There is much to observe and experience here, and we urge you to do both with care and deliberation. Hike along a dry wash and listen as curled leaves of parched mud crackle beneath your boots. On the compacted hardpan, look back and notice how you leave almost no trace at all. Watch closely as a long-tailed magpie takes flight, white wing patches flashing like outspread, gloved fingers against coalblack wings. Feel the wind brush your face like ghosts bearing ancient dreams.

A long thread of life weaves through the Badlands, both in its rich fossil beds and in stories handed down. Take time to learn and think about the living things, human and otherwise, that have found this to be a good land.

GETTING HERE, GETTING AROUND

There are several entrances to Badlands National Park. Most travelers arrive in the North Unit via I-90; if you're approaching from the east, take exit 131 and follow SR 240 (Badlands Loop Road) for about 3 miles to the park's **Northeast Entrance** and another 5 miles to **Ben Reifel Visitor Center** (see the write-up under Attractions later in this chapter). From the west, take exit 110 at Wall and head straight south on SR 240 for 8 miles to the **Pinnacles Entrance.** Badlands Loop Road links these two entrances.

Once you've arrived, you can pick up a free official map and ask for information and directions at the visitor center. Roads and attractions in the North Unit are well marked with signs to help you find your way. One caution, though: Unpaved roads can be slippery from winter ice or summer rain, so use extra care under those conditions.

From the north or south, Bureau of Indian Affairs (BIA) Road 27 takes you to the **White River Visitor Center** in the southeast corner of the Stronghold (South) Unit, which is on the Pine Ridge Indian Reservation. The Stronghold and nearby Palmer Creek Units, although part of the park, are isolated, undeveloped, and not well suited to tourism. Grazing and subsistence hunting (with a permit) are allowed here, and there is only one official road, unpaved at that; Sheep Mountain Road (off CR 589) narrows and turns from gravel to dirt, winding around until it dead-ends after 7 miles at a sheer drop on top of Sheep Mountain Table. There's the added complexity of private land that can't be crossed without permission—check on local access at visitor centers before you try to enter. And there's always the possibility of stumbling upon unexploded ordnance (UXO) from the gunnery-range days; information about what to do in that event is available at visitor centers.

i Of all the hazards you might encounter in Badlands National Park, lightning looms largest. During a storm, stay off ridges and away from lone trees to avoid being struck.

For a less complicated backcountry experience, consider **Badlands (Sage Creek) Wilderness Area** in the North Unit. (See the Recreation section in this chapter for more information.)

North of the park, **Wall Municipal Airport,** at an altitude of 2,810 feet, has a hard-surface runway rated up to 12,500 pounds for single- and twin-engine planes. Services here are minimal; fuel is available on an emergency basis only, and there are no car rentals or taxis. However, motels, restaurants, and tourist attractions, including world-famous **Wall Drug** (see the Close-up in this chapter) are within easy walking distance (9 blocks or fewer). For airport information, call (605) 279-2666.

Badlands National Park is open all year, and a $30 annual pass allows you unlimited visits. Seven-day passes cost $15 per noncommercial vehicle ($7.50 for Oglala Sioux tribal members). Single-person entry on motorcycle is $10, and on bicycle or foot is $7.50. Admission is free on National Parks Day, August 25.

HISTORY

The Lakota Sioux called it *Mako Sica,* "land that is bad." 18th-century French fur traders who traveled the area spoke of *les mauvaises terres à traverser,* "the bad lands to cross."

Not until the mid–19th century did scientists become convinced that this eerie place, with its rugged cliffs, baked soil, and ferocious weather, was in fact a storehouse brimming with information about the ancient past.

By studying the striated rock formations of the Badlands, researchers have learned that the area was covered by a warm inland sea millions of years ago. Then, as the Black Hills laboriously rose skyward, the sea drained away, and the seabed oxidized. Eons passed, and layers of silt, sand, clay, and volcanic ash were deposited. Today these mineralized layers are seen as varicolored bands sweeping across the craggy landscape.

Through millennia the land underwent many transformations, from dense forest to vast plain to grassland. The climate changed as well, from subtropical to cool and dry. Four-legged creatures roamed and grazed where invertebrates had lived submerged in the sea, and over time the four-leggeds' bones joined those of the sea-dwellers, settling into the earth to turn to stone. The Badlands are now an extensive source of fossils; local rocks from the Oligocene epoch, roughly 25 million to 35 million years ago, contain some of the world's best-known specimens. A fairly recent discovery, known as the Big Pig Dig, yielded the remains of an *Archaeotherium*, or ancient wild boar, and other animals from the Eocene period some 55 million years ago. Scientists digging at the site find more fossils each year, mostly of rhinoceros and boar ancestors. Paleontologists plan to dig each summer until there are no more bones to find, which probably won't be for years. If you'd like to visit the site, contact one of the park's visitor centers (phone numbers appear later in this chapter). Otherwise, you can see some of the Big Pig Dig bones at the Museum of Geology on the campus of South Dakota School of Mines and Technology in Rapid City (see the Attractions chapter).

Eventually, water and wind gouged out cliffs and canyons in the soft sediment, and the climate ripened into extremes of hot and cold. More than 10,000 years ago—recently, in geologic terms—humans appeared in the Badlands, hunting mammoths. (You can see bones and hair from these ancient creatures at Mammoth Site of Hot Springs, which is listed in the Attractions chapter.) Indian tribes followed—first the Arikara and

Badlands Climate

Badlands weather is a lot like the landscape: often harsh and subject to rapid change. Most of the park's million-plus annual visitors arrive during the summer, when the thermometer can easily register three digits. But just as easily, blazing sunshine can give way to a downpour that turns hiking trails and back roads into a gummy mess. Lightning, high winds, hailstorms, flash floods, and tornadoes are other warm-weather hazards for which it is wise to be prepared. The climate is semiarid (annual rainfall is about 15.5 inches). Add to this the prairie winds, and dehydration becomes a very real concern in hot weather, especially if you're hiking or otherwise working up a sweat. Carry plenty of drinking water with you, because opportunities to wet your whistle are few—essentially at facilities in the Cedar Pass area and at the White River Visitor Center (open only during the summer). Sunscreen and suitable clothing are essential.

During the winter, ice storms and blizzards can strike with little warning. Bitter cold and howling winds are to be expected, but so are mild, sunny days and picturesque snowfalls. That said, spring, when baby animals are born and the land greens up, and fall, when the weather is generally more moderate, are lovely times to visit the Badlands.

later the Lakota Sioux—then white trappers, traders, fossil collectors, ranchers, and homesteaders.

In the 1920s, South Dakotan US Sen. Peter Norbeck and Ben Millard, an early Badlands homesteader and founder of the Cedar Pass Lodge (see the listing below, under Accommodations), joined forces to create a national park in the Badlands, an effort actually begun by the South Dakota Legislature in 1909. President Franklin Roosevelt issued a proclamation establishing Badlands National Monument in 1939, three years after Norbeck's death. In 1976 the monument expanded to include the Stronghold (South) and Palmer Creek units, both on Pine Ridge Indian Reservation land that had been used as a gunnery range during World War II. In 1978 the monument achieved national park status through an act of Congress; today Badlands National Park contains 244,000 acres.

i | Badlands rock formations make a perfect reflective surface for sunlight. It's a good idea to wear sunscreen and a pair of sunglasses while touring the park, even during the winter.

THE NATURAL WORLD

The towering, 60-mile-long **Badlands Wall** dominates the Badlands moonscape with a series of eroded ridges and valleys running from the northeast to the southwest. Other, smaller rock formations have inspired comparisons to everything from castles and ancient ruins to oversized ribs and toadstools.

So it might surprise you to know that wide-open, mixed-grass prairies, not barren rocks, make up most of the Badlands. Some 170,000 acres nourish more than 50 species of grass (about 70 percent are native)

and numerous varieties of wildflowers that flourish from early spring until the first hard freeze. Yellow plains prickly pear, pale green yucca, golden prairie coneflower, and white snow-on-the-mountain are just a few of the varieties of flowers to be seen. Theodore Van Bruggen's *Wildflowers, Grasses & Other Plants of the Northern Plains and Black Hills* is a color-coded guide to local plants that you might find useful; also, a brochure titled *Badlands Nature Guide* is handy for identifying fauna as well as flora. Both publications can be purchased at the park.

A program of prescribed burns has been instituted in recent years to promote a balanced ecosystem in much the same way as wildfires of the past did, by recycling nutrients into the soil and promoting the natural succession of plant species.

Trees and shrubs are scarce in the Badlands, growing for the most part near creek drainages. Most notable are the aromatic Rocky Mountain junipers that give **Cedar Pass** its name. You can get a close look at these trees and enjoy their cooling shade on the **Cliff Shelf Trail** (see the listing below under Recreation). Cliff Shelf is a slump, a place where surface runoff collects as it drains underground, thus providing sufficient water to nourish a sizable stand of trees.

Other forms of life find sustenance in **Badlands National Park,** which is a key player in efforts to save the black-footed ferret from extinction. These black-masked members of the weasel family prey on prairie dogs and live in their holes, and ferrets bred in captivity have been reintroduced to the wild here. You're not likely to see ferrets in the park, though, because the nocturnal little burrowers spend almost all their time underground. In the event of a sighting, however, please watch from a respectful distance—binoculars or a telephoto camera lens will give you a close-up look—so as not to disturb these endangered creatures. (For more on these creatures, see the Close-up in the Natural World chapter.) Prairie dogs, on the other hand, are commonly seen—try **Roberts Prairie Dog Town** on Sage Creek Rim Road in the western portion of the park.

Audubon bighorn sheep were native to the Black Hills and Badlands, but unregulated hunting pushed the entire species to extinction sometime in the 1920s. Four decades later some closely related Rocky Mountain bighorn sheep were introduced to the park to take their place. Around the same time bison—barely saved from extinction—were reintroduced to the Badlands.

Wolves, elk, and bears no longer roam here. (Whether bears actually inhabited the Badlands is in dispute.) You might see antelope, deer, rabbits, coyotes, foxes, badgers, grouse, and many other animals as you explore the park, but remember that they are wild and potentially dangerous. Keep your distance no matter how placid they seem—the rule of thumb is, if an animal responds to your presence, you're too close. Be on the lookout for poisonous prairie rattlesnakes, especially around prairie dog holes, rocky areas, grass, and brush.

And remember, the only things you're allowed to take home from the park are your memories. Removing or harming the plants, animals, minerals, fossils, and other features is a federal offense, and it spoils the park for others. If you come upon fossils, notify a park ranger so the specimens can be handled professionally.

ACCOMMODATIONS

With all the fascinating things to see and do in and around Badlands National Park,

you may need a place to stay for a night or two, or even longer. Several good motels are listed below. Major credit cards are accepted.

i The best time to take pictures in the Badlands is when the sun is low in the sky and the softer light enhances the color in the rock formations. The harsher light of midday makes them appear almost white.

Price Code

Prices are for double occupancy during the peak season—generally, June, July, and Aug. Inquire about off-season rates and senior discounts.

$..................... **Less than $50**
$$ .... **$50 to $75**
$$$ .... **More than $75**

Badlands National Park

CEDAR PASS LODGE $–$$$
Cedar Street, Interior
(in Badlands National Park)
(605) 433-5460
www.cedarpasslodge.com
An unobstructed view of the open prairie, rocky spires, and deep canyons of the Badlands is the primary feature of these 24 cabins in the eastern end of the park. Aside from two primitive campgrounds operated by the National Park Service, these modest lodgings are the only accommodations within park boundaries. The lodge operators—a private company that manages marinas, inns, and resorts in national parks across the country—assume that you'll spend most of your time exploring the park, not holed up in your room. Subsequently, the cabins are furnished with little more than the bare essentials: twin beds, air-conditioning, a sink,

and a bathtub. Of course, amenities matter little when you realize that there's nowhere else in the world where you can wake up to the deep pink and purple hues of a Badlands sunrise, accompanied by the sounds of a western meadowlark or mountain bluebird. Also on-site at the lodge are a small restaurant (see the listing later in this chapter), pay phones, a gift shop, and a cottage with a full kitchen that sleeps up to 10 guests. Pets are allowed, but there is a $5 fee. The entire lodge, including the restaurant, closes down in mid-Oct and doesn't open again until early May; the exact dates depend on weather. The complex is located 5 miles from the park's Northeast Entrance off SR 240.

Nearby

ANN'S MOTEL $$
114 Fourth Ave., Wall
(605) 279-2501
Nineteen clean, cozy units and more than the usual amenities make this a homeaway-from-home kind of place. Whether you choose two double beds or one queen, you get a small refrigerator, microwave, coffeepot, phone, and remote cable TV in your room. Add a tub-shower combo and you've got all the basics and then some. Pets are allowed, but you can't leave them alone in your room.

BADLANDS BUDGET HOST MOTEL $$
SR 377, Interior
(605) 433-5335, (800) 388-4643,
(800) BUD-HOST
www.badlandsbudgethostmotel.com
The 21 units here are simply appointed but adequate and reasonably roomy, and you can choose either two double beds or two queen-size. If a hot soak is on your list of must-dos, ask for a room with a tub-shower

combination; some have a shower only. You won't have a phone in your room, but you will have a coffeepot, and there is a pay phone you can use. There's also a laundry at your disposal and a restaurant that serves simple, all-you-can eat breakfasts and suppers. The motel shares the grounds with Badlands Interior Campground, which is listed in the Campground section of this chapter. Open from May 1 to Sept 31, the motel is near the Interior Entrance to Badlands National Park, on the southeast end of the park and the north end of Interior.

BEST WESTERN PLAINS MOTEL $$-$$$
712 Glenn St., Wall
(605) 279-2145, (800) 528-1234
http://bestwesternplains.com
You'll get the royal treatment at this sparkling-clean place, where the beds come in either king- or queen-size. Best of all, you can choose family accommodations with two beds in a separate room for the kids. All 74 rooms have a tub-shower combination, coffeepot, phone, and TV with movie channel. There's a heated outdoor swimming pool and a game room. The lobby has free coffee and a gift shop with clothing and western gifts. Pets are allowed, and plenty of nonsmoking rooms are available.

SUPER 8 MOTEL $$
711 Glenn St., Wall
(605) 279-2688, (800) 800-8000
www.super8.com
This attractive, 29-room motel has a couple of outstanding features: a wheelchair-accessible room and extra-long double beds. (You can get a queen-size bed if you prefer.) Nonsmokers will appreciate the availability of smoke-free rooms. Other comforts include free local

calls, cable TV with Showtime, tub-shower combinations, and free coffee in the lobby during the morning and evening. Babies have the use of a free crib and are welcome, but pets are not.

CAMPGROUNDS

Badlands National Park has two campgrounds with minimal amenities, plus backcountry camping opportunities for the strong of heart and back (see the Recreation section later in the chapter). Regardless of your camping preferences, it's important to keep in mind that campfires are not allowed anywhere in the park. If you plan to cook, bring along a camp stove or, if you're staying in a campground, a small charcoal grill. The same arid conditions that make fire such a hazard also make drinking water essential, and unless you stay at Cedar Pass Campground, which has potable water, make sure you take a good supply with you.

Group camping is available in Cedar Pass Campground for $2.50 per person, with a minimum fee of $25 per night. Groups must have a designated leader and make advance reservations by writing to Group Camping, Badlands National Park, P.O. Box 6, Interior, 57750, faxing (605) 433-5404, or calling (605) 433-5235 or (605) 433-5361. Otherwise, campsites are available on a first-come, first-served basis; for information call (605) 433-5361.

Private campgrounds are available outside the park, and you'll find two shady ones listed here. Both are just a short distance away.

Badlands National Park

CEDAR PASS CAMPGROUND
SR 377, Interior
(605) 433-5361

About 100 sites are available for tents and RVs. You won't find hookups here, but the restrooms have flush toilets and electricity. When winter comes, however, the restrooms (and the RV dump station) are closed, but if you're a diehard camper, you'll gladly make do with pit toilets. Running water is available year-round from a spigot near the group loop area (which is the only section of the campground open during the winter). On hot days you'll welcome the relative shade of the covered picnic tables. Stays are limited to 14 days and cost $14 per night year-round. The campground is a short distance south of Ben Reifel Visitor Center and is well marked.

SAGE CREEK PRIMITIVE CAMPGROUND
Sage Creek Rim Road
(605) 433-5361

There's no charge for your stay of up of to 14 days here. Presently, there are unlimited sites to pitch a tent or park an RV, but the only comforts are picnic tables and two pit toilets. Be sure to bring your own water. The campground, which is 10 miles west of the park's Pinnacles Entrance, offers a semi-wilderness experience without the hazards of more remote places, plus it's a good starting point for treks into Badlands Wilderness Area, listed later. There are two areas with tie-offs for horse camping. Ask at the visitor centers for information and a brochure explaining horse regulations.

Nearby

BADLANDS INTERIOR CAMPGROUND
SR 377, Interior
(605) 433-5335, (800) 388-4643
www.badlandsbudgethostmotel.com

This modest little campground is surrounded by great views of the Badlands in all

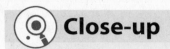 **Close-up**

Wall Drug

The signs are everywhere. Paris. Vietnam. The North Pole. And of course you'll see the signs for miles along I-90 long before you get to the town of Wall in western South Dakota: ALL ROADS LEAD TO WALL DRUG. SHOOTIN' GALLERY, WALL DRUG. WALL DRUG OR BUST. And the most famous sign of all, the one that got things started: FREE ICE WATER. It was a sweltering summer day in 1936 when Dorothy Hustead told her husband, Ted, that hot and thirsty travelers on the nearby highway would stop at their store, a pharmacy and soda fountain, if they knew they could get a free drink of ice water there. To spread the word, Dorothy said, they should post a series of signs along the road. Tourists have been flocking to Wall Drug ever since, and the business now takes up an entire city block, forming the heart of Wall (population about 900)—and still giving away ice water 361 days a year. (It's closed on Thanksgiving, Christmas, New Year's Day, and Easter.)

Wall Drug (officially, Wall Drug Store, Inc.) is still a Hustead family business, too. Now it's in the capable hands of Ted and Dorothy's grandsons, Teddy and Rick—the third generation. But what's the big attraction?

If Wall Drug had been founded 10 years ago rather than deep into the dirty 1930s, it would be nothing more than a big roadside tourist trap. However, its Depression-era roots, combined with some hokey western enthusiasm, give the store (which can just as easily be called an attraction) an almost irresistible appeal. Where else in the world can shelves of blue jeans and racks of leather chaps sit side by side with boxes full of tacky plastic snakes and rubber tomahawks?

But if shopping for turquoise jewelry and snow globes isn't your thing, not to worry. There's the Travelers Chapel (with antique stained glass), a poorly mechanized Cowboy Orchestra, and concrete dinosaurs to keep you entertained. Or, if you're in the minority of visitors who are really there for medicine, you can talk to a pharmacist and obtain any number of prescription or over-the-counter products.

Although visitors almost never tire of poking around to discover the latest cheap souvenir, they rarely leave without a visit to the Western Art Gallery Cafe. Its wooden walls are crowded with original western paintings, antique cowboy gear, and the brands of many area ranchers. The cafe serves any number of home-style dishes, from simple buffalo burgers and BLTs to steak dinners and homemade apple pie. Traditionalists will appreciate the authentic soda fountain and the stainless-steel tub and ladle in the corner, where visitors still serve themselves free cups of ice water.

The best part of the cafe, however, is the doughnuts. Locals swear by them. The dining room is filled with area ranchers and businessmen in the early morning hours, and almost all of them start their day with a cup of five-cent coffee and a couple of these cholesterol-laden pastries, which come plain, maple iced, or chocolate iced. Feel free to take a dozen back home with you, but know this: They taste much better if you heat them up a little bit first.

Wall is 50 miles east of Rapid City along I-90 and 8 miles north of the Pinnacles Entrance to Badlands National Park on SR 240 (the Badlands Loop Road). But approach from any direction, and we guarantee you won't have any trouble finding Wall Drug—all signs point that way. Once there, be sure to stop by the drug counter or the checkout stand in the souvenir department and ask for, you guessed it, a free WALL DRUG sign.

directions, and a generous sprinkling of trees and grass provides a nice contrast to the stark moonscape. Some 60 sites for tents and RVs, a swimming pool, playground, laundry, restrooms with showers, small convenience store, an arcade, and a restaurant serving basic breakfasts and suppers for a small charge take care of your basic needs when you're not out roaming. Full and partial hookups and a dump station are available. There are also two air-conditioned camping cabins and a 21-unit motel, which is described in the Accommodations listed earlier. If you're interested in an extended stay, the friendly owners let out a handful of mobile-home units. Be sure to inquire well before the summer season, however, because they get reserved quickly. The basic camping rate for two people is $16, with an additional charge for hookups. Cabins are $29.95 with air-conditioning. The campground is open from May 1 until Sept 31 and is on the north end of Interior, a short drive from the park's Interior entrance.

BADLANDS/WHITE RIVER KOA
SR 44, Interior
(605) 433-5337, (800) 562-3897
With more than 700 shade trees, this is a cooling, restful place to come home to after a day spent exploring under a searing Badlands sun. Situated on the south bank of the White River, the campground has 56 grassy tent sites (six with water and electricity), 81 RV sites (38 with full hookups, 43 with water and electricity), and 8 camping cabins. A swimming pool, playground, nine-hole minigolf course, and game room provide recreation, but you might find yourself perfectly content to simply lap up the peace and quiet at this "oasis in the Badlands," as it calls itself. Showers, laundry facilities,

and a dump station are provided, and a convenience store sells groceries, supplies, and souvenirs. A modestly priced pancake breakfast is available. The campground is open from Apr 15 to Oct 15. Rates for two adults start at $20 per night for a tent site and $26 for an RV site; hookups are extra. A night in a cabin costs $34. Campers ages five and younger stay for free. The campground is 4 miles southeast of Interior.

RESTAURANTS

It would be hard to visit the Badlands and not work up an appetite. There are plenty of places serving good food throughout the area. Unless otherwise noted, major credit cards are accepted.

Price Code
Prices are for two dinners not including appetizers, drinks, dessert, tax, or tip.

$.................. Less than $15
$$ .... $15 to $30

Badlands National Park

CEDAR PASS RESTAURANT $$
1 Cedar St., Interior
(in Badlands National Park)
(605) 433-5460
The first things you're likely to notice when you enter the dining room are the huge windows along two walls. Since you seat yourself, you can pick the booth or table with the view you want. The house specialty is Indian tacos (made with meat for dinner or scrambled eggs for breakfast), but trout and grilled halibut sound equally irresistible after a day of vigorous exploring. Sandwiches, buffalo burgers, steaks, chops, and ribs also are among the choices. You can have bottled beer or a glass of wine with your meal, but

not a smoke. The restaurant serves breakfast, lunch, and dinner daily from around Apr 1 until Oct 31. It's on SR 240, 5 miles from the park's Northeast Entrance.

Nearby

CACTUS CAFE AND LOUNGE $$
519 Main St., Wall
(605) 279-2561
Steaks and Mexican entrees such as Butch's Barnbuster—a large burrito smothered in green-chili gravy—are the specialties at this cafe, which has been run by three generations of the Beach family for more than 40 years. (It's been in existence much longer than that, though.) Other choices include daily specials and a soup, salad, and fruit bar (although it's not available during the winter). There's ordinary fare such as chicken strips, sandwiches, fish, and pasta, but you'll also find veggie burgers and, among the appetizers, breaded gizzards. Carrot cake and homemade pies appear on the dessert list. The decor is simple but dressed up a bit with brick arches and hanging planters. In the lounge, which has a full bar (plus a pool table and other diversions), there's a mural depicting scenes of early prairie life, including the building of the railroads. The cafe serves breakfast, lunch, and dinner daily all year.

ELKTON HOUSE RESTAURANT $–$$
203 South Blvd., Wall
(605) 279-2152
Low-fat and low-calorie items distinguish this eatery. You'll have to ask for them, but nonfat sour cream, zero-cholesterol margarine, low-fat salad dressing, and steamed seafood and chicken are available. The rest of the menu is a mix of typical chicken sandwiches and grilled fish along with more distinctive dishes including buffalo burgers. The

restaurant ages all of its own beef for steaks. There's a soup and salad bar, too. Bottled beer is available. Elkton House serves breakfast, lunch, and dinner daily, year-round.

✳WALL DRUG $$
510 Main St., Wall
(605) 279-2175
www.walldrug.com
This legendary attraction—known for free ice water and nickel coffee—has cafeteria service and a cafe with seating for more than 500. The fare is simple—burger baskets, soup and sandwiches, and the like—but wine is available. Breakfast, lunch, and dinner are served daily all year; during the summer a sub shop and restaurant serving low-fat food are open in the Back Yard. Although the food services here do a brisk business, there's far more to Wall Drug than you can imagine. See the Close-up in this chapter to learn more.

ATTRACTIONS

Strictly speaking, the Badlands are one big attraction all in themselves. But we've listed the primary tourist draws, which are located along Badlands Loop Road in the North Unit of the park and within a few miles of its northern boundary.

Badlands National Park

✳BADLANDS LOOP ROAD
SR 240, Badlands National Park
www.nps.gov/badl
Badlands Loop Road is the most heavily traveled road in the park, doubtless because it takes you to the most popular hiking trails and overlooks. Points of interest along the road are well marked, and all are worth stopping for. The wheelchair-accessible Fossil

Exhibit Trail, for instance, is a short, circular boardwalk along which you'll find "fossils under glass"—replicas of fossils found in the area and displayed in boxes with domed, heavy plastic lids. Bigfoot Pass Overlook tells a poignant tale of a doomed people and a dying leader trapped between two worlds. (You'll find more information about the 1890 Wounded Knee Massacre in the Day Trips & Weekend Getaways chapter.) At the Yellow Mounds Overlook you'll see low, ancient hills that oxidized and turned yellow after the inland sea receded. There are other sights that you won't want to miss, so plan to take your time.

i If you encounter a rattlesnake, stop and back away slowly or allow the snake to retreat. Don't make sudden moves. Once the coast is clear, proceed on your way. If you get bitten, contact a park ranger at (605) 433-5361 or seek medical attention. The closest facility with antivenin is Rapid City Regional Hospital; call (605) 341-8222 for the emergency department.

BEN REIFEL VISITOR CENTER
SR 240, Interior
(605) 433-5361
www.nps.gov/badl

A stop at this visitor center 5 miles from the park's Northeast Entrance will make your journey through the Badlands more meaningful. By studying the geologic displays, you'll be able to recognize a variety of natural features throughout the park and understand how they came to be formed. Cultural displays will help you appreciate the area's human history. In the exhibit area, you'll get acquainted with the park's flora and fauna. Every half hour during the summer

season and by request during the winter, you can view an 18-minute video on the natural and cultural history of the area; it's shown in audio and closed-caption versions simultaneously. Afterward, you might want to browse the Badlands Nautral History Association Bookstore. Services at the center also include information, restrooms, water, a public pay phone, and brochures in German and French.

The center is named for the late Oglala Lakota leader Benjamin Reifel, known to his tribe as Wiyaka Wanjila, or Lone Feather. Reifel was superintendent of the Pine Ridge Indian Reservation, a US congressman, and the US commissioner of Indian affairs. The center is open year-round; summer hours are 7 a.m. to 8 p.m. daily, with reduced hours at other times. The visitor center is closed Thanksgiving, Christmas, and New Year's days.

NATURALIST PROGRAMS
(605) 433-5361

Free educational programs are available each day during the summer, including evening talks and Night Sky programs that begin at dusk at the Cedar Pass Campground amphitheater. Times and topics (such as Badlands natural or human history, fossils, geology, and animals) are posted on park bulletin boards at Ben Reifel Visitor Center, Cedar Pass Lodge, and park campgrounds. Programs offered recently included the Prairie Walk, Geology Walk, and Fossil Talks. Check bulletin boards for information. The park newsletter, The Badlands Visitor Guide (you'll get a copy when you pay your entrance fee), lists regularly scheduled programs; you can ask at the visitor center about additional, special programs.

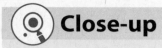

Close-up

Stronghold Table

In a last, desperate attempt to make their world right again, Lakota Sioux ghost dancers gathered at **Stronghold Table**, a remote sod table in what is now the Stronghold (South) Unit of Badlands National Park, to hold ceremonies in late 1890.

The ghost dance belonged to a religion preached by Paiute prophet Wovoka, who promised that the Messiah would restore the old ways. Purifying themselves and eschewing violence, adherents danced in a circle, appealing to their deceased relatives and praying for a miracle to drive out the white invaders and bring back the buffalo.

Whites, viewing the ghost dance as a threat to their own safety and objectives, and hearing reports that ghost dancers wore special shirts to protect them from bullets, were suspicious and tried to repress the ceremonies. Efforts to prevent ghost dancing led to the death of Chief Sitting Bull, who was killed December 15, 1890, by Native American police sent to keep him from joining the ghost dancers on Stronghold Table. Two weeks later, on December 29, the Wounded Knee Massacre took place when the Seventh Cavalry intercepted Chief Big Foot's band, believed to be en route to Stronghold Table but in fact bound for Pine Ridge to meet with Chief Red Cloud in a quest for peace. You can read more about Wounded Knee in the Day Trips & Weekend Getaways chapter.

WHITE RIVER VISITOR CENTER
Junction of BIA Roads 27 and 2
Badlands National Park
(605) 455-2878
www.nps.gov/badl
The center, cooperatively managed by the Pine Ridge Indian Reservation and the National Park Service (and on reservation land), features displays on Lakota Sioux history and culture. There's also a video you won't want to miss, *The Great Plains Experience*, which originally aired on public TV. Information, maps, restrooms, and water are available, too. The center is open from late May through Aug, from 10 a.m. to 4 p.m. daily.

i Although Badlands National Park is in South Dakota, other badlands are found in other states, including North Dakota, Wyoming, and Montana. The South Dakota badlands are sometimes referred to as the Big Badlands or the White River Badlands to distinguish them from the others.

Nearby

BUFFALO GAP NATIONAL GRASSLAND
South of Wall and southeast of
Hot Springs
(605) 279-2125
Don't be deceived. If you think you know about grass—that it's boring stuff—think again. Natural prairie grasslands aren't your suburban backyard. Home to prairie dogs, fox, prairie chicken, pheasant, bison, and coyotes, grasslands are vibrant places rich

Grassland Visitor Tips

- It's important to get information and a map at the visitor center before entering the grassland. Camping here is primitive, with no designated campgrounds or concessions. There are no established hiking trails and only one bike trail, but you can trek cross-country or follow a road or animal path.

- Grassland regulations are different from those for a national forest: You can pick wildflowers and hunt for rocks, and it's illegal to remove or disturb only the vertebrate fossils. You can dig for agate southwest of Kadoka and east of the old town of Conata, too; the exact sites are on the map.

- If you drive in (four-wheel drive or high-clearance vehicles are recommended), stay on the roads and close all gates behind you. Don't disturb the cattle. Don't cross private land without prior permission, and do be aware that it's hard to identify that land without a map.

- You'll need to pack everything in with you and pack it back out. Take plenty of water, and watch your campfire; this is semiarid, windy country. The folks at the visitor center ask that you use common sense about fires, and they'll tell you if fire danger is high while you are there.

- The grasslands are home to many wildlife species. You might see pronghorn antelope, deer, meadowlarks, sharp-tailed grouse, hawks and eagles, badgers and weasels, fox, and prairie dogs. Watch out for prairie rattlers, too. For advice on handling wildlife encounters, see the Natural World chapter.

- Remember that you're miles from anywhere and possibly from anybody. If your vehicle becomes stuck in wet clay after a rain or you get into trouble, help is a long way off. Use common sense and lots of caution.

- The best approach to the grasslands is to drive into one of the vast Buffalo Gap areas and park your car. Get out and look around. This is your exercise in subtlety. Take close looks at everything. This country will not shout at you or perform for your benefit; it's up to you to pay attention. If you're used to smaller, closer landscapes, all that treeless vastness may unnerve you at first.

with life. Modern living is often about speed and special effects, high color and haste. The grasslands, though indifferent to your presence, force you to slow down and look carefully. Their mysteries are not revealed to those in a hurry. Be sure to stop at the National Grasslands Visitor Center on Main Street in Wall (there's no admission charge).

When the Great Plains, in the heart of the United States, were first explored in the 1800s, the early explorers called it "the Great American Desert." They considered it a wasteland. But as the United States grew and civilization in the East pushed westward, there was a clamor for more room. All that vast emptiness in the middle of the country was available, so the government passed the Homestead Act of 1862. The cry of "Free land!" soon went up, and adventurous folks were on the move westward to the Great Plains.

The migration continued until the early 1920s. Up to that time, prairie farmers and ranchers had been relatively successful. There was enough rain, and the market for wheat and cattle was strong. Unfortunately, no one understood that the Great Plains are much more fragile than they appear. By the mid-1920s the plains had been overgrazed and overcultivated and were ripe for the disaster that soon struck. The combination of the Depression, drought, and high winds of the 1930s added to the land's burden. It is estimated that during those dust-bowl years, 2.5 million homesteaders gave up in despair and abandoned their ranches and farms.

In 1934 the federal government's Resettlement Administration began to purchase both never-owned and abandoned acreage, eventually amassing more than 10 million acres and relocating thousands of failed homesteaders. In 1937 the Soil Conservation Service began to "rehabilitate" the wind-eroded land. Using Civilian Conservation Corps and Works Progress Administration labor, shelter belts and stock ponds were created and new grass was seeded.

In 1954 the management of the grass-lands was transferred to the USDA Forest Service, and in 1960 nearly four million acres were designated national grasslands. The 20 national grasslands throughout the United States serve as multiple-use public land. Ranchers graze their livestock there, by permit, and have built stock tanks on the land at their own expense; the stock tanks water both livestock and wildlife. Hunting and fishing are also allowed (state laws apply).

Buffalo Gap National Grassland covers more than 591,000 acres of prairie and bad-lands, and there is no admission charge to enjoy it. On a detailed map (which you're encouraged to pick up at the National Grass-lands Visitor Center), you'll see it is not a "solid" mass of land; its blocks of acreage are mixed with private and state-owned property. The eastern half of the grassland, for example, is near Badlands National Park, and the western half is south of the Black Hills. Buffalo Gap is one of three South Dakota national grasslands; the others are Fort Pierre and Grand River, which you can read about in the Day Trips & Weekend Get-aways chapter.

You're not likely to see other people or vehicles, an exhilarating experience in itself. The wind may be ferocious, the sky an extraordinarily blue bowl above you, but the silence is the best of all. Listen—you won't hear a freeway, siren, or radio, only the sound the wind makes as it rushes past. The grass ripples like the ocean, prairie surf without roar or spray but comparable in majesty and beauty.

PRAIRIE HOMESTEAD
SR 240, Philip
(605) 433-5400
www.prairiehomestead.com
You'll experience something rare at this orig-inal 1909 sod dugout: an authentic sense of life on a prairie homestead, with all of its hardships and rewards. It's not hard to imag-ine the covered wagon coming to a stop at this spot, to picture Ed and Alice Brown

and their son, Charles, newly arrived from Nebraska, scanning the landscape and saying, "Yes, here. This is home."

The family dug a hole into a low hillside, plowed bricks from the hard soil, and built themselves a sod house with a kitchen and a bedroom. Later, they dug a root cellar, built a chicken coop and barn, and moved a wooden claim shack into place beside the "soddie"—then they had a proper parlor where they could relax and entertain their neighbors.

Ed Brown died in 1920, but Alice stayed on the homestead with Charles until 1934, when she moved to California. The sod house was last occupied by bachelor George Carr until 1949, and then, abandoned, it started to decay. But in 1962 Keith Crew (who never lived more than 2 miles from the site) and his wife, Dorothy, started restoration work on the place. Today you can tour the grounds and authentically furnished buildings (still owned by the Crew family) at your own pace while prairie dogs scamper and scold, chickens roam and peck in the sweet-smelling grass, and the calls of songbirds drift on the air like voices from the past. Take it all in, and you'll understand why the Browns and thousands like them were willing to sacrifice creature comforts to build a life on the Great Plains.

Prairie Homestead was entered into the National Register of Historic Places in 1974, and numerous prestigious publications carried articles about it—many of them are posted on the wall outside the gift shop. The shop has an excellent assortment of books about prairie life, featuring collections of Laura Ingalls Wilder, Willa Cather, and Mari Sandoz.

The homestead, which is 2 miles south of I-90, exit 131, is open for tours during daylight hours between mid-Apr and mid-Oct. Admission prices are $6 for adults, and $5 for seniors, and $4 for youths ages 11 to 17, and under 11 are free with parent.

WILD WEST HISTORICAL WAX MUSEUM
601 Main St., Wall
(605) 279-2915

From Sitting Bull and the Sundance Kid to John Wayne and the James Gang, the displays here tell the ripsnortin' version of western history. You'll meet famous outlaws such as Billy the Kid as well as some whose names might be less familiar, like Clay Allison. But there are "good guys" in this hall of fame, too, including "Little Sure Shot" Annie Oakley, courageous Sacagawea, and a trusty Pony Express rider. Signs and taped narratives give lots of details about each of the 50 wax figures (although historians might take issue with a couple of pieces of information). You can see displays of barbed wire, antique cavalry swords, silver dollars, old photos, and more. There's a gift shop with jewelry, souvenirs, books, and CDs.

The museum is open from early May until mid-Oct or later. Summer hours are 8 a.m. to 8 p.m. Admission (which also gets you a coupon for post-tour free popcorn) is $4.50 for adults ages 16 to 61, $4 for seniors 62 and older, $2.50 for youths 6 to 15, and free for kids 5 and younger. Inquire about discounts for groups of 10 or more.

KIDSTUFF

Badlands National Park

JUNIOR RANGER PROGRAM
Badlands National Park
(605) 433-5361
www.nps.gov/badl

Summer programs for kids preschool, ages 5 to 8 and 9 to 12 allow youngsters to learn about the fascinating Badlands in entertaining ways. By picking up a free Junior Ranger booklet at Ben Reifel Visitor Center, kids are on their way to adventure. Once they complete the book, which usually takes a couple of hours, and have it signed by a park ranger, they receive a free certificate and badge. Ask at the visitor center about other summer kids' programs. Discovery hikes, games, and other activities are offered on certain days.

Nearby

WALL DRUG
510 Main St., Wall
(605) 279-2175
www.walldrug.com
You're not afraid of a little dinosaur, are you? Well, how about a big one? For a roarin' good time, visit the (mechanical) T. rex in the Back Yard at Wall Drug—he speaks his mind about every 15 minutes. Less intimidating are the 6-foot rabbit, Singing Sam the Gorilla Man, and a hitch of singing reindeer. A tepee from the movie *Dances with Wolves* and a video arcade offer hands-on fun. The Back Yard closes for the winter, but there's lots more stuff inside. Read all about Wall Drug, where admission is free, in the Close-up in this chapter.

RECREATION

Many who visit Badlands National Park are "windshield" tourists, folks who like to view the scenery from the comfort of their vehicles but who never get out and explore. Such visitors are missing out on the best part, as the enticing recreational opportunities in the listings below demonstrate.

This section deals only with the park because, Wall Drug notwithstanding (see the Close-up in this chapter), that's the main attraction in this part of the country. Here we give information on hiking, backpacking, and horseback riding. If you bring your bicycles, you'll be required to stay on the paved and unpaved roads; bikes are not allowed in the park's backcountry or on hiking trails. Climbing in the park is limited to scrambling, since the soft, crumbly rock that makes up Badlands cliffs won't support standard climbing gear.

The following advice applies to any remote area, but especially to the Badlands. First, take a compass and topographic map (available for around $10 at park visitor centers) whenever you venture away from the roads. Weather changes very quickly here in any season; in fact, temperatures have been known to jump or drop 40 degrees or more in a single day, windchill notwithstanding. Be prepared with equipment and clothing. Beware of any trails after a good rain, as the soft, clay-ridden earth is prone to become a sticky mud called gumbo, which is infamous for trapping both car tires and hiking boots. Most important, take your own water, and lots of it—at least a gallon per person per day. Most of the creek beds here are dry, but even when they flow the water in them is too chalky to filter. And, as always, if you pack it in, pack it out.

Hiking & Backpacking

Badlands National Park Hiking Trails
A number of mostly short, mostly easy trails are accessible from **Badlands Loop Road** in the park's North Unit—this well-traveled route and the wheelchair-accessible **Fossil Exhibit Trail** are covered in the Attractions section of this chapter.

Other popular trails include the half-mile **Cliff Shelf Nature Trail,** which meanders along a dirt track interspersed with wooden stairs and takes you through a cool, fragrant bower of Rocky Mountain junipers. At the end of the 600-yard-long **Door Trail,** it's not too hard to block out traffic noise and imagine the vast, bleak silence that greeted early denizens and explorers in the Badlands. Both of these trails, which are north of the Ben Reifel Visitor Center, have self-guiding brochures available.

To the west of the visitor center is **Saddle Pass Trail.** A mere two-tenths of a mile long, it's still a demanding climb from the base of the Badlands Wall, and you'll want to be in good condition before you attempt it. Make sure you carry your water bottle and camera in a pack, because the trail is covered with a layer of loose, crumbly soil and you'll need to use your hands when the scrambling gets tough, especially on the way down. But your effort will be rewarded by a terrific view at the top. You might want to keep going by picking up the **Castle Trail** (you can go east or west) or the **Medicine Root Loop,** which heads east for 2 miles and leads you back to the Castle Trail. The Castle Trail links the Badlands Loop Road (from the Door Trail parking lot) and the Fossil Exhibit Trail and can be done as a 5-mile, end-to-end excursion through badlands and prairie or taken in sections. Free maps available in the park will help you decide.

Badlands (Sage Creek) Wilderness Area

If you've ever longed to experience the prairie the way its early inhabitants did, here is a place to realize that dream. Few visitors venture into this panoramic paradise, making it an ideal place to escape civilization—a plus when you're seeking solitude,

a potential hazard if you run into trouble. At 64,144 acres, this is the nation's largest prairie wilderness, a home on the range to bison, pronghorn antelope, eagles, and other wild creatures. Although mixed-grass prairie dominates, you'll also find barren badlands formations to explore.

Vehicles are not allowed here, and the only trails are those of the bison. (You can leave your car at Sage Creek Primitive Campground.) You don't need a permit to hike or camp in this territory, but park officials recommend checking in with a ranger at Ben Reifel Visitor Center and signing a backcountry register before you head into the trackless wilds. Registers can be found at Conata Picnic Area off Badlands Loop Road, Rodeo Point Overlook off Sage Creek Rim Road (ask for directions), and Sage Creek Campground.

Camping is prohibited within a half mile of any road or trail, and your campsite must not be visible from a road. Stay clear of bison trails when making camp, since the giant creatures are not likely to make a detour— after all, they were here first. And make this your mantra: "No open fires." They are absolutely forbidden in Badlands National Park.

i Pets are only allowed in developed areas of the park and must be on a leash and under physical control of their owners at all times in Badlands National Park. Pets are not allowed at all in the Badlands (Sage Creek) Wilderness Area.

Horseback Riding

Horses are allowed throughout the park except on marked trails and roads or in developed areas. Horses usually don't like Badlands water any better than do humans (for whom it's not safe), so it's wise to pack at least five gallons of drinking water for your horse each day, along with your own gallon. You can park your horse trailer at an overlook or parking area if you just want to ride around the Badlands for the day; if you're staying overnight, you'll find Sage Creek Primitive Campground equipped for horse camping. See the Campgrounds section above as well as the Horse Camps section of the Campgrounds chapter for information about camping with your equine. Also check under Trail Rides and Pack Trips in the Recreation chapter to find out about commercial expeditions into the Badlands. Backcountry camping and grazing are allowed (remember, no campfires), but check with park rangers for the latest regulations. They can also tell you where to buy certified weed-free hay, the only kind allowed in the park.

Appendix

LIVING HERE

In this section we feature specific information for residents or those planning to relocate here. Topics include real estate, education, health care, and much more.

RELOCATION

The Black Hills have been luring people with their enchanting beauty and enduring mystery for centuries. Native tribes and European settlers alike have fought drought, flood, fire, famine, and each other for the right to make this timeless place their home. Fortunately, people who wish to live here today don't have to contend with such adversity.

All the same, finding a place to live in the Black Hills isn't without its challenges. One of the first challenges is deciding on your preference for housing, as there is property for any type of person. It isn't hard to rent a downtown loft in a multistory historic building, but it's also relatively easy to find a spot on a mountain slope, miles from the nearest town. And then there are the places in between: small houses bounded by acres of public forest, but only five minutes from the nearest traffic light.

If you're from Europe or the American coasts, prices for land and homes here will seem cheap. For instance, an average-size house on a small, forested lot might be appraised at four or five times its South Dakota value if it were located in California. On the other hand, Canadians, Australians, and visitors from the rural American Great Plains might find costs to be typical or slightly expensive. The bottom of the housing market has come and gone in South Dakota, which suffered little during the recent financial crisis. Few foreclosures have troubled the state's economy and Black Hills home prices are actually forecasted to rise 3.5% over the coming year.

By and large, western South Dakota avoided the downturns in the real estate market in recent years, primarily because it wasn't overbuilt to begin with and, secondly, because this region of the world is becoming increasingly attractive to retirees, adventure addicts, and the self-employed. While the Rapid City area continues to experience significant housing growth, many retirees opt for the small-town feel of outlying communities such as Spearfish, Deadwood, Custer, Hot Springs, and Hill City. The Black Hills offer multigenerational options in housing from residential developments on pristine golf courses to secluded, luxury get-away town houses in the pines.

OVERVIEW

In terms of jobs, South Dakota continues to rank lowest in the nation in unemployment, and, while many positions in this region of the world don't offer wages comparable to urban areas, job openings are abundant. In fact, as recently as November 2008, CNN reported Bureau of Labor Statistics' data that ranked Sioux Falls, SD, first and Rapid City second in the nation among the "25 Best Cities to Find a Job." Western South Dakota's largest community—Rapid City— had an unemployment rate of 2.5 percent, while job growth, even in a faltering national economy, had increased by 1 percent during the previous year, CNN reported. That's good news for job-seekers and for those hoping to buy a house. The median home value in the Black Hills will hover around $174,000, which means most buyers will get themselves a very good deal.

Wherever you're from, if you stick around the Hills long enough, you'll see real estate prices rise, thanks mostly to low mortgage rates and an influx of seasonal residents. Like western Wyoming and Montana, the Black Hills are slowly becoming a haven for wealthy out-of-state residents who fall in love with the pristine scenery but are unable to leave their urban jobs and families. Their solutions can be seen in the giant summer homes peeking out of the forest on mountaintops and along canyon rims.

But the Black Hills are still being discovered, and property remains both affordable and readily available. You'll find a few suggestions on the following pages, but by no means is the list exhaustive. Be sure to check the newspaper classifieds, real estate publications, and word of mouth. A real estate agent can be especially helpful if you're not familiar with the area; there are several listed at the end of this chapter.

For those of you relocating to the Black Hills from out of state, this chapter will also direct you to motor vehicle and licensing offices, chambers of commerce, and public libraries—all good resources for newcomers. The Black Hills cover a wide area (about the size of Delaware), so information about hospitals, schools, retirement homes, and other services of interest to potential immigrants were vast enough to include in separate chapters. If you're serious about relocating, be sure to look at the chapters on Education,

Health Care, Child Care, Retirement, Media, and Worship and Spirituality for more details on the facilities and services available in Black Hills communities.

REAL ESTATE IN THE NORTHERN HILLS

People who want the hospitality and safety of small-town life but don't wish to be isolated from urban comforts find that the northern Black Hills provide a number of pleasing variations on that theme. The towns of Belle Fourche, Spearfish, Lead, Deadwood, and Sturgis all have their own personalities, yet all are reasonably close to the population hub of Rapid City. Some working folks choose to live in the Northern Hills and commute an hour or more to their Rapid City jobs.

Belle Fourche

A growth spurt in Belle Fourche has slowed, but the town continues to attract home owners looking for the last of the wide-open spaces, as one real estate agent so aptly put it. Many of those moving to the Belle Fourche area have pulled up stakes from metropolitan regions; others work in the surrounding towns but choose to own a home here, where prices tend to be lower.

Belle Fourche responded to growth with the in-town **Ridgefield** subdivision, where homes on the approximately 21 lots are wood frame. A bit farther out and established are the **Sonoma Estates** and **Grandview** subdivisions. **Jewell Estates** and rugged **Redwater Ranchettes** accommodate both wood-frame and mobile homes. At **SRK Ranchettes** east of town, lots of anywhere from 10 to 30 acres with water, electricity, and phone service—and in some cases, views of the Black Hills—are available for building a new home. Historic homes and fixer-uppers can be found closer to downtown. Home prices range from $29,000 to around $189,000 in Belle Fourche, with the mean price in 2010 at $127,500. Rentals, primarily multifamily houses, are plentiful, which means that average rent is low—right around $450.

Spearfish

In Spearfish, growth and prices continue to rise, as is evidenced by robust construction and brisk property sales. A high percentage of homes in this picturesque college town (see the Black Hills State University write-up in the Education chapter) were built in the 1980s and 1990s, and many were custom-built for their owners. Accordingly, prices are similar to those in nearby Rapid City, which is about six times the size: The average value of a home in Spearfish today is $184,900, but you can easily find something for $100,000 or less. Nice homes have made developments such as the **Jorgensen, Evans,** and **Mountain Plains** subdivisions popular. Mountain Plains, above Spearfish City Park, features large lots with wood-exterior houses that are among the most expensive in town—around $250,000 to $800,000—even though city services aren't provided. Properties in the newer **Sandstone Hills** subdivision on the southern slope of Lookout Mountain do have city services, and houses being built here run $350,000 to $2 million. **Mountain Shadows Estates** is the newest, most modern mobile-home park, with about 300 well-groomed lots designed primarily for larger homes.

The university guarantees there will always be an abundance of mid-priced rentals in Spearfish, and in fact, a number of town houses and apartment complexes have been built for just that purpose. In 2009, median rent ran about $450 per month, slightly higher than the state average.

Lead and Deadwood

At the turn of the 20th century, Deadwood and Lead were populated by thousands of miners. Even after the surface deposits ran out and Homestake became the dominant mining company, the corporation continued to employ more than 1,200 workers, many of whom lived and played in the Twin Cities. Population numbers took a hit when Homestake closed in early 2002. Within a decade both communities lost a third of their population. However, the figures are misleading. With the introduction of gambling to Deadwood's Main Street in 1989, many once-crumbling storefronts were converted into casinos, eliminating the apartment space above and driving up rental costs. Developments outside city limits are thriving; the high-income homes in **Shirttail Gulch** and **Meadow Crest** near Deadwood are valued from $400,000 to $1.2 million, while houses in the **Hearst** development on a mountain above Lead run from $200,000 to $400,000. In 2010, the mean price of all housing units in Deadwood was $181,943. Of course, there are plenty of isolated private lots outside the towns as well, and many summer homes and cabins are springing up on them. Less-expensive housing can be found among the historic residences within city limits, though some of the Victorian-era homes—which sell from $55,000 to $225,000—require substantial restoration work. Both towns have plans to create more affordable apartments and town houses; as it is now, the median rent payment in 2009 was $552. **Apple Springs Resort** a residential resort community on Boulder Canyon Golf

Course, (800-689-7469), is being developed just minutes from Deadwood and Sturgis and offers golf cottages, condos, lots, and luxury homes from the low $400,000s to $800,000s. **Sugarloaf Village,** (888) 578-6944 or (888) 406-4671, a luxury residential development south of Lead, provides a more secluded, setting in the pines just minutes from downhill skiing, snowmobile trails, mountain biking and golf, with full-maintenance townhomes staring in the high $300,000s.

Sturgis

Situated along I-90 between Spearfish and Rapid City, Sturgis is both smaller and slower-paced than either. That helps keep prices down, making it possible to find a nice home at a reasonable cost in a convenient location—as escapees from more crowded parts of the West are discovering. Many who choose Sturgis want to live in the country or on the outskirts of town, but new subdivisions called **Pine Acres, Hurley,** and **Vernon Heights Estates** are filling up quickly. The median price of a house in Sturgis in 2010 was $139,000, while rent averaged $470 per month. Three new apartment buildings help make up the rental market in Sturgis, where few houses are rented, except during the Rally, when any real estate commands prime rates—even by Manhattan standards.

REAL ESTATE IN THE CENTRAL HILLS

With the entire Black Hills to choose from, people pick Rapid City for its economic and cultural advantages. Nevertheless, folks relocating here want to feel as if they live in the country; trees and privacy are top on the list of what they say they want in a home. As construction heads south, new housing developments offer just that type of setting, whether in town or miles away.

Rapid City

Early in Rapid City's history, west became the fashionable place to expand the growing municipality. It wasn't long before the hills got in the way, however, and the city started pushing north and east. But the flat, wind-swept land wasn't very attractive, and as property values dropped, these sections of town turned to commerce, which thrives there today. That left the southern district of the city as its only solid residential development option, and develop it has. **South Rapid City,** both to the east and west of Skyline Drive's divisive ridge, is one of the fastest-growing regions in the Black Hills. **Terracita Hills,** just south of the city's burgeoning medical district, is filled with homes that range from $250,000 to $500,000. On Rapid City's eastern edge, the unincorporated area known as **Rapid Valley** continues to see expanded residential development, with more than 9,000 people now living there. Several miles to the southwest, along US 16 outside the city limits, are housing developments such as **Copper Oaks, Enchanted Hills,** and **Hart Ranch.** The area around Neck Yoke Road off US 16 near Rockerville is noted for its secluded homes.

The **Sheridan Lake Road** area southwest of town is also the site of new, upscale housing developments such as **Wildwood, Countryside** (where all the streets are named for bird species), and **Countryside South.** Homes in Countryside South, which run in the $250,000 to $350,000 range, realize an exceptionally high appreciation rate. **Chateaux Ridge** and **Autumn Hills** subdivisions are along Sheridan Lake Road inside the city limits. Lots average $30,000 to $50,000.

Nemo Road (CR 234) and **Rimrock Highway** (SR 44), which link Rapid City and US 385 to the northwest and west, respectively, are the sites of smaller developments as well as gated **Cinnamon Ridge** on Rimrock Highway. This scenic road follows the route of the old Crouch Line, a rail line with so many twists and turns that it made what amounted to a dozen complete circles on every trip between Rapid City and Mystic, crossing more than 100 bridges each way.

Closer to downtown, **New Robbinsdale** in the southeastern part of the city is attracting home owners who like the newer housing and Parkview swimming pool there. Existing homes are in the $125,000 to $200,000 range (with the exception of those in the Rapid City Defense Housing subdivision for Ellsworth Air Force Base personnel, which are less). Several new apartment complexes and retirement communities have been built in New Robbinsdale in recent years. In **Old Robbinsdale,** folks on a budget can find quaint post–World War II houses and fixer-uppers in the $60,000 range or even as low as $50,000.

i New in town? If you've moved to the Rapid City area in the last few months, New Neighbors Welcome Service will send a representative to greet you and supply you with literature, maps, and merchandise certificates to help you get acquainted with your new community. Call (605) 341-5737.

West Rapid City experienced most of its growth from World War II through the 1970s, but several homes and buildings are new, and most have been well cared for and renovated. Because of west Rapid City's location in the upper foothills, forested land, and beautiful parks, land values here are generally high. Stevens High School occupies an expansive site in west Rapid. Prestigious developments in **Pinedale Heights, Chapel Valley,** and the older section of **Carriage Hills** have been established for some time and are filled up, but new multimillion-dollar mansions are taking hold in the uppermost reaches of Carriage Hills. Lots there carry price tags in excess of $100,000.

In the historic district around **West Boulevard,** buyers can find older but well-maintained, higher-end homes from about $150,000 for older and smaller homes on up to $700,000 for larger historic mansions and villas. The boulevard, one of downtown Rapid City's loveliest features, is popular with fitness-conscious residents who can be seen jogging or power walking down the tree-lined median just about any time of the day.

The northwestern and northeastern parts of town are well developed, and the area beyond is flat, windy, and less desirable for development. **North Rapid** includes some subsidized-housing neighborhoods and is becoming increasingly commercial. New businesses in this part of town include national giants Best Buy, Borders, Lowe's, Chili's, Applebee's, Pier One Imports, Shopko, OfficeMax, and Super Wal-Mart. Rushmore Mall is out that way, and I-90 runs through the area.

Rapid Valley to the east offers attractive, affordable homes that are closest to Rapid City Regional Airport. Rapid Valley boasts a Blue Ribbon elementary school, which you can read about in the Education chapter.

In 2010, the mean price of a house in Rapid City was $174,900. Houses have been appreciating at the rate of 3 percent or more per year, a figure attributed at least in part to easy access to the interior of the Black Hills and to Mount Rushmore National Memorial.

Apartments and rental houses are plentiful in Rapid City, but so are people who want to occupy them. Rentals come in all types, so whether you're looking for a place over a store downtown, a furnished room, an apartment in someone's house, a duplex or multifamily house, a luxury space in an apartment, a town house complex beside a golf course, or a furnished or unfurnished house, you're sure to find listings. But expect lots of competition, too. The property management division of a real estate agency can sometimes be your best bet if you are in the market for something new and upscale. Median rent in Rapid City in 2010 was $664 per month.

North of Rapid City, homes and businesses are going up in the **Black Hawk** area, where property taxes are lower and building codes and zoning laws are less restrictive. Home owners not concerned with conformity in their neighborhoods or a certain proximity to commercial development may find their heart's desire here.

A few miles north of Black Hawk is the new, recently incorporated town of **Summerset.** This place remains among the fastest-growing residential areas in South Dakota. People are attracted to Summerset because of its proximity to I-90, seclusion in the pines away from Rapid City, growing commercial services, and comparatively low costs. Many of the houses here are middle-income homes, with the average price tag hovering around $200,000. Both Black Hawk and Summerset are in Meade County, although they serve primarily as bedroom communities for Rapid City and Pennington County. **Sun Valley Estates,** (866) 740-8800, located just off I-90 at exit 46 on the foothills

north of Rapid City, provides more affordable single-family residences from $150,000 to $250,000.

i Before buying country property be sure to inquire about the availability and quality of water. Ask adjacent landowners and check with a local well driller to find out whether you'd be able to drill a productive well on your piece of paradise and how deep it would have to be.

Hill City

At one point in the mid-1990s, disillusioned exiles from populous places discovered tiny Hill City and dubbed it a cool place to live. But the influx of newcomers to this town of fewer than 1,000 people was short-lived, largely because 85 percent of the land around Hill City is controlled by the USDA Forest Service. That leaves little room for private development, although Hill City could be an up-and-coming bedroom community for Rapid City, a place where families can find small-town atmosphere and lower housing costs. It will take time, however, because growth here is slow, and development takes place on demand rather than on speculation. Older and smaller homes in town will run from $60,000 to $125,000, but a fair number of larger houses outside the community carry price tags from $200,000 to $800,000. The mean price of a Hill City house in 2010 was $184,500.

Top of the Hills subdivision in the city limits is helping to fill a need for subsidized housing for those on a modest income; an adjacent development offers buildable lots with utilities and maintained roads in the $20,000 range for middle-income home buyers. **Matkins Addition No. 4,** alongside

Major Lake and also inside the city, offers improved lots as part of a four-acre parcel to be developed in phases. Few existing homes are for sale, and even fixer-uppers are scarce. Desirable out-of-town lots can run around $5,000 to $10,000 an acre along with potentially high costs for improvements because of rocky soil. That's something for prospective buyers to inquire about.

REAL ESTATE IN THE SOUTHERN HILLS

About 90 percent of Custer County is public land. But Custer State Park, Wind Cave National Park, Jewel Cave National Monument, and the Black Hills National Forest also make this area a special place where people want to buy a plot of land, build a nice house, and settle in to enjoy the wilderness. Trouble is, those places are pricey (by Black Hills standards, anyway), starting at around $150,000, and buildable land is becoming scarce. Finding water can be a tricky business, too, especially to the south and west. So although Custer was the state's fastest growing county during the late 1980s, the pace has slowed since then.

Custer

New subdivisions are appearing in Custer, such as **Weaver** subdivision, which accepts double-wide mobile homes on a foundation as well as frame houses. Lots in **Boot Hill Ranch Estates,** ranging in size from a half acre to two-and-a-half acres, run between $30,000 and $60,000. The subdivision, located a couple of miles east of town near Custer State Park, is heavily regulated by covenants.

A typical newer home runs anywhere from $250,000 to $450,000, and a fixer-upper

in town runs around $90,000. The mean price of a Custer house in 2010 was $315,457. Rentals, which averaged $520 in 2009, are scarce in Custer, which makes it hard for college kids who work in the parks, restaurants, and gift shops to find summer lodging.

Hot Springs

The demand for farms and ranches is high around Hot Springs, especially from out-of-staters who want thousands of pristine acres on which to roam in privacy. Then again, many who are looking in this area want a lot in a subdivision so they can build a house. The 12-acre **Hot Brook Overlook** 5 miles north of town, **Water's Edge** on Angostura Reservoir, and **Battle Mountain Ranch** on US 385 next to Wind Cave National Park are among subdivisions where lots of several acres may be found. **Cedar Hills** is a development west of town with lots from 6 to 11 acres; prices hover at $50,000. Houses in town run from $35,000 to $350,000, depending on age and condition. There are plenty of ranches and homes on secluded lots outside town as well, and they can range in price from $175,000 to over $1 million. The mean price of a Hot Springs house in 2010 was $120,000. Median rent was $488 per month in 2009.

REAL ESTATE PUBLICATIONS

The following publications are available for free from real estate agencies and, in some cases, selected newspapers, information centers, and businesses.

The monthly *Home Journal* comes out in a Saturday edition of the *Rapid City Journal* around the middle of the month. The *Home Journal* contains listings for the entire Black Hills—turn it one way and you can leaf through the Rapid City pages; flip it over and turn it upside down to get listings for the rest of the Hills.

Black Hills Homes and Land Magazine is also published monthly and is available for free at newsstands throughout the Hills. You can also request a copy for free at www .homesandlandoftheblackhills.com.

REAL ESTATE AGENCIES

You'll recognize some agencies as big-name franchises with solid reputations in real estate sales. But don't overlook smaller, independent agencies. Many of them are operated by agents who have been in the local real estate business for a long time and know the area intimately. You'll find additional agencies listed in the Yellow Pages, or you can contact local boards of Realtors, listed in the sidebar in this section.

Hills-wide

CENTURY 21
607 State St., Belle Fourche
(605) 892-2021
www.century21.com
One of the world's largest residential real estate franchises has six independent offices in the Black Hills. In addition to national name recognition, the franchise offers buyers and sellers a large coverage area. Although the offices operate separately, they do make referrals to each other whether for a house, commercial property, or country acreage. For rental information call individual offices located in Belle Fourche, Deadwood, Spearfish, Sturgis, Custer, and Hill City. Specific listing info for Century 21's five other South Dakota locations can be found on their website.

THE REAL ESTATE CENTER
140 West Jackson Blvd., Spearfish
(605) 642-2525
www.realestatecenters.com
These six independent offices are part of a limited partnership that started as a single office in Spearfish in 1992. Other agents liked founder Rich Harr's concept and, one by one, asked to be part of it. The partnership specializes in helping people relocate to the Black Hills, and all offices work together, making referrals between them. Combined, they cover the entire area, including the Wyoming Black Hills, through regional multiple listing services. Check out the Real Estate Center's website for listing info for their Deadwood, Sturgis, Custer, Sundance, and Bell Fourche offices.

i Need a plumber? A builder? A siding expert? The Black Hills Home Builders Association can provide you with a list of members for just about any homebuilding task. Stop in at 3121 West Chicago St., Rapid City, or call (605) 348-7850.

Northern Hills

JOHNSON JOY REAL ESTATE
1230 North Ave., Suite 5, Spearfish
(605) 642-5723
www.johnsonjoy.com
This agency has been dealing in homes, ranches, land, and recreational properties in Spearfish and western Wyoming since the mid-1960s. Its agents can help you learn about this beautiful area and will send you a packet of information if you're thinking of relocating here.

THE KEENE TEAM RE/MAX GOLD
134 Sherman St., Deadwood
(605) 717-1544
www.keene-team.com

This small real estate agency is run by area natives and avid skiers John and Terri Keene. They list properties throughout the Northern Hills, including homes and businesses in Spearfish, Deadwood, Lead, and the surrounding canyons. If you're looking to build your own home on a wooded lot, they can help you find your place in the pines. They also work closely with an interior-design firm in Spearfish to help clients decorate their new home. The Keenes are also able to help arrange financing.

REAL ESTATE 2000
506½ State St., Belle Fourche
(605) 892-2000

The agents here handle a diverse mix of properties, from rural land, farms, and ranches to traditional residential listings. The company has covered northwest South Dakota and northeast Wyoming since the early 1990s.

Central Hills

CENTRAL HILLS REAL ESTATE, INC.
349 Main St., Hill City
(605) 574-6000, (800) 682-9149
www.blackhills.com/
centralhillsrealestate

The residents-turned-real-estate agents here handle commercial and residential listings primarily in Hill City, Custer, and Rapid City. The company also sells real estate at auction.

COLDWELL BANKER LEWIS-KIRKEBY
   HALL REAL ESTATE, INC.
2700 West Main St., Rapid City
(605) 343-2700, (888) 343-2700
www.coldwellbankerrapid.com

One of the nation's largest franchises, Coldwell Banker has been established in Rapid City since 1963. Approximately 40 agents handle residential, commercial, business, land, farm, and ranch sales in Rapid City and the Black Hills. A separate property management department can help in your search for any type of rental, and relocation kits are available for prospective newcomers.

HALLMARK REALTORS INC.
821½ Columbus St., Rapid City
(605) 343-4545, (800) 343-8301

These agents sell business, commercial, and residential properties of all kinds in Rapid City and the surrounding Black Hills. The independent agency, which has been in operation since 1985, also provides information packets to clients who are interested in relocating to the area.

MATKINS REALTY
114 Main St., P.O. Box 56, Hill City
(605) 574-2628
www.matkinsrealty.com

This agency deals in all types of real estate in Hill City and the surrounding area, including Keystone and Custer. The office, which opened in 1983, can help you locate a rental house or apartment, too. Relocation information is available.

PRUDENTIAL KAHLER REALTORS
2401 West Main St., Rapid City
(605) 343-7500, (800) 658-5550
www.kahlerinc.com

After 35 years as an independent company, Kahler joined the Prudential franchise. The 30 or so agents here specialize in residential and commercial sales throughout the Black Hills area. The property management division handles all types of rentals, from houses and

Boards of Realtors

Local boards of Realtors primarily serve the agencies in their territory, but they can also provide home buyers with a list of member firms and handle ethical complaints against real estate agents. Some also offer mediation service for a fee when buyers and sellers get into a dispute, or provide statistical data about property sales. Here's a list of our local boards:

- Northern Black Hills Association of Realtors, 1230 North Ave., (605) 722-0181
- Black Hills Board of Realtors, 1836 West Kansas City St., Rapid City, (605) 341-2580
- Southern Black Hills Board of Realtors has merged with the Northern Black Hills Board of Realtors.

primarily residential listings in this company, which opened in 1972. They can also provide you with a list of available apartments.

i Realtor is a trademark name for a member of the National Association of Realtors. GRI stands for Graduate Realtor Institute, and CRS stands for Certified Residential Specialist; both mean the agent has taken advanced courses through a Realtor organization.

RE/MAX REALTORS
1240 Jackson Blvd., Rapid City
(605) 341-4300, (800) 456-0860
www.remax.com
The Real Estate Maximum concept that originated in Denver in the mid-1970s has made RE/MAX an internationally successful franchise. Under the formula, each agent is an independent producer committed to providing top-quality service, and the 30 or so agents in the Rapid City office are no exception. The office deals in residential and commercial properties in Rapid City and within a 50- to 60-mile radius. Relocation packets are available upon request.

apartments to offices, warehouses, and strip malls. The relocation division sends information packets upon request.

RABEN REAL ESTATE
302 Main St., Rapid City
(605) 342-7272, (800) 888-1619
www.rapidcityrealestate.com
Relocation is a major part of Raben Real Estate's business. Folks with serious inquiries receive a two-hour video tour of the Black Hills, from the backcountry to attractions and shopping; a book on many aspects of life here; several smaller publications; and even customized information for those with specific requests. About 25 agents handle

ROSSUM & NEAL, REALTORS
2400 West Main St., Rapid City
(605) 342-9112, (800) 888-1430
www.rossumneal.com
The motto at this independent agency is, "Our reputation is your guarantee." About 20 agents sell homes, commercial properties, and land in Rapid City and the immediate area. Rossum & Neal can make the relocation process easier, by providing an information packet with a free video about the Black Hills or by helping you find an agency in your future hometown. Local rentals of all kinds are handled here as well.

Southern Hills

WYATT'S REAL ESTATE
646 Jennings Ave., Hot Springs
(605) 745-3140

Wyatt's has been selling real estate for nearly three decades. You'll find specialists in ranches and appraisals among the agents at this independent company, which also deals in residential, commercial, and undeveloped properties within about a 20-mile radius of Hot Springs. Requests for relocation information are handled individually.

MOTOR VEHICLE INFORMATION

If you're moving to the Black Hills, you'll need to register and license your vehicle in South Dakota. You can do this by heading to the treasurer's office of your local county courthouse (or the appropriate extension office). If you need a South Dakota driver's license or ID card, however, you'll need to go to an approved exam location—typically a fire station or community center. The exam locations are active only one day a week (or less often) in all Black Hills communities except for Rapid City, where you can take a driver's test Tues through Fri. Most of these locations don't have their own phone numbers, so for more information contact the South Dakota Department of Public Safety, Office of Driver Licensing, (605) 773-6883 or (800) 952-3696.

Northern Hills

BELLE FOURCHE DRIVER'S LICENSE EXAM STATION
(Thursday only)
City Hall Council Room
508 6th St., Belle Fourche

BUTTE COUNTY COURTHOUSE, TREASURER'S OFFICE
839 5th St., Belle Fourche
(605) 892-4456

DEADWOOD DRIVER'S LICENSE EXAM STATION
(Tuesday only)
Deadwood Fire Station
737 Main St., Deadwood

LAWRENCE COUNTY COURTHOUSE, TREASURER'S OFFICE
90 Sherman St., Deadwood
(605) 578-1862
www.lawrence.sd.us

MEADE COUNTY COURTHOUSE, TREASURER'S OFFICE
1425 Sherman St., Sturgis
(605) 347-5871

SPEARFISH DRIVER'S LICENSE EXAM STATION
(Wednesday only)
Spearfish Fire Hall
622 Canyon St., Spearfish

STURGIS DRIVER'S LICENSE EXAM STATION
(Friday only)
Sturgis Community Center
1401 Lazelle St., Sturgis

Central Hills

PENNINGTON COUNTY COURTHOUSE TREASURER'S OFFICE
315 Saint Joseph St., Rapid City
(605) 394-2161
www.co.pennington.sd.us

RAPID CITY DRIVER'S LICENSE EXAM STATION
(Tues through Fri)
South Dakota Highway Patrol Station
1301 East Catron Blvd., Rapid City

WALL DRIVER'S LICENSE EXAM STATION
(call for days)
Wall Community Center
501 Main St., Wall
(605) 394-2162

Southern Hills

CUSTER COUNTY COURTHOUSE, TREASURER'S OFFICE
420 Mount Rushmore Rd., Custer
(605) 673-8172

CUSTER DRIVER'S LICENSE EXAM STATION
(first three Wednesdays of the month)
Custer City Hall
622 Crook St., Custer

FALL RIVER COUNTY COURTHOUSE, TREASURER'S OFFICE
906 North River St., Hot Springs
(605) 745-5145

HOT SPRINGS DRIVER'S LICENSE EXAM STATION
(Friday only)
Hot Springs High School Administration Building
1609 University Ave., Hot Springs

CHAMBERS OF COMMERCE & VISITOR INFORMATION

Each of the major communities in the Black Hills has its own chamber of commerce and visitor bureau staffed with helpful people and stocked with guides and printed material about the area. These business associations are more than happy to provide you with information about local stores and services, but they'll also give you an idea of a community's character and personality.

i Packaged Vacations: Black Hills Central Reservations offers all-inclusive travel packages complete with airline, lodging, rental car, activities and attraction passes, all at a bargain rate. For one-stop shopping with travel advisors available, check them out by calling (866) 329-7566 or going online at www.blackhillsvacations.com.

Northern Hills

BELLE FOURCHE CHAMBER OF COMMERCE
415 5th Ave., Belle Fourche
(605) 892-2676, (888) 345-5859
www.bellefourche.org

DEADWOOD AREA CHAMBER OF COMMERCE & VISITOR BUREAU
767 Main St., Deadwood
(605) 578-1876, (800) 999-1876
www.deadwood.com

LEAD AREA CHAMBER OF COMMERCE
160 West Main St., Lead
(605) 584-1100
www.leadmethere.org

SPEARFISH AREA CHAMBER OF COMMERCE & VISITOR BUREAU
106 West Kansas St., Spearfish
(605) 642-2626, (800) 626-8013
www.spearfish.sd.us/Chamber

STURGIS AREA CHAMBER OF COMMERCE
2040 Junction Ave., Sturgis
(605) 347-2556
www.sturgis-sd.org

Central Hills

HILL CITY CHAMBER OF COMMERCE
23935 US 385, Hill City
(605) 574-2368, (800) 888-1798
www.hillcitysd.com
www.move2hillcity.com

KEYSTONE CHAMBER OF COMMERCE
110 Swanzey St., Keystone
(605) 666-4896, (800) 456-3345
www.keystonechamber.com

RAPID CITY AREA CHAMBER OF COMMERCE
444 Mount Rushmore Rd.,
North Rapid City
(605) 343-1744
www.rapidcitychamber.com

WALL-BADLANDS AREA CHAMBER OF COMMERCE
503 Main St., P.O. Box 527, Wall
(605) 279-2665, (888) 852-9255
www.wall-badlands.com

Southern Hills

CUSTER AREA CHAMBER OF COMMERCE & VISITORS BUREAU
615 Washington St., Custer
(605) 673-2244, (800) 992-9818
www.custersd.com

HOT SPRINGS AREA CHAMBER OF COMMERCE
801 South 6th St., P.O. Box 342,
Hot Springs
(605) 745-4140, (800) 325-6991
www.hotsprings-sd.com

LIBRARIES

Most Black Hills communities—even the very small ones—have libraries, thanks largely to Andrew Carnegie's philanthropic generosity at the turn of the 20th century. Aside from offering general reading material, local libraries are usually depositories for community historical archives and public Internet access points. You should be able to find several books devoted to the flora, fauna, and people of the Black Hills.

Northern Hills

BELLE FOURCHE PUBLIC LIBRARY
905 5th Ave., Belle Fourche
(605) 892-4407

DEADWOOD PUBLIC LIBRARY
435 Williams St., Deadwood
(605) 578-2821
http://dwdlib.sdln.net

GRACE BALLOCK MEMORIAL LIBRARY
625 5th St., Spearfish
(605) 642-1330

PHOEBE APPERSON HEARST LIBRARY
315 West Main St., Lead
(605) 584-2013
http://leadlib.sdln.net

STURGIS PUBLIC LIBRARY
1040 Second St., Sturgis
(605) 347-2624

Central Hills

HILL CITY PUBLIC LIBRARY
324 Main St., Hill City
(605) 574-4529

KEYSTONE PUBLIC LIBRARY
1101 Modill St., Keystone
(605) 666-4499

RAPID CITY PUBLIC LIBRARY
610 Quincy St., Rapid City
(605) 394-4171
http://rcplib.sdln.net

WALL COMMUNITY LIBRARY
407 Main St., Wall
(605) 279-2929

Southern Hills

CUSTER COUNTY LIBRARY
447 Crook St., Custer
(605) 673-8178
www.custerlibrary.com

HOT SPRINGS PUBLIC LIBRARY
1543 Baltimore St., Hot Springs
(605) 745-3151

EDUCATION

Admittedly, South Dakotans aren't usually the first ones to champion a cause in the name of progress. People in the Black Hills tend to be conservative and resistant to change, embracing it only after much deliberation. All the same, South Dakotans can't be thought of as being backward, especially when it comes to education. That's because we're serious about educating our young people and preparing them to make their way in life. We provide school-to-work opportunities so students can experience the career world firsthand while earning credit toward graduation. For gifted students, we have academic enrichment programs to let them stretch their abilities to the fullest. And although we know there's always room for improvement, we see our efforts paying off in test scores that are slightly to significantly higher than the national average, particularly in math, science, and social studies. Approximately 75 percent of our high school students stay in school and graduate (our dropout rate is less than 2.5 percent a year); of those, more than 47 percent go on to a four-year college, and 20 percent attend other postsecondary institutions. Another 5 percent enter the military.

We face some difficult issues, nonetheless. One shortcoming is in teacher pay: South Dakota has been 50th or 51st in the nation (counting the District of Columbia) for more years than we care to recall. Another point of contention is the way we fund our public schools. Roughly half of school funding comes from property taxes, a system that has produced several citizen-initiated ballot measures aimed at shifting more, or all, of the burden elsewhere. So far, however, the state legislature has failed to come up with a satisfactory school-funding alternative, in part because the thought of a state income tax is anathema to most South Dakotans. Currently, the state's funding formula provides half of school funds, paying districts approximately $4,200 per student.

Still, we've moved ahead on other issues. With the advent of open enrollment in 1998, parents and students entered an arena of brand-new choices and challenges. Under open enrollment, most students can attend any public school in the state without paying tuition, subject to limitations aimed at maintaining reasonable attendance levels. The idea is to help students find schools best suited to their needs.

OVERVIEW

Not everyone in South Dakota is concerned with open enrollment, of course. In a recent school year, 2,724 students were receiving alternative instruction, with 1,938 of them in home schools taught mostly by dedicated mothers. Alternatively schooled students must achieve proficiency in English and take math and reading/language arts as well as nationally standardized achievement tests, the same as their peers in public school. But it's up to individual districts to decide what course work they'll accept for credit toward graduation for students who want a diploma from an accredited public high school. For more information about alternative schooling, call your local school district.

Districts throughout the Hills contract with **Black Hills Special Services Cooperative** for special- and alternative-education services, various forms of therapy, and a full range of other benefits for special-needs students. In addition, the co-op's **Technology and Innovations in Education (TIE)** office is involved in a sophisticated technology project in schools across South Dakota. The co-op has been a national leader in rural education services since the 1970s.

Learning doesn't end at adulthood. Older learners find intellectual stimulation in community education programs. In most cases the local school district is the place to call for information about that as well as about General Educational Development (GED) preparation and testing; in Rapid City, however, contact the **Career Learning Center,** 730 East Watertown St., (605) 394-5120, www.clcbh.org.

Below you'll find thumbnail sketches of many school districts, private schools, and colleges. We couldn't squeeze all of their accolades into this chapter, but administrators and teachers at each one would be happy to fill in the blanks. Naturally, the best way to get acquainted with a school is to pay a call, or several, and observe it for yourself. The profiles here serve as an introduction.

PUBLIC SCHOOLS

Northern Hills

BELLE FOURCHE SCHOOL DISTRICT
1113 National St., Belle Fourche
(605) 892-3355

Belle Fourche has the only school district in the country with a four-day alternative calendar. Regular classes are held four days per week, and the fifth is called an intercession day. Academically gifted students work on special projects, while those struggling with certain subjects can get help catching up. Attendance on this day is voluntary, but the schools are usually full, a sign of both parent and student support for the program. More than 1,400 students attend school in the Belle Fourche district, where the focus is on a child-centered curriculum that strives to meet each student's individual needs, especially in math and science. Spanish is offered in elementary school, and there's an eclectic approach to English that incorporates both whole language and phonics.

Advanced-placement classes allow high school students to earn college credit early. Vocational studies are another strength, as the district has articulation agreements with Western Dakota Technical Institute (WDTI). Students studying the building trades here can transfer their credits to WDTI without cost if they enroll there after graduation. Class projects have included building homes for people in the community from start to finish. Computer-aided drafting is a popular class.

District residents are serious about educating their youth, as evidenced by several community/school partnerships, such as the Community Council for Education and the School Improvement Council, which looks at curriculum changes before they go to the school board. Both are made up of professional educators and community members.

Belle Fourche teachers have won five national Presidential Science and Math Awards; honors among students include state football and girls' basketball championships; and the district has produced a Rhodes scholar.

The district has one elementary school spread out among several buildings, a new middle school, and one high school. High school students who don't do well in a traditional classroom setting may be referred to Education Connection, an alternative school in Spearfish. Read more about it in the Spearfish School District listing later in this chapter.

LEAD-DEADWOOD SCHOOL DISTRICT
320 South Main St., Lead
(605) 717-3890
www.lead-deadwood.k12.sd.us

This district in the heart of Black Hills gold mining country is still proud of the fact that Lead High School won a prestigious National Bellamy Award for overall excellence and teaching of Americanism in 1970. But the school hasn't rested on its laurels in subsequent decades. In recent years LHS physics and chemistry students have excelled in regional competition with their peers, and the school band represented South Dakota at the 150th anniversary of the laying of the Washington Monument cornerstone in Washington, D.C., in 1998. Student athletes have brought recognition to Lead-Deadwood by winning state championships for the girls' cross-country team in 1997 and 1996, when they won a combined championship with the boys' team, which went on to become the 1998 Class A champ. The boys' golf team reigned as state champs in 2006, while the girls' team took top state honors from 2005 through 2008. The Debate and Speech team won the 2004 District Award, which means the entire team competed at the National Forensics League's national tournament. The team has

sent individuals to the national speech and debate tourneys from 2006 through 2009. The district's approximately 860 students are divided among one elementary school, one middle school, and the high school in Lead.

MEADE SCHOOL DISTRICT
1230 Douglas St., Sturgis
(605) 347-2523, (877) 522-6251
http://meade.k12.sd.us

At 3,200 square miles, this is the state's largest school district geographically. Primarily encompassing Sturgis, Piedmont, Black Hawk, and rural Meade County (South Dakota's largest county), it also includes Whitewood, in Lawrence County. The Meade district is further distinguished by its eight rural schools, most of which are reached via miles and miles of gravel roads—the most remote one in the town of Opal is some 90 miles from school administrative offices in Sturgis. One principal oversees and visits them all. Students who attend these one- and two-room schools on the prairie benefit from a close-knit, family-style atmosphere and lots of individual attention from teachers, but those advantages can also make adjusting to a larger school difficult. The rural schools carry students through eighth grade in the same curriculum as their peers in town; after that it's on to high school in Sturgis or somewhere closer to home. Some rural families move into town during the week so their high schoolers can get to school more easily, or students might board with town families for the school year.

In addition to the rural schools, the Meade elementary system includes five attendance centers in Sturgis that are divided into various grade levels, one building each in Piedmont and Stagebarn plus one school in Whitewood. Some children in Black Hawk attend the Piedmont-Stagebarn schools, but others go to Black Hawk Elementary School, which is in the Rapid City Area School District. All Meade students, except those in the rural schools, are assigned to Williams Middle School in Sturgis. From there they go to Sturgis Brown High School. Black Hawk children attend middle and high school in either Sturgis or Rapid City.

Sturgis Brown High School is noted for its excellent wrestling and girls' cross country teams. The wrestling team is especially distinguished, having won both the state's dual or individual championship titles in 2001, 2002, 2004, 2006, 2007, 2009, and 2010, while the girls' cross country team reigned as champions in 2010. Also in 2010, the district completed a $1.1 million renovation of its track surface at Woodle Field.

The *USA Today* Community Solutions for Education Award and other honors have also gone to the district. An applied-academics curriculum helps Meade students find practical applications for their classroom studies, and a law-related education program helps them stay out of trouble—or see the error of their ways if they stray. An alternative academy associated with Brown High School serves students with a variety of needs, from work-related scheduling problems to struggles in the classroom.

Despite its large coverage area, the Meade district has a modest enrollment of about 3,000 students.

SPEARFISH SCHOOL DISTRICT
525 East Illinois St., Spearfish
(605) 717-1201
http://spearfish.k12.sd.us
As the home of Black Hills State University (see later listing), Spearfish is able to offer its public school students dual enrollment,

a popular option that enables high school juniors and seniors to take certain classes at the university level and earn college credit.

Spearfish has dedicated a good share of its resources to making sure its students acquire current technology skills, as highlighted by the one-to-one computer program at Spearfish High School. The facilities are suited to academic excellence, as evidenced by recent additions at Spearfish High School, West Elementary School, and the new Creekside Elementary School (opening in the fall of 2011). In addition to its academic advantages, Spearfish is justly proud of its athletic teams—the high school football team won the state 11AA championship in 1997 and 2003, the boys' basketball team won the state title in 2002, and Spearfish boys won state and conference championships in track in 1999. Spearfish is also proud of its music programs: Some 160 students participate in band alone, as well as two choirs. The students have been successful in drama and debate, and have dominated the "We the People" constitutional contest in the state for the past decade.

Recent enrollment was 1,960. Currently, kindergarten through grade five are distributed among four elementary schools.

Central Hills

DOUGLAS SCHOOL DISTRICT
400 Patriot Dr., Box Elder
(605) 923-0000
www.dsdk12.net
Named for the family that founded it in 1891, the Douglas School District started as a one-room school and expanded to meet the needs of military families who arrived when Rapid City Army Air Base—now Ellsworth Air Force Base—was built in 1942. Today, Douglas educates about 2,400 students a

year from Ellsworth, the town of Box Elder, the surrounding rural area, and part of Rapid Valley.

There are three elementary schools, each containing just two grades. Students attend Douglas Middle School for grades six through eight, then move on to Douglas High School, which in 1971 became first in the state to have an ROTC program. The air force discontinued its rating system for ROTC programs in 2000, but the Douglas High School program consistently garnered Honor Unit or Meritorious Unit awards before then, and it continues to be very popular among students.

The school has an outstanding family and consumer sciences classroom with a progressive home economics and life-skills curriculum that's a hit with both male and female students. In the building and trades classes, students are building houses that are for sale to the public. In one program sponsored by Cisco, students split up into teams to learn about computer networking, then compete to design a campus or office building with the most efficient network. The School-to-Work program has been implemented at all levels, from kindergarten through 12th grade, to help students "learn a living." (On-the-job training doesn't begin until the later grades.) Educators, parents, and other community members work together to improve education through the Douglas Community Partnership Council and the Curriculum Coordinating Committee.

HILL CITY SCHOOL DISTRICT
421 Main St., Hill City
(605) 574-3030
http://hillcity.k12.sd.us
Though Hill City has only 800 residents, the town is vibrant and thriving. Without a

doubt, its prosperity is directly tied to the millions of visitors who pass through here each summer on their way to or from nearby Mount Rushmore. However, the community's push to become the regional art-gallery capital certainly helps. Several major Black Hills artists have set up shop here, adding vitality to the commercial district along Main Street that bustles even after the tourists are long gone.

The constant ring of cash registers means more taxes for the Hill City School District. Even so, it took many years of careful saving and planning to construct a new $5.5 million high school in 2001 without any bonds or loans. This is remarkable not only because of the town's small size but also because the district managed to add 9,000 square feet and a new hardwood gym floor (also without debt) to the middle school just two years earlier. But officials have long recognized that nice buildings aren't very useful without proper equipment, and it was this attitude that led the tiny district to become the second in the state to connect its school computer network to the Internet.

On the other hand, the district really isn't that small—comparatively. More than 500 students (nearly the town's total population) attend the elementary, middle, and high schools on the upper end of Main Street. Most of the children live outside of town in the Black Hills National Forest, which makes up 87 percent of the district, or in the nearby communities of Keystone, Silver City, and Rochford. Students call themselves "Rangers," and Hill City is the only district in the country that can claim Smokey Bear as its mascot. The honor was bestowed by the USDA Forest Service after several schoolchildren helped fend off a forest fire threatening the town in 1939.

RAPID CITY AREA SCHOOL DISTRICT
300 6th St., Rapid City
(605) 394-4037 (elementary),
(605) 394-5147 (secondary)
www.rcas.org

Approximately 13,000 students attend classes in South Dakota's second-largest school district, which includes 16 elementary schools (including one for children with disabilities), five middle schools, two high schools, three alternative academies that allow at-risk students to work at their own pace (in some cases, over the Internet) toward a diploma, and a technical school (see the Western Dakota Technical Institute listing below).

The district is committed to giving its youths a solid academic foundation from the very beginning of their educational career. The school board lowered student-teacher ratios in the earliest grades as a means of increasing literacy from the start. Outstanding primary programs such as this one have garnered honors for the district. Rapid Valley Elementary School won a national Blue Ribbon Award in 1997 from the US Department of Education, one of 262 schools to be recognized for excellence. The school combines multiage classrooms, looping (where teachers remain longer with the same group of students), and traditional self-contained classes with progressive teaching techniques and a welcoming, "community of learners" atmosphere that makes children want to go to school—really! Some of its other progressive approaches to education include a money responsibility program, in which students can earn "Best Bills" play money they can use to pay fines for late homework or save to purchase items at the school store, and extended school days on Mon, Tues, Thurs, and Fri, which leaves Wednesday afternoon free for staff development and networking.

On the secondary level, Central and Stevens High Schools consistently excel in track, cross-country, and music (both band and orchestra). Stevens is usually noted for its wrestling, golf, and theater programs, which are consistently ranked as the best in the state, while Central takes top honors in volleyball and soccer and has a federally funded learning center for Native American students.

Overall, the district prides itself on doing a good job teaching basic skills and on the success of its science students in local and national competition. Noteworthy, too, is an active, successful exchange program with educators from Rapid City's Japanese sister city, Imaichi.

Southern Hills

CUSTER SCHOOL DISTRICT
147 North 5th St., Custer
(605) 673-3154
www.csd.k12.sd.us

Technology programs and boys' basketball have made Custer a standout school district. Presently, it is one of three districts in the Black Hills to operate on a four-day week. When the schedule changed in 1995, closing school on Fri and adding almost an hour a day Mon through Thurs was supposed to save the district money. In fact, savings were realized in transportation but little else, yet district voters overwhelmingly chose to continue the four-day week. According to the school superintendent, both rural and town residents like having their children home an extra day each week, and teachers like the longer class periods. In addition, cocurricular activities on Fri no longer interrupt instructional time.

Custer schools use computer technology across the curriculum at all levels, from kindergarten through 12th grade. All students have received a laptop computer as part of their education since 2008. A few students even use the Internet to take classes that earn them high school and college credit. In the athletics arena, the names of Coach Larry Luitjens and the Custer High School boys' basketball team are practically synonymous with the title "state championship." Together, they won five between 1990 and 2003. In 2002, the South Dakota Legislature passed a resolution congratulating Luitjens on garnering the most wins of any basketball coach in state history. Coaching at Custer since 1973, Luitjens' record stood at 690 wins and 270 losses after the 2010 season. Other Custer teams have had success as well. In 2004, the boys' soccer team won the state championship and the girls' cross-country team earned the state title in 2007. Academic honors have included placing in the Odyssey of the Mind world finals and a Sallie Mae national teaching award for a teacher at the rural school in Spring Creek.

The Custer district has three rural schools that teach kindergarten through eighth grade, including one in Fairburn. It's one of only a few two-room rural schoolhouses built in the last 50 years in South Dakota. In the city of Custer are one elementary, one middle, and one high school.

A program for at-risk students is in place. The school district embraces Custer State Park and Wind Cave National Park within its boundaries, and the district has 890 students, 1,100 square miles, and 1,500 bison.

HOT SPRINGS SCHOOL DISTRICT
1609 University Ave., Hot Springs
(605) 745-4145
www.hssd.k12.sd.us

Maybe it's the Southern Hills' gorgeous scenery and pleasant climate that produce top athletes at Hot Springs High School. The girls' track and cross-country teams consistently rank as the top in the state, and the volleyball team participated in and won two state championships. But students also focus on academics and technology skills. Hot Springs High School has an 11 to 1 student-teacher ratio and runs several special programs, including a business and marketing class that integrates computer technology and an annual trip to Washington, D.C., that affords students a close-up look at American government. The district, after observing the benefits in nearby Custer, went to a four-day school week in 2003. Approximately 840 students attend pre-kingergarten, elementary, middle, and high school in Hot Springs and a rural school in Oral that goes through grade eight. A program for at-risk students helps keep struggling scholars on track to graduation.

PRIVATE SCHOOLS

With the exception of Montessori schools, private schools in the Black Hills generally are religious institutions. Many of them are affiliated with a specific church and can be located through the churches. Check the Yellow Pages or inquire at the local school district for information. Here we've listed several private schools, including one that principally serves Native American students.

Central Hills

RAPID CITY CHRISTIAN HIGH SCHOOL
23757 Arena Dr., Rapid City
(605) 341-3377
Approximately 145 students in grades 7 through 12 attend this interdenominational

Christian school, which opened in 1981. Accredited by the state and the Association of Christian Schools International, the school combines religious instruction with a traditional approach to basic learning. Students are required to enroll in a Bible class every semester and attend chapel once a week, and they must be committed to learning through a Christian worldview. A full activities schedule also keeps them busy in football (the team competes in two conferences), basketball, volleyball, track, drama, and more. The school bought the Hart Ranch Arena and 20 acres of land south of Rapid City and converted it into a campus in 2006.

ST. ELIZABETH SETON SCHOOL
431 Oakland St., Rapid City
(605) 348-1477

ST. THOMAS MORE HIGH SCHOOL
300 Fairmont Blvd., Rapid City
(605) 343-8484
These two fast-growing, accredited Catholic schools comprise a single school system under the auspices of the Saint Elizabeth Seton Central Catholic School Corp. Recently, enrollment at St. Elizabeth Seton was 520 students in preschool through grade eight, with a waiting list in every grade. St. Thomas More had 257 scholars in grades 9 through 12. About 90 percent of the students came from Rapid City, and about one-fourth were non-Catholics.

Both schools strive to deepen understanding of the meaning and importance of the Catholic faith, and in addition to receiving religious instruction, students participate in regular prayer services and retreats. Eighth-graders take on a community service program, and seniors must complete a 30-hour Christian service project to graduate. Academic performance is boosted by

strong discipline and a heavy homework load, backed by vigorous parental involvement and commitment to the schools' vision.

St. Elizabeth Seton School opened in 1961, replacing the Cathedral school that had been established in 1916. St. Thomas More High School began humbly, taking up temporary quarters at National American University in 1991 after the closure of St. Martin's Academy, a coed high school started by Benedictine nuns more than a century ago.

Commitment to St. Thomas More was such that enough money was donated to permit groundbreaking for a new building in 1994. The high school with a chapel in its center opened the next year.

St. Thomas More offers an accelerated college preparatory program with advanced placement courses, traditional college prep, and general studies for those who plan to go on to junior college or vocational school. For students needing extra help, tutoring is provided. In general, however, all students take the same level of course work. As a member of the South Dakota High School Activities Association, St. Thomas More competes with other local schools in football, basketball, wrestling, golf, debate, and many other activities.

Southern Hills

BETHESDA LUTHERAN SCHOOL
1537 Baltimore Ave., Hot Springs
(605) 745-6676
Between 40 and 50 youngsters attend this grade school, which is a ministry of Bethesda Lutheran Church and is accredited through National Lutheran Schools. Located in the church complex, the school teaches a standard curriculum like that found in public schools, with the addition of a literature-based reading program and Lutheran

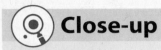

Close-up

Willard Water

It heals burns, grows gargantuan squash, helps you sleep, relieves pain, and keeps your pets healthy. Those are some of the claims made by folks who swear by **Willard Water**, a mysterious fluid discovered in the 1960s and patented by John Willard, a chemistry professor at South Dakota School of Mines and Technology in Rapid City.

Doc Willard, as he was called, developed "catalyst altered water" as a solvent but found it had health properties when he used it to soothe a burn on his arm. Once on the market it naturally attracted considerable curiosity, and in 1980 veteran TV reporter Harry Reasoner interviewed Doc Willard and a number of Willard Water devotees on *60 Minutes*. The testimonials claimed all sorts of benefits and no bad effects. Independent lab tests and a congressional investigation found it to be harmless. But no one could explain why Willard Water worked. As Doc himself said, "I see it but I still don't believe it."

One hypothesis holds that by altering the molecular structure of ordinary water, Willard Water boosts the assimilation of nutrients and hastens the elimination of toxins. It's also said to be a powerful antioxidant that helps the body rid itself of damaging free radicals. Users who drink it mixed with filtered water say they can't taste it, but they can tell a difference in the way they feel. And they say they feel better.

Doc Willard passed away in 1991, but Willard Water is still manufactured in Rapid City by his heirs and associates and distributed on a limited basis. There are imitations and diluted forms on the market, too, and representatives of Nutrition Coalition, a Moorhead, Minnesota, marketer, say the only way to know whether you're getting the real thing is . . . if you get results. If you're curious about Willard Water, call Nutrition Coalition at (800) 447-4793 for more information.

doctrine. Pupils receive religious instruction four days a week and attend chapel one day a week. Kindergartners attend class for half a day, sharing a room with first-graders. Second and third grades are combined, as are fourth, fifth, and sixth. The school, which opened in 1980, is affiliated with the Missouri Synod and is open to all students.

MONTESSORI SCHOOLS

Maria Montessori was the first woman in Italy to receive a medical degree. Her work as a doctor led to her belief that children learn best at their own pace, a philosophy that has been the cornerstone of Montessori education since she opened her first school in 1907. The classroom materials she designed then are still in use today.

CHILDREN'S HOUSE MONTESSORI
3520 West Main St., Rapid City
(605) 341-0824
www.chkids.net

Bringing the outdoors in is one area of focus at this school for children from age three through grade five. Raising butterflies, tending a butterfly garden, growing pumpkins, and building a compost heap on the one-and-a-half-acre wooded campus are just a few of the activities that are integrated into the classroom. Studies include individual and group learning in a variety of subjects. Children also participate in a cultural exchange by visiting and writing to their peers in the Montessori school at Red Cloud Indian School on the Pine Ridge Indian Reservation. A multigenerational exchange takes place when parents and grandparents volunteer their time for reading, gardening assistance, and other activities. Preschool and kindergarten are offered on a part-time basis, with limited extended care before school and at lunchtime. Teachers are required to obtain Montessori certification. But after a snowfall, even they can turn into kids again when everybody goes sledding. Children's House is closed during the summer.

LIFE TREE MONTESSORI SCHOOL
2110 St. Martins Dr., Rapid City
(605) 343-1541
Life Tree Montessori School offers part-time and full-time programs for children from age 18 months through sixth grade. Tykes up to age 3 enroll in the toddler program; from 3 to 6 they're in preprimary, which includes kindergarten; and 6- to 12-year-old students receive elementary instruction. Extended care is available before and after school for students who attend Life Tree. All activities take place in open, sunny classrooms under the nurturing tutelage of Montessori-certified teachers. Parental involvement is evident, too, in the wooden play equipment that was built by a parent for the big outdoor playground.

i **Most South Dakotans who take General Educational Development (GED) tests are between the ages of 20 and 24 and have completed 10th grade. The minimum age to take the tests is 16.**

HEAD START PROGRAMS

As the name implies, these publicly funded programs give preschoolers a solid foundation before they enter kindergarten. Call the programs for income guidelines. For private preschool programs, check the Yellow Pages, and see the Child Care chapter for information about locating a day-care center.

DAKOTA TRANSITIONAL HEAD START
612 Crazy Horse St., Rapid City
919 Main St., Suite 201, Rapid City (mailing address)
(605) 341-3163
This center-based program serves 75 Native American children ages three to five and their families who move to the Rapid City area from an Indian reservation. Because the transition may involve several moves back and forth, enrollment is open at all times. Students learn typical preschool skills like math concepts and motor development, but they also learn about Lakota language and culture. Four classroom sessions are offered Mon through Thurs for the youngsters, and their parents can find assistance with their own educational and social needs, including obtaining a GED, planning for career development, and finding work and housing. Dakota Transitional is under the auspices of Rural America Initiatives, 919 Main St., Rapid City, (605) 341-3339, an organization that offers education-related services to Native American youth.

YOUTH AND FAMILY SERVICES
1920 Plaza Blvd., Rapid City
(605) 342-4195
www.youthandfamilyservices.org
This comprehensive agency offers a wide range of services (see the Child Care chapter), including home-based and center-based

Head Start programs for educational enrichment, starting at age four, with strong parental involvement. A center-based Early Head Start program promotes healthy relationships between parents and children from birth to age three. Youth and Family Services also administers home-based Head Start programs in Butte, Custer, Fall River, Lawrence, and Meade Counties.

COLLEGES & TECHNICAL SCHOOLS

The Black Hills are a favorite location for students who love the area's recreational opportunities, but they also come here for a quality education. Many of them are nontraditional and international students who find the courses they need at our postsecondary schools. For information about attending intercollegiate sports events, turn to the Spectator Sports chapter.

i If you know someone who needs help learning to read, have him or her call the South Dakota Literacy Council in Pierre at (800) 423-6665, or inquire at the local library. In Rapid City call (605) 394-4171; as soon as the recorded greeting starts, the caller should dial 255 and leave a message after the beep. Messages are retrieved daily.

Northern Hills

BLACK HILLS STATE UNIVERSITY
1200 University Station, Spearfish
(605) 642-6343, (800) 255-2478
www.bhsu.edu
This small public university is situated on a pristine 123-acre campus on the west side of Spearfish. Aside from its desirable setting and academic programs, it prides itself on an outstanding athletic facility, the Donald E. Young Sports and Fitness Center. The $10.5 million center opened in 1990, the result of a cooperative funding effort by the school, the city, the state, and private sources, including alumni. It serves the entire community with two swimming pools, a wide range of athletic facilities, and classroom and meeting space (see the Spectator Sports chapter for more information).

BHSU, one of six state-run colleges in South Dakota, was founded in 1883 as a teachers' training institution called Spearfish Normal School. Many old-timers still call it that, even though for many years it was Black Hills State College before getting the university designation. Although primarily a school for aspiring teachers, it draws more business majors than any other South Dakota school.

Today BHSU has three colleges: Arts and Sciences, Business and Technology, and Education. The university is also home to the Center for Tourism Research, the Center for Indian Studies, and the Center for the Advancement of Mathematics and Science Education, which provide academic resources to students and private companies alike. Major courses of study for a bachelor of arts or bachelor of science degree include, but are by no means limited to, such fields as accounting, American Indian studies, art, biology, business administration, chemistry, communication arts, mass communication, environmental physical science, history, human resource management, English, Spanish, outdoor education, political science, psychology, speech, theater, vocal music, tourism and hospitality management, human services, and education. The school has two-year preprofessional programs in agriculture, dentistry, forestry, law, nursing, medicine, and other subjects. Associate degrees are offered in administrative assistance, drafting technology, general studies, tourism and hospitality management, and a number of computer and technology-related fields. Master's programs are offered in education and tourism.

The school's athletes are known as the Yellow Jackets, and its colors are green and gold. Football, men's and women's basketball, and volleyball are high-profile competitive sports at BHSU. The football field, Lyle Hare Stadium, seats 3,200 and hosts high school as well as college football games.

Many of the university's 3,900 students live in residence halls, since state law requires unmarried undergraduates to live on campus for at least their first two years. Extension courses are offered over the Internet or in person at Ellsworth Air Force Base, Rapid City Regional Hospital, South Dakota School of Mines and Technology, and other locations.

Central Hills

SOUTH DAKOTA SCHOOL OF MINES AND TECHNOLOGY
501 East St. Joseph St., Rapid City
(605) 394-2400, (800) 544-8162
www.sdsmt.edu
Started as the Dakota School of Mines in 1885, Tech, as it's called today, has been known for its science and engineering programs for the last half century or more.

Four colleges—Materials Science and Engineering, Earth Systems, Interdisciplinary Studies, and Systems Engineering—provide courses of study toward 10 undergraduate degrees in engineering and 6 in science. There are master's programs in 12 disciplines and 3 doctoral programs in science and engineering.

The Institute of Atmospheric Sciences, established in 1959, is located on campus, and students are encouraged to take part in research there. The institute collaborates with the National Weather Service, which has a station nearby, through a student internship program and by helping develop models for more accurate weather prediction. A fiber-optic cable connected to weather service computers affords the institute instant access to data so scientists can watch storms as they develop; that information is then used in research and teaching.

The institute also works with the EROS (Earth Resources Observation Systems) Data Center in Sioux Falls, the world's largest storehouse of earth science information, to interpret and use data to delve into problems such as pollution, climate change, and weather phenomena. The institute has performed major weather-modification field research for several federal agencies and has developed studies for air quality and air pollution. Also, scientists there use the world's only armor-plated, instrumented airplane capable of penetrating hailstorms in their studies of thunderstorm development. Currently, institute staffers are looking into the ways human activity affects Earth's atmosphere, a science called biogeochemistry.

The Museum of Geology on the Tech campus welcomes visitors who want to ogle dinosaur skeletons, meteorites, minerals, and other fascinating objects from the natural world. Read about the museum in the Attractions chapter.

About 2,400 students attend Tech, 500 of them housed in campus dorms. Under the watchful eye of their mascot, Grubby the miner, the blue-and-yellow Hardrockers compete in football, basketball, volleyball, track and field, and cross-country.

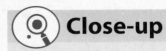

Close-up

Billy Mills and Randy Lewis

Billy Mills and **Randy Lewis** didn't have to take up mining to find gold. They used their talents and worked hard to win gold medals in Olympic competition—20 years apart. So far, they're the only South Dakotans ever to do so.

Billy, an Oglala Lakota from the Pine Ridge Indian Reservation, became the only American in Olympic history to win the 10,000-meter running race. A virtual unknown, he stunned the crowd at the 1964 Tokyo games when, with a mighty burst of speed, he shot ahead of the front-runners and crossed the finish line in a record 28 minutes, 24.4 seconds, beating a world champion. The spectacular win caused such a sensation that it halted his victory lap. Winning the gold made Billy a national hero, but it didn't make him conceited. Instead, he became a role model for Native American youth.

Billy had been orphaned at age 12 and sent to an Indian school in Kansas. Later, at the University of Kansas, he'd competed in track and field, then joined the US Marine Corps after graduating in 1962. In 1965, when he was already an Olympic champion, he won the US national championship in the 6-mile run and set another world record. Billy retired from track and field due to injuries in 1968, but he was later inducted into the National Track and Field Hall of Fame and the US Olympic Hall of Fame. A movie, *Running Brave,* was made about him.

All the while Billy never forgot his roots or the folks back home struggling with deprivation. After 23 years in the insurance business, he sold his company to become a full-time motivational and inspirational speaker. He formed the Billy Mills Speakers Bureau in Fair Oaks, California, and became national spokesperson for Running Strong for American Indian Youth. In the latter capacity he visited the Loneman School on the Pine Ridge reservation in 1997 to hand out awards in a student poster contest.

O'Harra Stadium, with its playing field and all-weather running track, is surrounded on three sides by terraces where some 300 cars can park while their occupants watch college and high school sports.

SOUTH DAKOTA STATE UNIVERSITY COLLEGE OF NURSING

1011 11th St., Rapid City
(605) 394-5390, (888) 819-1725
www.sdstate.edu

Nursing students need not attend the main South Dakota State University campus in Brookings to obtain a Bachelor of Science or master of science degree in nursing. This Rapid City department offers all the courses needed. Through a consortium agreement, students take support courses such as biology, anatomy, and microbiology at South Dakota School of Mines and Technology in Rapid City. They may elect to take other classes through Black Hills State University, either on the Spearfish campus or at the Ellsworth Air Force Base branch. The remaining classes are offered at the nursing school's main building downtown. The R.N. Upward Mobility Program allows registered nurses with associate degrees to earn a four-year degree in three semesters. With a bachelor's degree in nursing and a year of work experience, students may enter the graduate program to study for a master's degree in any

Billy also wrote a book, *Wokini: A Lakota Journey to Happiness and Self-Understanding,* published in 1991.

While Billy was making history, Randy Lewis was a little boy growing up in Rapid City. He was still young, just 10 years old, when he started wrestling. He was a natural at it, and Olympic gold soon became his goal. He worked hard at his studies too, keeping up his grades at Stevens High School as he won three state wrestling championships. He even set a national record with 45 consecutive pins. The year he graduated, 1977, he won a junior world championship and two national championships. While studying business at the University of Iowa, Randy won two National Collegiate Athletic Association (NCAA) championships and others besides. In 1980 he qualified as the youngest member of the US Olympic wrestling team, but his hopes were dashed when President Jimmy Carter decided the United States would boycott the games. Randy got his chance four years later in Los Angeles, though, and in 1984 he won the gold medal in the 136$^{1}/_{2}$-pound weight class.

In his wrestling career Randy was victorious over eight other world or Olympic champions and scored wins over dozens of other top wrestlers. For about eight years he was rated among the world's top three wrestlers, and he won numerous championships. But possessing excellence didn't go to his head, and, like Billy, Randy wanted to pass on something of value to the next generation. Even before he became an Olympic star, he had developed a series of summer wrestling camps for elementary and high school athletes, and after graduating from college in 1982 he coached his alma mater's postgraduate Hawkeye Wrestling Team for 13 years.

His days on the mat ended after that, and at this writing Randy was living in Arizona, running a business. He was inducted into the National Wrestling Hall of Fame in 1998.

of several tracks: family nurse practitioner, educator, administrator, or clinical nurse specialist. Presently, 200 students are pursuing degrees here. All are on their own for housing and meals, since the school does not have student housing or a cafeteria.

SOUTH DAKOTA STATE UNIVERSITY
WEST RIVER GRADUATE CENTER
501 East St. Joseph St., Rapid City
(605) 394-6823
www.sdstate.edu

This SDSU extension offers master's programs in education administration, curriculum and instruction, and counseling. All classes are held in the evening on the South

Dakota School of Mines and Technology campus; student housing and meals are not provided. Recent enrollment was approximately 130 students in all three programs; enrollment is limited for the counseling program, based on factors that vary from semester to semester.

THE UNIVERSITY OF SOUTH DAKOTA
1011 11th St., Rapid City
(605) 394-6720, (800) 233-7937
www.usd.edu

The state's largest public university operates two education-related programs in Rapid City through the Division of Technology for Training and Development. The first is a Master of Science program designed to help students use technological resources for teaching and learning; the second is a specialist program designed to build on the master's degree. The USD graduate extension offers a master's program in business administration with a health-service option and Master of Science programs in administrative studies with three options: human resources, health services, and interdisciplinary studies. About 90 students take advantage of this program. All classes are offered at night. Students live and dine off campus. The USD School of Medicine, which is located on the main campus in Vermillion, has a West River campus at 3625 5th St., Suite 200, in Rapid City, (605) 394-5105, where third- and fourth-year medical students can complete a portion of their studies.

WESTERN DAKOTA TECHNICAL INSTITUTE

800 Mickelson Dr., Rapid City
(605) 394-4034, (800) 544-8765
www.westerndakotatech.org
One of four state-created technical schools in South Dakota, Western Dakota Technical Institute provides training for jobs in the fields of medicine, engineering, science, law, agriculture, mechanics, and more. Students can choose from among 25 programs that lead to an associate of applied science degree or a diploma. Courses of study at the accredited school include accounting, agriculture, business management, automotive technology, business management and marketing, cabinetmaking, collision-repair technology, computer-aided drafting (architectural and mechanical), industrial electronics, law-enforcement technology, medical transcription, paralegal/legal assistance, pharmacy technician, phlebotomy/patient care technician, practical nursing, welding, and others. A ranch management program is offered on a 496-acre working ranch in Sturgis. The approximately 4,000 students who go to school here have the use of on-site child care and a retail clothing store where they can get outfitted for a job interview or internship for a reasonable price. Students can buy meals on campus; however, they must find their own housing.

CHILD CARE

In a state where wages are relatively low, few families can afford to have a parent who doesn't work. In fact, recent statistics show that South Dakota has the highest percentage nationally of working mothers with preschoolers (well over 70 percent versus the national average of about 65 percent). Other numbers show that more than 80 percent of South Dakotan women with school-age children work, well above the national statistic of around 75 percent. As a result, child care is an important issue among South Dakotans in general, and Black Hills residents especially.

There's an enormous demand for quality child care, an issue that's an increasingly high priority for state officials and communities. The state even has a coordinator of child-care services to help us do a better job of watching over our kids. There's widespread agreement that more infant and toddler care is needed here, and the state is doing its best to create more slots with a new reimbursement rate structure and more accessible training for child-care providers.

In the Black Hills especially, both providers and parents have an outstanding number of training opportunities. In addition, numerous agencies provide services or referrals for special-needs children. You'll find some of both listed in the following information.

We're also innovative when it comes to looking after children when they're not in school. In Rapid City, for instance, the YMCA and the school district joined forces to create the Kidstop program that provides before- and after-school supervision and activities in many elementary schools. You can learn more about their approach by calling the YMCA at (605) 718-9622 or by visiting www.rcymca.org. In the Northern Hills the Lead-Deadwood School District has instituted a similar program called Stop and Grow. For more information call the Administration office at (605) 717-3890.

OVERVIEW

Although the Black Hills is a strongly traditional and conservative area, long based on standard nine-to-five jobs, a growing tourist industry and increasing population base mean that more and more workers are taking shifts on weekends and during the evenings. In response, more child-care providers have been experimenting with extended hours. And as day care becomes a more permanent fixture in our lives, we're seeing a growing array of public and private child-care options, from licensed day-care centers and home-based facilities to preschools and after-school programs. Some schools have day-care programs for students who are raising children.

With so many choices, be sure to shop around. Use the resources listed in this chapter to find the right place for your child and which meet your criteria.

LOCATING CHILD CARE

If you're new to the area or to the demands of finding child care, Rapid City–based **Early Childhood Connections,** (605) 342-6464 or (888) 999-7759, is a good place to begin your search. This nonprofit group can produce a customized list of child-care providers to anyone who calls. Just answer a few simple questions (such as the hours you'll need and the neighborhood and town in which you live) and staffers will supply you with a list of all the licensed providers that meet your criteria. Their list of providers, which they maintain with the help of the Department of Social Services, covers all of the Black Hills and much of western South Dakota. They also print a regular newsletter and offer some enrichment and training classes for day-care providers and new parents. All of these services are provided free of charge.

In the Northern Hills, check out child care options at the **Deadwood Recreation Center,** the **Northern Hills Family Recreation Center** in Lead, and the **Spearfish Recreation Department** and Kids Connection after-school programs. A new, nonprofit Center, the **First Step Child Care Center,** opened on the south end of Main Street in Deadwood in March 2011. For more information go to www.nhfirststep.com.

Classes, workshops, and published materials for parents are also available through the **South Dakota Parent Resource Network,** (605) 347-6260 or (800) 219-6247, in Sturgis. The network especially focuses on getting parents involved in their children's education, but it also covers topics like violence and community service. It doesn't keep a list of child-care providers, however; to obtain one, see the Early Childhood Connections description above or call the South Dakota Department of Social Services. The latter maintains the **Office of Child Care Services,** which has on hand lists of both licensed and unlicensed child-care providers across the state. There are several offices scattered throughout Black Hills towns. For their numbers, either contact a local chamber of commerce or consult the government pages of a Black Hills phone book.

WHAT TO ASK

One of the most important steps in choosing a caregiver is often overlooked: visiting the home or center you are considering before you enroll your youngster. While there, observe how staff members interact with children, look over the facility to ensure that it's clean and spacious enough for the number of children who stay there, and inspect the outdoor play area. Be sure to ask lots of questions, especially about licensing, activities, and child to adult ratios.

You'll also need to know whether there's a policy that requires you to have backup care if your regular provider gets sick or has an emergency, and whether the day care closes for staff vacation time.

It's a good idea to ask for parent references and to find out whether parents are welcome to drop in unannounced—if not, you might want to look elsewhere.

TRAINING & OTHER SUPPORT

Whether or not you work outside the home, the time you spend with your child is precious. Here is a partial list of services and training opportunities that can help enrich the hours you have together. These agencies serve the entire Black Hills.

SOUTH DAKOTA PARENT RESOURCE NETWORK

2885 Dickson Dr., Sturgis
(605) 347-6260, (800) 219-6247

Program staffers make free home visits to families with children up through age five, providing information about growth and development as well as age-appropriate activities for parents and children to do together. Other services include developmental screenings, group meetings for parents, and toy-lending programs. A second location in Custer is at 215 North Third St. (605-673-2660).

Single Points of Contact

BLACK HILLS BIRTH TO THREE CONNECTIONS

730 East Watertown, Rapid City
(605) 394-6089

Responsible for providing service coordination for children with developmental disabilities throughout western South Dakota via a grant from South Dakota Department of Education. The program concentrates on educating parents about developmental programs available for children from birth to age three, and provides free screening and evaluation services.

YOUTH & FAMILY SERVICES

1920 Plaza Blvd., Rapid City
(605) 341-2251
www.youthandfamilyservices.org

Youth & Family Services is a comprehensive agency whose services include a child care center, Girls, Inc., Head Start and the YFS Counseling Center for children and families. Free training in drug-abuse and violence prevention is available to school districts, individuals, and community groups through the Western Prevention Resource Center.

REGULATION

The state of South Dakota keeps a vigilant eye on those who tend and nurture children by setting strict standards and making regular inspections to enforce them.

State law requires licensing for any day-care center that serves 21 or more children, as well as for group family daycare centers that serve 13 to 20 children. Providers who care for up to 12 children in their homes must register with the state if they or their clients receive public funds. In other cases, family home day-care registration is voluntary, but those who don't register don't get listed with the Office of Child Care Services.

From a parent's point of view, registration may offer added reassurance since it extends system-wide screening for reports of child abuse and neglect to anyone age 10 or older who lives in the provider's home.

All licensed and registered providers must meet in-service training requirements that range from 6 to 20 hours a year, comply with nutrition standards, and keep up-to-date immunization records on the children in their care. Everyone who works in a regulated child-care facility has to maintain current certification in CPR and first aid.

There are limits to the number of children who can be supervised by one adult. For infants and toddlers, the limit is 5 children to 1 adult; for children ages 3 to 6, it's 10 to 1; and for school-age youngsters, it's 15 to 1. Call city hall to find out what's required in your community.

LIVING HERE

HEALTH CARE

Tourism and retail are easily the Black Hills' largest industries, especially in Rapid City. The growing number of giant retailers on the community's east and north sides and the construction of new office complexes downtown are evidence enough. However, a quick look at Rapid City's southern district will tell you that the medical industry runs a close second. Rapid City Regional Hospital, just one player among dozens of local clinics and medical centers, is the largest private-sector employer in the region, boasting a staff of about 2,000 (not including consultants, contractors, and employees of the other clinics the organization owns—see its listing for details). Other major medical facilities include the Rapid City Indian Hospital, the Black Hills Surgical Hospital (see their listings later in the chapter), as well as several clinics for spine injuries, orthopedics, and radiology, among others.

But Rapid City isn't the only place you can receive medical care in the region. Most major Black Hills towns have a hospital or clinic as well as independent doctors (some of whom still make house calls). Even tiny Deadwood, less than 15 miles from facilities in Sturgis and Spearfish, has its own hospital (which it shares with its sister city, Lead). Although there aren't many wellness or spa facilities in the Black Hills, this sector of the health care community is also growing. More middle- and high-income residents coming to the area means there is a broader customer base for these sorts of facilities, and the commercial sector is beginning to respond.

With ranching still playing a major role in the economy, keeping animals healthy is also a big business in the Black Hills. You'll find a small number of veterinarians listed at the end of this chapter. Because of the nature of the region, many of them are just as experienced with dogs and ferrets as they are with horses and bison.

HOSPITALS

Northern Hills

FORT MEADE VA MEDICAL CENTER
113 Comanche Rd., Fort Meade
(605) 347-2511, (800) 743-1070
www.va.gov
Fort Meade VA Center is part of the Department of Veterans Affairs (VA) Black Hills Health Care System that provides primary and secondary medical and surgical care along with domiciliary, extended nursing home, and tertiary psychiatric inpatient care services for veterans residing in South Dakota and portions of Nebraska, Wyoming, North Dakota, and Montana. Other specialty programs include addictive disorders, post-traumatic stress, and compensated work therapy. VA Black Hills features medical centers at Fort Meade and Hot Springs along with many community based outpatient clinics, including Rapid City. It is ranked

among the nation's top five VA health care facilities for patient satisfaction. Fort Meade VA Center, 2 miles east of Sturgis, has been a VA facility since the birth of the VA in the 1940s, but there has been a hospital at the 120-year-old fort since its founding. Today it features inpatient and outpatient care, an inpatient psychiatric unit, and a rehabilitation-focused nursing-home care unit.

i Rapid City serves as the region's health care center, employing more than 8,000 people. Rapid City Regional Hospital is the main health care center between Denver and Minneapolis, providing 42 specialty areas including radiation, cardiology and emergency medicine. Other prominent facilities include the Black Hills Regional Eye Institute, Rapid City Community Health Care Center, Sioux San Hospital, and Black Hills Surgical Hospital.

LEAD-DEADWOOD REGIONAL HOSPITAL
61 Charles St., Deadwood
(605) 722-6101
www.rcrh.org
A $1.8 million project gave the hospital a new lobby, an entrance and parking for the disabled, renovated rehabilitation facilities, and expanded services. The primary-care hospital has been in existence since 1878. Services include an emergency room, cardiac care, obstetrics, cardiac and pulmonary rehabilitation, home health, respiratory and physical therapy, and medical equipment. The facility has 18 beds.

SPEARFISH REGIONAL HOSPITAL
1440 North Main St., Spearfish
(605) 644-4000
www.rcrh.org
A primary-care facility with 40 beds, Spearfish Regional was named one of the top-100 hospitals in the nation and one of the top-38 rural care facilities. It has an adjacent family medical center, an emergency room, home health care (for in-home visits), rehabilitation services, a women's health care center with eight birthing suites, and an award-winning cardiopulmonary rehabilitation program. Spearfish Regional belongs to the Black Hills Regional System of Care.

STURGIS REGIONAL HOSPITAL
949 Harmon St., Sturgis
(605) 720-2400
www.rcrh.org
This 25-bed primary-care facility has an adjacent family medical center, emergency room, a medical equipment component, a home-health program, and rehabilitation services for the elderly and the disabled. The hospital also has an 84-bed Medicare-certified nursing home and offers wellness and education programs.

Central Hills

BLACK HILLS SURGICAL HOSPITAL
216 Anamaria Dr., Rapid City
(605) 721-4700, (800) 818-1890
www.bhsc.com
Rapid City's smaller licensed hospital was built by doctors. It is a specialty hospital where many surgical procedures can be performed, including neurosurgery and dental, pediatric, gynecological, and other operations. This 23-bed center does not accept heart attack victims or patients requiring intensive care, as it does not have an

emergency room or intensive-care facilities. It specializes instead in most routine (and some advanced) surgical procedures, both inpatient and outpatient.

RAPID CITY INDIAN HOSPITAL (SIOUX SAN)
3200 Canyon Lake Dr., Rapid City
(605) 355-2500
www.ihs.gov

This Indian Health Service primary-care hospital is one of just three such facilities in the nation not located on a reservation. It was founded in the early 1950s as a tuberculosis sanitarium. Operated by the federal government, the 32-bed hospital treats only Native American patients. Services and facilities include an emergency room, community health nursing (home care), specialty clinics such as dentistry and optometry, walk-in clinics, and the only mental health inpatient unit in the Indian Health Service. There are no facilities for surgery or obstetrics, which are handled at Rapid City Regional Hospital.

RAPID CITY REGIONAL HOSPITAL
353 Fairmont Blvd., Rapid City
(605) 341-1000
www.rcrh.org

Rapid City Regional Hospital was created in 1973. It is a 417-bed regional medical center providing services in more than 40 medical specialties. The hospital complex encompasses the Cancer Care Institute, Black Hills Rehabilitation Hospital, Regional West Behavioral Health Center, the Heart Care Center, Same-Day Surgery Center, and other components. Emergency services include a 24-hour emergency department and regional LifeFlight, a 24-hour emergency air- and ground-transport service.

i Rapid City Regional Hospital has a benefit for patients' families: discount rates at the Best Western Town & Country Inn, 2505 Mount Rushmore Rd., just 2 blocks from the hospital. Request a Hospital Visitor Card at the hospital's information desk and present the card at the motel to receive a discounted rate. The hospital also has "accommodation rooms," which are rented for a minimal charge. Inquire at the information desk.

Southern Hills

CUSTER REGIONAL HOSPITAL
1039 Montgomery St., Custer
(605) 673-2229
www.rcrh.org

Custer's hospital is a 16-bed primary-care facility with a 24-hour emergency room and an adjacent urgent care and family practice facility. It also has a home-health program. It operates two smaller rural clinics in nearby towns: the Hill City Medical Clinic and the Edgemont Memorial Clinic.

HOT SPRINGS VA MEDICAL CENTER
500 North 5th St., Hot Springs
(605) 745-2000, (800) 764-5370
www.va.gov

The Hot Springs VA Medical Center—like the VA Medical Center in Fort Meade—is part of the Department of Veterans Affairs (VA) Black Hills Health Care System that provides primary and secondary medical and surgical care along with domiciliary, extended nursing home, and tertiary psychiatric inpatient care services for veterans residing in South Dakota and portions of Nebraska, Wyoming, North Dakota, and Montana. The Hot Springs facility was founded in 1907 as the Battle Mountain Sanitarium. Today it features

Medical Centers & Day Clinics

Some of these clinics are open early and late for minor emergencies, sudden illnesses, routine physicals, or when your regular doctor isn't available. Many take walk-in patients; some require appointments. For major emergencies, go to a hospital emergency room instead.

Northern Hills

Belle Fourche Regional Medical Clinic
2200 13th Ave., Belle Fourche
(605) 892-2701

Lead-Deadwood Regional Medical Clinic
71 Charles St., Deadwood
(605) 578-2364

Massa Berry Regional Medical Clinic
890 Lazelle St., Sturgis
(605) 347-3616

Queen City Medical Center
1420 North 10th St., Spearfish
(605) 642-8414

Spearfish Regional Medical Clinic
1445 North Ave., Spearfish
(605) 644-4170

Sturgis Medical Center
1010 Ball Park Rd., Sturgis
(605) 347-3684

Central Hills

Black Hills Pediatrics and Neonatology
2905 5th St., Rapid City
(605) 341-7337

Family Practice Residency Center
502 East Monroe St., Rapid City
(605) 719-4060

Foothills Family Clinic
8075 Stage Stop Rd., Black Hawk
(605) 718-7625

Hill City Medical Clinic
114 East Main St., Hill City
(605) 574-4470

Medical Arts Clinic
717 St. Francis St., Rapid City
(605) 388-4640

Medical Associates of the Black Hills
640 Flormann St., Rapid City
(605) 718-3100

Rapid City Community Health Center
504 East Monroe St., Rapid City
(605) 394-6666

Rapid City Medical Center
2820 Mount Rushmore Rd., Rapid City
(605) 342-3280

Rapid City VA Health Clinic
3625 5th St., Rapid City
(605) 718-1095
(accepts veterans only)

Southern Hills

Custer Regional Medical Clinic
1041 Montgomery St., Custer
(605) 673-4150

Edgemont Regional Medical Clinic
908 H St., Edgemont
(605) 662-7250

inpatient and outpatient medical care and residential-based programs.

INFORMATION & SERVICES

AMERICAN CANCER SOCIETY, SOUTH DAKOTA DIVISION, INC.
2465 West Chicago St., Rapid City
(605) 399-2062, (800) 227-2345
www.cancer.org

Above and beyond raising money for research, the local office of the American Cancer Society provides educational materials and programs to heighten cancer awareness, and it has a number of volunteer services for patients. In the Reach to Recovery program, for instance, volunteers who have survived breast cancer help current patients understand what to expect and how to care for themselves during treatment. Additional volunteer services include transportation to treatment centers and assistance with appearance, such as help with skin care from trained cosmetologists. Pamphlets that explain different cancers and treatments are available from the office, which is located in west Rapid City. The office serves the entire Black Hills area.

NONTRADITIONAL & ALTERNATIVE TREATMENTS

A growing number of alternative health care practitioners are relocating to the Black Hills. Some offer services such as acupuncture, reflexology, herbal remedies, yoga classes, and more. In all cases, ask about the practitioner's certification. *NOTE:* Some alternative treatments are offered by spas and fitness centers, listed later in this chapter.

ACUPUNCTURE CLINIC OF THE BLACK HILLS
2720 West Main St., Rapid City
(605) 342-4333

Gary Gamache, a certified acupuncturist, also operates the Westside Chiropractic Clinic at the same location. Patients come to be treated for chronic health problems and pain, among other ailments.

HALINA HLADYSZ
4801 Powderhorn Dr., Rapid City
(605) 342-7543
www.halina-health.com

Halina Hladysz is an herbalist and certified iridologist who offers health and fitness consultations and iris photography and analysis. In the field of iridology, the iris is a sort of mirror of the changes taking place in the body; it is analyzed to determine the cause of illness. She uses vitamins and minerals, homeopathic remedies, flower essences, essential oils, books, and herbs.

JSL ENTERPRISES
2425 Mount Rushmore Rd., Suite C, Rapid City
(605) 343-2322
www.shaklee.com

This small independent store distributes products of the Shaklee company, a national company that manufactures food products and household cleaners based primarily on herbs and plant material. You can purchase or order any Shaklee product from owner Jan Spicer, from pain medication and skin-firming lotion to glass cleaner and water filters.

SPAS & FITNESS CENTERS

Some spas and fitness centers require memberships in order to use their facilities, but they also offer day or temporary passes for

Support Organizations & Other Information

AIDS Hotline:	(800) 592-1861, (800) 342-2437
Al-Anon/Alateen:	(605) 394-8250
Alcohol/Drug Helpline:	(605) 394-6128
Alcoholics Anonymous:	(605) 721-4552
Church Response:	(605) 342-5360
Crisis Hotline:	(605) 342-4303
Family Violence Hotline:	(800) 430-7233
Gamblers Anonymous:	(888) 781-4357
Gay and Lesbian Coalition:	(605) 391-8080
Poison Control:	(800) 222-1222
South Dakota Parent Resource Network:	(605) 347-6260, (800) 219-6247
Working Against Violence:	
Domestic Violence Crisis	(605) 341-4808
Sexual Assault Crisis	(605) 341-2046

visitors. In addition, the charge is often lower if you are visiting the spa with a current member.

Northern Hills

ROCKIN' LOCKS
83 Charles St., Deadwood
(605) 578-2355
www.rockinlockssalon.com
Rockin' Locks is a small salon located on Charles Street in Deadwood. They cut and style hair, give pedicures and manicures, and apply makeup. Upstairs, Jessica Farrier provides the best in massage therapy techniques. Individual treatments and salon services vary but are generally less expensive than similar businesses in Rapid City.

Central Hills

MYSTIQUE EDGE SALON AND SPA
509 7th St., Rapid City
(605) 737-0095
www.mystiqueedge.com
This spa's downtown location means that it attracts a lot of businesspeople; it even has specially designed massage packages for executives with only a few minutes to spare. Salon services include haircuts, pedicures, manicures, facials, and waxes. It offers body wraps and treatments, a sauna, a hydrotherapy tub, and more. Owner Lori Eggersgluess and her staff are both friendly and professional, and they ensure that customers feel relaxed from the moment they walk in the door.

STRETCH STUDIO
611 Main St., Rapid City
(605) 484-0108
www.stretchstudiofitness.com
Your first visit is free at Stretch Studio, one of Rapid City's newest wellness and fitness centers. Certified staff assist with yoga, pilates, zumba, dance, belly bolly, cowboy cardio and more creative group exercise, and personal training.

ULTIMATE FITNESS
512 Main St., Rapid City
(605) 342-8080
It offers aerobics, treadmills, weight machines, free weights, mixed martial arts, a circuit training program called Pace, a whirlpool, a sauna and more. Tanning beds and a nursery are available, too, but there's an extra charge for those services. The spa has a certified personal trainer on staff. It offers nutrition classes and fun classes in stationary biking and spinning, which will really help you work up a sweat.

THE WEIGHT ROOM
601 12th St., Rapid City
(605) 348-5070
www.theweightroom.net
This center specializes in the heavy stuff: weight lifting, free weights, Hammer-Strength equipment, and bodybuilding. Personal trainers are on staff and vitamins and protein supplements are for sale.

YMCA
815 Kansas City St., Rapid City
(605) 342-8538
www.rcymca.org
The YMCA offers a new gym, drop-in childcare center, and the Randy Travis Wellness Center. The wellness center has free weights, cardiovascular machines, Nautilus weight-lifting machines, and more, including an indoor track, racquetball courts, and three gyms. Fitness trainers are available for fitness testing, health appraisals, consultations, and exercise prescriptions (in collaboration with Rapid City Regional Hospital). Massage therapy is available by appointment. Three indoor pools are on-site. One has water aerobics and other water workouts; the others are 25-meter pools for general use.

Southern Hills

ALOHA SPA
745 North River, Hot Springs
(605) 891-3980
www.flatiron.bz
Indulge in a unique paradise spa located in the Flatiron Guest Suites. Hot Springs has been known for its healing mineral baths and spas for over a century. The Aloha Spa offers a variety of treatments that will leave you feeling like royalty.

WELLNESS CENTERS
Central Hills

BLACK HILLS HEALTH & EDUCATION CENTER
13815 Battle Creek Rd., Hermosa
(605) 255-4101
www.bhhec.org
A true wellness facility, the center uses education to improve the lives and health of its participants. It is open year-round, and programs run from 5 to 20 days. Participants hike, work out, attend lectures on medicine, nutrition, cooking, and stress; and enjoy massages and hydrotherapy monitored by staff physicians. Meals are vegan (no meat, eggs, or animal products), as the staff are members of the Seventh-day Adventist

Church. The center, however, is nondenominational and nonprofit.

VETERINARIANS

Most area veterinarians work with small and large domesticated animals and livestock. Most can care for horses, either offsite or in their facilities, but we recommend you call ahead and ask.

Northern Hills

BELLE FOURCHE VETERINARY CLINIC
406 Summit St., Belle Fourche
(605) 892-2618

NORTHERN HILLS VETERINARY CLINIC
713 Anna St., Sturgis
(605) 347-3606

METZGER HOLCOMB ANIMAL CLINIC
144 E. Grant, Spearfish
(605) 642-3422

SPEARFISH ANIMAL HOSPITAL
3010 7th Ave., Spearfish
(605) 642-5771

STURGIS VETERINARY HOSPITAL
2421 Vanocker Canyon Rd., Sturgis
(605) 347-4436

TRI-STATE VETERINARY CLINIC
US 212 West, Belle Fourche
(605) 892-2844

Central Hills

ANIMAL CLINIC
1655 East 27th St. (Valley Drive),
Rapid City
(605) 342-1368

BLACK HILLS ANIMAL HOSPITAL
2909 US 79 South, Rapid City
(605) 343-6066

CANYON LAKE VETERINARY HOSPITAL
4230 Canyon Lake Dr., Rapid City
(605) 348-6510

DAKOTA HILLS VETERINARY CLINIC
1571 US 44 East, Rapid City
(605) 342-7498

GREEN MEADOWS VETERINARY CLINIC
3400 Elk Vale Rd., Rapid City
(605) 348-3727

MEINERS ANIMAL CLINIC
220 Krebs Dr., Rapid City
(605) 343-5089

MOUNTAIN VIEW ANIMAL HOSPITAL
1130 Jackson Blvd., Rapid City
(605) 343-8050

NOAH'S ARK ANIMAL HOSPITAL
1315 Mount Rushmore Rd., Rapid City
(605) 343-3225

Southern Hills

FALL RIVER VETERINARY CLINIC
Fall River Rd., Hot Springs
(605) 745-3786
US 385 South, Custer
(605) 673-4018

RETIREMENT

For a certain number of Black Hills residents, retirement means winters on the sunny golf courses of Arizona. For others, it can mean moving to the Hills to live full-time in the family vacation cabin. Some build a dream home and settle down after years of moving around in the military or another line of work. Still others see retirement as a time to start a new career—it's not uncommon to see someone in her golden years taking a computer class, giving tours at a history attraction, or volunteering at an archaeological dig.

Whatever your lifestyle, retirement brings change. In this chapter we'll direct you to some of the opportunities and challenges reserved for retirees. We'll tell you about a couple of retirement communities where you can live in comfort and privacy with others who share your interests. And we'll provide information about some of the many services that are available to you.

For a comprehensive look at housing and medical care, turn to the Relocation and Health Care chapters.

INFORMATION & SERVICES

Advocacy groups, financial and legal services, support groups, and other resources can be found throughout the Hills.

Hills-wide

DAKOTA PLAINS LEGAL SERVICES
528 Kansas City St., Suite 1, Rapid City
(605) 342-7171, (800) 742-8602
Dakota Plains Legal Services provides free legal help to US citizens age 60 or older regardless of income, as well as to income-qualified younger people. Areas of assistance include Social Security, Medicaid and Medicare, elder abuse, spousal abuse, powers of attorney and living wills, housing and homelessness issues, employment, and more. The agency covers the entire Black Hills and beyond. Call for an appointment.

MEALS PROGRAM
303 North Maple Ave., Rapid City
(605) 394-6002
Seniors can enjoy a hot noon meal five days a week at sites throughout the Black Hills, and volunteers deliver meals to those who are homebound because of a mental or physical disability. Participants must be 60 or older, but their spouses younger than 60 are also welcome. Operating under the auspices of Western South Dakota Senior Services, the agency provides information about home health care agencies in Rapid City and gets referrals to the state Department of Social Services. Payment is by donation; those younger than 60 pay a flat fee of $6.50. Call to reserve a place at the table, or sign up at one of the meal sites. Several senior centers in 16 Black Hills communities participate in the program,

including Belle Fourche Senior Center, Custer Senior Citizens Center, Hill City Senior Citizens Center, Springs Senior Citizens Center, Keystone Senior Citizens Center, Canyon Lake Senior Citizens Center, and Minneluzahan Senior Citizens Center. See the Senior Centers section of this chapter for addresses and phone numbers. In addition, some apartment buildings in Rapid City are in the program. Call the main number above for other serving sites, brochures, menus, and service.

SHIINE PROGRAM
2628 West Main St., Rapid City
(605) 342-3494, (800) 822-8804
SHIINE stands for Senior Health Information and Insurance Education. Trained volunteers in almost every county in the state help seniors sort out the complexities of health insurance, including Medicare, private long-term or supplemental insurance, and other benefits. One-on-one meetings can be arranged when questions are too involved to be handled by phone. All services are free of charge.

Central Hills

AARP
2200 North Maple St. (Rushmore Mall), Rapid City
(605) 394-7798
www.aarp.org
The AARP is practically a one-stop shopping information outlet for people age 50 and older. Not only does the advocacy organization have its own education and assistance programs—for instance, a safe-driving course and help at tax time—but volunteers keep an astounding list of resource people and organizations that can answer your questions and direct you to service providers. So whether you want to find out

if there's a local adult soccer team, get help with a legal or medical problem, obtain a list of nursing facilities, or get information on just about any topic, the AARP can tell you where to turn. The office is open and staffed by volunteers from 10 a.m. to 3 p.m. Mon through Fri. One chapter holds regular meetings, so ask about joining.

FINANCIAL SERVICES EXCHANGE
2040 West Main St., Suite 310, Rapid City
(605) 348-4573
Using dedicated computer software, an independent financial consultant can help you decide how much money you'll need for retirement and how to invest for it. You'll get help analyzing your current savings situation and understanding different kinds of Individual Retirement Accounts and pension plans. Setting aside funds for your children's college education, learning to manage your portfolio, and estate planning can be addressed as well. Charges for services vary.

RETIREE HOUSING

When it's time to move into a smaller home, many seniors want to retain their independence while finding comfort, convenience, and companionship among their own age group in a retirement community. Regional Senior Care, a division of Rapid City Regional Hospital, operates several assisted-living facilities around the Black Hills, including Fairmont Grand Manor and Fox Run in Rapid City, Wedgwood in Custer, and Golden Ridge in Lead. While these retirement communities offer a range of independent and assisted-living options, the majority of residents are older and generally need regular health monitoring. For more independent options, try some of the facilities listed below.

Northern Hills

JUNIPER COURT
430 Oriole Dr., Spearfish
(605) 642-4744

Each of the 14 apartments here is at ground level and has a walk-out patio and a small plot for a flower garden. Seniors 62 and older can rent a one- or two-bedroom apartment but must bring their own clothes washer and dryer—a plus if you swear by your own appliances. There's a community room for socializing. Juniper Court is part of Evergreen Management Services, which operates a handful of other housing units in Belle Fourche, Sturgis, and Gillette, Wyoming.

Central Hills

PRIMROSE
224 East Minnesota St., Rapid City
(605) 342-6699
www.primroseretirement.com

Primrose has 48 one- and two-bedroom apartments for seniors 60 and older, 16 of which are for those who require residential care or assisted living. Each unit has a fully equipped kitchen and, depending on whether it's on the first or second floor, a patio or a balcony. In the common area are a library, cozy fireplace, exercise room, entertainment center, and multipurpose room. During the summer, residents can have a garden spot on the grounds.

WESTHILLS VILLAGE RETIREMENT COMMUNITY
255 Texas St., Rapid City
(605) 342-0255
www.westhillsvillage.com

You don't have to be retired to move into one of the 202 lovely private apartments at Westhills Village, a life-care community that compares itself to a first-class hotel with five sizes and floor plans from which to choose (all with fully equipped kitchens). If you're 62 years old and capable of living on your own, you're eligible. Get your application in early; you can expect to be on the waiting list for at least a year, so plan ahead.

Established in 1984, the nonprofit and Christian- based Westhills Village offers a full spectrum of options for moderate-income seniors. In addition to the apartments already mentioned, 31 private suites at adjacent Westhills South offer assisted living with staffers on hand around the clock. For those needing the highest level of care and supervision, Westhills Village Health Care Facility is a state-licensed, Medicare-approved skilled-nursing facility with 44 beds in private and semiprivate rooms. Registered nurses are on staff 24 hours a day. The Home Health Agency of Westhills Village provides in-home care in Rapid City and the surrounding area.

The monthly service fees for Westhills Village apartments include a daily meal, utilities, and many services such as limited housekeeping and scheduled transportation. Woodworkers, gardeners, and crafters find ample space for their pastimes in the common area, and the beautifully manicured grounds feature gardens and walking paths.

i Under South Dakota law, door-to-door salespeople must advise you of your right to cancel purchases of $25 or more made in your home and provide you with a cancellation form. You have three days in which to mail the form, preferably by certified mail, if you want to return the merchandise for a refund.

SENIOR CENTERS

Nearly every community in the Black Hills has a senior center where you can engage in fun activities, make friends, and find out about local services such as transportation. We've listed a number of senior centers here, but check phone book listings or contact the local chamber of commerce for others. There is no residency requirement for the centers listed below, so you can join any or all of them, regardless of where you live. Most of these sites serve meals, and you'll find information about that under the Information and Services section. Bloodpressure checks and other wellness clinics often are provided, too, as well as assistance with income tax preparation.

Northern Hills

BELLE FOURCHE SENIOR CITIZENS CENTER
828 Kingsbury St., Belle Fourche
(605) 892-6285
Members here take part in line dancing, cards and other games, pool, holiday dances, and a greeting card recycling program. Members must be at least 45 years old (voting privileges come at age 55) and pay an annual fee of $7.

MEADE COUNTY SENIOR CITIZEN CENTER
919 Second St., Sturgis
(605) 347-5877
The center serves about 5,000 breakfasts during the annual Sturgis Rally & Races (see the Annual Events & Festivals chapter) each Aug. It also provides Meals on Wheels weekly to senior citizens and shut-ins. The rest of the year, members get together for card games, dances, choral performances, crafts, and sewing for the center's semiannual craft fairs. Special activities include potlucks and fund-raising meals, dances, exercise classes, and a thrift shop. Annual dues are $10 for membership at age 55 or older.

SPEARFISH SENIOR SERVICE CENTER
1306 10th St., Spearfish
(605) 642-2827
Members here enjoy pool, card games, bingo, chorus and band, exercise classes, and dances. Other activities include monthly breakfasts, potluck luncheons, a bridge club, and fund-raisers (all on different days). Achieving age 50 and paying annual dues of $10 are the only membership requirements.

TWIN CITY SENIOR CITIZEN CENTER
609 West Main St., Lead
(605) 584-1261
Bingo, card games, and aerobics are available to members age 50 and older who pay their yearly $10 dues. Monthly potlucks and fund-raisers are on the agenda, and efforts are being directed at arranging regular Sunday social activities.

Central Hills

CANYON LAKE SENIOR CITIZENS CENTER
2900 Canyon Lake Dr., Rapid City
(605) 721-8710
www.canyonlakecenter.com
Seniors age 60 and older find a wealth of activities and services here, including aerobics, bingo, cribbage, bridge, a discussion group, ceramics, dances, table tennis, pool, shuffleboard, line dancing, exercise classes, and limited computer training. There's a rug loom for weavers, a library for book lovers, and a garden where you can rent space for summer flowers and veggies. Those with a flair for the performing arts will want to take

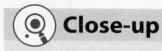

Close-up

Comanche and Tipperary

Two of the most famous Black Hills retirees were horses. **Comanche** was a steady, faithful Seventh Cavalry steed. **Tipperary**, Comanche's temperamental opposite, was an outlaw bronc that was never tamed.

When troopers reached the battlefield at Little Bighorn—site of the "last stand" of Lt. Col. George A. Custer's Seventh Cavalry—two days after the 1876 battle, they found only one participant still alive: the seriously injured Comanche. He had been ridden into the battle by Capt. Myles Keogh, the commander of I Company.

The stoic horse eventually recovered and spent the rest of his life as the pet of the Seventh. By regimental order, he was retired, never to be ridden or worked again. He participated only in ceremonies, draped in mourning and led by a trooper. During the Seventh Cavalry's nine years at Fort Meade, Comanche lived a life of ease, had the run of the grounds, and reportedly developed a taste for treats and beer, panhandled from his fond fellow soldiers.

In 1888 the Seventh was sent to Fort Riley, Kansas, where Comanche died in 1891 at the age of 31 (or 28, depending on the source). His battle-scarred body was stuffed, mounted, and caparisoned, and it is still on display at the University of Kansas Natural History Museum in Lawrence.

Tipperary was born in 1905 near Camp Crook, north of the Black Hills. A range horse, he gave little indication of his ability to buck off the best until 1915, when Ed Marty tried to break him. The wild ride lasted only seconds. The cowboy gingerly picked himself up from the mud and broke into the popular refrain, "it's a long way to Tipperary," and the horse had his name.

The outlaw bronc loved cowboy busting and constantly learned new tricks to outwit them. He could rear straight up, twist, jump, sunfish, and buck, anything to get a rider off his back. Although he was mounted about 100 times, only eight men were not thrown from him.

Tipperary was retired in 1926. But he made his final appearance at the 1931 Black Hills Roundup in Belle Fourche (see the Annual Events chapter), where he had thrown so many riders. He stood there, head down, feeble, tired . . . until the band struck up "Tipperary." Then the old bronc raised his head and, keeping time to the music as he had done in his younger days, strutted proudly before the cheering crowd one last time.

Tipperary died during a 1932 blizzard on the rangeland of his birth. A monument to the great horse stands in Buffalo, South Dakota.

---

part in community presentations by the Joyful Guys and Gals singing group and the center's drama group. Special activities include crosscountry ski trips, golf lessons, hikes, and more. Yearly dues are $10, and there's a small fee for certain activities. The center claims more than 1,800 active members.

i The Social Security Administration has an office at 605 Main St., Suite 201, in Rapid City. Call (605) 342-1819 between 9 a.m. and 4 p.m. Mon through Fri, or call (800) 772-1213 for automated service.

HILL CITY SENIOR CITIZENS CENTER
303 Walnut Ave., Hill City
(605) 574-2988
Recent remodeling added new windows, an office, and an entryway for greater comfort at the center, where members participate in a greeting card recycling program, pool, the Merry Music Makers singing group, and birthday potlucks. New ideas are welcome, as are members of any age. Only those 60 and older can vote, though. Dues are $12 per year.

KEYSTONE SENIOR CITIZENS CENTER
517 First St., Keystone
(605) 666-4808
The center is used mostly for community functions, but seniors congregate here to share meals (especially at holiday times), celebrate birthdays, and talk. Dues are $5 a year for members 55 and older.

MINNELUZAHAN SENIOR CITIZENS CENTER
315 North 4th St., Rapid City
(605) 394-1887
There's no excuse for idleness when exercise classes, dances, bingo, cards, table tennis, crochet classes, pool, shuffleboard, volleyball, and so much else is available here. The musically inclined will find a place in the Rambling Larks singing group or the Merry Music Makers "kitchen band." Potlucks for members and suppers that are open to the public provide additional social opportunities, and a monthly bus trip to Deadwood provides a change of scenery. Members make good use of "retired" items through a greeting card recycling program and a thrift room where used clothing and household items are sold. Those 55 and older pay $5 a year to belong.

Southern Hills

CUSTER SENIOR CITIZENS CENTER
538 Mount Rushmore Rd., Custer
(605) 673-2708
You don't need to be a senior citizen to enjoy the benefits of membership at this center. Associate members of any age pay $10 a year to belong; those 60 and older pay $20 and get voting privileges. Line dancing, exercise classes, bingo, greeting card recycling, ceramics, movies, a Stitches 'n' Sew group, pool, and card games are some of the activities found here. The center has a support group for widowed people, as well as programs for greeting new area residents and visiting or staying in touch by phone with those who are alone or isolated. The local ministerial association's food pantry is located in the center, and the Coalition on Aging holds its meetings here. Enjoy the monthly potluck for a buck.

SPRINGS SENIOR CITIZENS CENTER
206 South Chicago Ave., Hot Springs
(605) 745-6123
Bridge, cribbage, and pinochle are some of the card games members enjoy playing here. Pool, exercise classes, and, occasionally, a dance offer additional opportunities for fun and well-being. Bingo players find their game of choice at the regularly scheduled potlucks, and fund-raisers, greeting card recycling, and a small rummage area for non-clothing items help support the center. Seniors 55 and older pay $10 a year or $60 for lifetime membership.

WORKING & VOLUNTEERING

Looking for work and volunteer opportunities? Here are a few agencies that can help in the search for both. If you're interested in volunteering, also check with hospitals, libraries, schools, community sports programs, national organizations, and the USDA Forest Service.

Hills-wide

RETIRED & SENIOR VOLUNTEER PROGRAM (RSVP)
333 6th St., Rapid City
(605) 394-2507
www.seniorcorps.org

This national organization has put the skills of seniors age 55 and older to use on worthy community projects for a quarter of a century. The organization tries to match individual skills and training to specific tasks, be it helping other seniors fill out their tax returns, working in a literacy program, guiding children safely across the street as a crossing guard, or joining a chorus to entertain nursing home residents. Other locations are in Spearfish at 236 West Jackson Blvd. (605-642-5198), and in Sturgis at 919 Second St. (605-347-5048).

WORK EXPERIENCE—SOUTH DAKOTA DEPARTMENT OF LABOR
(Hills-wide)
2500 Minnekahta Ave., Hot Springs
(605) 745-5101, (605) 347-9362

Seniors 55 and older who are eligible to work in the United States can get help finding employment through Work Experience, the nation's largest organization of its kind. You'll find Work Experience representatives serving the entire Black Hills; in the Northern Hills, however, there's no permanent office, and you'll need to call ahead. An offshoot of Work Experience, Experience Works Staffing Service, 1719 West Main St., Rapid City, (605) 394-5755, is a temp agency for mature workers of all ages and income levels. A second Work Experience office location is in Rapid City at 111 New York St. (605-394-1745).

Central Hills

COMMUNITY DEVELOPMENT DEPARTMENT
300 6th St., Rapid City
(605) 394-4181
www.rcgov.org

Concentrates on issues, human needs and gaps in services that impact the living standards of the residents of Rapid City. At this writing, the department oversees nine city task forces dealing with issues ranging from early childhood development and care, to affordable housing and mental health issues.

MEDIA

Visitors to the Black Hills will find plenty to listen to, watch, and read—on the radio and television and in print publications, that is. You'll find a diversity of music, a smattering of homegrown magazines, plenty of newspapers, and a wide variety of television programming. Just for fun, we've included information about our film industry. After your visit here you may catch some big—or small—screen films or advertisements in which the landscapes look very familiar.

NEWSPAPERS

If you're interested in learning about daily life in Black Hills towns, local newspapers are your best source. The largest, the *Rapid City Journal,* offers state, national, and international coverage, as well as general coverage of smaller towns. However, many small newspapers provide thorough and personal coverage of their own hometowns, from community news and local government information to features and the quaint community and small-town neighbor news that defines the distinct personality of each area. However, as is the case with the rest of the US, newspapers in western South Dakota are witnessing buy-outs, closures, and consolidations.

Northern Hills

Dailies
BLACK HILLS PIONEER
315 Seaton Circle, Spearfish
(605) 642-2761
www.bhpioneer.com
A daily tabloid (Mon through Sat), the *Black Hills Pioneer* is distributed in the Northern Hills and focuses on the news and events in Lead, Lawrence County, and Spearfish. It's

one of the larger papers, with a circulation of 3,500, and it includes an advertising supplement, the *Weekly Prospector,* on Tuesday.

Weeklies
BUTTE COUNTY POST
1004 5th Ave., Belle Fourche
(605) 892-2528
www.blackhillsweeklygroup.com
This weekly newspaper focuses on Belle Fourche and surrounding areas.

LAWRENCE COUNTY JOURNAL
376 Main St., Deadwood
(605) 578-3305
This weekly comes out on Wednesday and has a circulation of 800. It covers the Northern Hills and is distributed throughout the Spearfish, Deadwood, and Lead areas.

MEADE COUNTY TIMES-TRIBUNE
1238 Main St., Sturgis
(605) 347-2503
www.meadecountytimes.com
The *Times-Tribune* publishes each Wednesday, focusing on the Sturgis and Meade County area.

TRI-STATE LIVESTOCK NEWS
1022 Main St., Sturgis
(605) 347-2585
www.tsln.com

The *Tri-State Livestock News* is published weekly on Saturday. It has served the Midwest's agricultural industry for four decades, and if you're a farmer or rancher, you'll find its reports and news helpful. If you're not an agriculturist, it's a great way to learn what the real "cowboy life" is like.

Central Hills

Dailies
RAPID CITY JOURNAL
507 Main St., Rapid City
(605) 394-8300, (800) 843-2300
www.rapidcityjournal.com

The *Journal* is the largest newspaper in the Hills, with a circulation of 35,000 and bureaus in Spearfish and Pierre. It focuses on the entire Hills area and also covers eastern Wyoming, northern Nebraska, and the rest of South Dakota. It provides national and international news and features. A daily morning paper founded in 1878 as the *Black Hills Journal*, the *Rapid City Journal* is sold in vending boxes and stores in all Hills towns.

Wednesday editions include advertising supplements (the majority of which are grocery store ads) and the *Rapid City Advertiser* (the *Northern Hills Advertiser* goes to towns north of Rapid City). Friday editions have weekend entertainment information, and Saturday editions offer religious articles and church service listings. Sunday editions include *Parade* magazine and the most extensive help-wanted ads of the week.

Weeklies
HILL CITY PREVAILER NEWS
114 Main St., Hill City
(605) 574-2538
www.hillcitynews.com

The *Prevailer* is published on Wednesday; its 1,100 copies are distributed throughout both the Central and Southern Hills. The *Western Trader* is its weekly shopper supplement.

PENNINGTON COUNTY COURANT
212 4th Ave., Wall
(605) 279-2565

The *Courant* circulates 1,000 copies throughout eastern Pennington County. It's an award-winning broadsheet that was founded in 1906 and is a window to the happenings in Wall, the Badlands, and surrounding area.

Southern Hills

Weeklies
CUSTER COUNTY CHRONICLE
522 Mount Rushmore Rd., Custer
(605) 673-2217
www.custercountynews.com

The *Chronicle* calls itself "your hometown newspaper" and is one of the oldest newspapers in the Hills. In fact, it celebrated its 125th anniversary in 2004. Distributed in the Southern Hills on Wednesday, the *Chronicle* has won South Dakota Newspaper Association awards for excellence and best feature story.

HOT SPRINGS STAR
107 North Chicago Ave., Hot Springs
(605) 745-4170
www.hotspringsstar.com

The *Star* was founded in 1885, is published on Tuesday, and serves the Southern Hills. It focuses on the people and events in and around Hot Springs and also publishes a shopper, the *Hot Springs Star Extra*.

It isn't easy to find the *New York Times* in the Black Hills. It's easier to find the Sunday *Denver Post* or *USA Today*. You can find the Sunday *Times* in some convenience stores, bookstores, grocery stores, and hotels. You can read the daily *Times* at the Rapid City Library, which receives its copies by mail, three days late.

MAGAZINES

An array of locally published magazines can be found in the Black Hills. Some are published "East River," far from the Hills, but they're popular and available here (some by subscription only, though). Each is a resource to learn more about an aspect of the Hills, from business and culture to hobbies and attractions.

BLACK HILLS FACES MAGAZINE
524 7th St., Rapid City
(605) 348-0558
www.bhfaces.wordpress.com
Featuring some of the unusual people who live and work in the Black Hills, this refreshing quarterly magazine is fun and features outstanding photography, as well as in-depth stories on locals. Available by subscription at $22 per year.

DAKOTA OUTDOORS
333 West Dakota St., Pierre
(605) 224-7301
This midwestern sportsperson's magazine offers information on outdoor recreation in the Dakotas, with a focus on hunting and fishing. In the Black Hills area it's available by subscription only for $10 per year. (It's on newsstands east of the Missouri River.) *Dakota Outdoors* is published monthly, and two stand-alone issues are included with

subscriptions: the *Fishing Guide* in Jan and the *Hunting Guide* in Aug.

RAPID CITY HOME JOURNAL/BLACK HILLS HOME JOURNAL
507 Main St., Rapid City
(605) 394-8300, (800) 843-2300
This is a two-in-one monthly real estate publication (produced by the *Rapid City Journal*) with listings arranged by real estate agency. One half contains Rapid City listings; flip it over to check out listings for the Black Hills.

SOUTH DAKOTA CONSERVATION DIGEST
412 West Missouri, Pierre
(605) 773-3485
www.state.sd.us/gfp
This magazine started in 1934 as mimeographed sheets produced by the state's Department of Game, Fish & Parks. Today the bimonthly has a circulation of 16,000 and is still devoted to outdoor recreation, wildlife, and conservation. Its articles are about hunting, fishing, camping, wildlife, parks, and issues relating to all these. The Nov/Dec issue contains a calendar of events for the following year. You can't buy *South Dakota Conservation Digest* on newsstands, but you can subscribe for just $5 per year.

SOUTH DAKOTA HALL OF FAME MAGAZINE
1480 South Main St., Chamberlain
(605) 734-4216, (800) 697-3130
This magazine provides a wealth of information about our South Dakota heritage. The nonprofit Hall of Fame began in 1974 to recognize those "who have contributed to the development and heritage of South Dakota." Since then, hundreds of noteworthy people, living and deceased, have become

hall of famers commemorated in this quarterly magazine. The magazine is published once a year. Fifteen people are inducted each year, in 15 categories, including agriculture, Indian heritage, religion, professional cowboy, and "unsung heroes and good hearts." The Hall of Fame sells books and displays a photo collection, and its magazine files are open to the public. The historically valuable archives are computerized, and a database is available for public use. You won't find this magazine on newsstands, but it's available at most South Dakota libraries. Both subscriptions and single copies are available at the number above.

i The daily *Rapid City Journal* includes a list of the day's television programming. A separate television supplement, with program listings for the coming week, is published with the *Journal*'s Saturday edition.

✺SOUTH DAKOTA MAGAZINE
410 East 3rd St., Yankton
(605) 665-6655, (800) 456-5117
www.southdakotamagazine.com
South Dakota Magazine was founded in 1985 and has been highly successful, now reaching 100,000 readers with bimonthly issues. It celebrates the heritage of South Dakota with a rich mix of articles about interesting characters, small towns, historical events, fascinating wildlife, and local lifestyles. It's a well-loved magazine, produced by people who obviously care deeply about the state. The extensive monthly collection of letters to the editors saying "thanks for the memories" and enthusing "I remember that!" attests to its popularity. *South Dakota Magazine* is available on newsstands around the state or by subscription for $19 per year.

RADIO

This being the Wild West, you'll find several country music stations (both contemporary and classic styles), but the airwaves also carry choices for fans of talk radio, rock, oldies, alternative, and Christian. These radio stations are listed by format, not region, so you can easily find the type of music you prefer. Many stations are powerful enough to span more than one of our usual geographical designations, but the Hills themselves may interfere occasionally with your reception of less-powerful stations, especially as you drive.

The talk, country, and Christian stations are probably the most popular local stations. However, the harder and classic rock stations have a substantial following in the Northern and Central Hills, due in part to some colorful radio personalities. South Dakota Public Radio is another favorite choice, as it can be received almost anywhere in the state, including the entire I-90 corridor. The soothing, conservative NPR programming is on par with the values of many South Dakotans.

Alternative

KBHU THE BUZZ 89.1 FM

Christian

KLMP 97.9 FM
Inspirational and talk

KSLT 105.7/107.3 FM
Adult contemporary Christian

Country

KBHB 810 AM
Traditional

KIMM 1150 AM
Classic

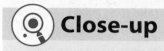 **Close-up**

South Dakota Public Television

South Dakota Public Television celebrated its official 40th anniversary in 2007. Although educational television station KUSD-TV first went on the air in 1961, the South Dakota State Legislature secured a federal grant (with matching funds from the state) in 1967 to increase the station's power, create more transmitters, and form a board of directors. The board was given the task of creating a network of stations across this huge state so that every single school could access instructional television programming for classroom use. Today, there are nine television/radio transmitters in place, with coverage areas that blanket the entire state.

Public television in South Dakota provides national programming and news from the Public Broadcasting System; South Dakota–oriented programs such as *Arts Advocate Report, Buffalo Nation Journal,* and legislative reports from the state capital; and programs for children and teens. In addition to instructional television programs broadcast to schools, it offers adult continuing education telecourses, overnight educational programs that teachers or daycare providers can tape and use later, and live video-conferences for professionals via the Rural Development Telecommunications Network.

More than 20,000 people are Friends of South Dakota Public Broadcasting, supporting quality cultural and educational programming with both their financial contributions and their time and energy as volunteers. To become a Friend, call (800) 333-0789.

KIQK KICK 104.1 FM
Contemporary

KOUT KAT COUNTRY 98.7 FM
Contemporary

KZZI KZ COUNTRY 95.9 FM
Mainstream

Oldies

KDSJ 98 AM
Golden

KKLS KOOL 92 AM
'50s, '60s, '70s

Public Radio

KBHE 89.3 FM
Rapid City

KPSD 97.1 FM
Northern Hills

Rock

KDDX X-ROCK 101.1/103.1 FM
Album-oriented

KFXS THE FOX 100.3 FM
Classic hits

KKMK MAGIC 93.9 FM
Adult

KQRQ 92.3 FM
Classic hits

KRCS HOT 93.1 FM
Top 40

KSQY K-SKY 92.1/95.1 FM
Adult-oriented

MEDIA

KZLK 106.3 FM
Adult contemporary/soft

Talk

KOTA 1380 AM
News/talk

KTOQ K-TALK 1340 AM
News/talk

TELEVISION

Although cable or satellite service isn't necessary to receive network stations in most Black Hills locations (it does improve reception, however), many consumers here do subscribe. There are several Black Hills companies to choose from, including **Knology,** (605) 721-2000; **Direct Satellite TV,** (888) 441-7233, (605) 343-3806, or (605) 343-0755; **DirecTV,** (605) 341-1323; and **Midcontinent Communications,** (800) 888-1300 or (605) 343-3402.

Local Television Stations & Affiliates

There are six local stations, listed below with their network affiliates and their local channel numbers. Channel numbers will be different if you're watching a television with cable or satellite service.

KBHE CHANNEL 9, SOUTH DAKOTA PUBLIC BROADCASTING (PBS)
(605) 394-2551, (605) 677-5861,
(800) 456-0766 (administration),
(800) 568-6922 (network production)

KCLO CHANNEL 15 (CBS)
(605) 341-1500, (800) 888-KCLO

KEVN/KIVV CHANNEL 7 (FOX)
(605) 394-7777, (888) 394-7775

KKRA CHANNEL 24 (PAX)
(605) 355-0024

KNBN CHANNEL 27, RAPID CITY; CHANNEL 31, LEAD/DEADWOOD
(605) 355-0024, (877) 4-KNBN-TV

KOTA CHANNEL 3 (ABC)
(605) 342-2000

FILM

SOUTH DAKOTA FILM OFFICE
711 East Wells Ave., Pierre
(605) 773-3301, (800) 952-3625
The beauty of the Black Hills and Badlands has enticed many a filmmaker to bring camera and crew to South Dakota, most recently, for the 2008 blockbuster, *National Treasure: Book of Secrets,* starring Nicolas Cage. Thus, the state's Department of Tourism created a film office to promote South Dakota to the film- and video-producing industries and to assist and support filmmakers when they arrive.

The popularity of Kevin Costner's *Dances with Wolves* brought the state's visual attributes to the attention of many. A state with open spaces and gorgeously varied vistas; herds of buffalo, horses, and cattle; eager extras; Old West–style towns and buildings; skilled horse riders; and Mount Rushmore is a real find in the film industry.

The Badlands have been especially popular among Hollywood directors since the 1950s, and they served as the backdrop for prominent westerns like *Chief Crazy Horse* and *How the West Was Won.* They've also been tapped to serve as other planets (or an asteroid, as the casé may be) for the films *Starship Troopers* and *Armageddon.* You'll also find South Dakota scenery in the opening scenes of the movie *Twister.*

INDEX